Grand Blue Dreaming 16

PRESENTED BY KENJI INOUE & KIMITAKE YOSHIOKA

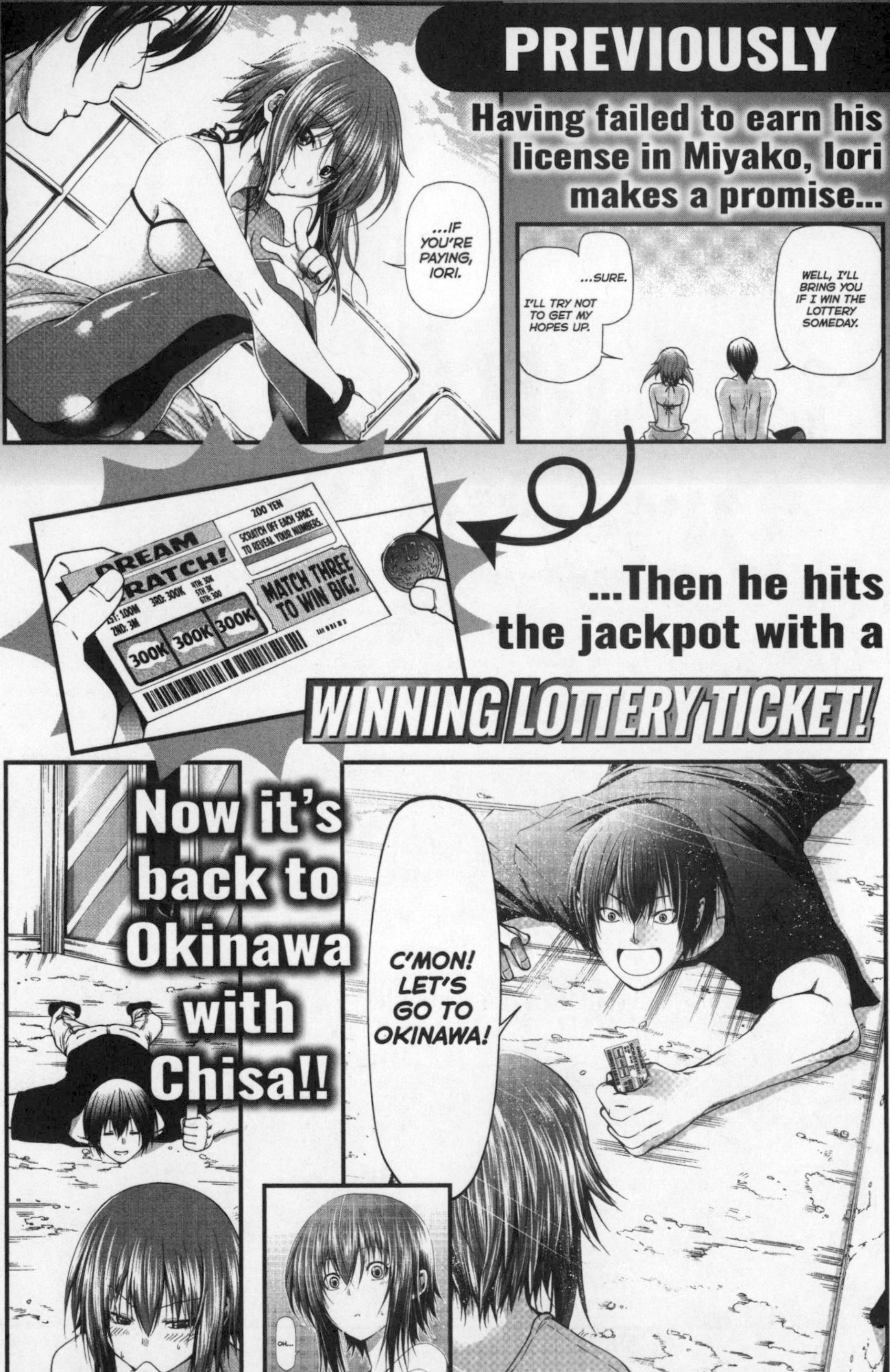
PREVIOUSLY
Having failed to earn his license in Miyako, Iori makes a promise...
WELL, I'LL BRING YOU IF I WIN THE LOTTERY SOMEDAY.
...SURE.
I'LL TRY NOT TO GET MY HOPES UP.
...IF YOU'RE PAYING, IORI.
...Then he hits the jackpot with a
WINNING LOTTERY TICKET!
200 YEN
SCRATCH OFF EACH SPACE TO REVEAL YOUR NUMBERS.
MATCH THREE TO WIN BIG!
DREAM
1ST: 100M 2ND: 3M 3RD: 300K 4TH: 30K 5TH: 3K 6TH: 300
300K 300K 300K
C'MON! LET'S GO TO OKINAWA!
Now it's back to Okinawa with Chisa!!
OH...

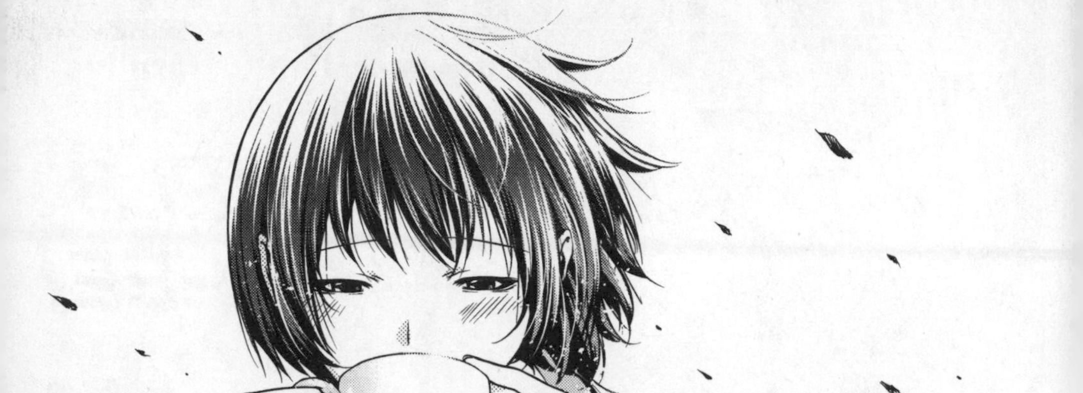

Ch. 62: War Council

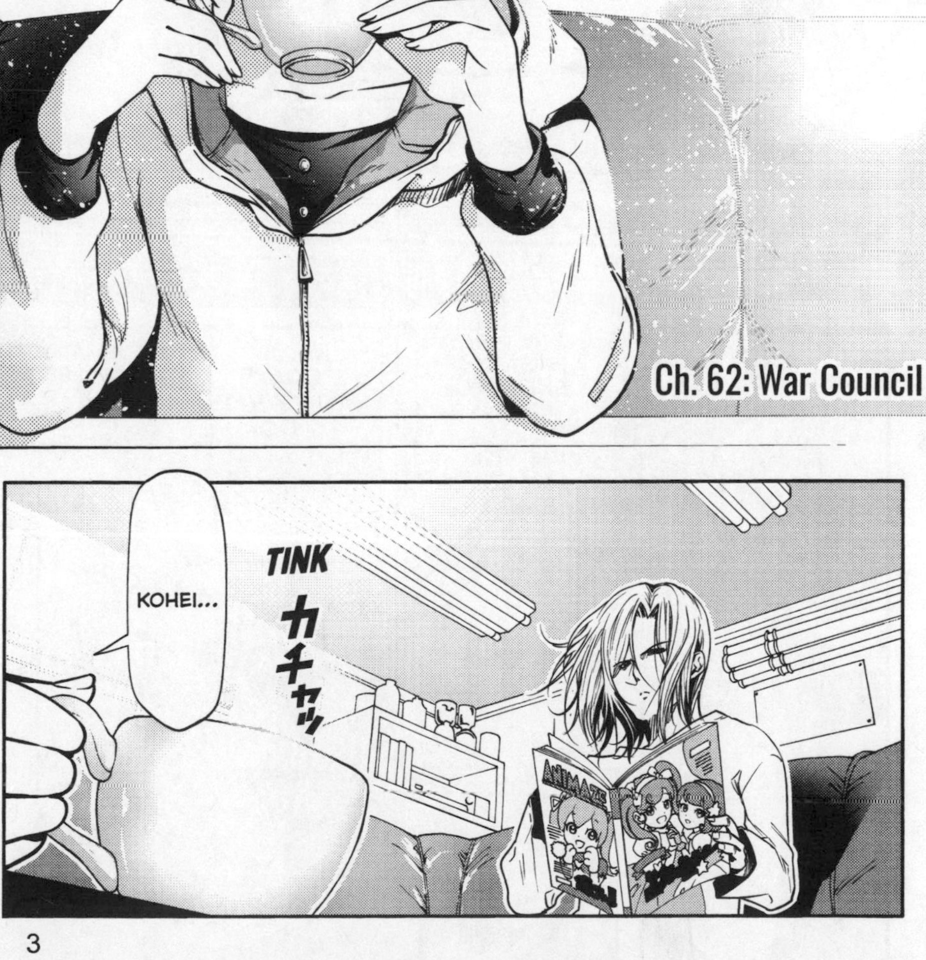

KOHEI...
TINK
カチャッ

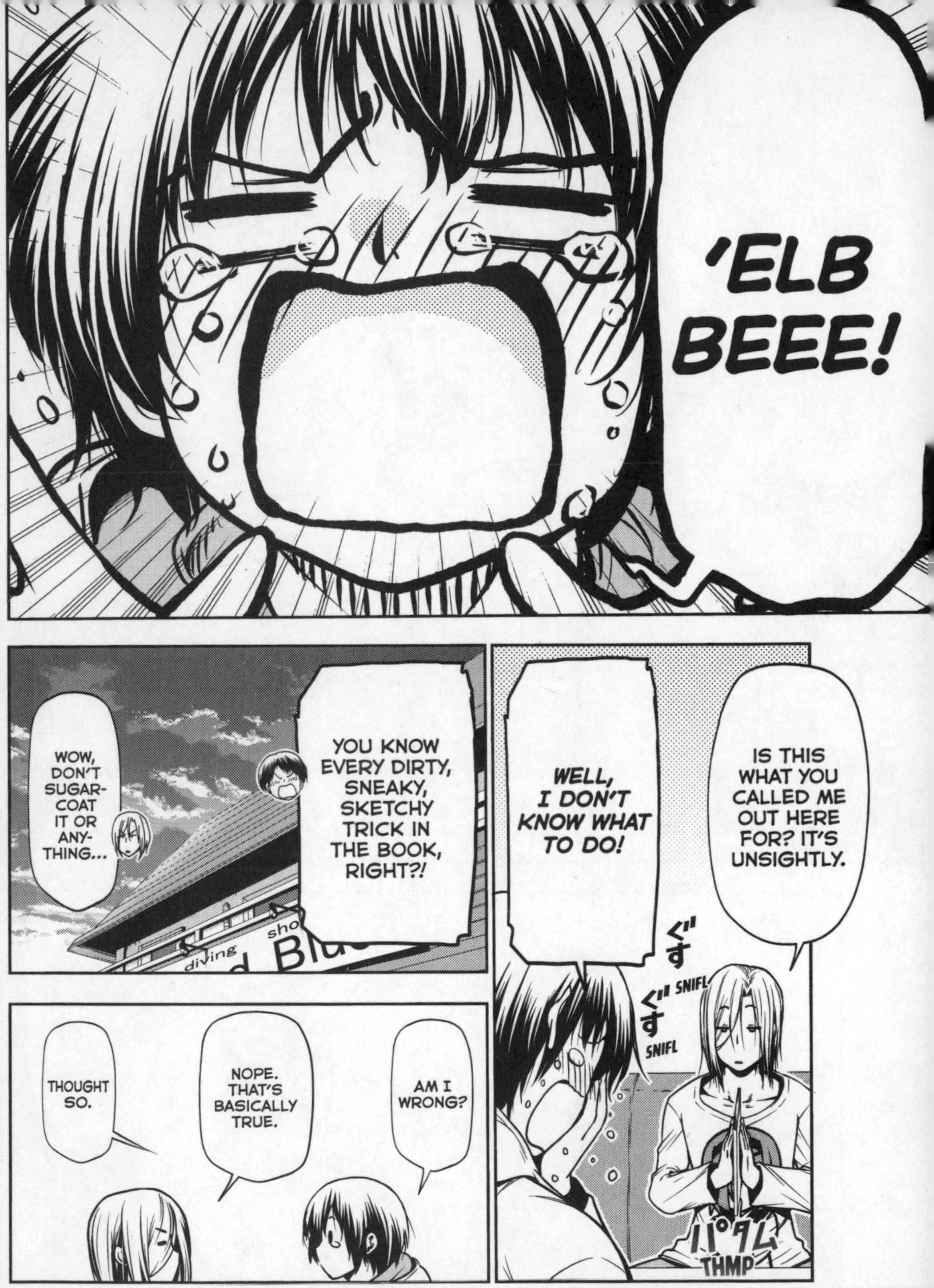

'ELB BEEE!
IS THIS WHAT YOU CALLED ME OUT HERE FOR? IT'S UNSIGHTLY.
WELL, I DON'T KNOW WHAT TO DO!
ぐす SNIFL
ぐす SNIFL
パタム THMP
YOU KNOW EVERY DIRTY, SNEAKY, SKETCHY TRICK IN THE BOOK, RIGHT?!
WOW, DON'T SUGAR-COAT IT OR ANY-THING...
AM I WRONG?
NOPE. THAT'S BASICALLY TRUE.
THOUGHT SO.

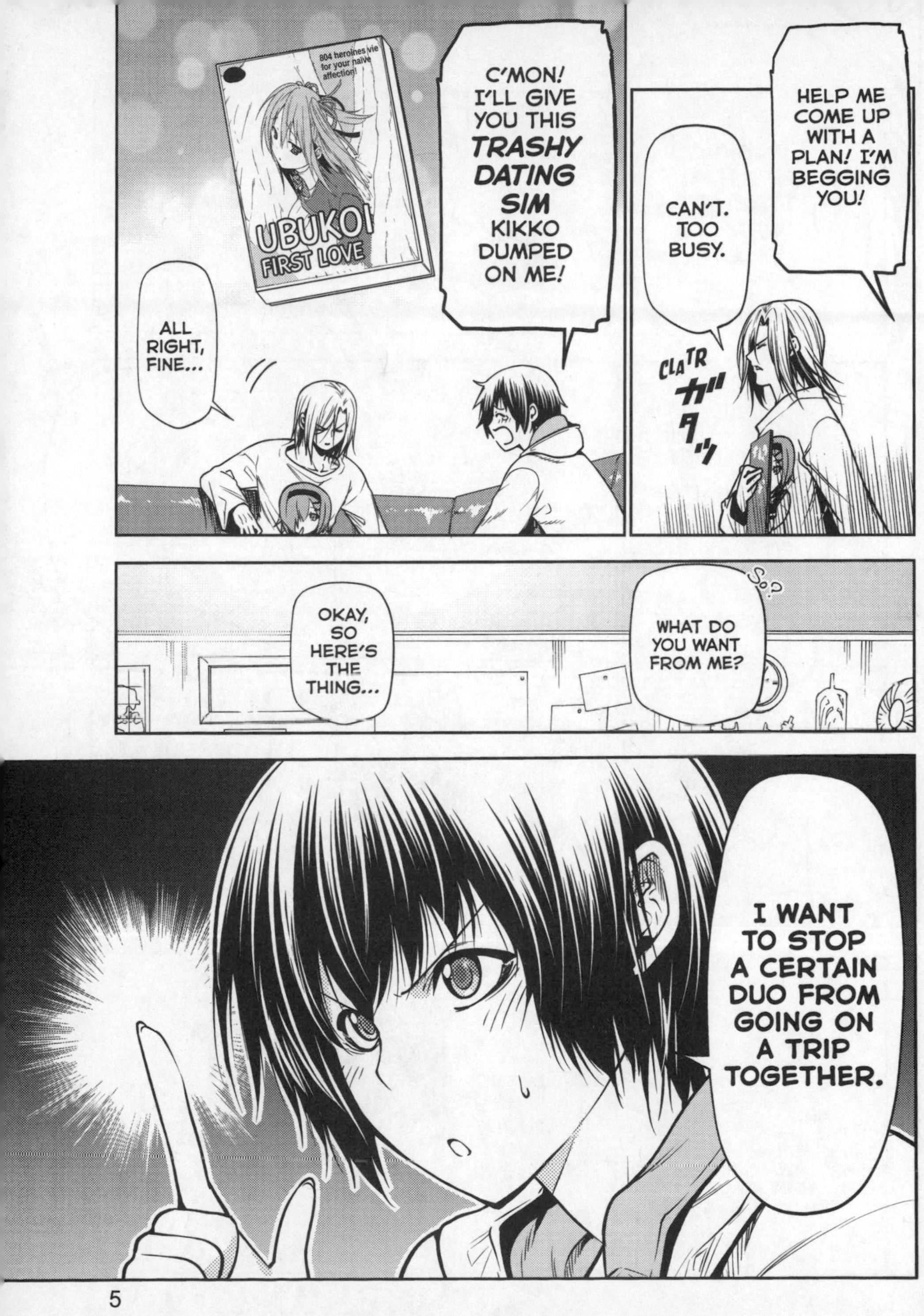
HELP ME COME UP WITH A PLAN! I'M BEGGING YOU!
CAN'T. TOO BUSY.
CLATR
ガタッ
804 heroines vie for your naive affection!
UBUKOI FIRST LOVE
C'MON! I'LL GIVE YOU THIS TRASHY DATING SIM KIKKO DUMPED ON ME!
ALL RIGHT, FINE...
So?
WHAT DO YOU WANT FROM ME?
OKAY, SO HERE'S THE THING...
I WANT TO STOP A CERTAIN DUO FROM GOING ON A TRIP TOGETHER.

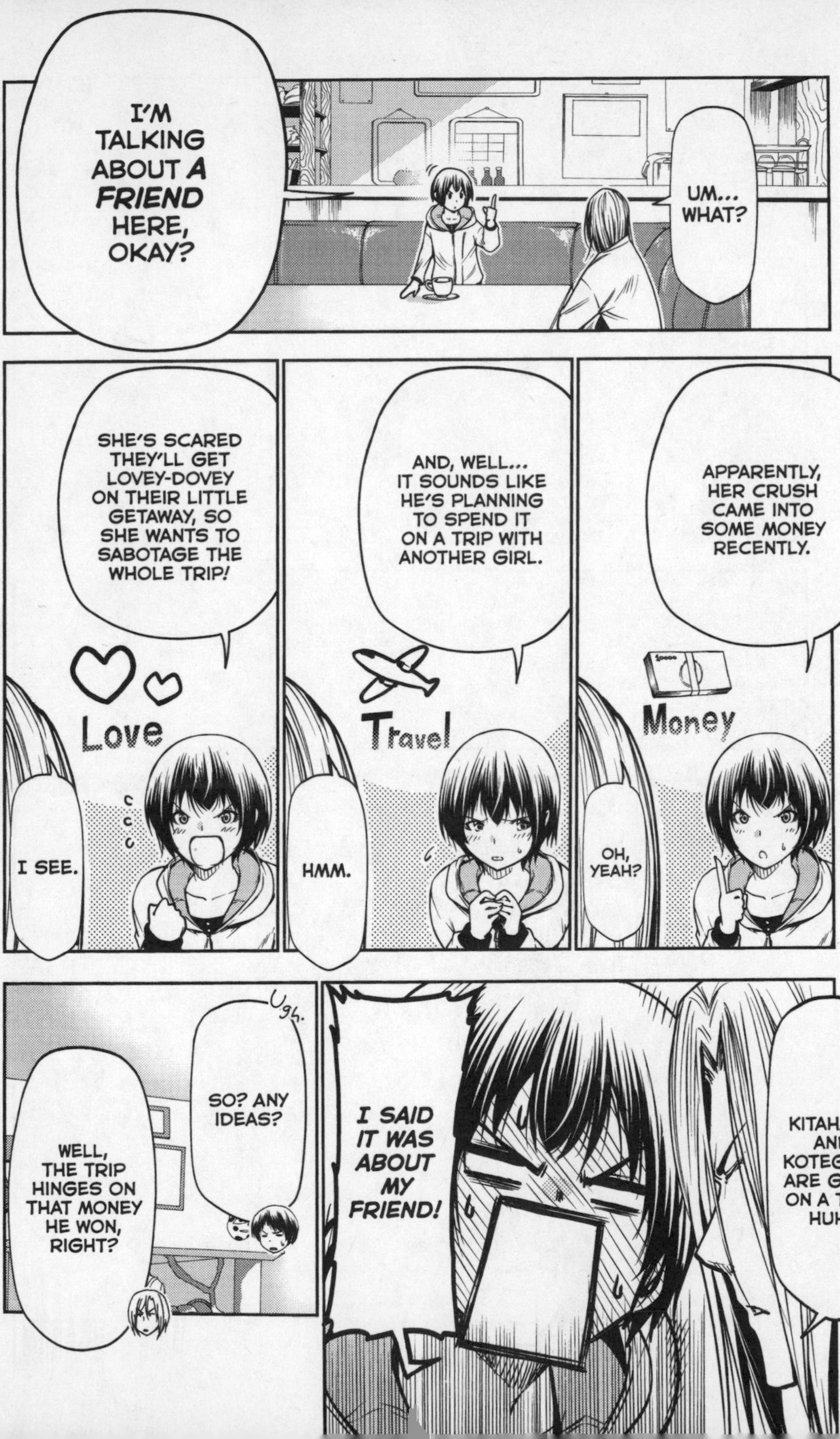
I'M TALKING ABOUT *A FRIEND* HERE, OKAY?
UM... WHAT?
Money
APPARENTLY, HER CRUSH CAME INTO SOME MONEY RECENTLY.
OH, YEAH?
Travel
AND, WELL... IT SOUNDS LIKE HE'S PLANNING TO SPEND IT ON A TRIP WITH ANOTHER GIRL.
HMM.
Love
SHE'S SCARED THEY'LL GET LOVEY-DOVEY ON THEIR LITTLE GETAWAY, SO SHE WANTS TO SABOTAGE THE WHOLE TRIP!
I SEE.
KITAHARA AND KOTEGAWA ARE GOIN' ON A TRIP, HUH?
I SAID IT WAS ABOUT MY FRIEND!
Ugh.
SO? ANY IDEAS?
WELL, THE TRIP HINGES ON THAT MONEY HE WON, RIGHT?

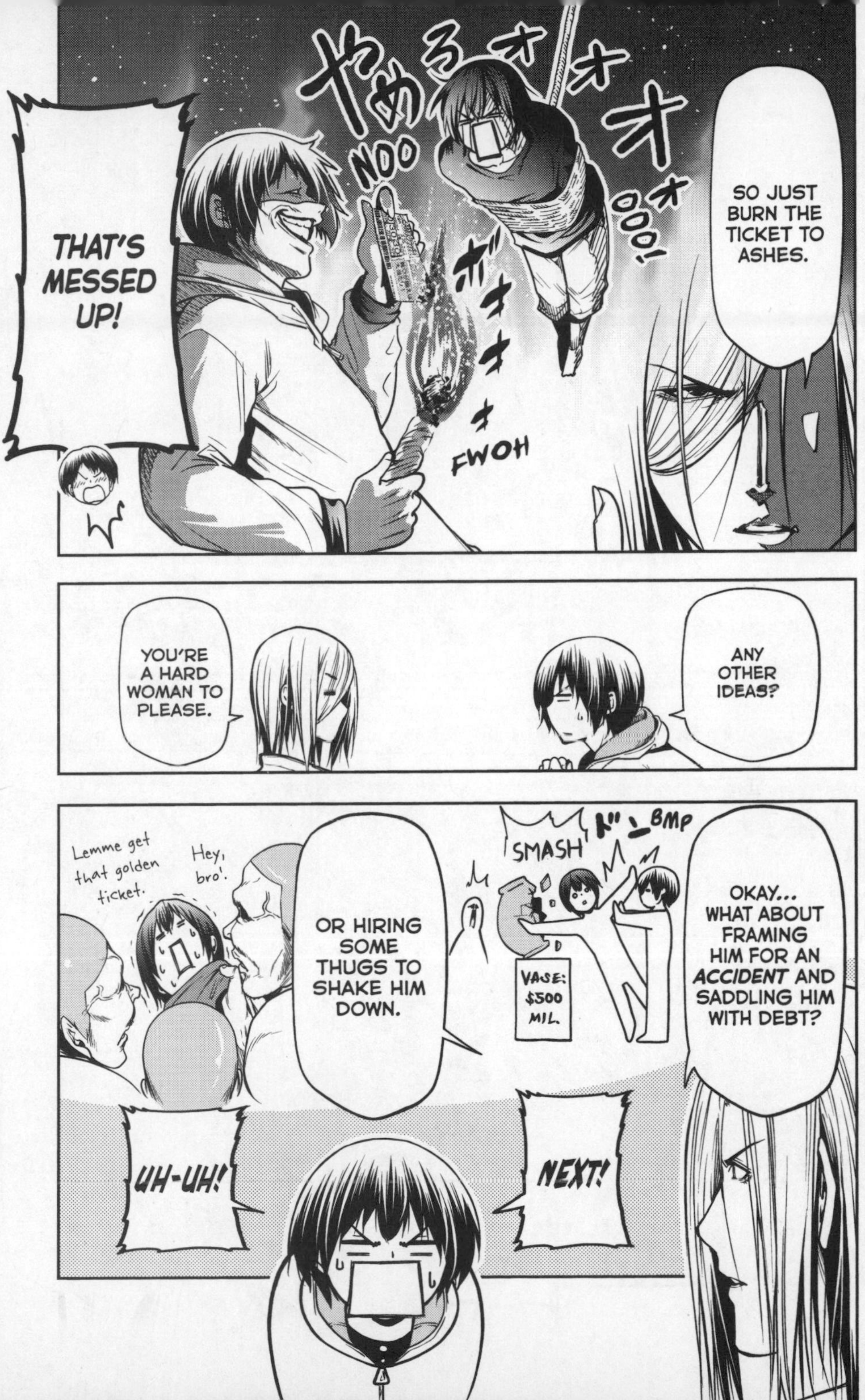
SO JUST BURN THE TICKET TO ASHES.
やめろォォォォ
NOOOOO!
ボォォォォ
FWOH
THAT'S MESSED UP!
ANY OTHER IDEAS?
YOU'RE A HARD WOMAN TO PLEASE.
OKAY... WHAT ABOUT FRAMING HIM FOR AN *ACCIDENT* AND SADDLING HIM WITH DEBT?
ドン
BMP
SMASH
VASE: $500 MIL.
OR HIRING SOME THUGS TO SHAKE HIM DOWN.
Hey, bro!
Lemme get that golden ticket.
NEXT!
UH-UH!

SHE COULD JUST BE HONEST...
PLEASE DON'T GO!
きゅるーん
UGUU
...AND BEG HIM TO CALL IT OFF?
NO WAY! SHE CAN'T DO THAT!
WHY NOT?
WHY? I MEAN...
THEY'RE NOT EVEN DATING. WHAT GIVES HER THE RIGHT TO STOP HIM?
HMM.
THEN SHE SHOULD CONFESS HOW SHE FEELS AND STOP HIM LEAVING.
CON- WHAT NOW?!

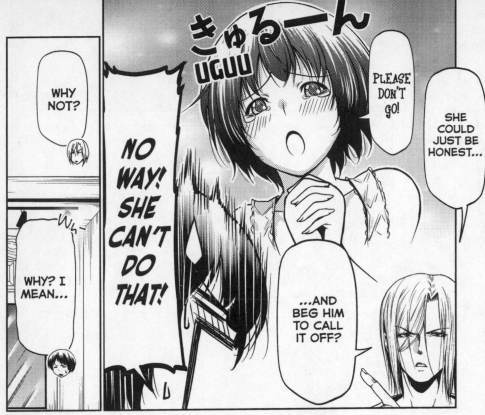

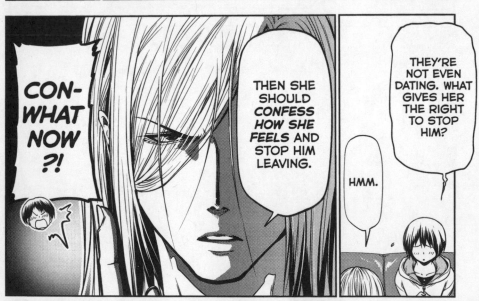

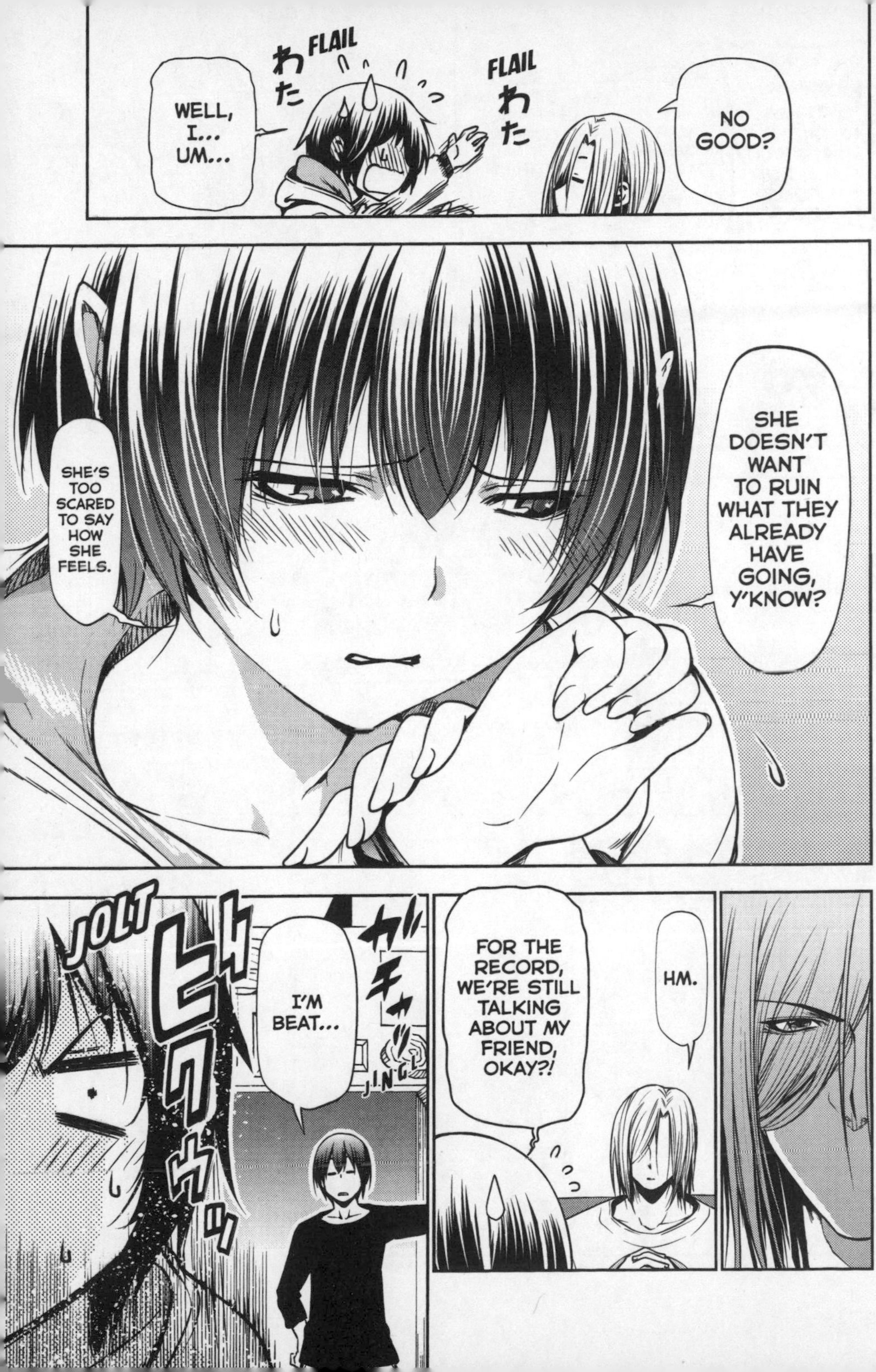
NO GOOD?
FLAIL
わた
FLAIL
わた
WELL, I... UM...
SHE DOESN'T WANT TO RUIN WHAT THEY ALREADY HAVE GOING, Y'KNOW?
SHE'S TOO SCARED TO SAY HOW SHE FEELS.
HM.
FOR THE RECORD, WE'RE STILL TALKING ABOUT MY FRIEND, OKAY?!
I'M BEAT...
JOLT
ビクゥッ

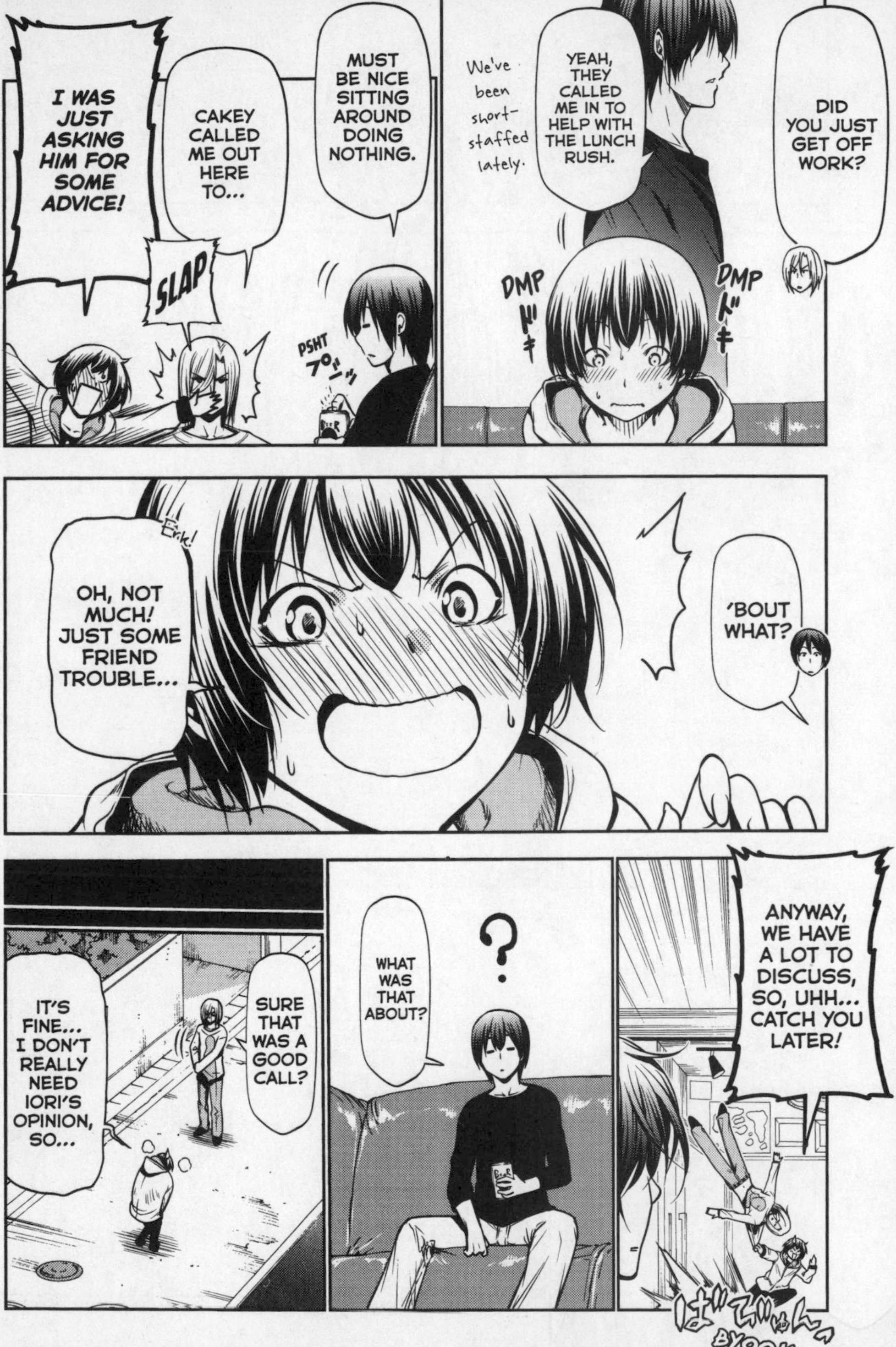
DID YOU JUST GET OFF WORK?
YEAH, THEY CALLED ME IN TO HELP WITH THE LUNCH RUSH.
We've been short-staffed lately.
DMP ドキ
DMP ドキ
MUST BE NICE SITTING AROUND DOING NOTHING.
PSHT
CAKEY CALLED ME OUT HERE TO...
SLAP
I WAS JUST ASKING HIM FOR SOME ADVICE!
'BOUT WHAT?
Erk!
OH, NOT MUCH! JUST SOME FRIEND TROUBLE...
ANYWAY, WE HAVE A LOT TO DISCUSS, SO, UHH... CATCH YOU LATER!
BYOOM
?
WHAT WAS THAT ABOUT?
SURE THAT WAS A GOOD CALL?
IT'S FINE... I DON'T REALLY NEED IORI'S OPINION, SO...

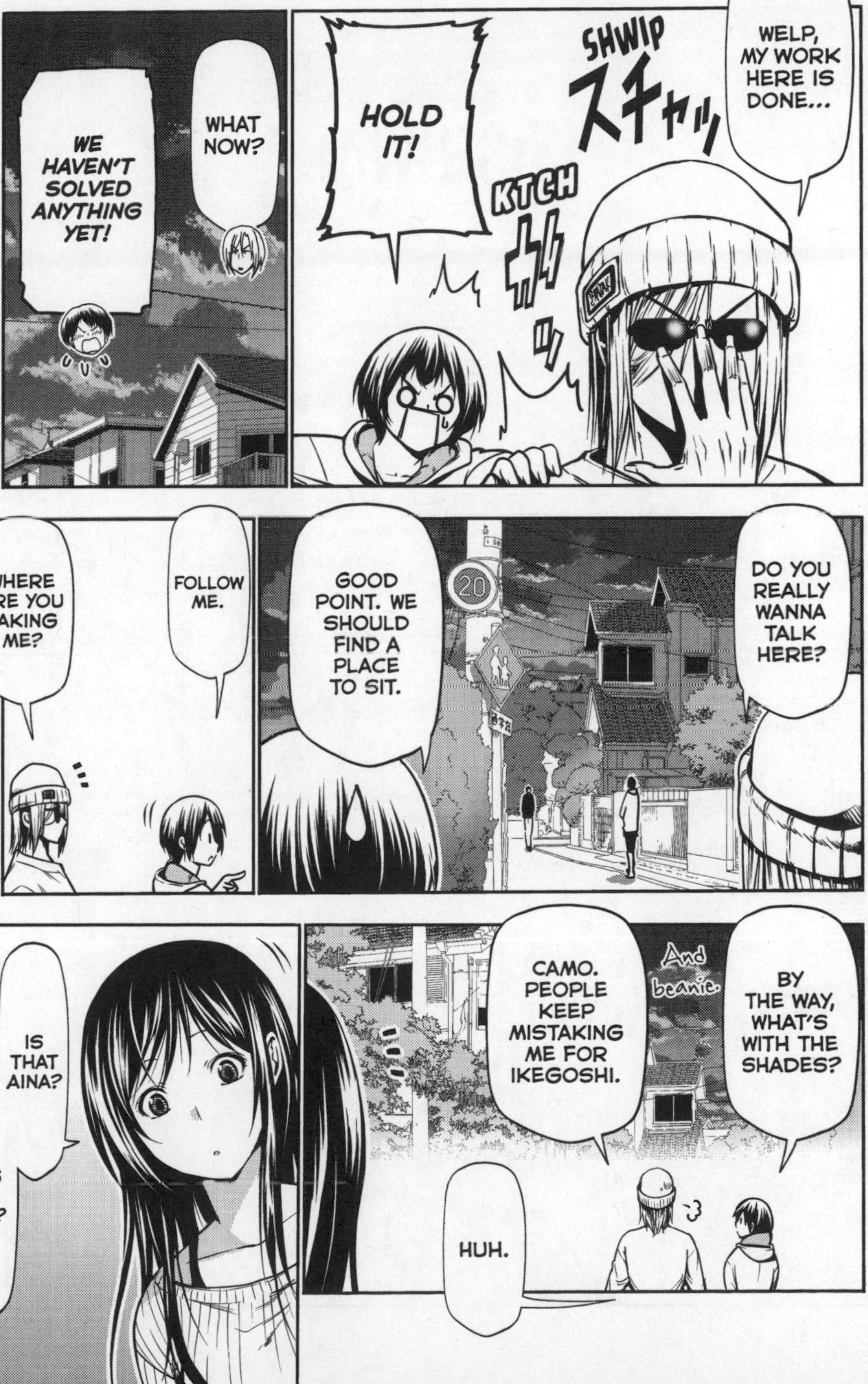
WELP, MY WORK HERE IS DONE...
SHWIP
スチャッ
KTCH
カチッ
HOLD IT!
WHAT NOW?
WE HAVEN'T SOLVED ANYTHING YET!
DO YOU REALLY WANNA TALK HERE?
GOOD POINT. WE SHOULD FIND A PLACE TO SIT.
FOLLOW ME.
WHERE ARE YOU TAKING ME?
BY THE WAY, WHAT'S WITH THE SHADES?
CAMO. PEOPLE KEEP MISTAKING ME FOR IKEGOSHI.
And beanie.
HUH.
IS THAT AINA?
WHO'S THE GUY...?

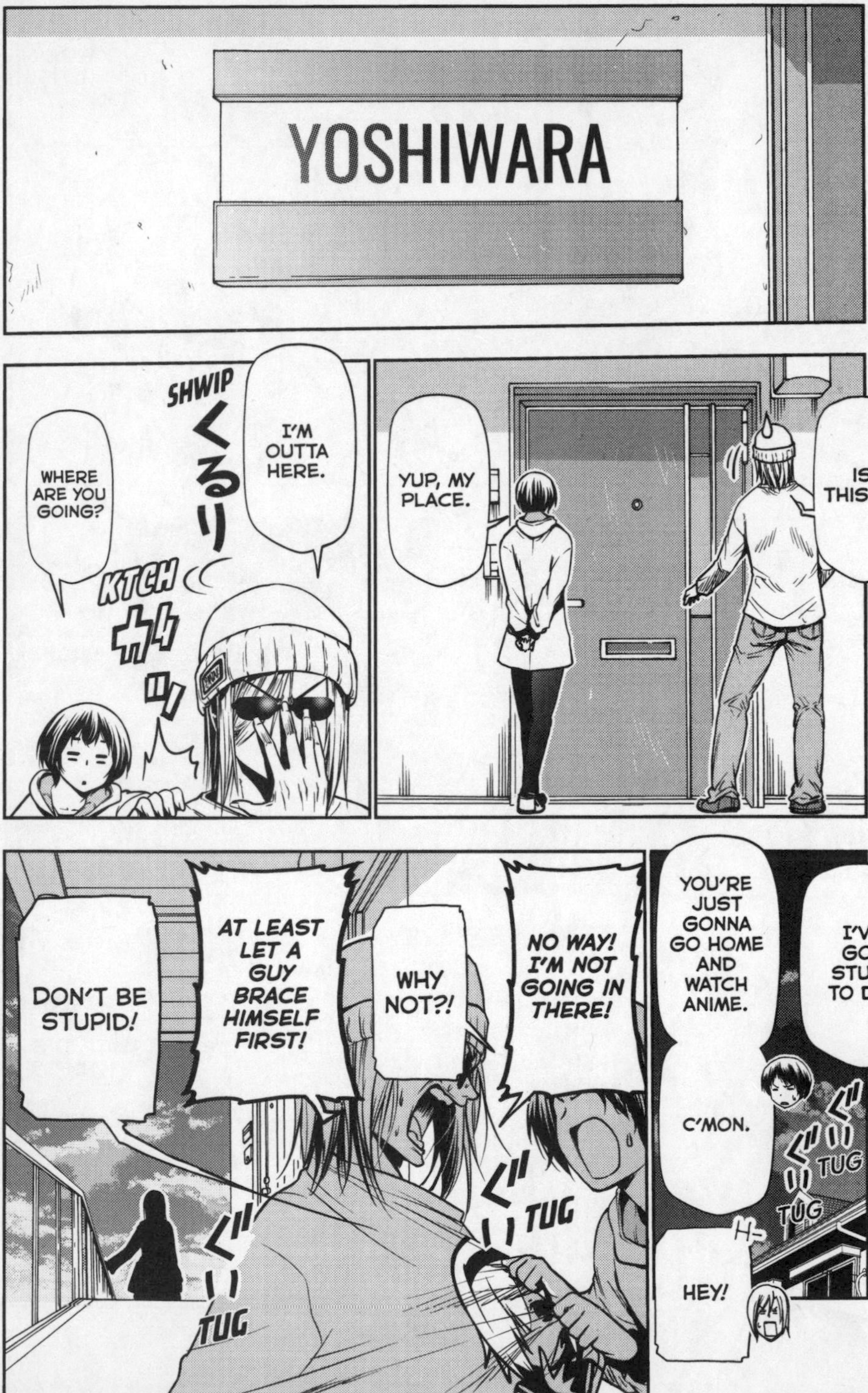
YOSHIWARA
IS THIS...?
YUP, MY PLACE.
I'M OUTTA HERE.
SHWIP
くるり
KTCH
WHERE ARE YOU GOING?
I'VE GOT STUFF TO DO.
YOU'RE JUST GONNA GO HOME AND WATCH ANIME.
C'MON.
TUG
TUG
HEY!
NO WAY! I'M NOT GOING IN THERE!
WHY NOT?!
AT LEAST LET A GUY BRACE HIMSELF FIRST!
DON'T BE STUPID!
TUG
TUG

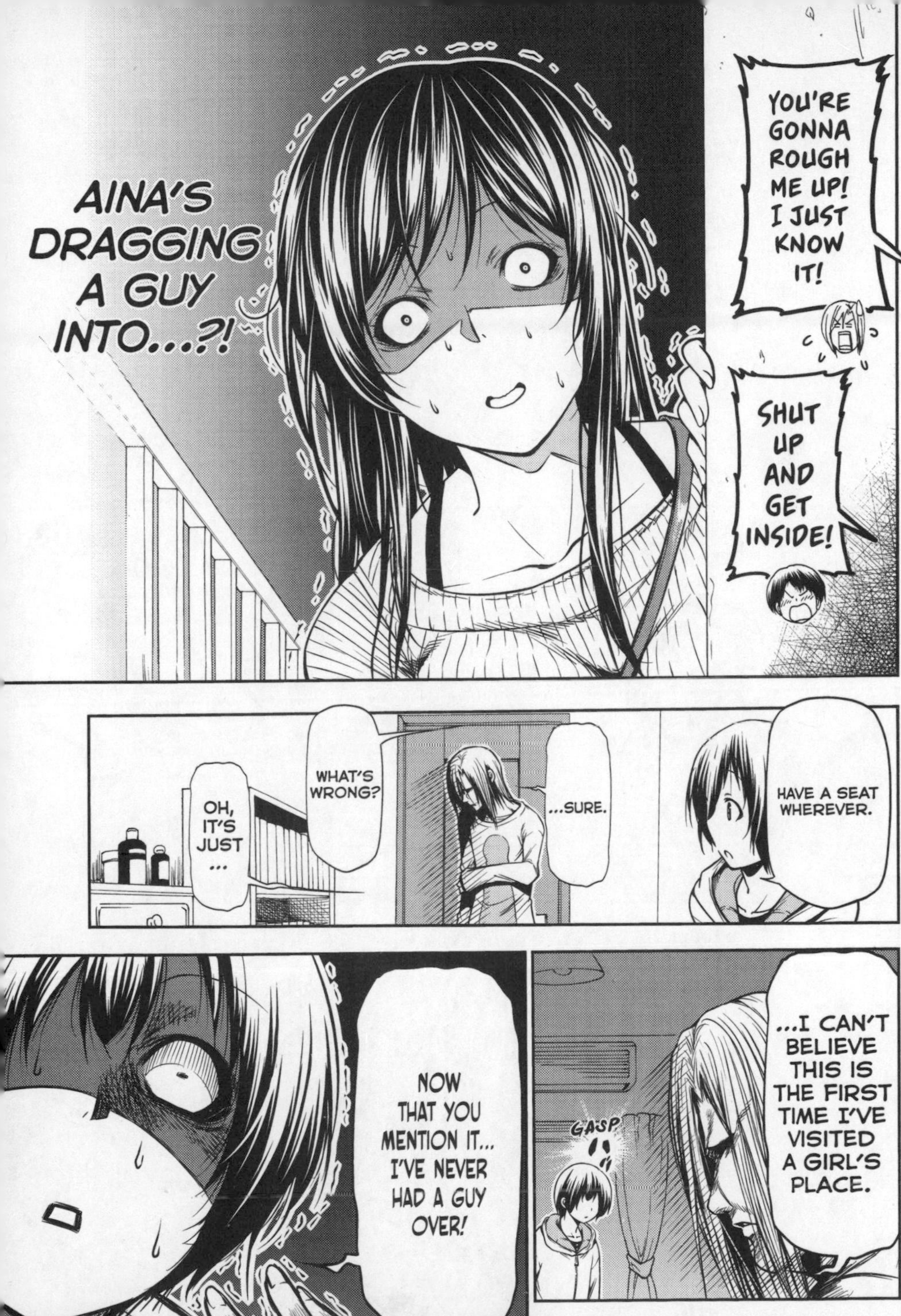
YOU'RE GONNA ROUGH ME UP! I JUST KNOW IT!
SHUT UP AND GET INSIDE!
AINA'S DRAGGING A GUY INTO...?!
HAVE A SEAT WHEREVER.
...SURE.
WHAT'S WRONG?
OH, IT'S JUST ...
...I CAN'T BELIEVE THIS IS THE FIRST TIME I'VE VISITED A GIRL'S PLACE.
GASP
NOW THAT YOU MENTION IT... I'VE NEVER HAD A GUY OVER!

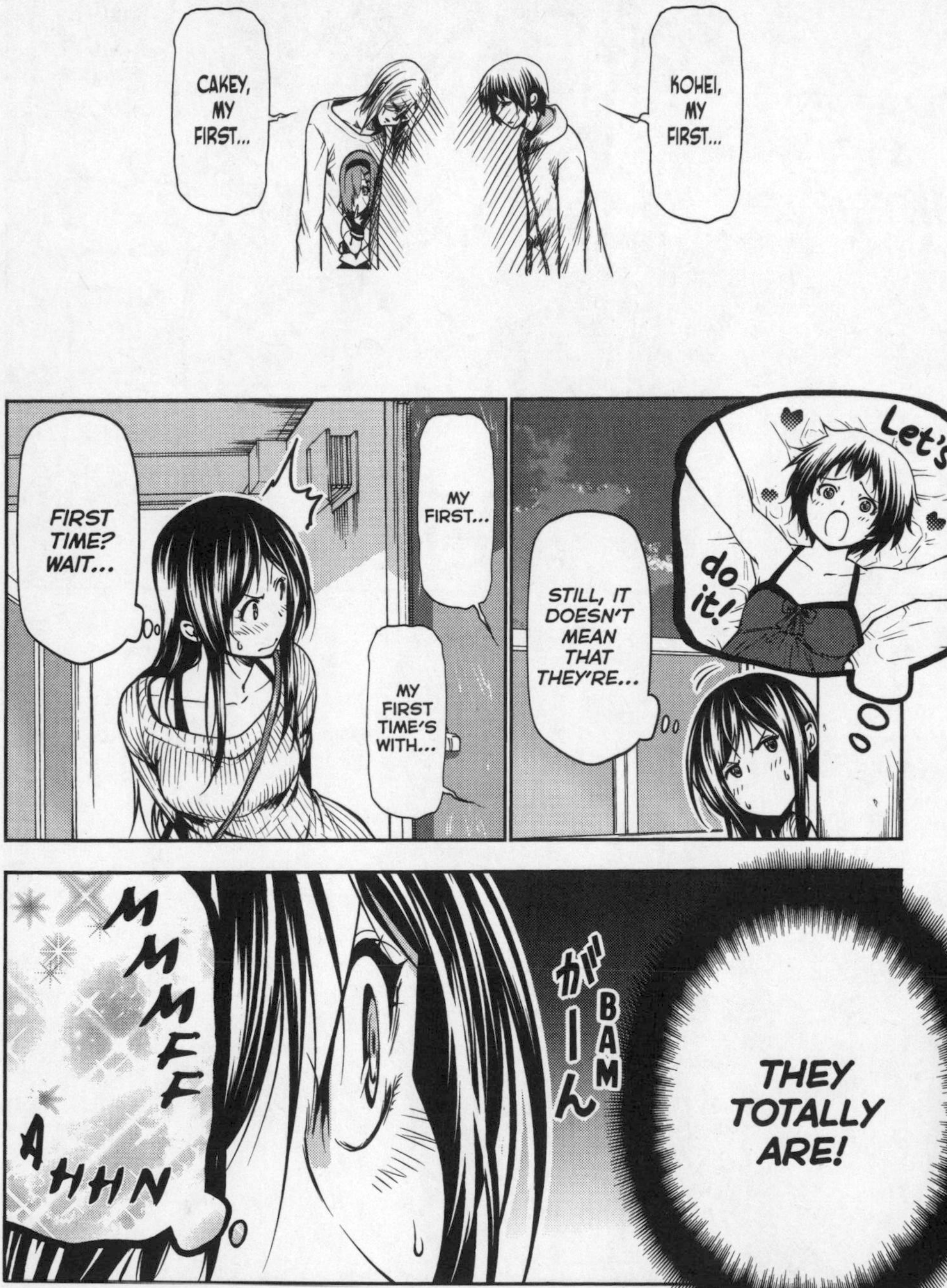
KOHEI, MY FIRST...
CAKEY, MY FIRST...
Let's do it!
STILL, IT DOESN'T MEAN THAT THEY'RE...
MY FIRST...
MY FIRST TIME'S WITH...
FIRST TIME? WAIT...
THEY TOTALLY ARE!
がーん
BAM
MMMFF AHHN

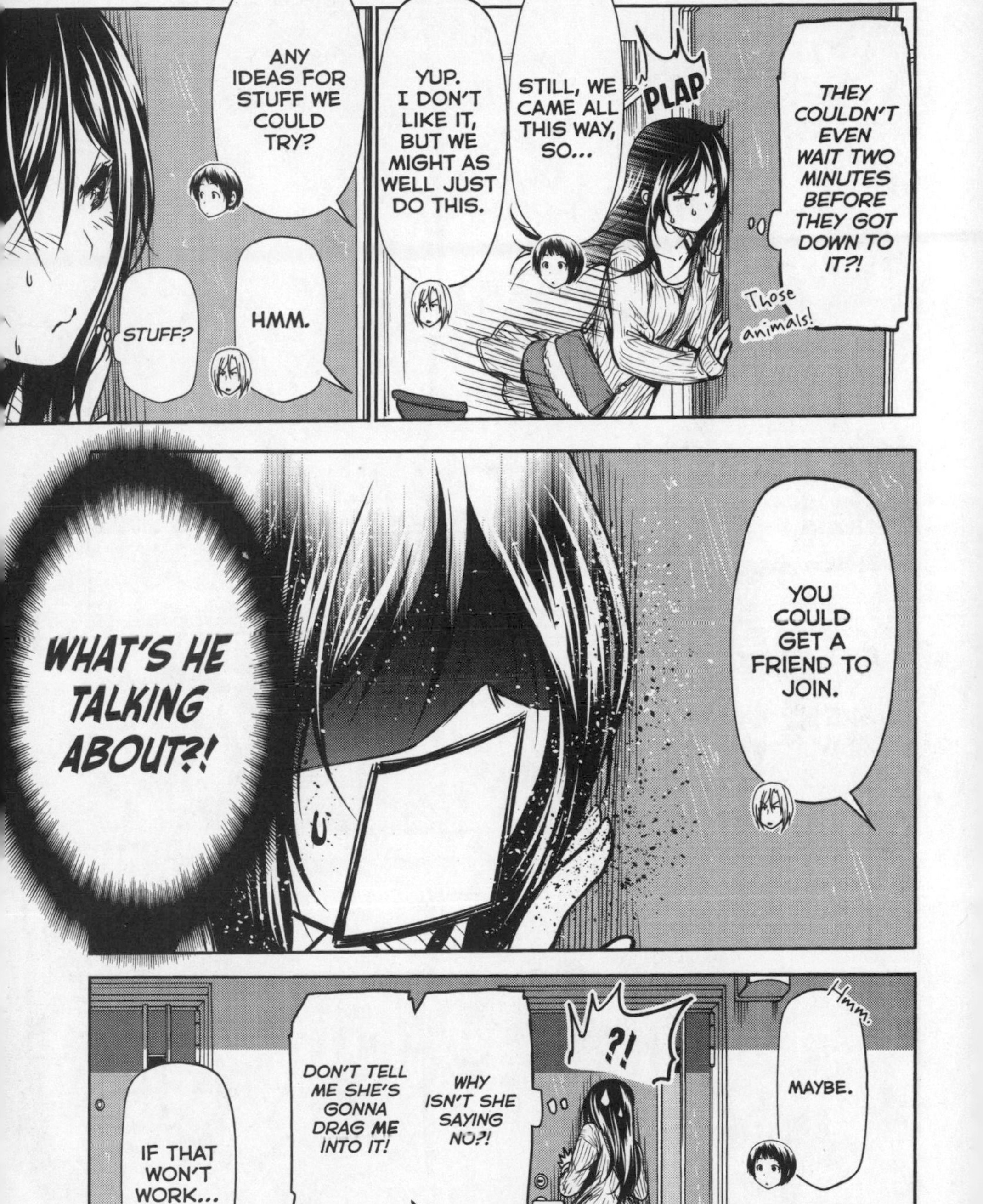
THEY COULDN'T EVEN WAIT TWO MINUTES BEFORE THEY GOT DOWN TO IT?!
Those animals!
PLAP
STILL, WE CAME ALL THIS WAY, SO...
YUP. I DON'T LIKE IT, BUT WE MIGHT AS WELL JUST DO THIS.
ANY IDEAS FOR STUFF WE COULD TRY?
HMM.
STUFF?
YOU COULD GET A FRIEND TO JOIN.
WHAT'S HE TALKING ABOUT?!
Hmm.
MAYBE.
?!
WHY ISN'T SHE SAYING NO?!
DON'T TELL ME SHE'S GONNA DRAG ME INTO IT!
IF THAT WON'T WORK...

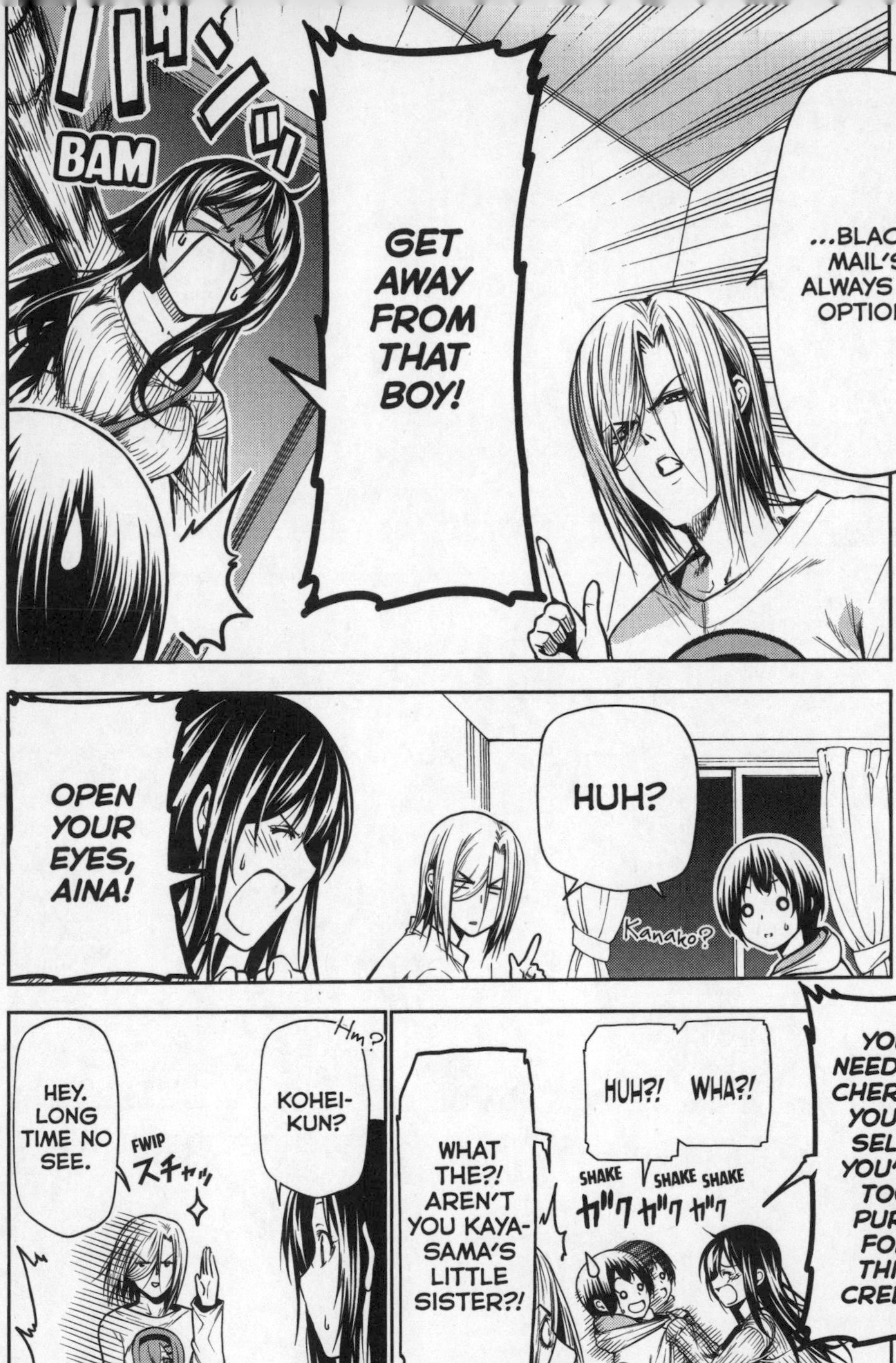
...BLACK-MAIL'S ALWAYS AN OPTION.
GET AWAY FROM THAT BOY!
BAM
HUH?
Kanako?
OPEN YOUR EYES, AINA!
YOU NEED TO CHERISH YOUR-SELF! YOU'RE TOO PURE FOR THIS CREEP!
HUH?! WHA?!
SHAKE SHAKE SHAKE
ガクガクガク
WHAT THE?! AREN'T YOU KAYA-SAMA'S LITTLE SISTER?!
Hm?
KOHEI-KUN?
HEY. LONG TIME NO SEE.
FWIP
スチャッ

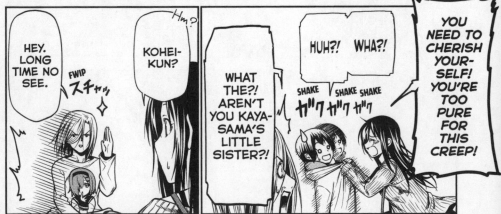

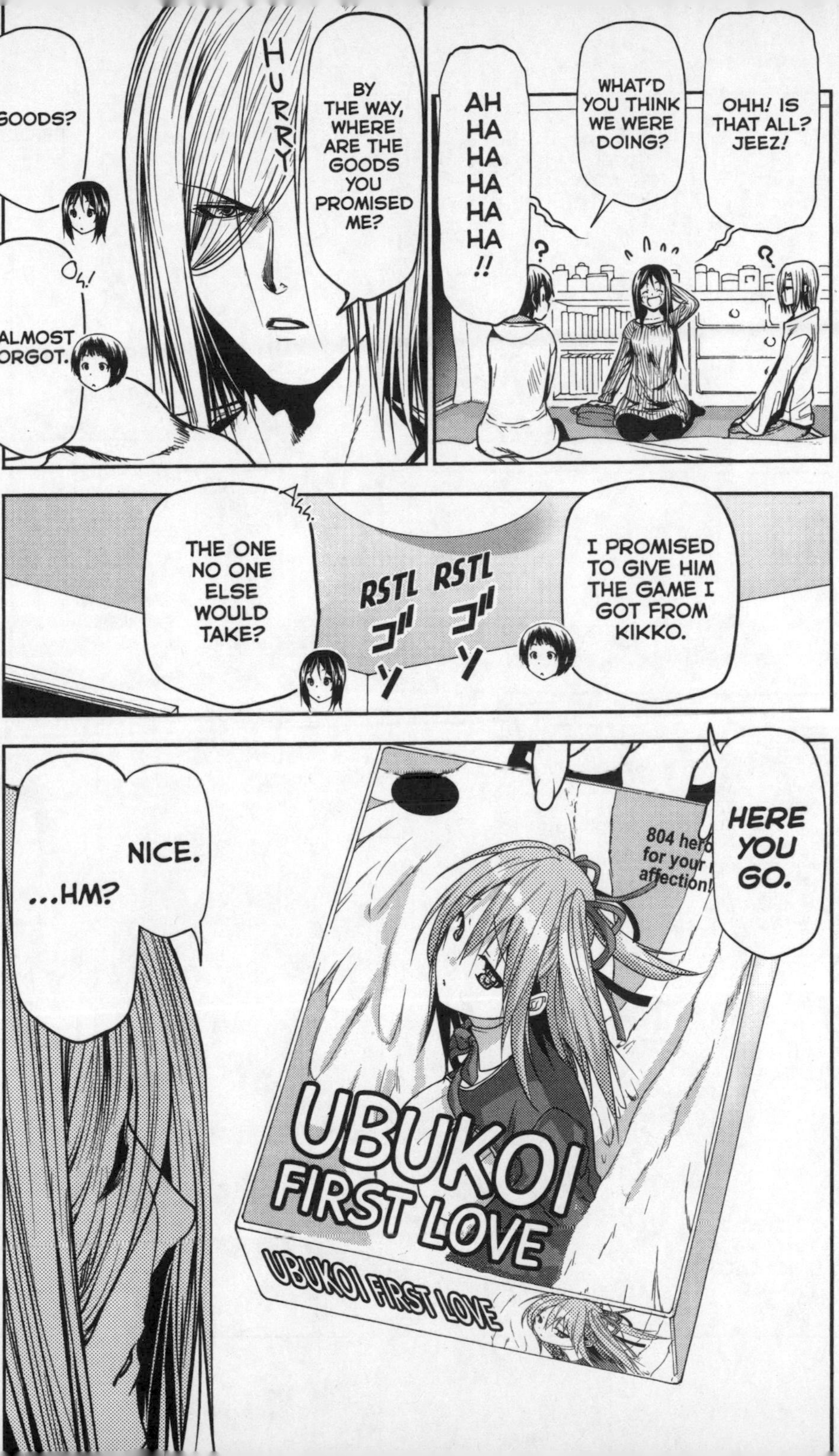

OHH! IS THAT ALL? JEEZ!
WHAT'D YOU THINK WE WERE DOING?
AH HA HA HA HA HA!!
HURRY
BY THE WAY, WHERE ARE THE GOODS YOU PROMISED ME?
GOODS?
Oh!
I ALMOST FORGOT.
I PROMISED TO GIVE HIM THE GAME I GOT FROM KIKKO.
RSTL RSTL
ゴソ ゴソ
THE ONE NO ONE ELSE WOULD TAKE?
HERE YOU GO.
UBUKOI FIRST LOVE
UBUKOI FIRST LOVE
NICE.
...HM?

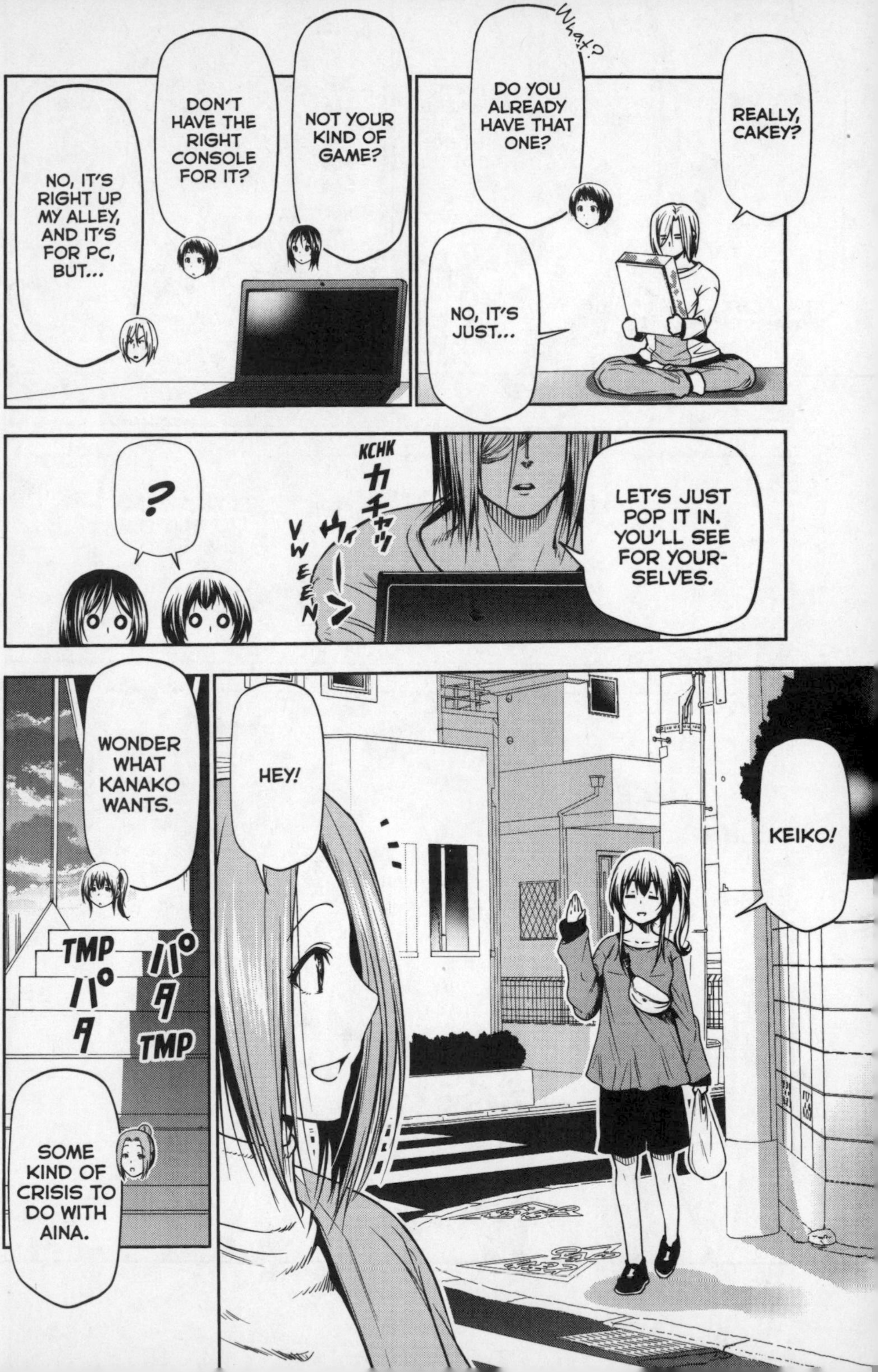
REALLY, CAKEY?
What?
DO YOU ALREADY HAVE THAT ONE?
NO, IT'S JUST...
NOT YOUR KIND OF GAME?
DON'T HAVE THE RIGHT CONSOLE FOR IT?
NO, IT'S RIGHT UP MY ALLEY, AND IT'S FOR PC, BUT...
LET'S JUST POP IT IN. YOU'LL SEE FOR YOURSELVES.
KCHK カチャッ
VWEEN ヴィーン
?
KEIKO!
HEY!
WONDER WHAT KANAKO WANTS.
TMP パタ
パタ TMP
SOME KIND OF CRISIS TO DO WITH AINA.

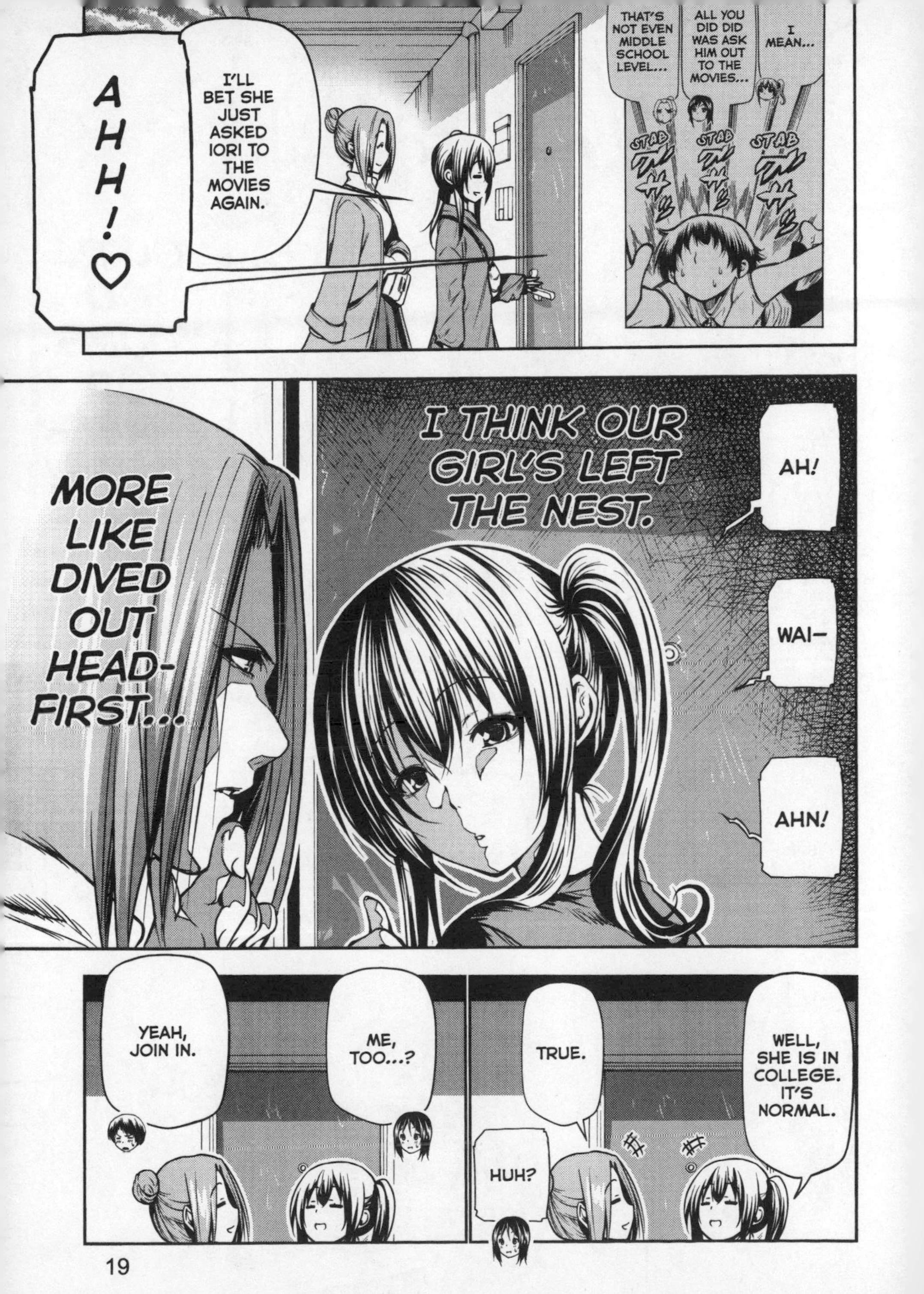
I MEAN...
ALL YOU DID DID WAS ASK HIM OUT TO THE MOVIES...
THAT'S NOT EVEN MIDDLE SCHOOL LEVEL...
STAB
STAB
STAB
I'LL BET SHE JUST ASKED IORI TO THE MOVIES AGAIN.
AHH!♡
AH!
I THINK OUR GIRL'S LEFT THE NEST.
WAI—
AHN!
MORE LIKE DIVED OUT HEAD-FIRST...
WELL, SHE IS IN COLLEGE. IT'S NORMAL.
TRUE.
HUH?
ME, TOO...?
YEAH, JOIN IN.

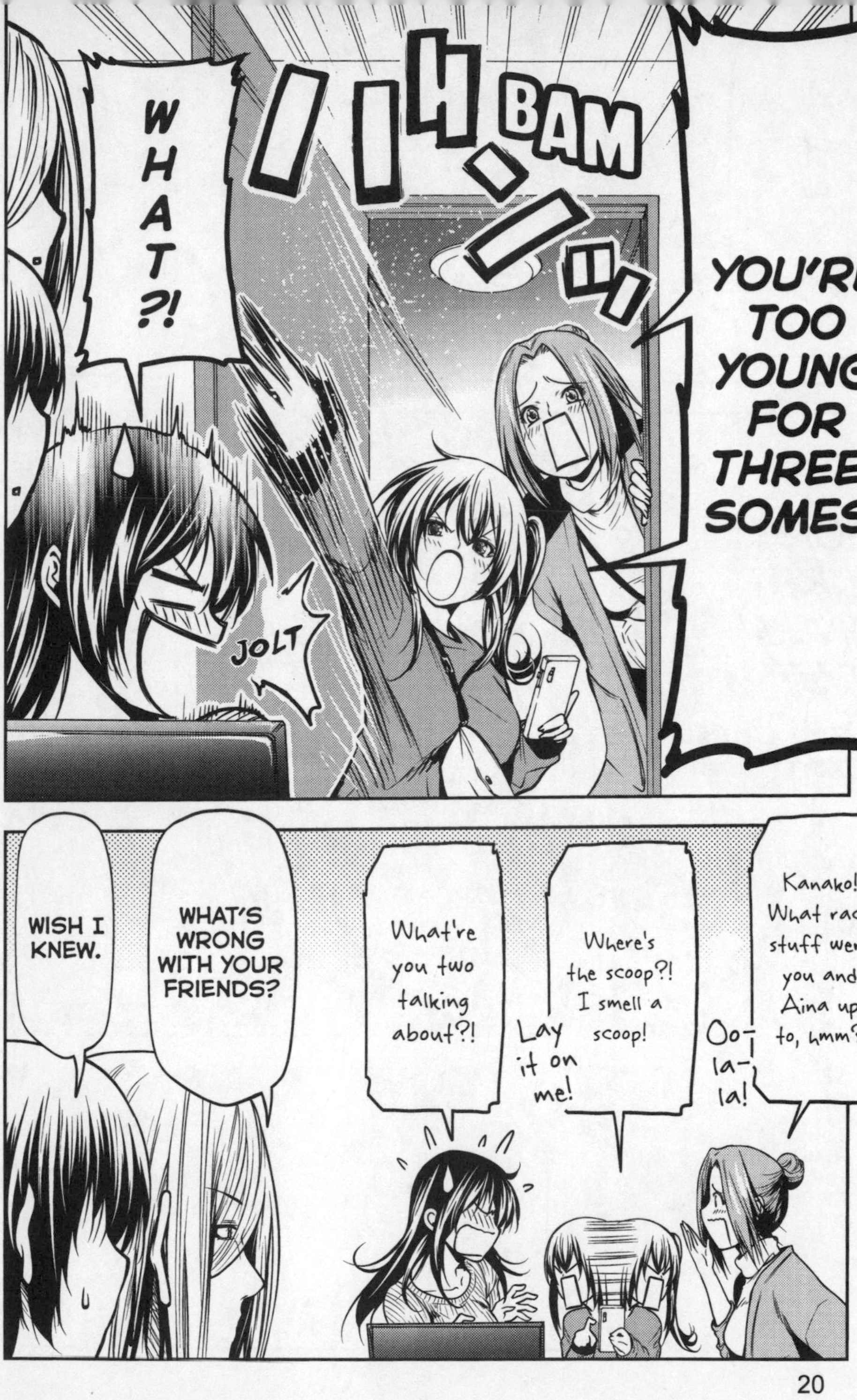
YOU'RE TOO YOUNG FOR THREE-SOMES!
BAM
WHAT?!
JOLT
Kanako! What racy stuff were you and Aina up to, umm?
Oo-la-la!
Where's the scoop?! I smell a scoop!
Lay it on me!
What're you two talking about?!
WHAT'S WRONG WITH YOUR FRIENDS?
WISH I KNEW.

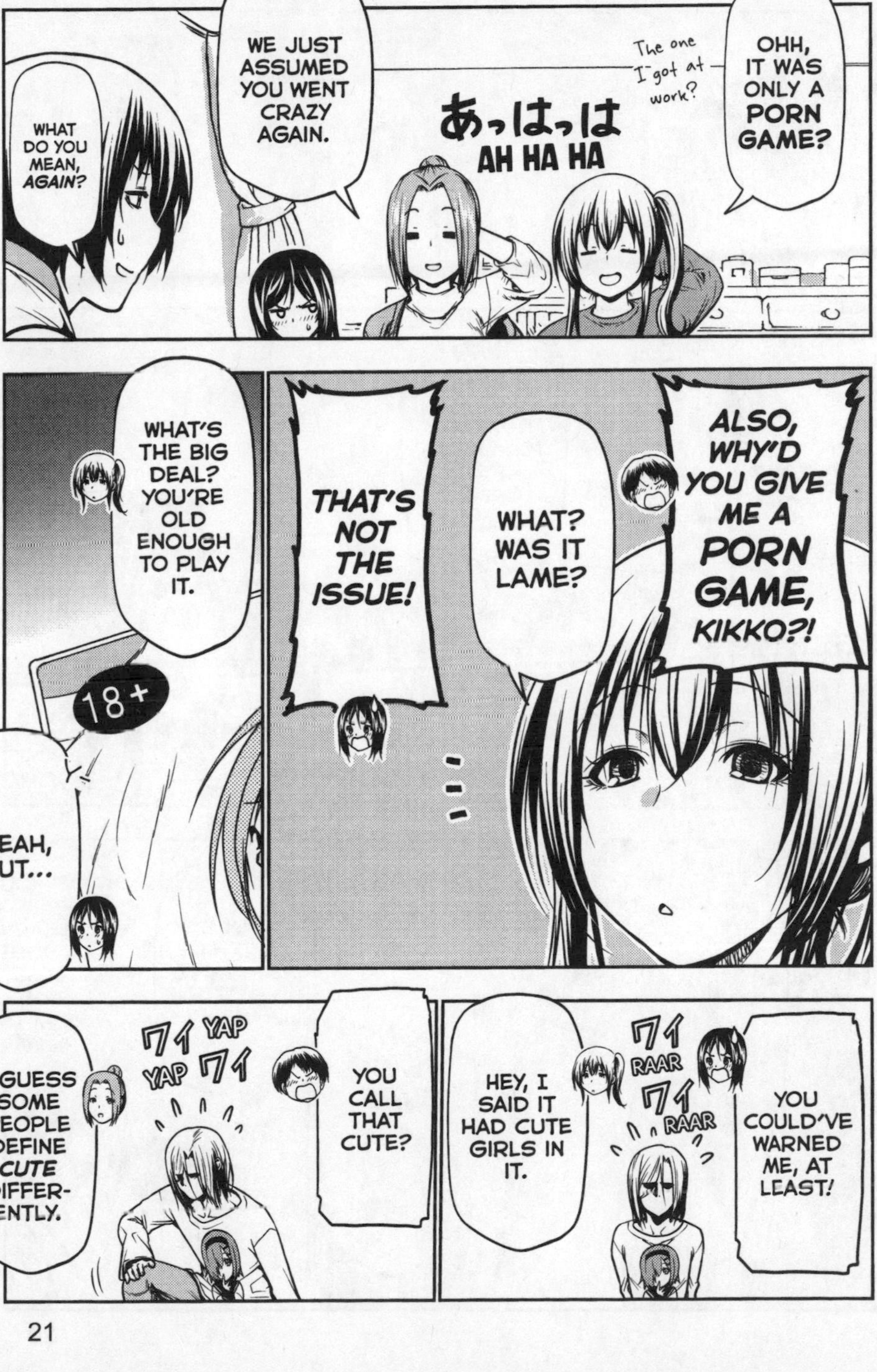

OHH, IT WAS ONLY A PORN GAME?
The one I got at work?
あっはっは
AH HA HA
WE JUST ASSUMED YOU WENT CRAZY AGAIN.
WHAT DO YOU MEAN, *AGAIN*?
ALSO, WHY'D YOU GIVE ME A PORN GAME, KIKKO?!
WHAT? WAS IT LAME?
THAT'S NOT THE ISSUE!
...
WHAT'S THE BIG DEAL? YOU'RE OLD ENOUGH TO PLAY IT.
18+
YEAH, BUT...
YOU COULD'VE WARNED ME, AT LEAST!
ワイ RAAR
ワイ RAAR
HEY, I SAID IT HAD CUTE GIRLS IN IT.
YOU CALL THAT CUTE?
ワイ YAP
YAP ワイ
I GUESS SOME PEOPLE DEFINE *CUTE* DIFFER-ENTLY.

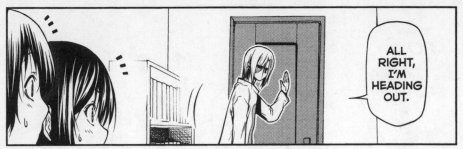

ALL RIGHT, I'M HEADING OUT.
OH, YEAH. WE WERE TALKING ABOUT AINA'S LOVE LIFE.
HUH?
HOW DO YOU GO FROM THAT TO PLAYING A PORN GAME?
Really, now...
I DIDN'T KNOW!
CHIPS
IF YOU WANNA LEARN ABOUT LOVE, JUST PLAY THE GAME.
LIKE IT'D HAVE ANYTHING WORTH LEARNING...
18+
DON'T BE SO SURE.

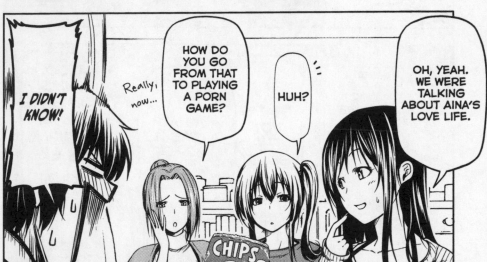

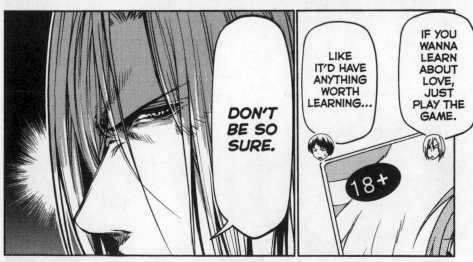

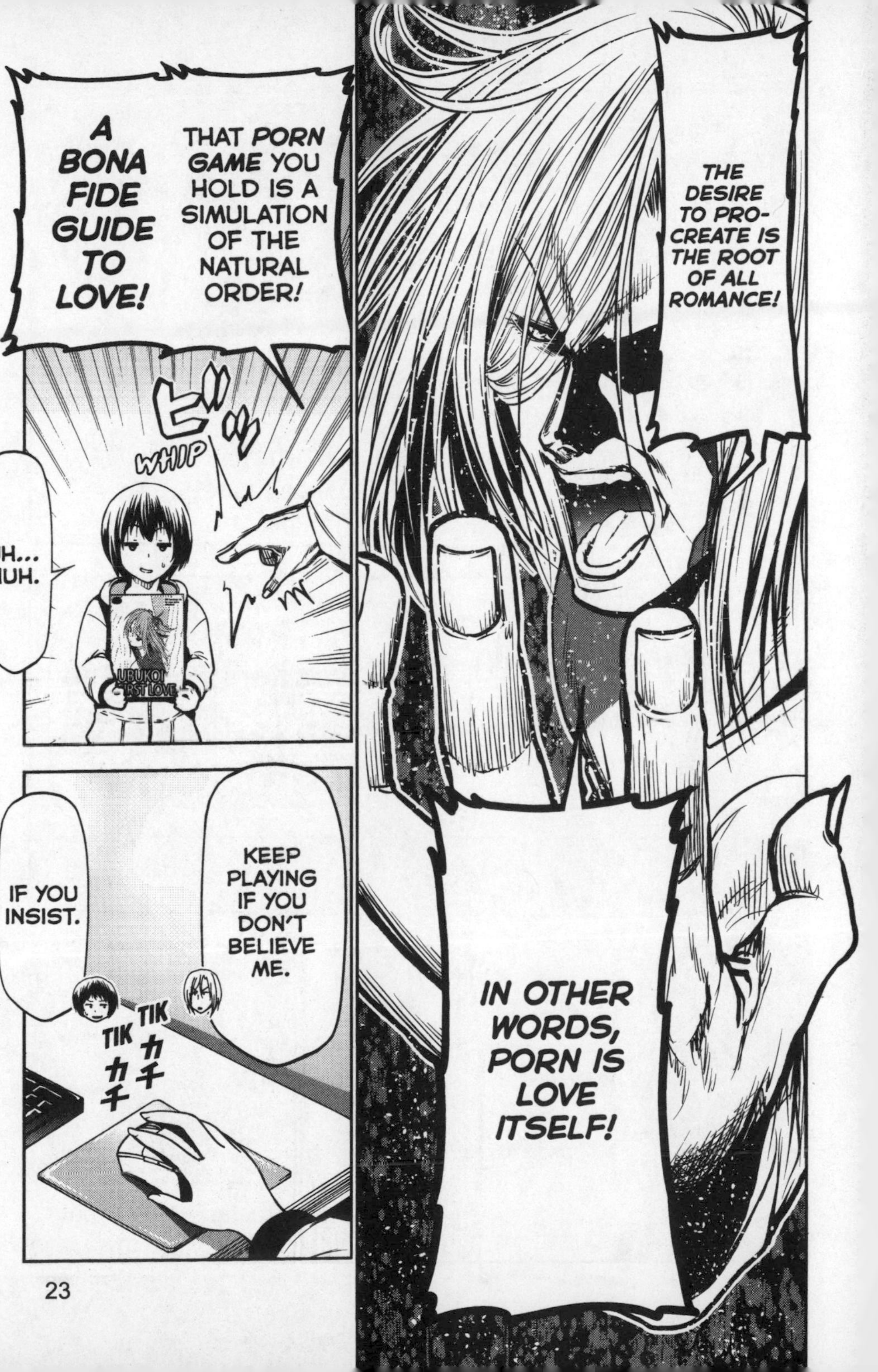
THE DESIRE TO PRO-CREATE IS THE ROOT OF ALL ROMANCE!
IN OTHER WORDS, PORN IS LOVE ITSELF!
THAT PORN GAME YOU HOLD IS A SIMULATION OF THE NATURAL ORDER!
A BONA FIDE GUIDE TO LOVE!
WHIP
UH... HUH.
UBUKOI
KEEP PLAYING IF YOU DON'T BELIEVE ME.
IF YOU INSIST.
TIK
TIK
カチ
カチ

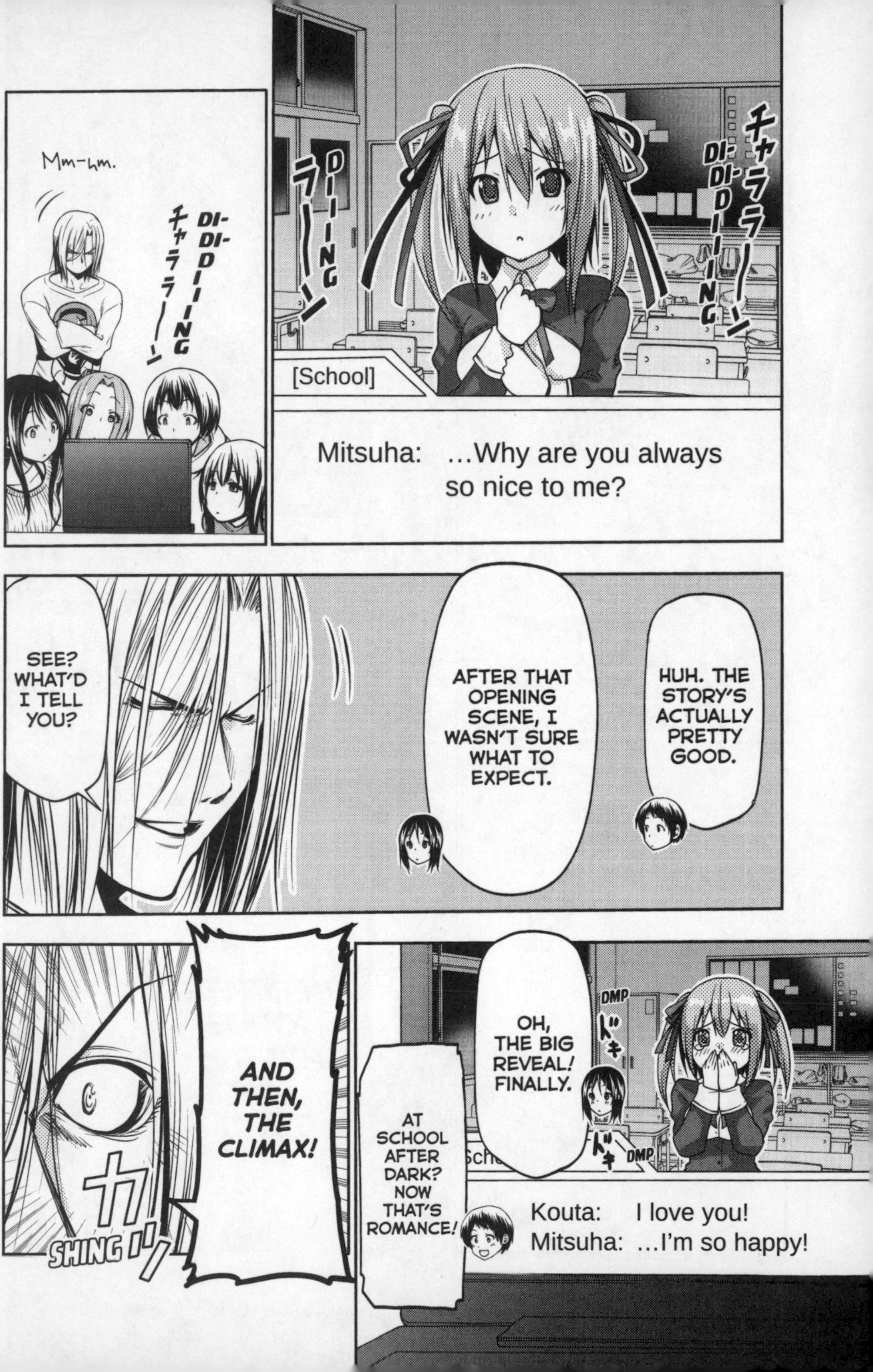
チャララ～ン
DI-DI-DI-DI-DIIING
ラ～ン
DI-IING
[School]
Mitsuha: …Why are you always so nice to me?
Mm-hm.
DI-DI-DI-DIIING
チャララ～ン
HUH. THE STORY'S ACTUALLY PRETTY GOOD.
AFTER THAT OPENING SCENE, I WASN'T SURE WHAT TO EXPECT.
SEE? WHAT'D I TELL YOU?
OH, THE BIG REVEAL! FINALLY.
DMP
ドキ
ドキ
DMP
AT SCHOOL AFTER DARK? NOW THAT'S ROMANCE!
Kouta: I love you!
Mitsuha: …I'm so happy!
AND THEN, THE CLIMAX!
カ
SHING

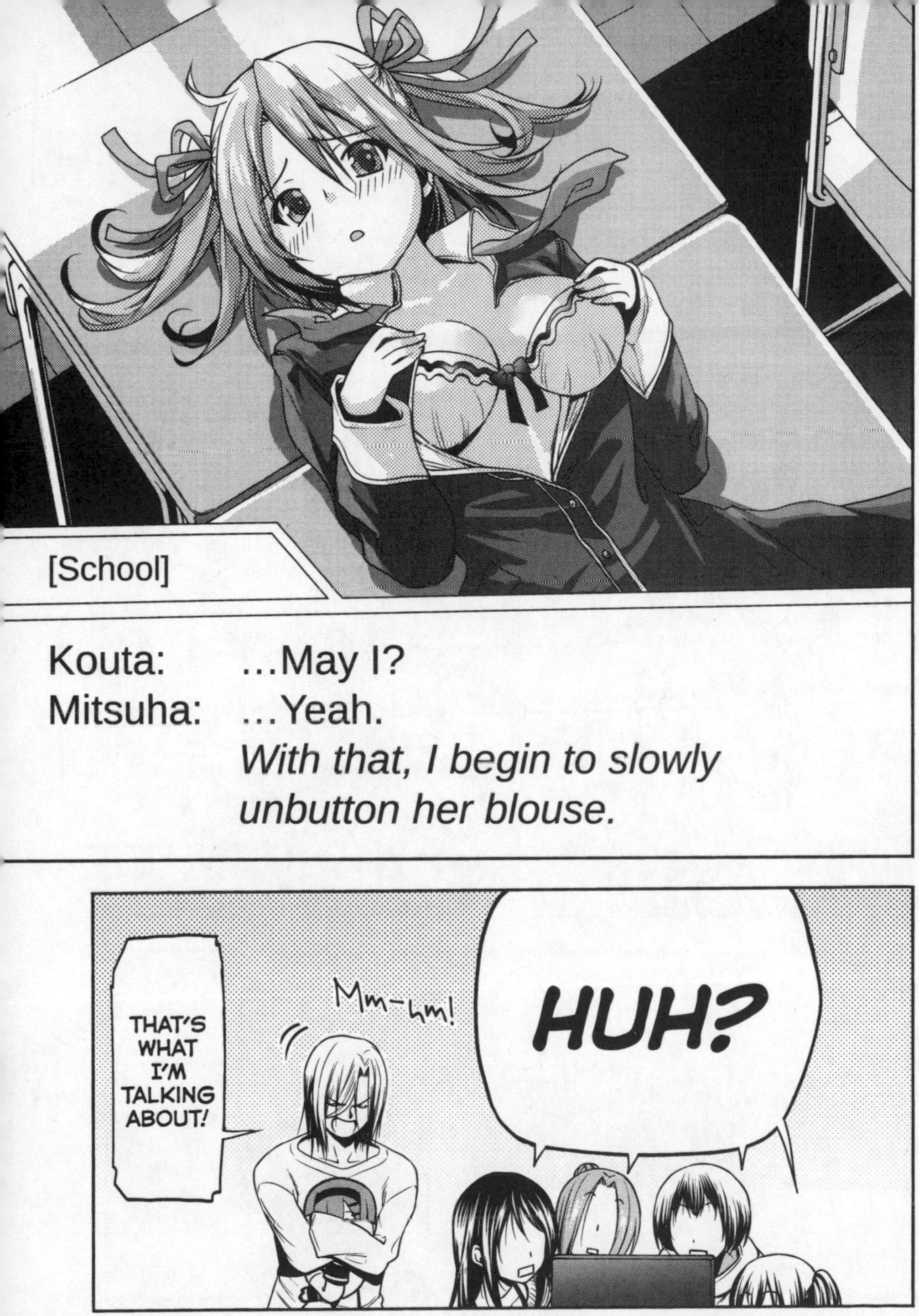
[School]
Kouta: …May I?
Mitsuha: …Yeah.
With that, I begin to slowly unbutton her blouse.
HUH?
Mm-hm!
THAT'S WHAT I'M TALKING ABOUT!

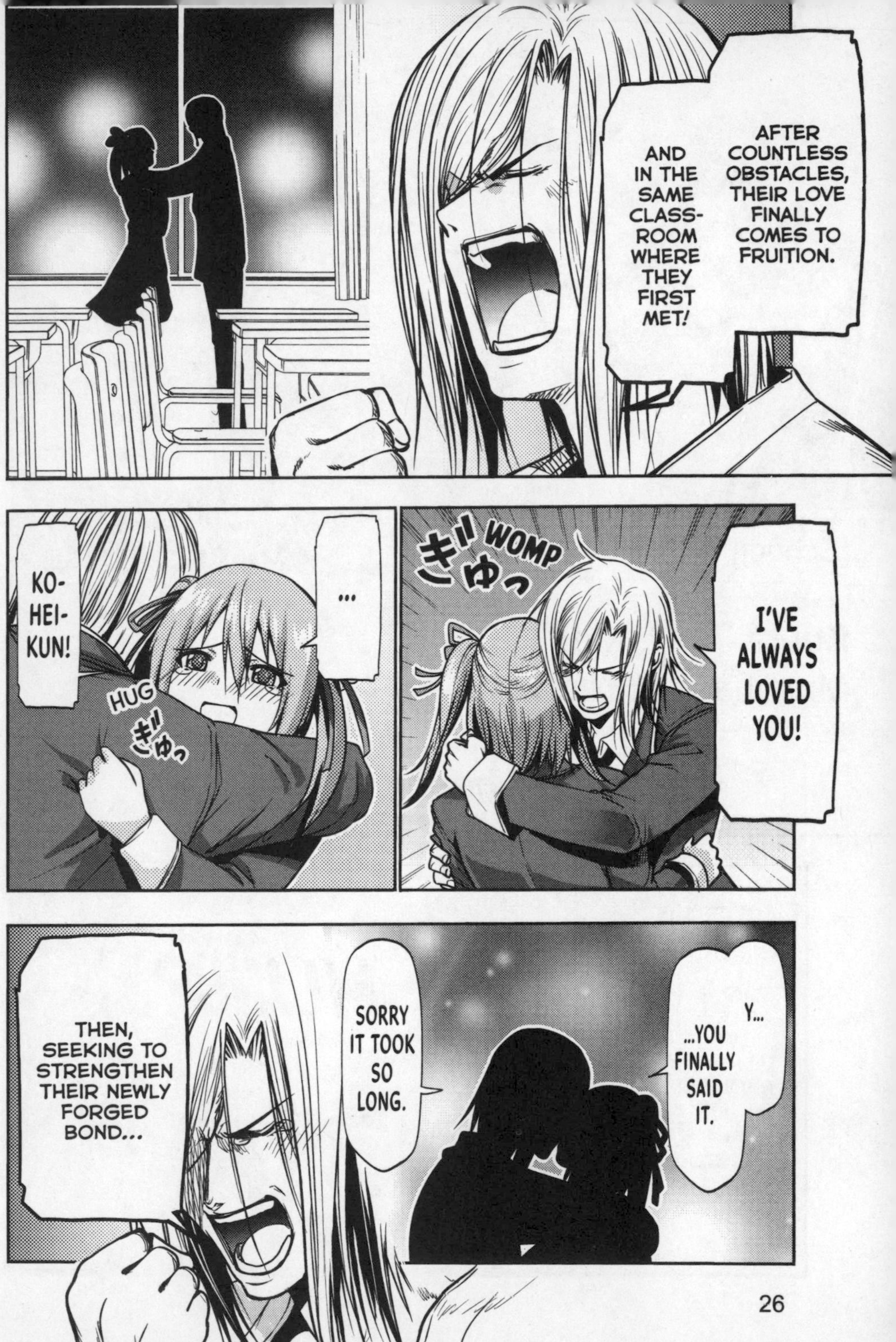
AFTER COUNTLESS OBSTACLES, THEIR LOVE FINALLY COMES TO FRUITION.
AND IN THE SAME CLASS-ROOM WHERE THEY FIRST MET!
きゅっ
WOMP
I'VE ALWAYS LOVED YOU!
...
KO-HEI-KUN!
きゅっ
HUG
Y...
...YOU FINALLY SAID IT.
SORRY IT TOOK SO LONG.
THEN, SEEKING TO STRENGTHEN THEIR NEWLY FORGED BOND...

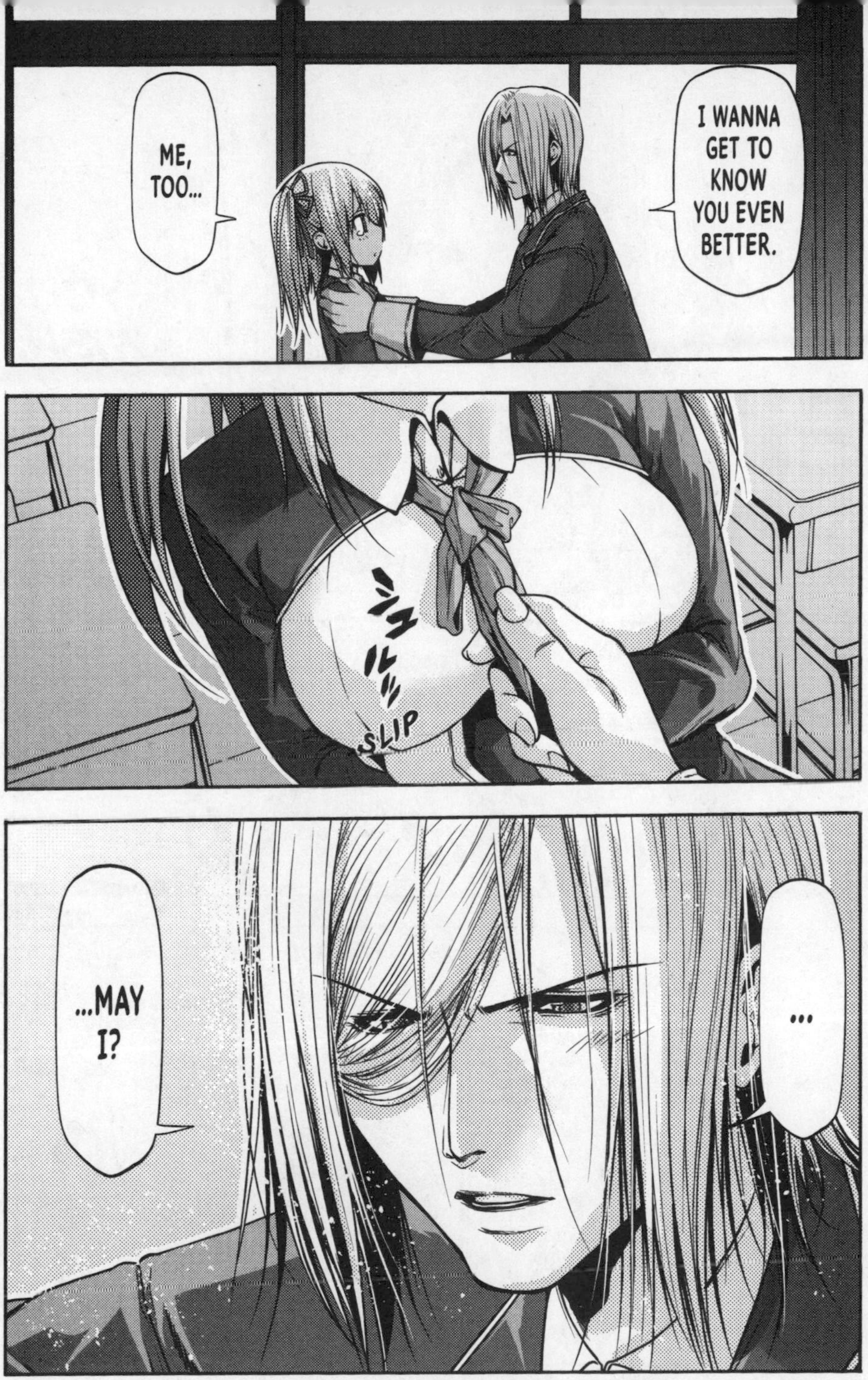
I WANNA GET TO KNOW YOU EVEN BETTER.
ME, TOO...
SLIP
...
...MAY I?

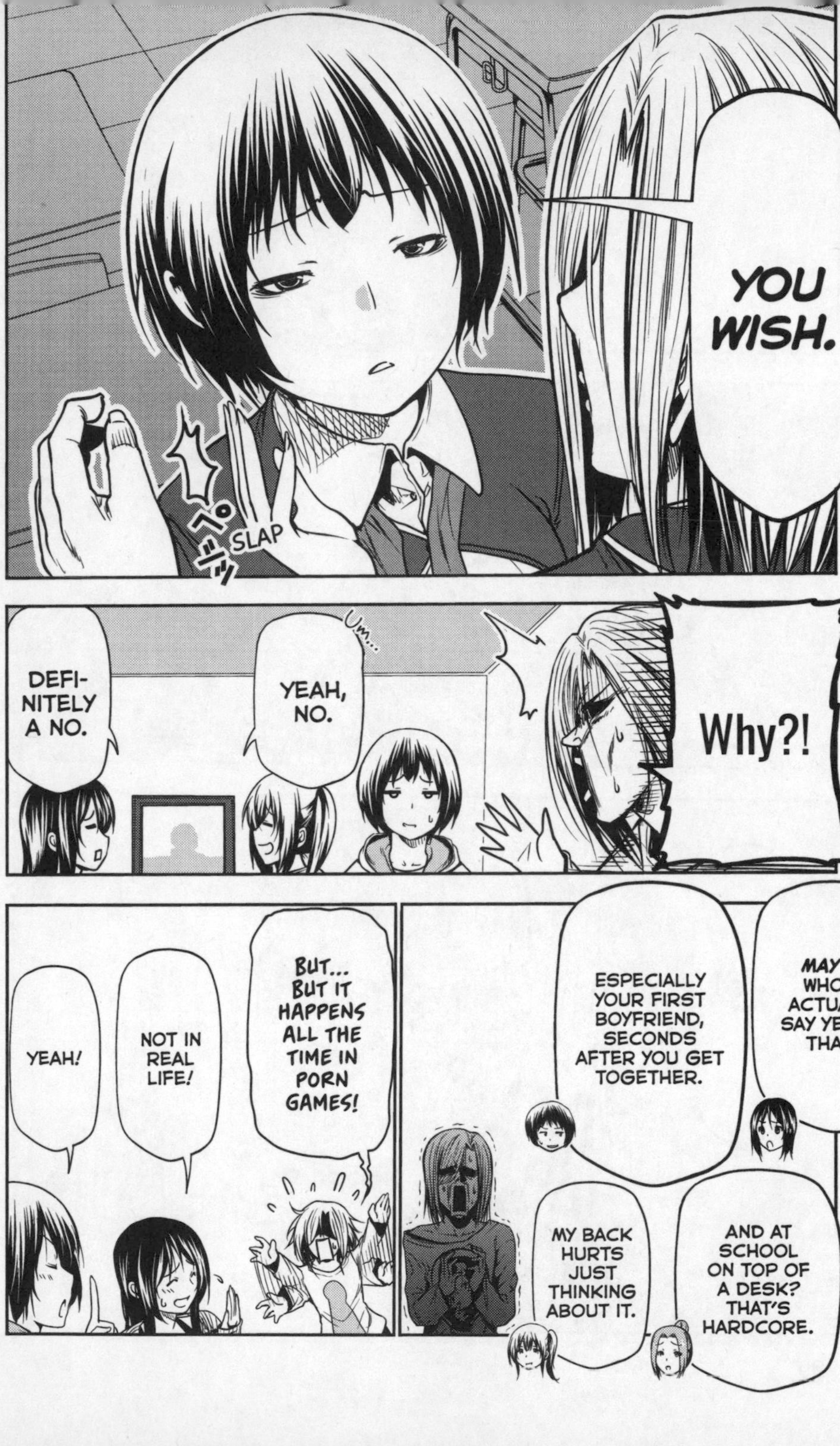
YOU WISH.
ペシッ
SLAP
Why?!
Um...
YEAH, NO.
DEFI-NITELY A NO.
MAY I? WHO'D ACTUALLY SAY YES TO THAT?
ESPECIALLY YOUR FIRST BOYFRIEND, SECONDS AFTER YOU GET TOGETHER.
AND AT SCHOOL ON TOP OF A DESK? THAT'S HARDCORE.
MY BACK HURTS JUST THINKING ABOUT IT.
BUT... BUT IT HAPPENS ALL THE TIME IN PORN GAMES!
NOT IN REAL LIFE!
YEAH!

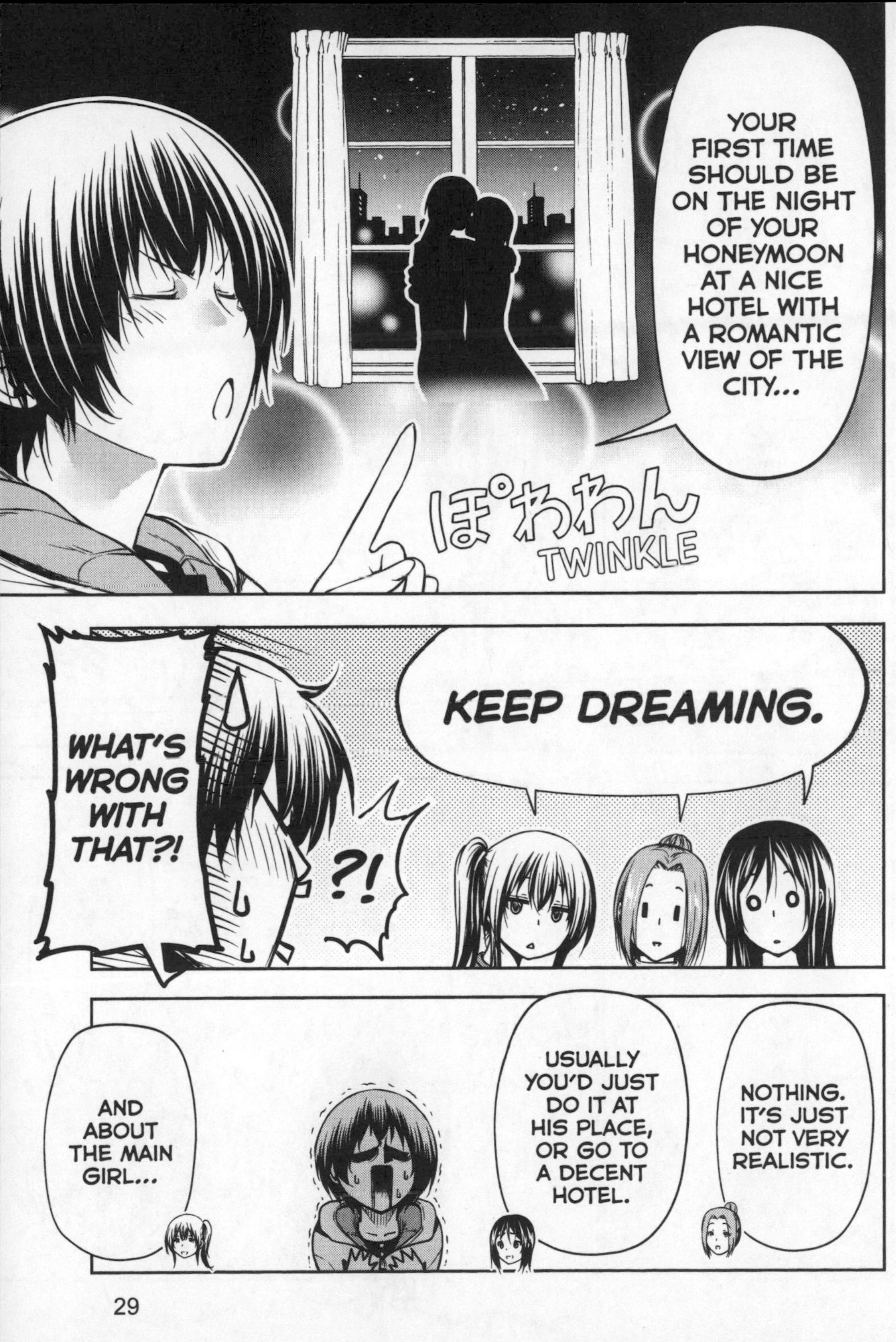
YOUR FIRST TIME SHOULD BE ON THE NIGHT OF YOUR HONEYMOON AT A NICE HOTEL WITH A ROMANTIC VIEW OF THE CITY...
ぽわわん
TWINKLE
KEEP DREAMING.
?!
WHAT'S WRONG WITH THAT?!
NOTHING. IT'S JUST NOT VERY REALISTIC.
USUALLY YOU'D JUST DO IT AT HIS PLACE, OR GO TO A DECENT HOTEL.
AND ABOUT THE MAIN GIRL...

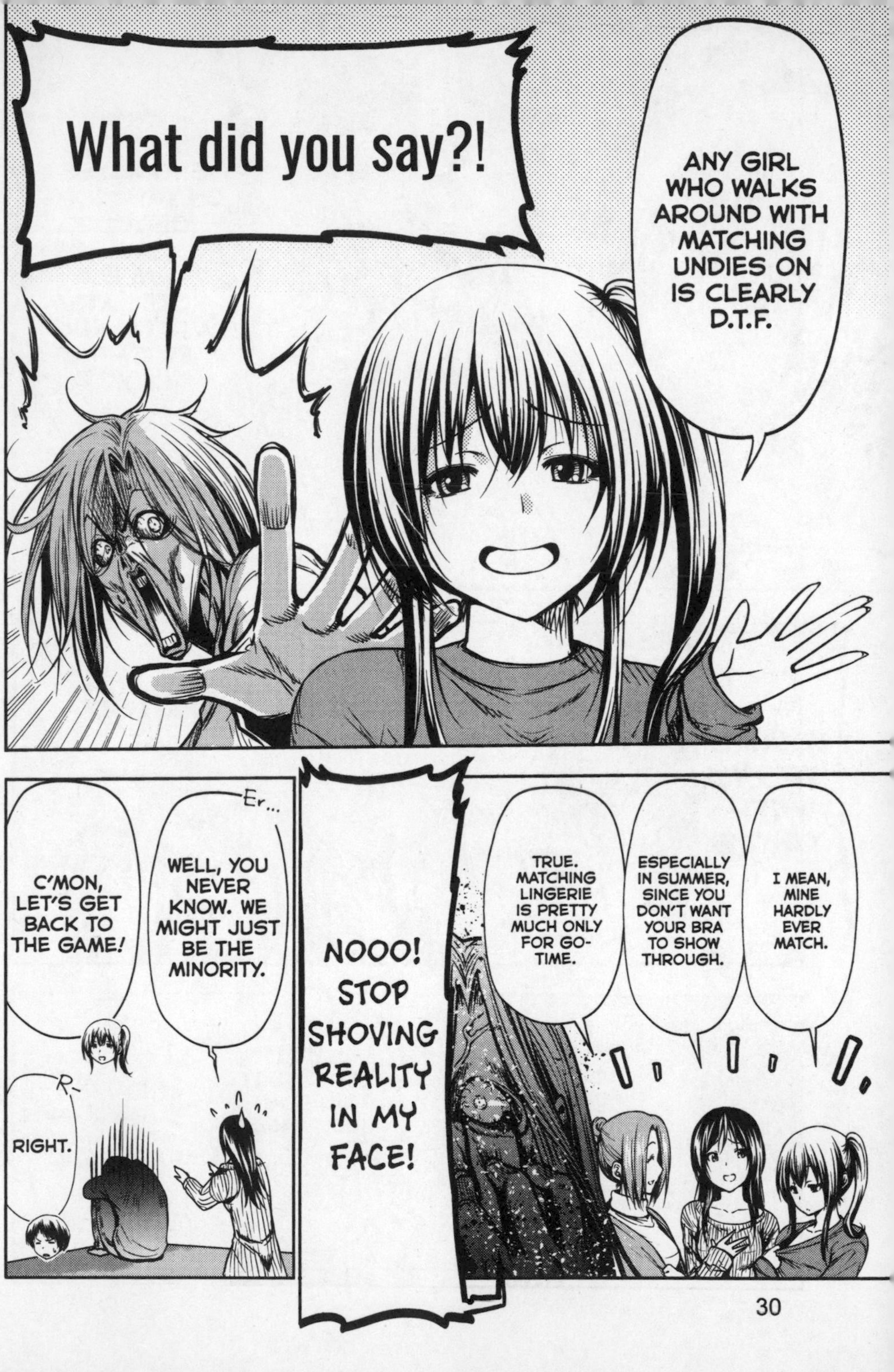
ANY GIRL WHO WALKS AROUND WITH MATCHING UNDIES ON IS CLEARLY D.T.F.
What did you say?!
I MEAN, MINE HARDLY EVER MATCH.
ESPECIALLY IN SUMMER, SINCE YOU DON'T WANT YOUR BRA TO SHOW THROUGH.
TRUE. MATCHING LINGERIE IS PRETTY MUCH ONLY FOR GO-TIME.
NOOO! STOP SHOVING REALITY IN MY FACE!
Er...
WELL, YOU NEVER KNOW. WE MIGHT JUST BE THE MINORITY.
C'MON, LET'S GET BACK TO THE GAME!
R-
RIGHT.

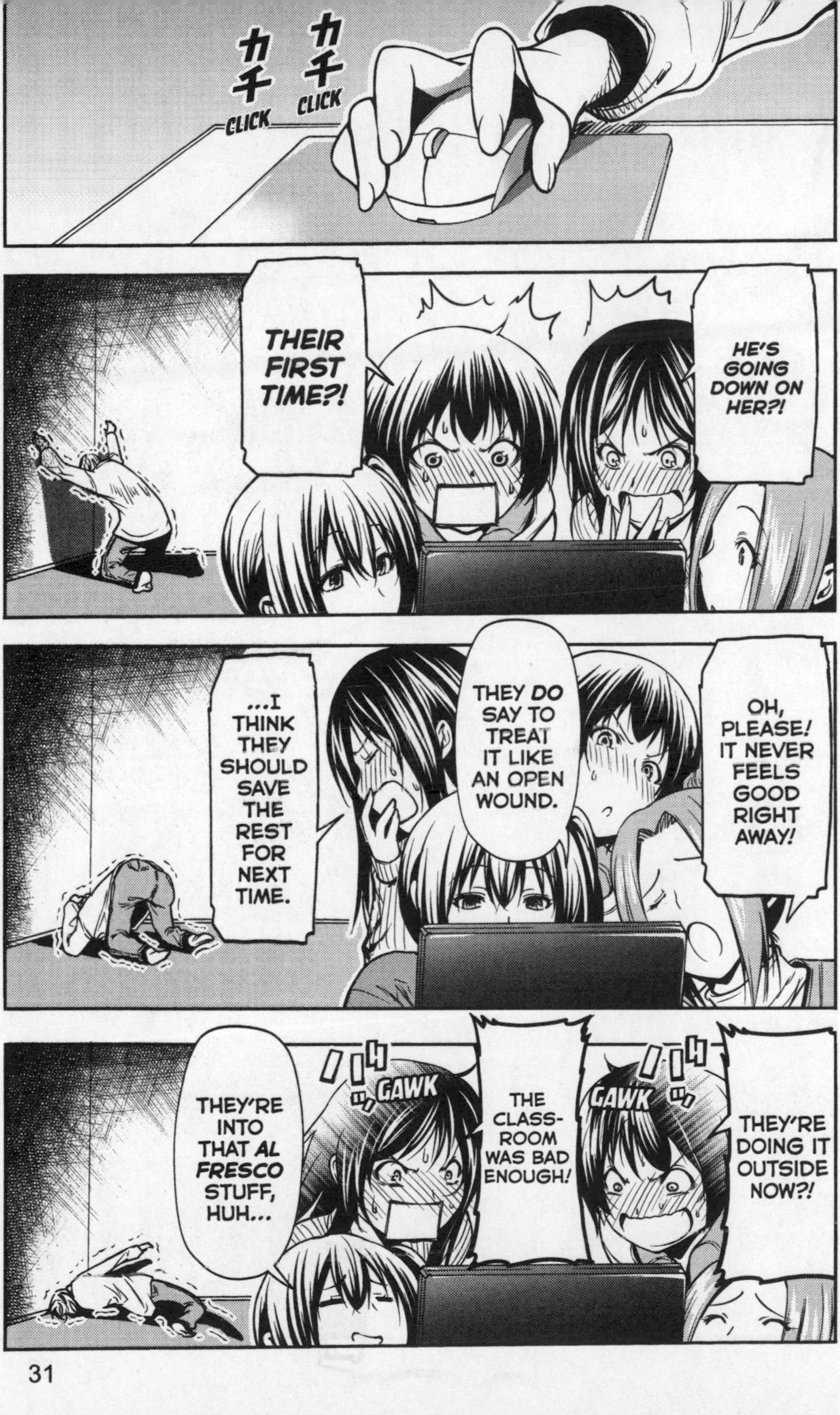
カチ
CLICK
カチ
CLICK
HE'S GOING DOWN ON HER?!
THEIR FIRST TIME?!
OH, PLEASE! IT NEVER FEELS GOOD RIGHT AWAY!
THEY DO SAY TO TREAT IT LIKE AN OPEN WOUND.
...I THINK THEY SHOULD SAVE THE REST FOR NEXT TIME.
THEY'RE DOING IT OUTSIDE NOW?!
GAWK
THE CLASS-ROOM WAS BAD ENOUGH!
GAWK
THEY'RE INTO THAT AL FRESCO STUFF, HUH...

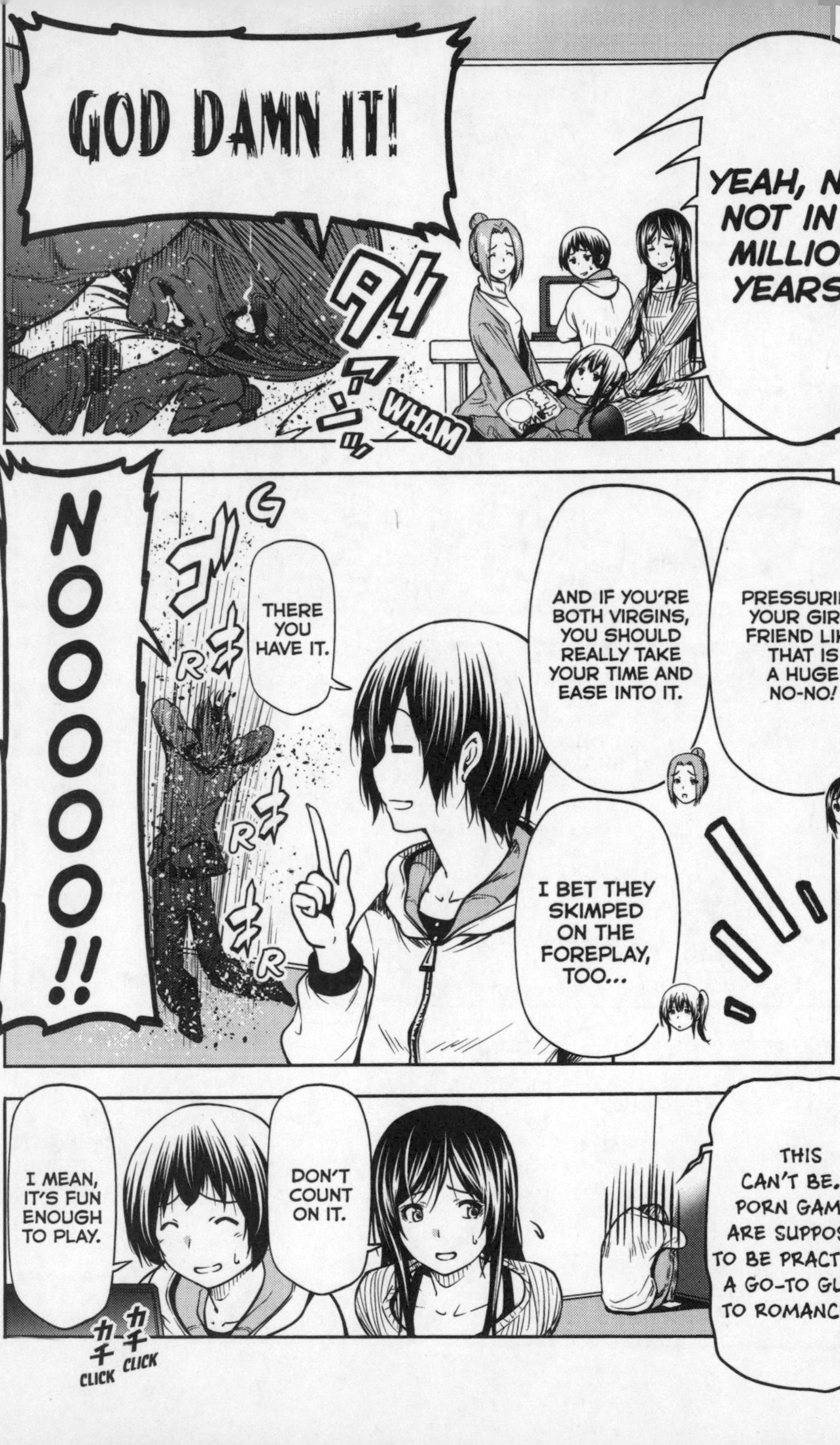
YEAH, NO. NOT IN A MILLION YEARS.
GOD DAMN IT!
WHAM
PRESSURING YOUR GIRL-FRIEND LIKE THAT IS A HUGE NO-NO!
AND IF YOU'RE BOTH VIRGINS, YOU SHOULD REALLY TAKE YOUR TIME AND EASE INTO IT.
I BET THEY SKIMPED ON THE FOREPLAY, TOO...
THERE YOU HAVE IT.
GRRR
NOOOOOO!!
THIS CAN'T BE... PORN GAMES ARE SUPPOSED TO BE PRACTICAL. A GO-TO GUIDE TO ROMANCE...
DON'T COUNT ON IT.
I MEAN, IT'S FUN ENOUGH TO PLAY.
カチ CLICK
カチ CLICK

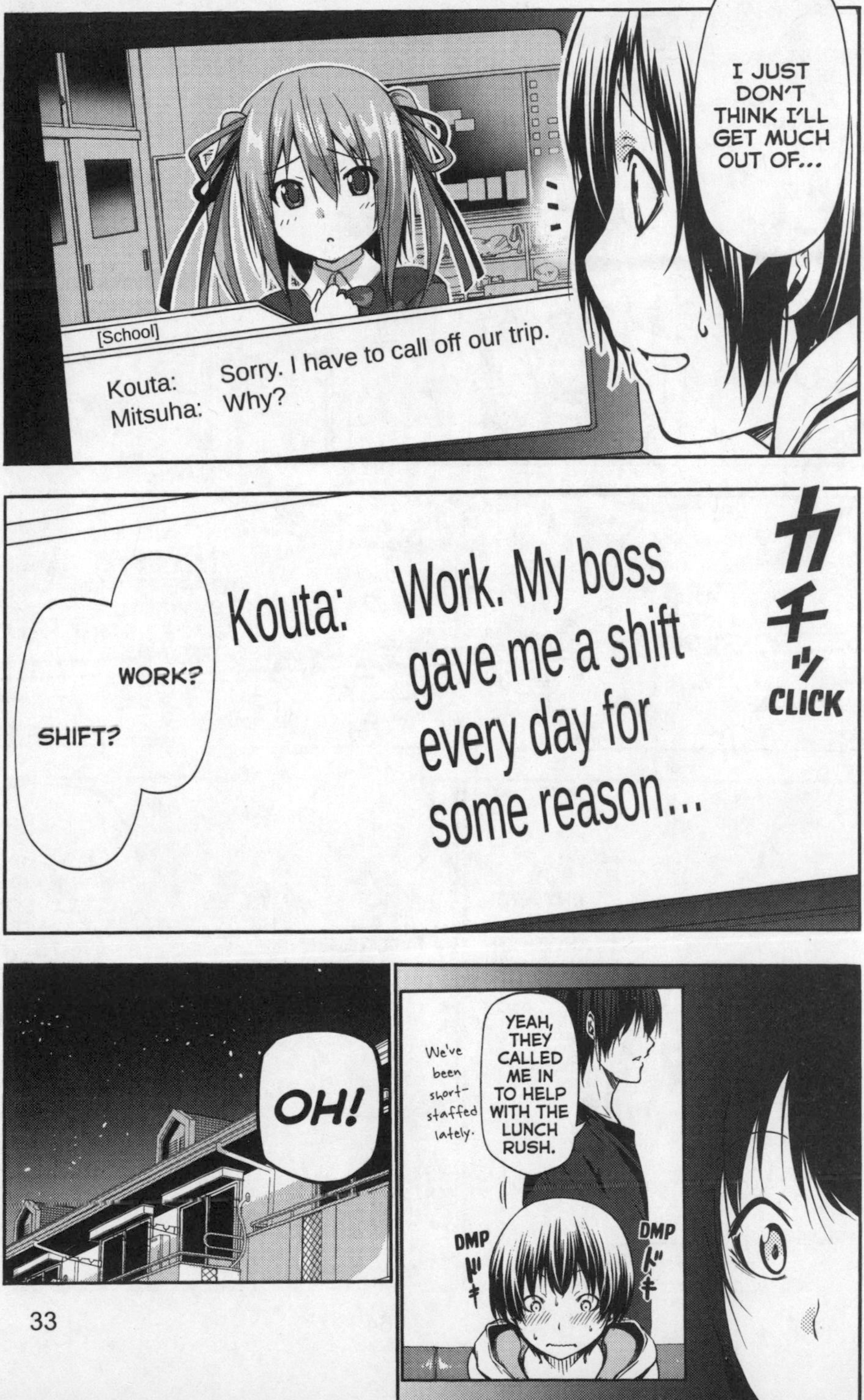
I JUST DON'T THINK I'LL GET MUCH OUT OF...
[School]
Kouta: Sorry. I have to call off our trip.
Mitsuha: Why?
カチッ
CLICK
Kouta: Work. My boss gave me a shift every day for some reason...
WORK?
SHIFT?
YEAH, THEY CALLED ME IN TO HELP WITH THE LUNCH RUSH.
We've been short-staffed lately.
DMP
ドキ
DMP
ドキ
OH!

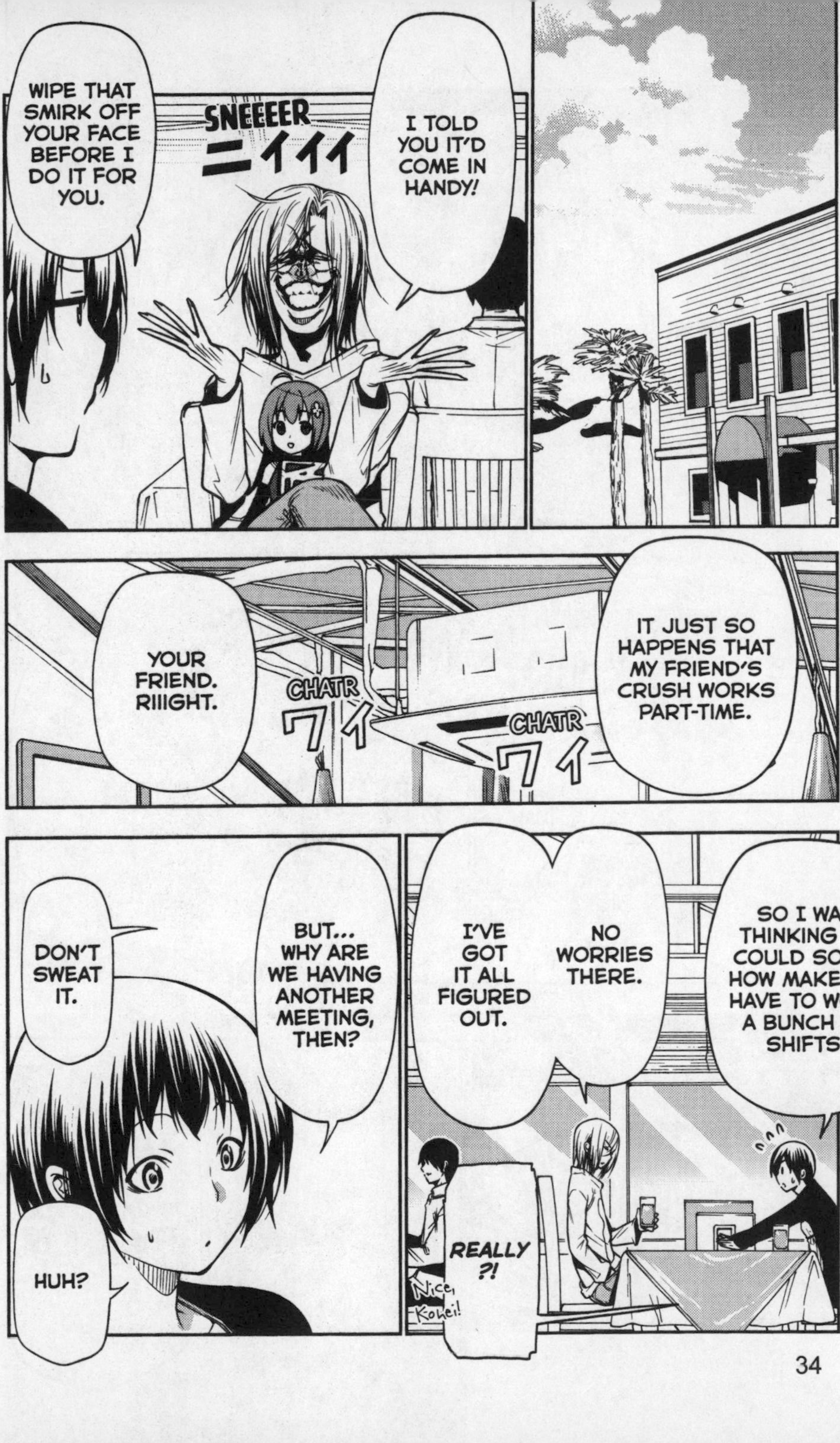
I TOLD YOU IT'D COME IN HANDY!
SNEEEER
ニイイイ
WIPE THAT SMIRK OFF YOUR FACE BEFORE I DO IT FOR YOU.
IT JUST SO HAPPENS THAT MY FRIEND'S CRUSH WORKS PART-TIME.
CHATR
ワイ
CHATR
ワイ
YOUR FRIEND. RIIIGHT.
SO I WAS THINKING WE COULD SOME-HOW MAKE HIM HAVE TO WORK A BUNCH OF SHIFTS.
NO WORRIES THERE.
I'VE GOT IT ALL FIGURED OUT.
REALLY ?!
Nice, Kohei!
BUT... WHY ARE WE HAVING ANOTHER MEETING, THEN?
DON'T SWEAT IT.
HUH?

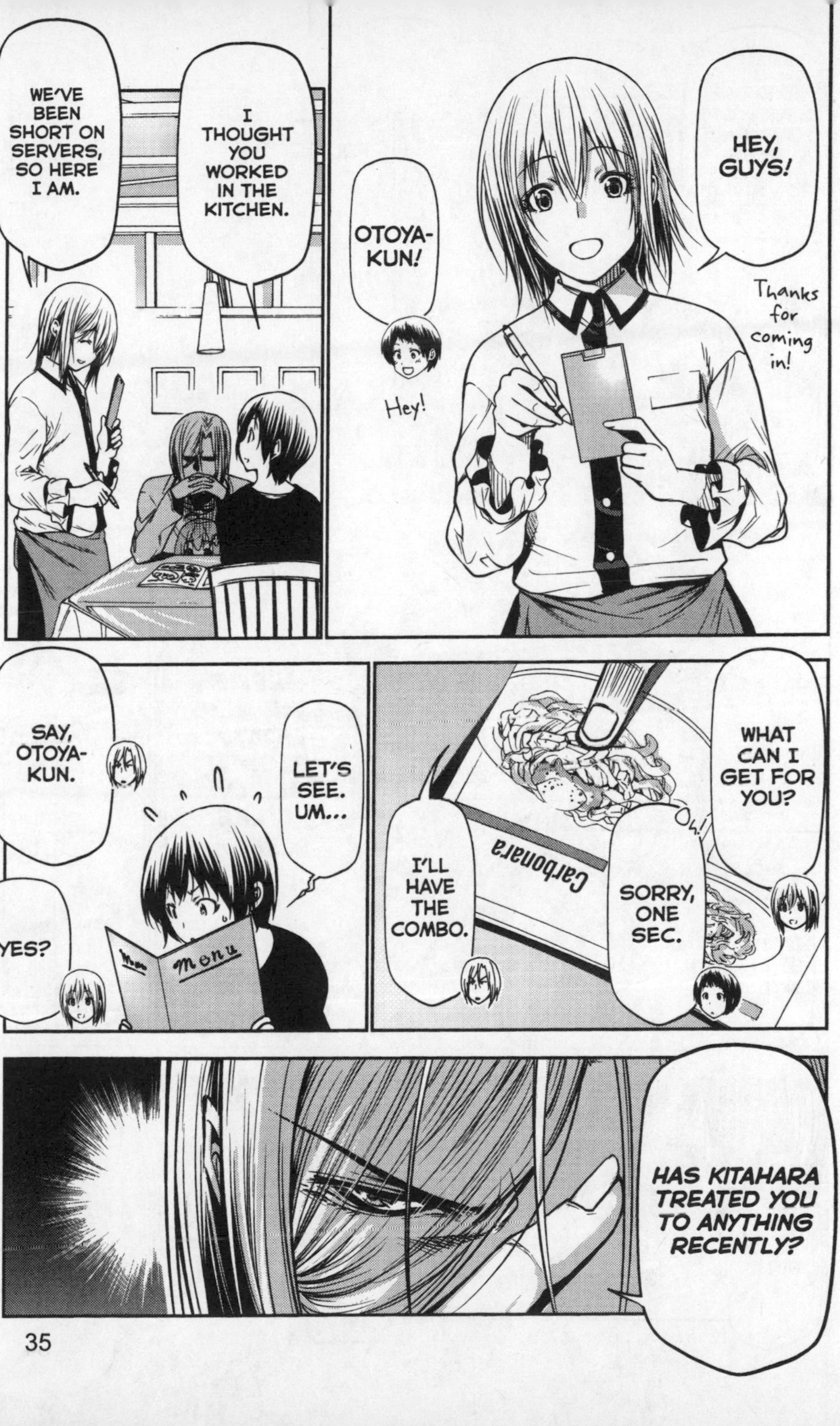
HEY, GUYS!
Thanks for coming in!
OTOYA-KUN!
Hey!
I THOUGHT YOU WORKED IN THE KITCHEN.
WE'VE BEEN SHORT ON SERVERS, SO HERE I AM.
WHAT CAN I GET FOR YOU?
Oh!
SORRY, ONE SEC.
Carbonara
I'LL HAVE THE COMBO.
LET'S SEE. UM...
SAY, OTOYA-KUN.
Menu
YES?
HAS KITAHARA TREATED YOU TO ANYTHING RECENTLY?

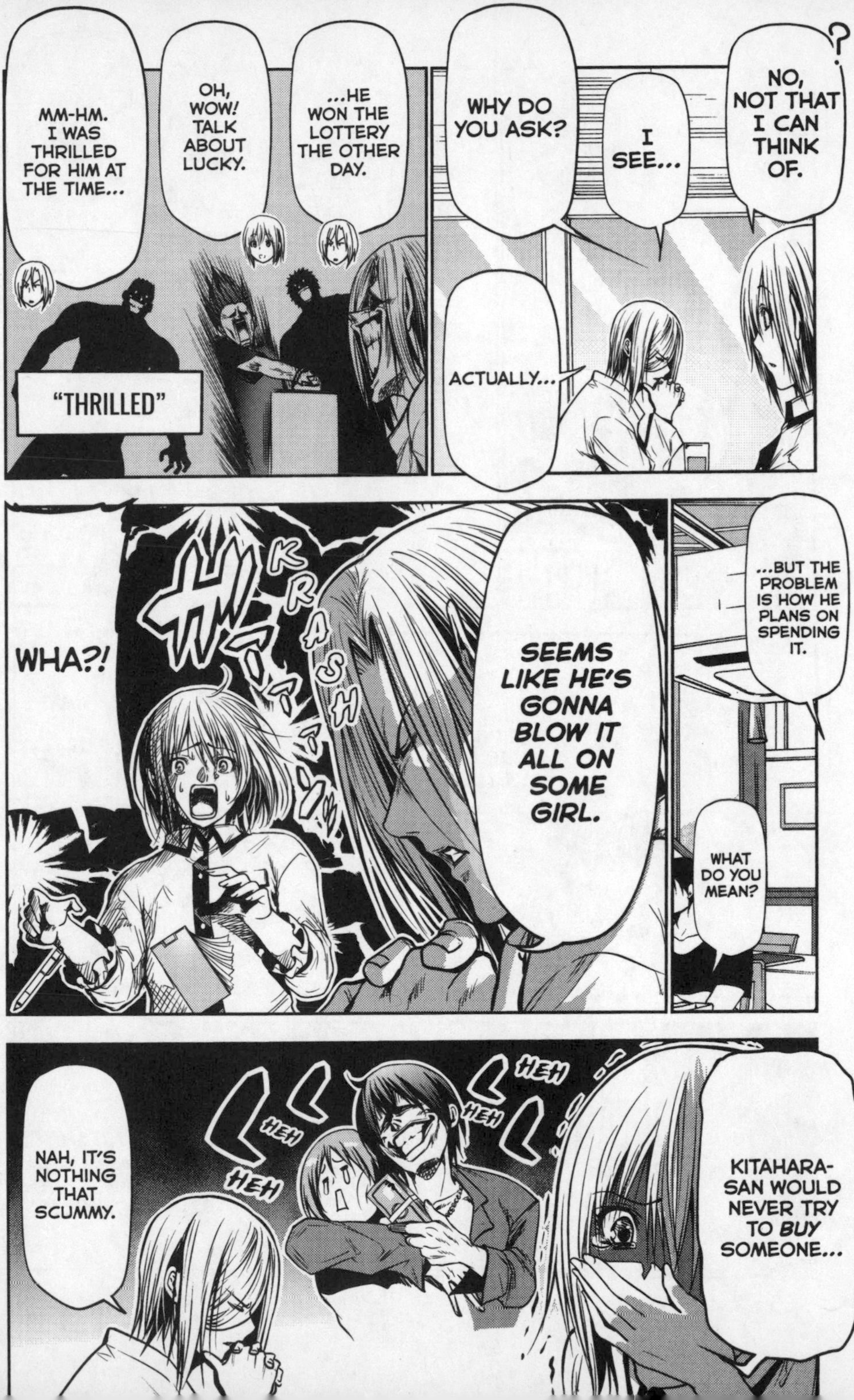
?
NO, NOT THAT I CAN THINK OF.
I SEE...
WHY DO YOU ASK?
ACTUALLY...
...HE WON THE LOTTERY THE OTHER DAY.
OH, WOW! TALK ABOUT LUCKY.
MM-HM. I WAS THRILLED FOR HIM AT THE TIME...
“THRILLED”
...BUT THE PROBLEM IS HOW HE PLANS ON SPENDING IT.
WHAT DO YOU MEAN?
SEEMS LIKE HE'S GONNA BLOW IT ALL ON SOME GIRL.
KRASH
WHA?!
KITAHARA-SAN WOULD NEVER TRY TO *BUY* SOMEONE...
HEH
HEH
HEH
HEH
NAH, IT'S NOTHING THAT SCUMMY.

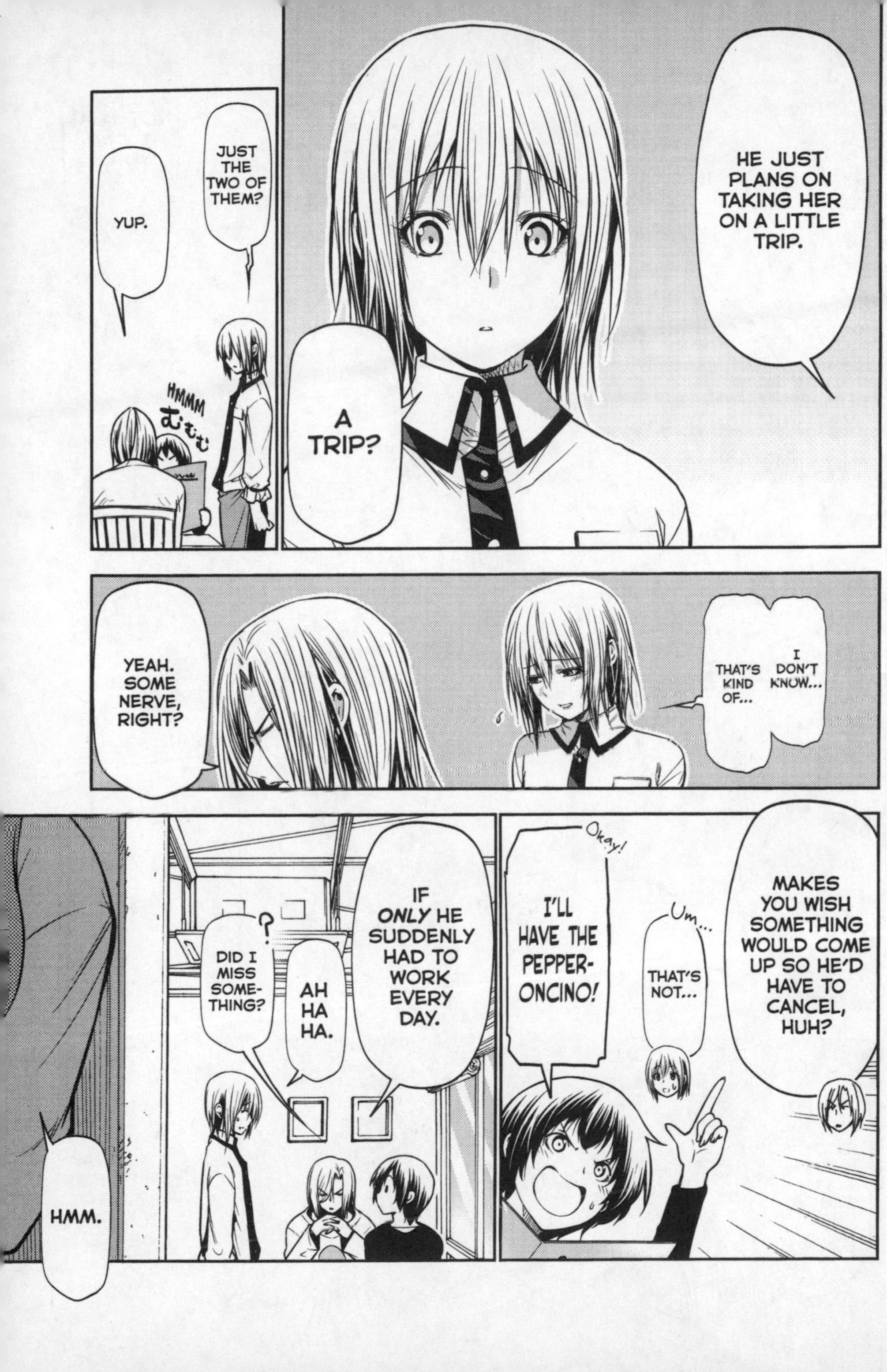
HE JUST PLANS ON TAKING HER ON A LITTLE TRIP.
A TRIP?
JUST THE TWO OF THEM?
YUP.
HMMM
むむむ
I DON'T KNOW... THAT'S KIND OF...
YEAH. SOME NERVE, RIGHT?
MAKES YOU WISH SOMETHING WOULD COME UP SO HE'D HAVE TO CANCEL, HUH?
Um... THAT'S NOT...
I'LL HAVE THE PEPPER-ONCINO!
Okay!
IF ONLY HE SUDDENLY HAD TO WORK EVERY DAY.
AH HA HA.
?
DID I MISS SOME-THING?
HMM.

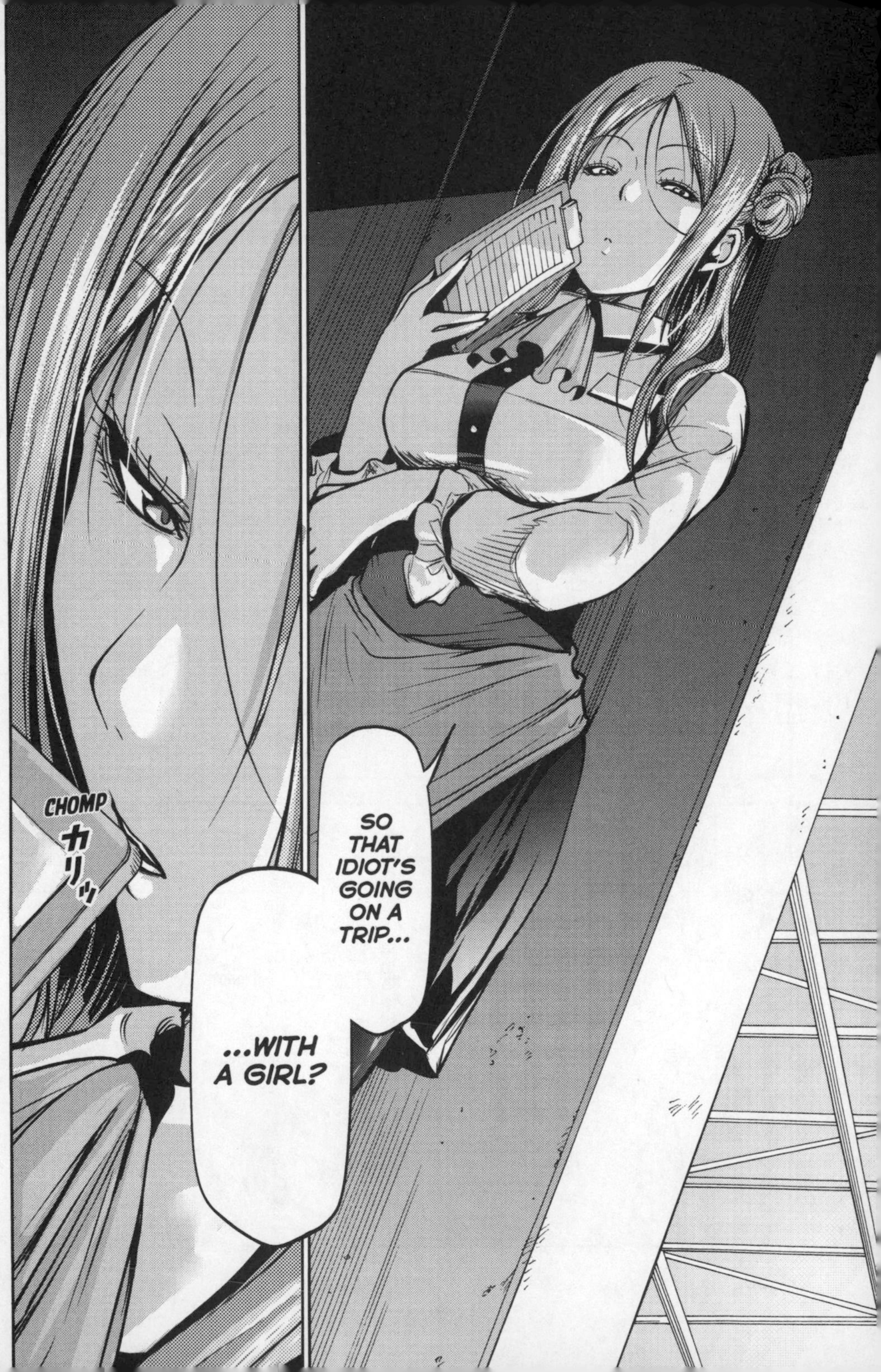
CHOMP
カリッ
SO THAT IDIOT'S GOING ON A TRIP...
...WITH A GIRL?

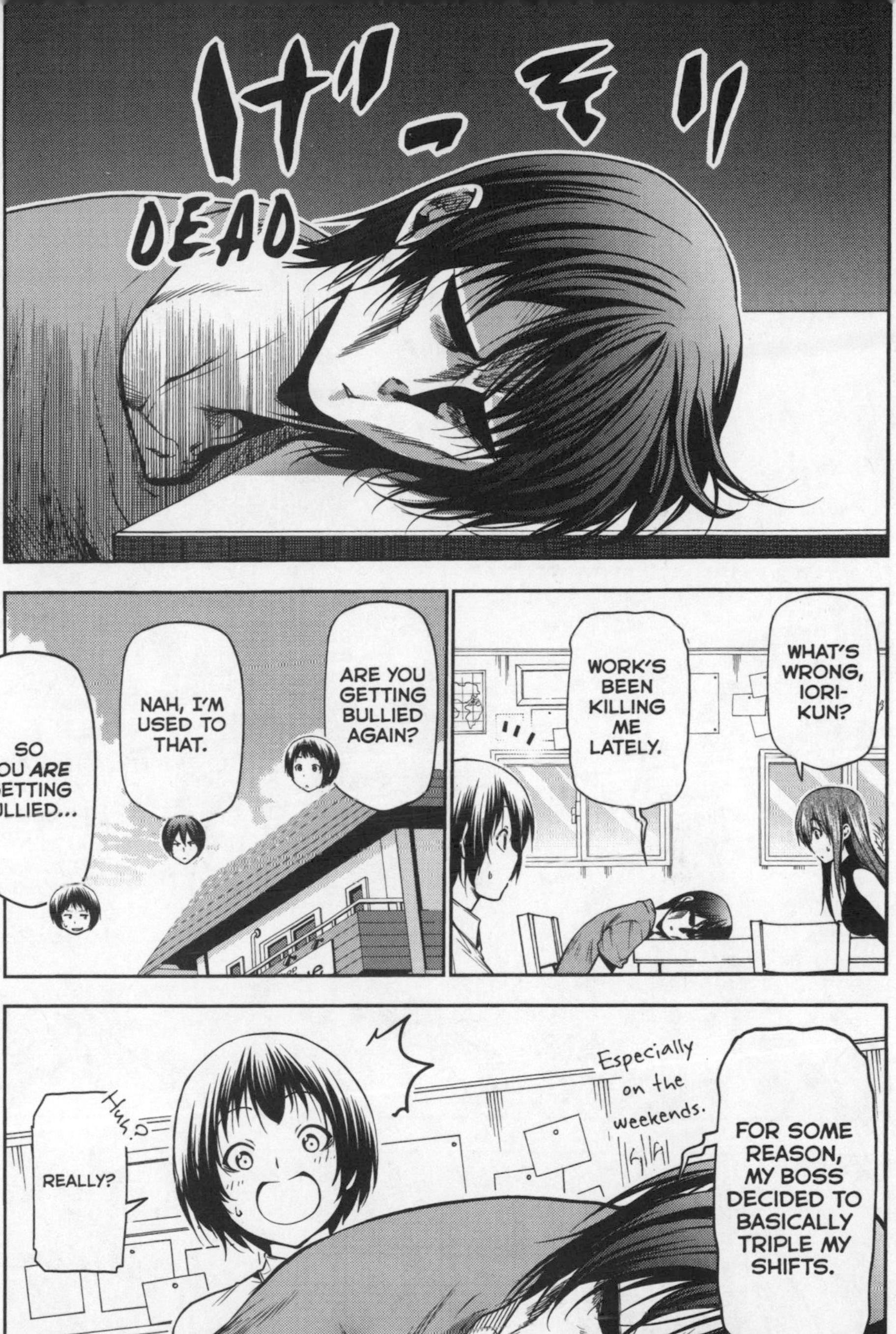
げっそり
DEAD
WHAT'S WRONG, IORI-KUN?
WORK'S BEEN KILLING ME LATELY.
ARE YOU GETTING BULLIED AGAIN?
NAH, I'M USED TO THAT.
SO YOU *ARE* GETTING BULLIED...
FOR SOME REASON, MY BOSS DECIDED TO BASICALLY TRIPLE MY SHIFTS.
Especially on the weekends.
Huh?
REALLY?

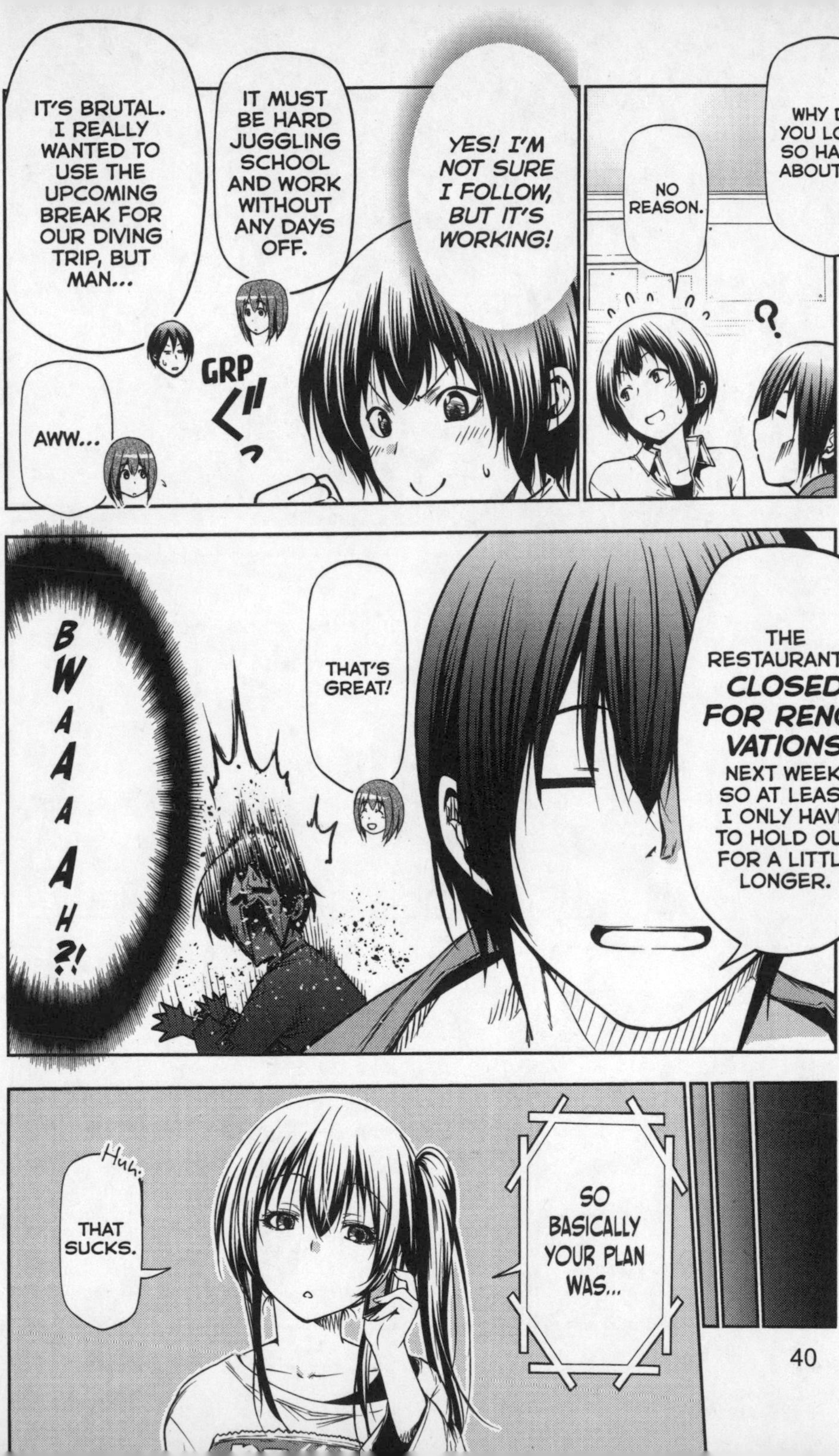
WHY DO YOU LOOK SO HAPPY ABOUT IT?
NO REASON.
?
YES! I'M NOT SURE I FOLLOW, BUT IT'S WORKING!
GRP
IT MUST BE HARD JUGGLING SCHOOL AND WORK WITHOUT ANY DAYS OFF.
IT'S BRUTAL. I REALLY WANTED TO USE THE UPCOMING BREAK FOR OUR DIVING TRIP, BUT MAN...
AWW...
THE RESTAURANT'S CLOSED FOR RENOVATIONS NEXT WEEK, SO AT LEAST I ONLY HAVE TO HOLD OUT FOR A LITTLE LONGER.
THAT'S GREAT!
BWAAAAAH?!
SO BASICALLY YOUR PLAN WAS...
Huh.
THAT SUCKS.

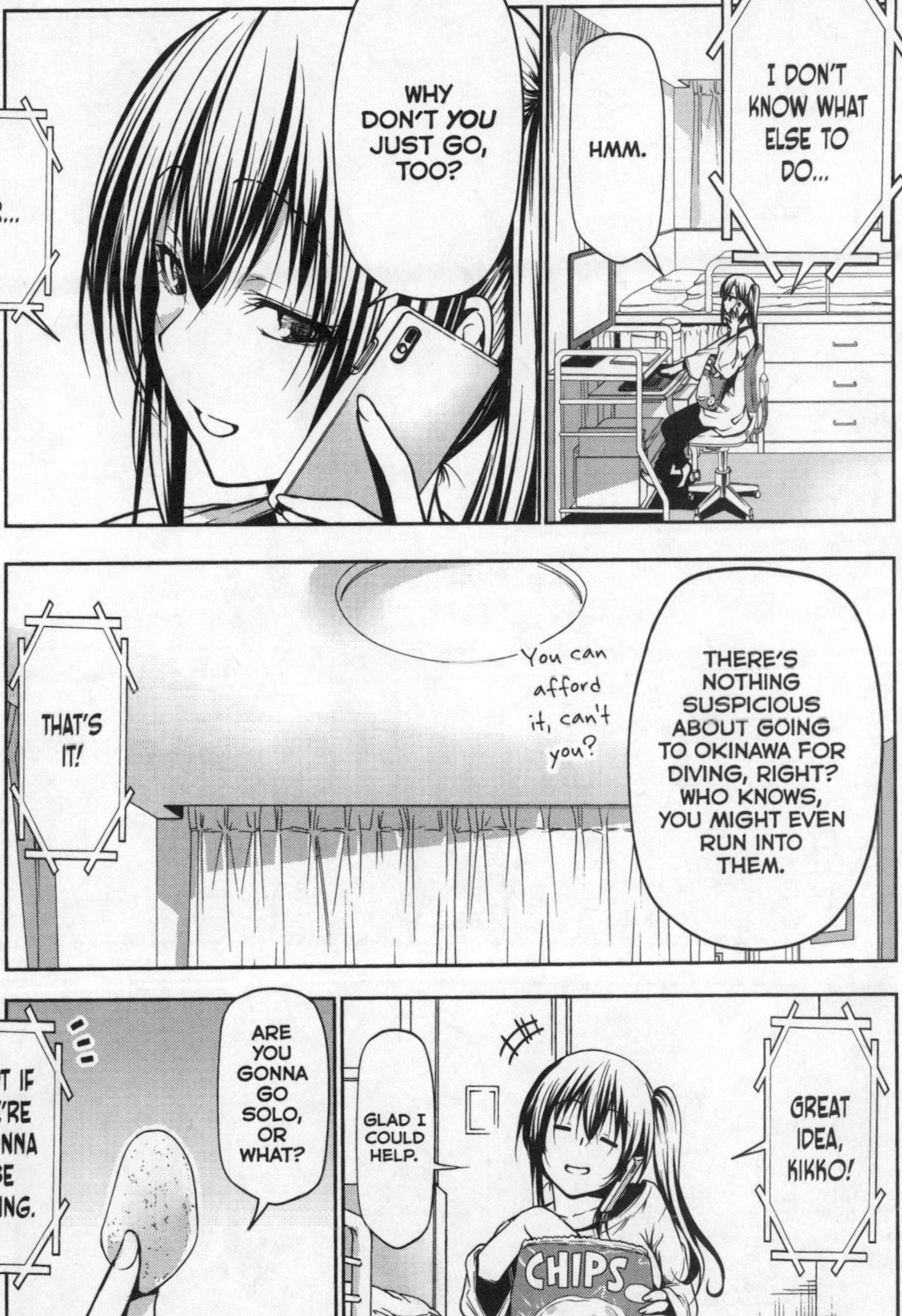
I DON'T KNOW WHAT ELSE TO DO...
HMM.
WHY DON'T YOU JUST GO, TOO?
ER...
THERE'S NOTHING SUSPICIOUS ABOUT GOING TO OKINAWA FOR DIVING, RIGHT? WHO KNOWS, YOU MIGHT EVEN RUN INTO THEM.
You can afford it, can't you?
THAT'S IT!
GREAT IDEA, KIKKO!
GLAD I COULD HELP.
CHIPS
ARE YOU GONNA GO SOLO, OR WHAT?
NOT IF WE'RE GONNA BE DIVING.

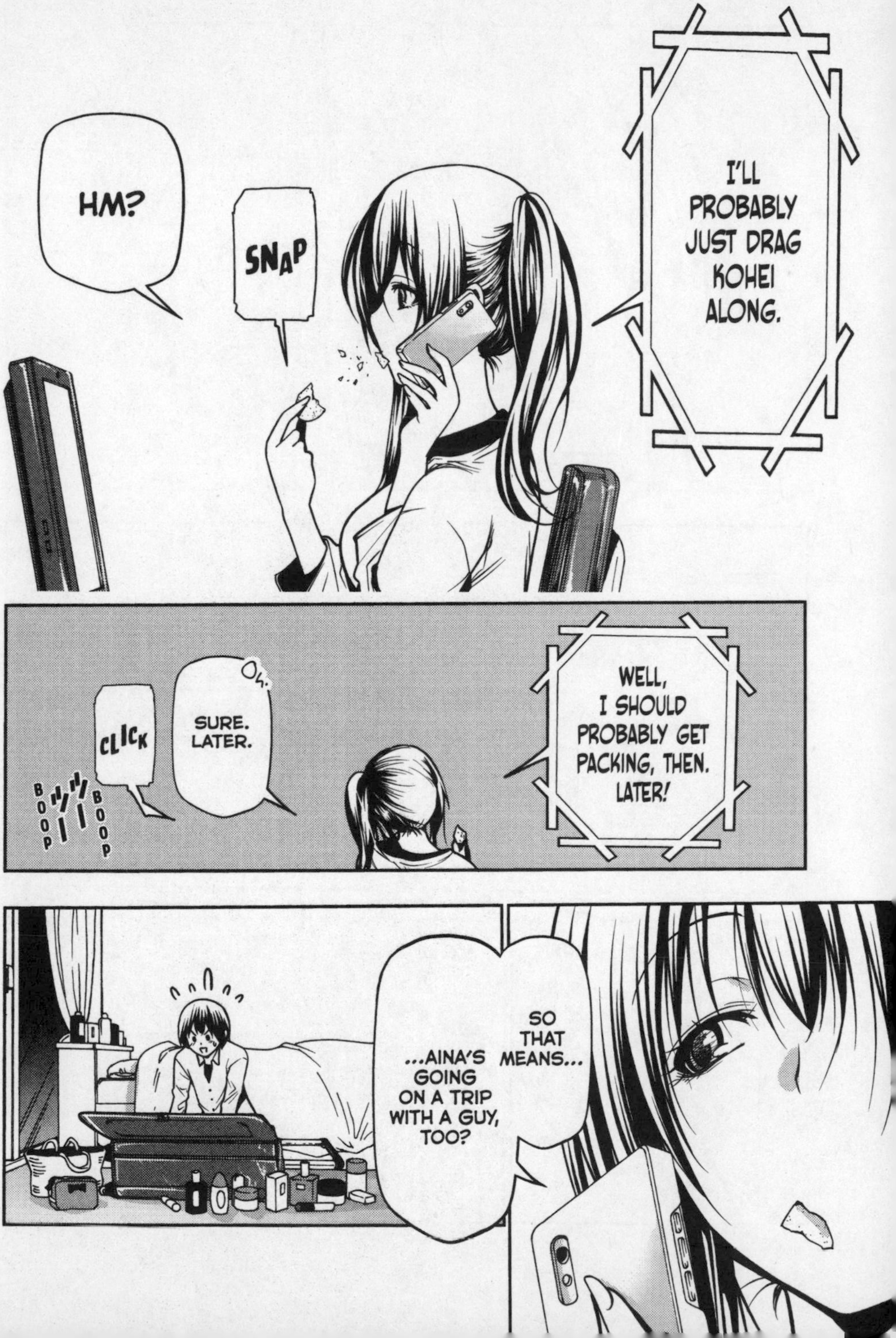
I'LL PROBABLY JUST DRAG KOHEI ALONG.
SNAP
HM?
WELL, I SHOULD PROBABLY GET PACKING, THEN. LATER!
Oh.
SURE. LATER.
CLICK
BOOP
BOOP
SO THAT MEANS...
...AINA'S GOING ON A TRIP WITH A GUY, TOO?

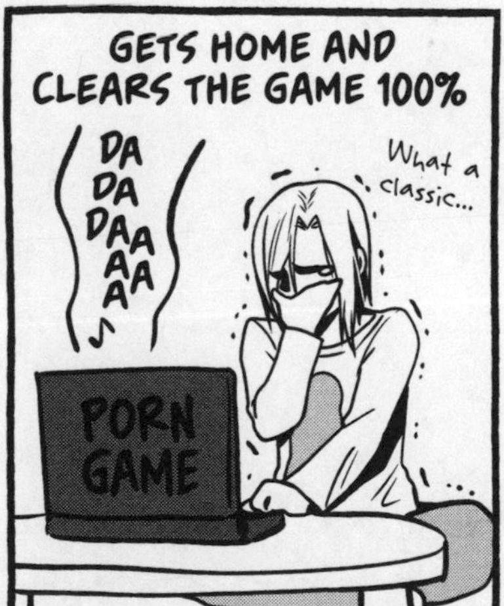
GETS HOME AND CLEARS THE GAME 100%
What a classic...
DA DA DAAAAAA
PORN GAME

Grand Blue Dreaming

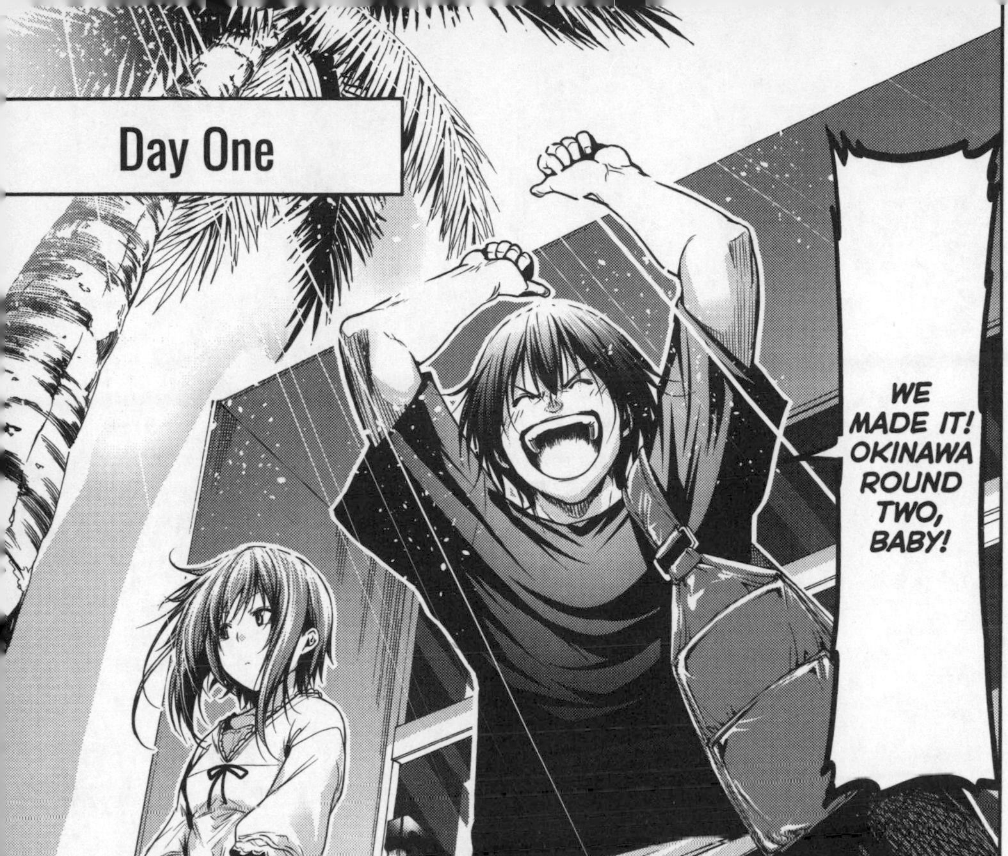
WE MADE IT! OKINAWA ROUND TWO, BABY!
Day One
Ch. 63: Okinawa Revisited

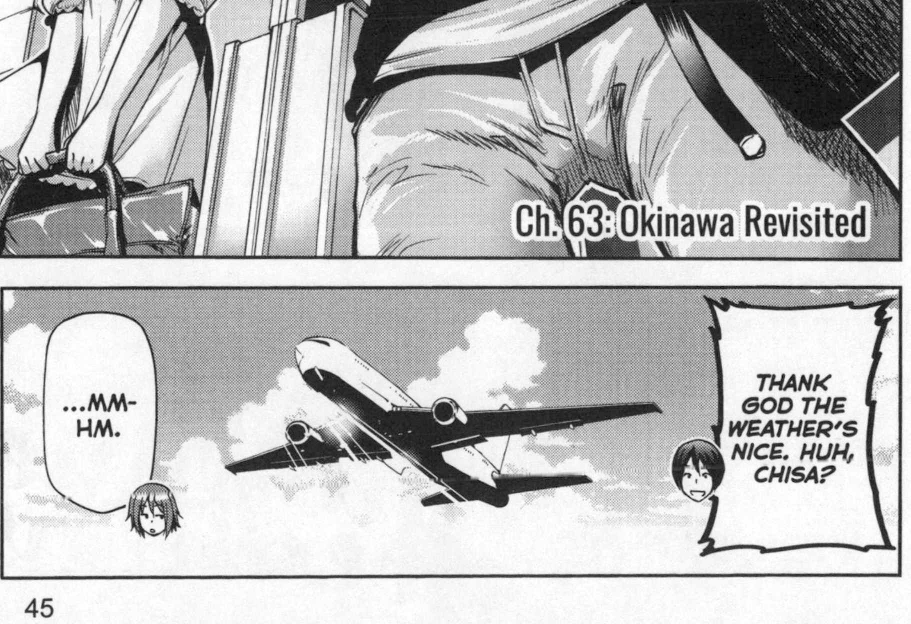
THANK GOD THE WEATHER'S NICE. HUH, CHISA?
...MM-HM.

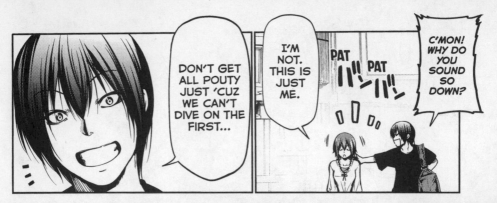

C'MON! WHY DO YOU SOUND SO DOWN?
PAT PAT
I'M NOT. THIS IS JUST ME.
DON'T GET ALL POUTY JUST 'CUZ WE CAN'T DIVE ON THE FIRST...
STARE
WHAT?
IRK
...ARE YOU NERVOUS?
HUH?!

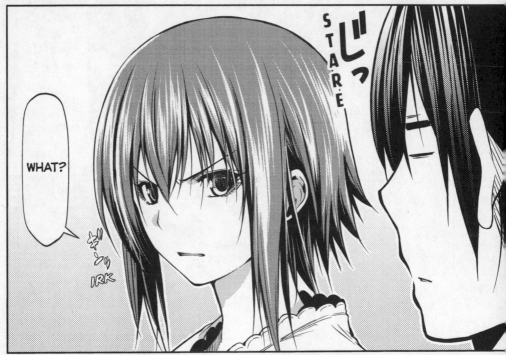

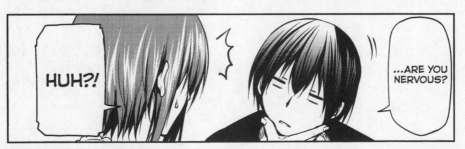

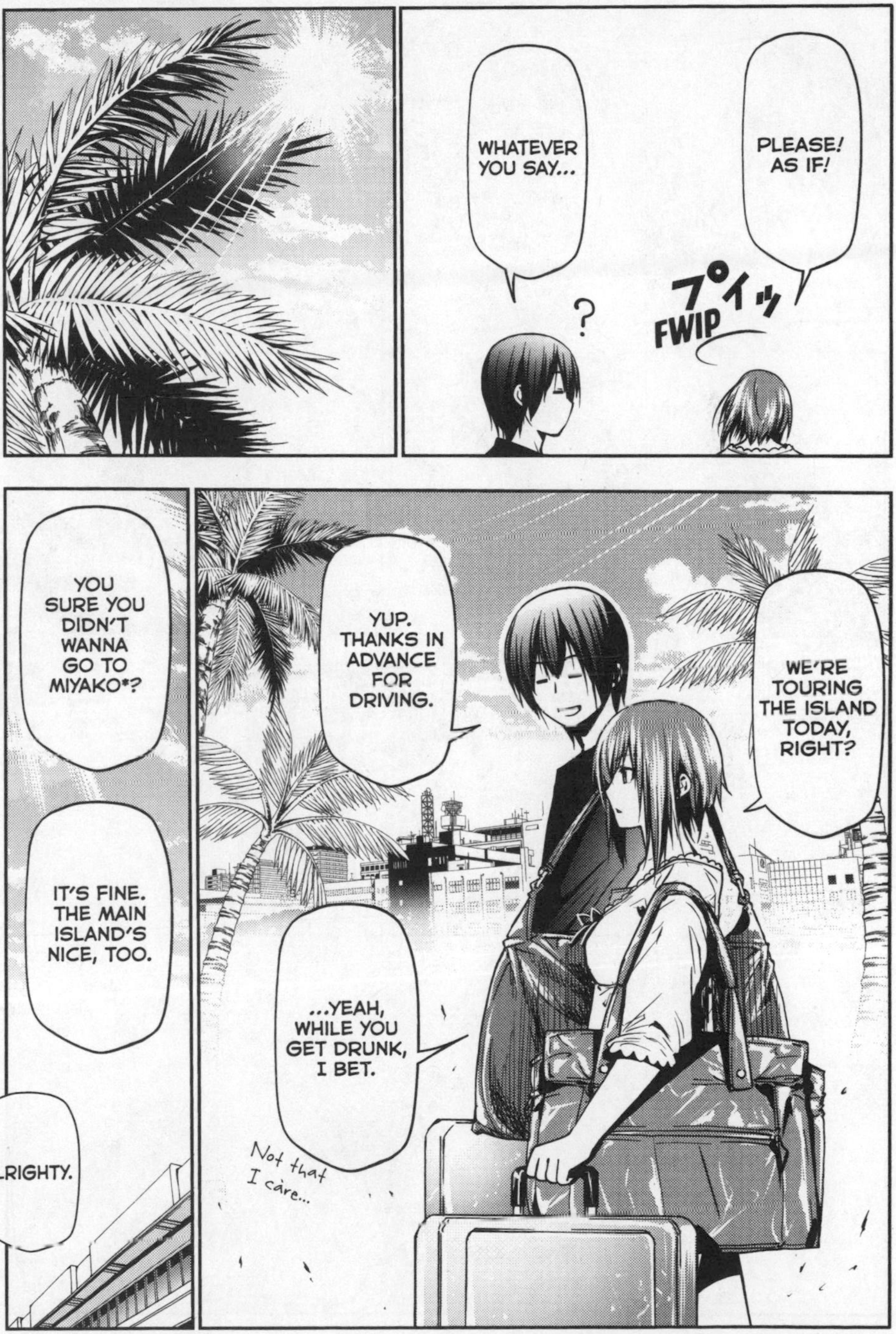
PLEASE! AS IF!
プイッ
FWIP
WHATEVER YOU SAY...
?
WE'RE TOURING THE ISLAND TODAY, RIGHT?
YUP. THANKS IN ADVANCE FOR DRIVING.
...YEAH, WHILE YOU GET DRUNK, I BET.
Not that I care...
YOU SURE YOU DIDN'T WANNA GO TO MIYAKO*?
IT'S FINE. THE MAIN ISLAND'S NICE, TOO.
ALRIGHTY.

*A group of islands off of Okinawa Island popular with tourists.

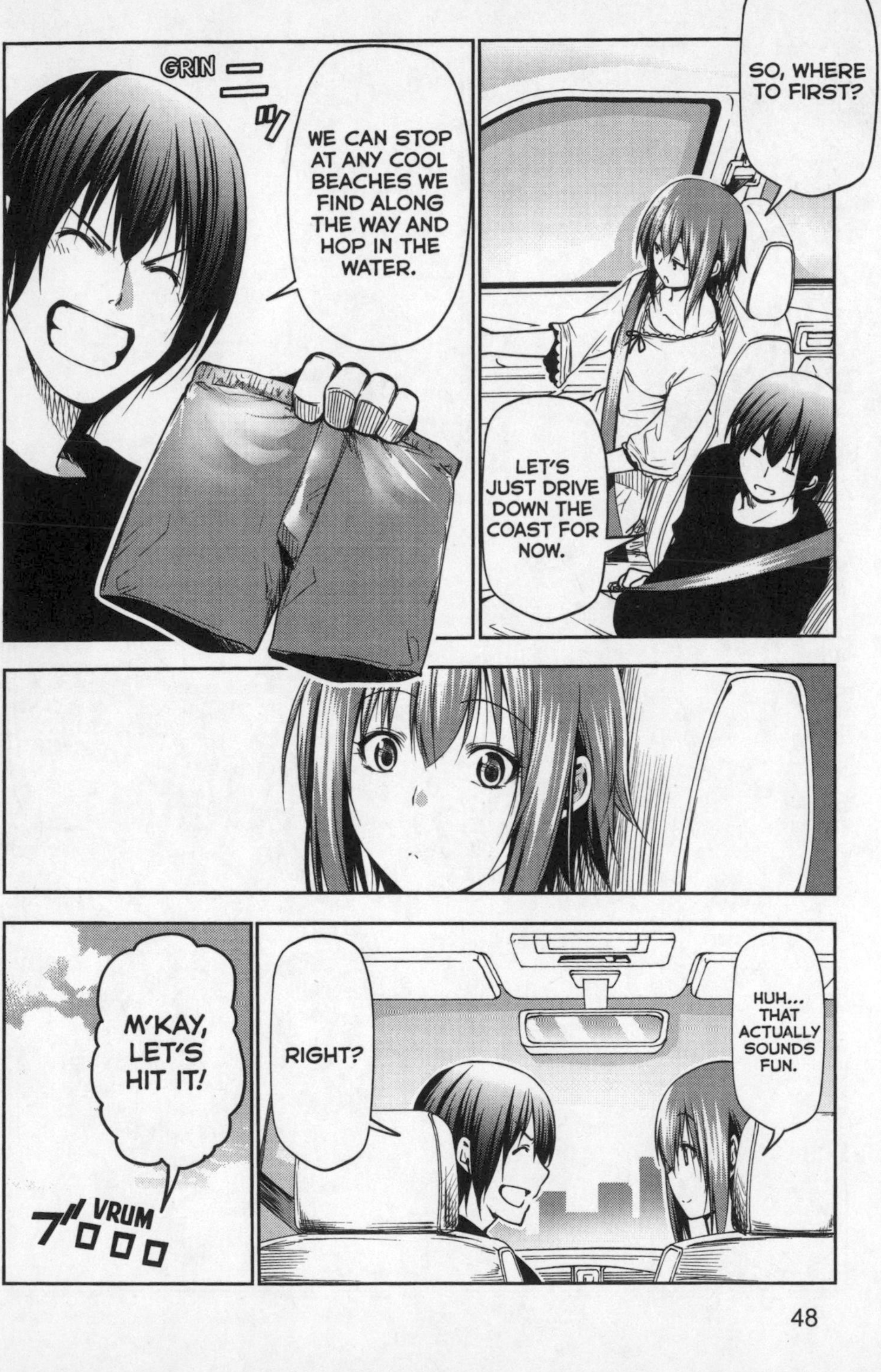
SO, WHERE TO FIRST?
LET'S JUST DRIVE DOWN THE COAST FOR NOW.
GRIN
WE CAN STOP AT ANY COOL BEACHES WE FIND ALONG THE WAY AND HOP IN THE WATER.
HUH... THAT ACTUALLY SOUNDS FUN.
RIGHT?
M'KAY, LET'S HIT IT!
VRUM

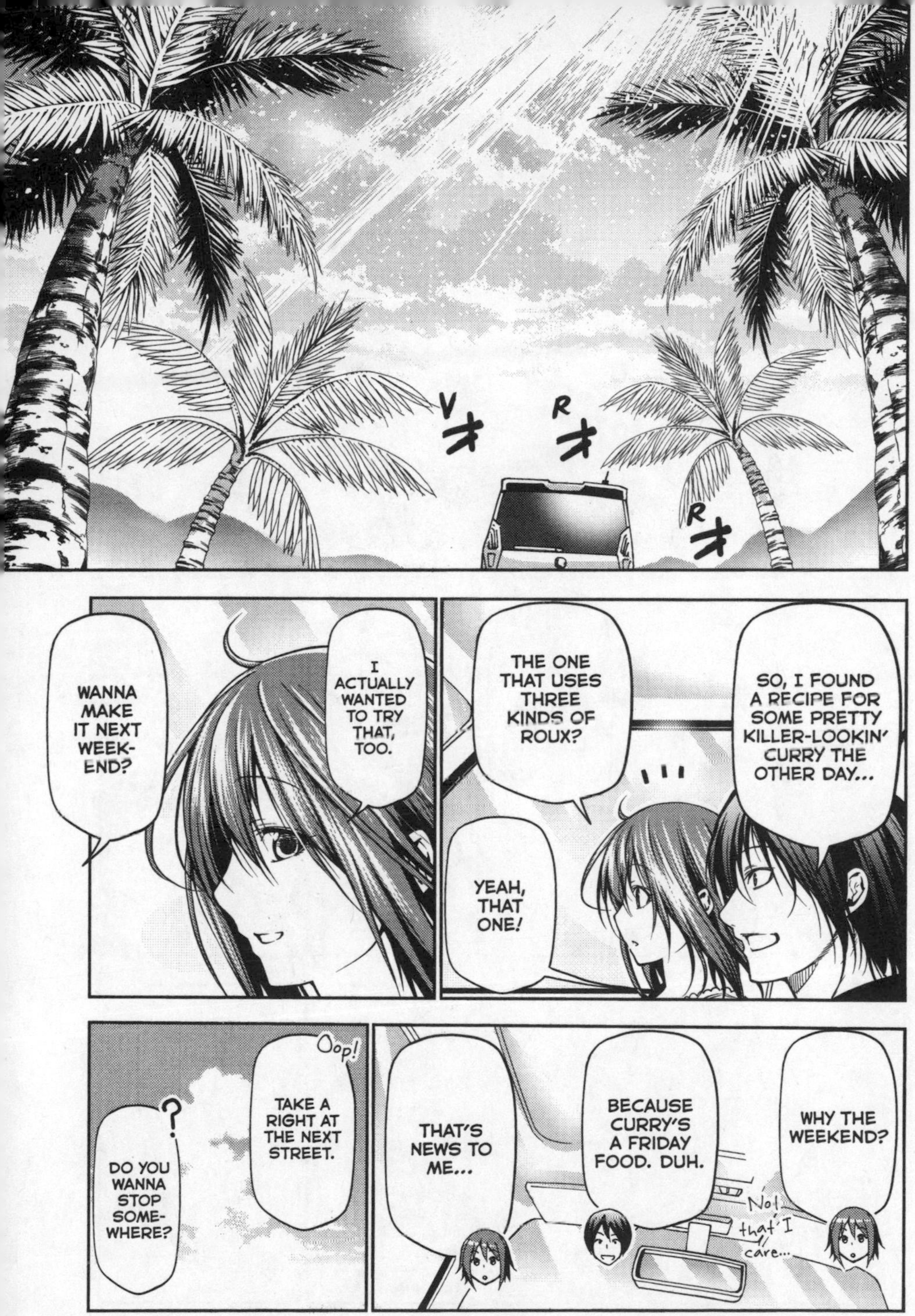
V オ R オ R オ
SO, I FOUND A RECIPE FOR SOME PRETTY KILLER-LOOKIN' CURRY THE OTHER DAY...
THE ONE THAT USES THREE KINDS OF ROUX?
YEAH, THAT ONE!
I ACTUALLY WANTED TO TRY THAT, TOO.
WANNA MAKE IT NEXT WEEK-END?
WHY THE WEEKEND?
Not that I care...
BECAUSE CURRY'S A FRIDAY FOOD. DUH.
THAT'S NEWS TO ME...
Oop!
TAKE A RIGHT AT THE NEXT STREET.
?
DO YOU WANNA STOP SOME-WHERE?

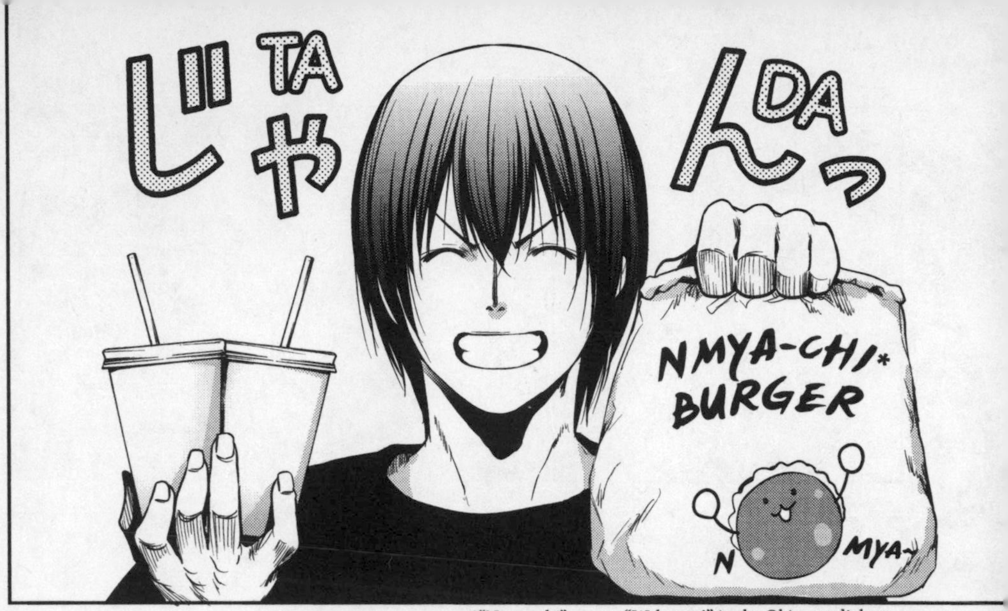
じゃ TA
ん DA っ
NMYA-CHI* BURGER
N MYA~
*"Nmya-chi" means "Welcome!" in the Okinawa dialect.

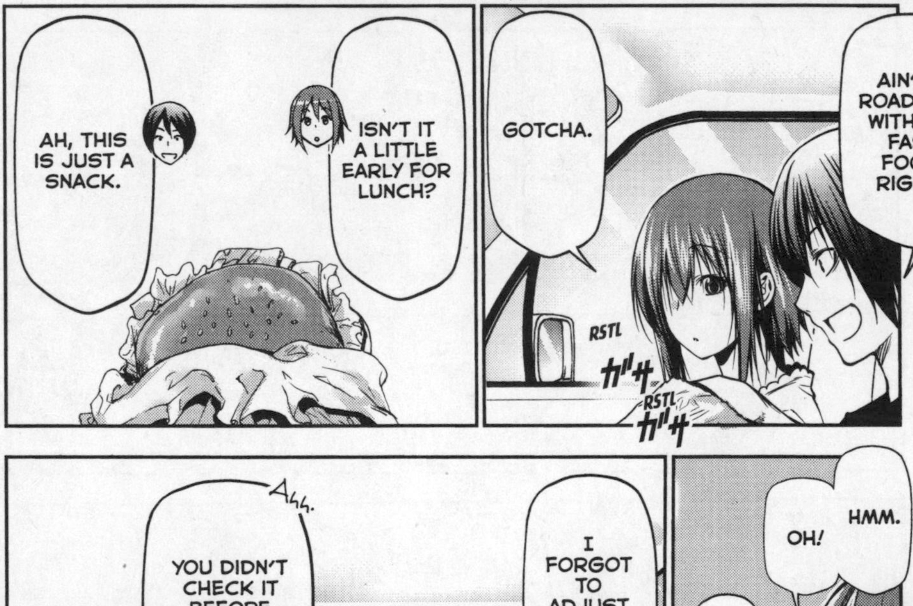
AIN'T A ROAD TRIP WITHOUT FAST FOOD, RIGHT?
GOTCHA.
RSTL ガサ
RSTL ガサ
ISN'T IT A LITTLE EARLY FOR LUNCH?
AH, THIS IS JUST A SNACK.
HMM.
OH!
WHAT'S UP?
I FORGOT TO ADJUST THE MIRROR.
Ahh.
YOU DIDN'T CHECK IT BEFORE WE HIT THE ROAD?
IT JUST SLIPPED MY MIND.

DON'T YOU JUST WISH YOU COULD EAT FOREVER WHEN YOU GO ON VACATION?
VRRRR
ブロロロ
TOTALLY.
FRY?
NOM
パクッ
MM.
SODA?
YUP.
MRG MRG
ムグムグ
ROGER THAT.
SIP
ズー

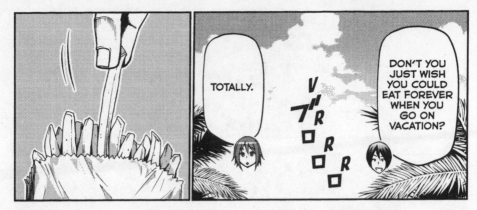

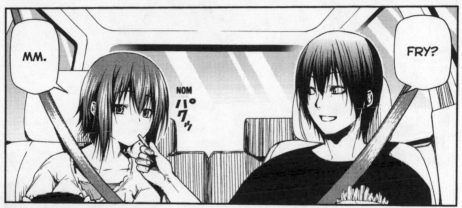

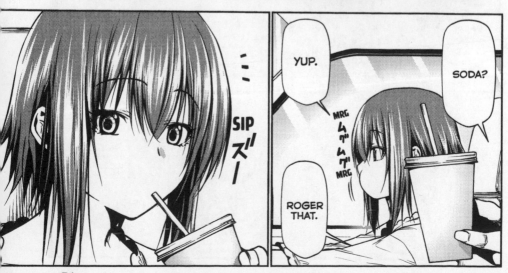

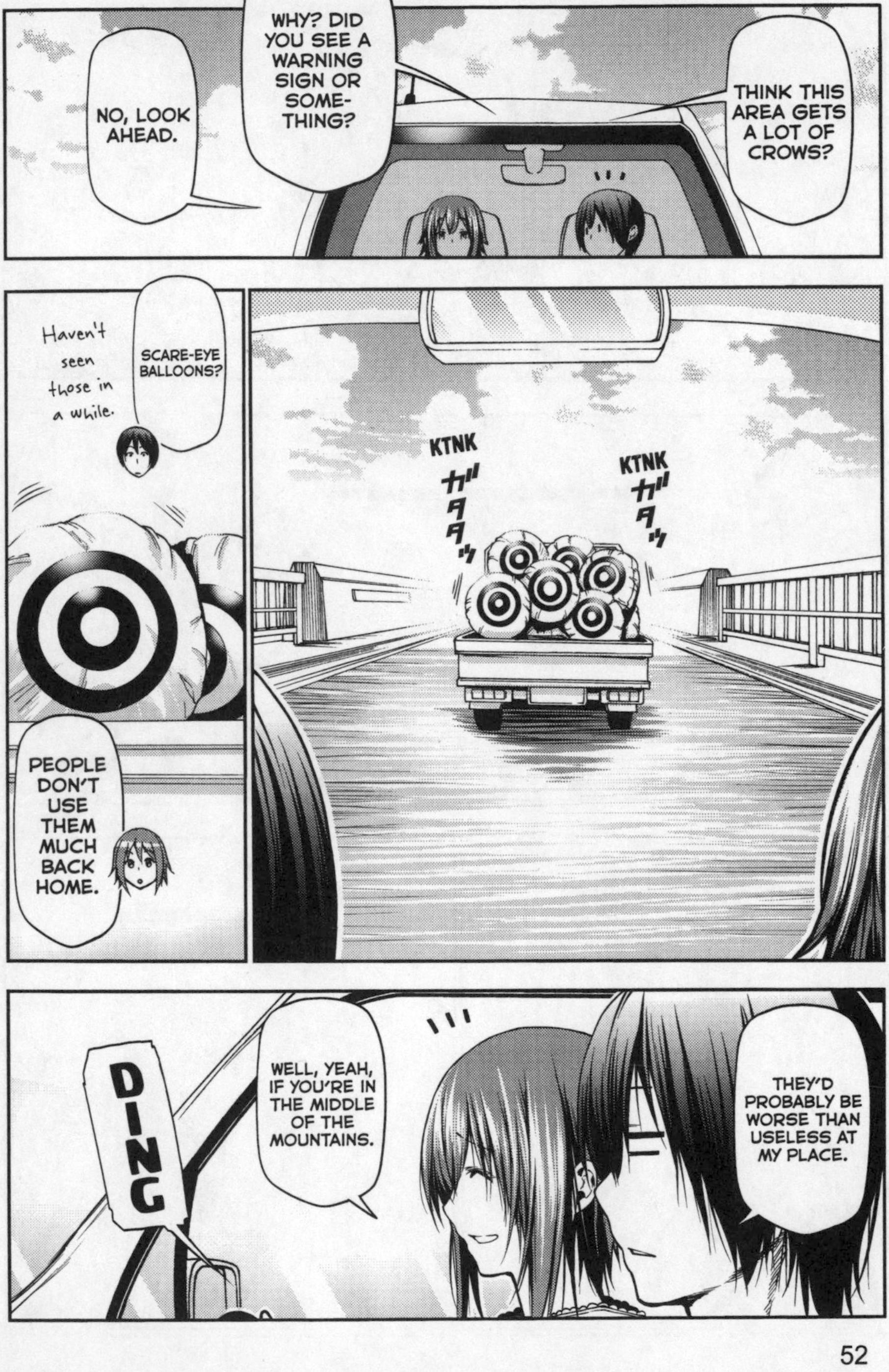
THINK THIS AREA GETS A LOT OF CROWS?
WHY? DID YOU SEE A WARNING SIGN OR SOME-THING?
NO, LOOK AHEAD.
KTNK ガタタッ
KTNK ガタタッ
SCARE-EYE BALLOONS?
Haven't seen those in a while.
PEOPLE DON'T USE THEM MUCH BACK HOME.
THEY'D PROBABLY BE WORSE THAN USELESS AT MY PLACE.
WELL, YEAH, IF YOU'RE IN THE MIDDLE OF THE MOUNTAINS.
DING

OOP. THAT'S ME.
SWIP
スッ
...
WHAT?
CAN'T SAY FOR SURE, BUT I THINK SOMEONE MIGHT DIE BECAUSE OF ME.
UM... WHAT?
KTNK
ガタタッ
KTNK
ガタタッ
WHOOSH
ゴオオッ
WHOA!!

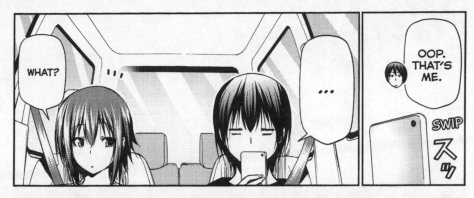

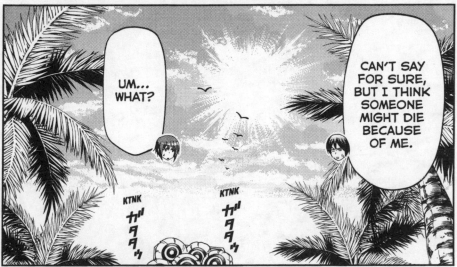

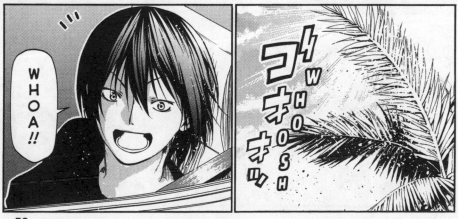

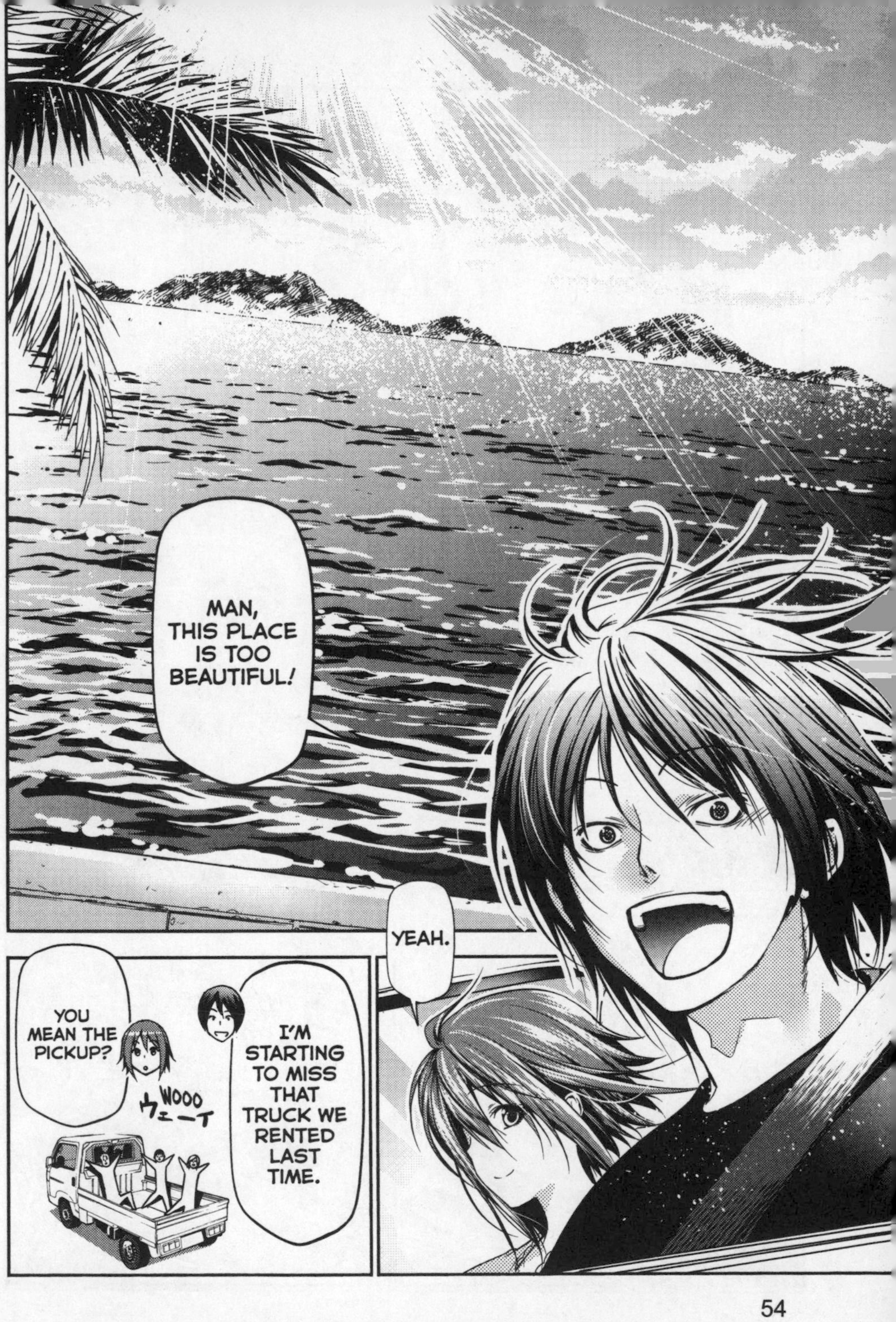
MAN, THIS PLACE IS TOO BEAUTIFUL!
YEAH.
I'M STARTING TO MISS THAT TRUCK WE RENTED LAST TIME.
YOU MEAN THE PICKUP?
WOOO ウェーイ

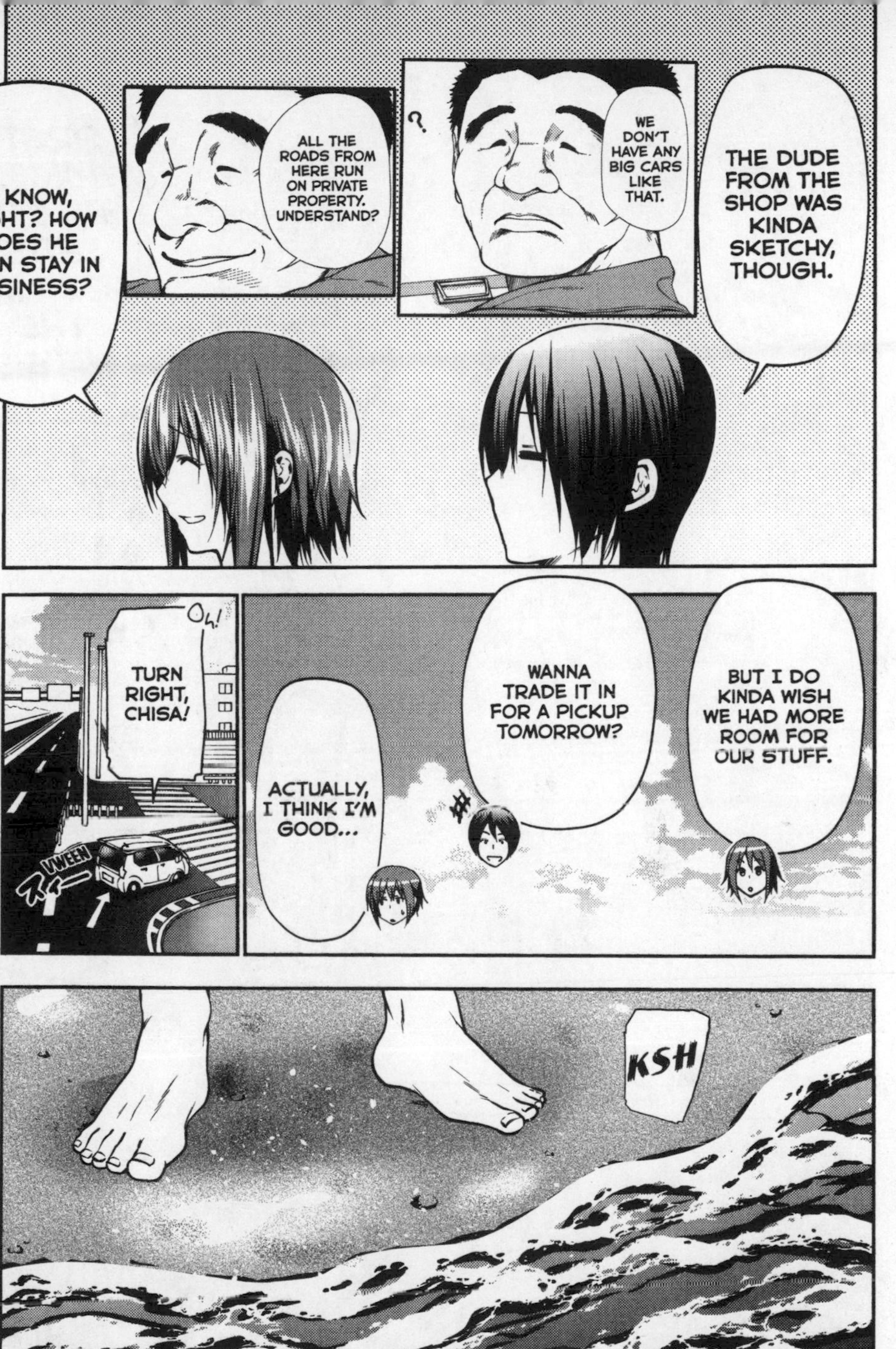
THE DUDE FROM THE SHOP WAS KINDA SKETCHY, THOUGH.
?
WE DON'T HAVE ANY BIG CARS LIKE THAT.
ALL THE ROADS FROM HERE RUN ON PRIVATE PROPERTY. UNDERSTAND?
I KNOW, RIGHT? HOW DOES HE EVEN STAY IN BUSINESS?
BUT I DO KINDA WISH WE HAD MORE ROOM FOR OUR STUFF.
WANNA TRADE IT IN FOR A PICKUP TOMORROW?
#
ACTUALLY, I THINK I'M GOOD...
Oh!
TURN RIGHT, CHISA!
VWEEN
スィー
KSH

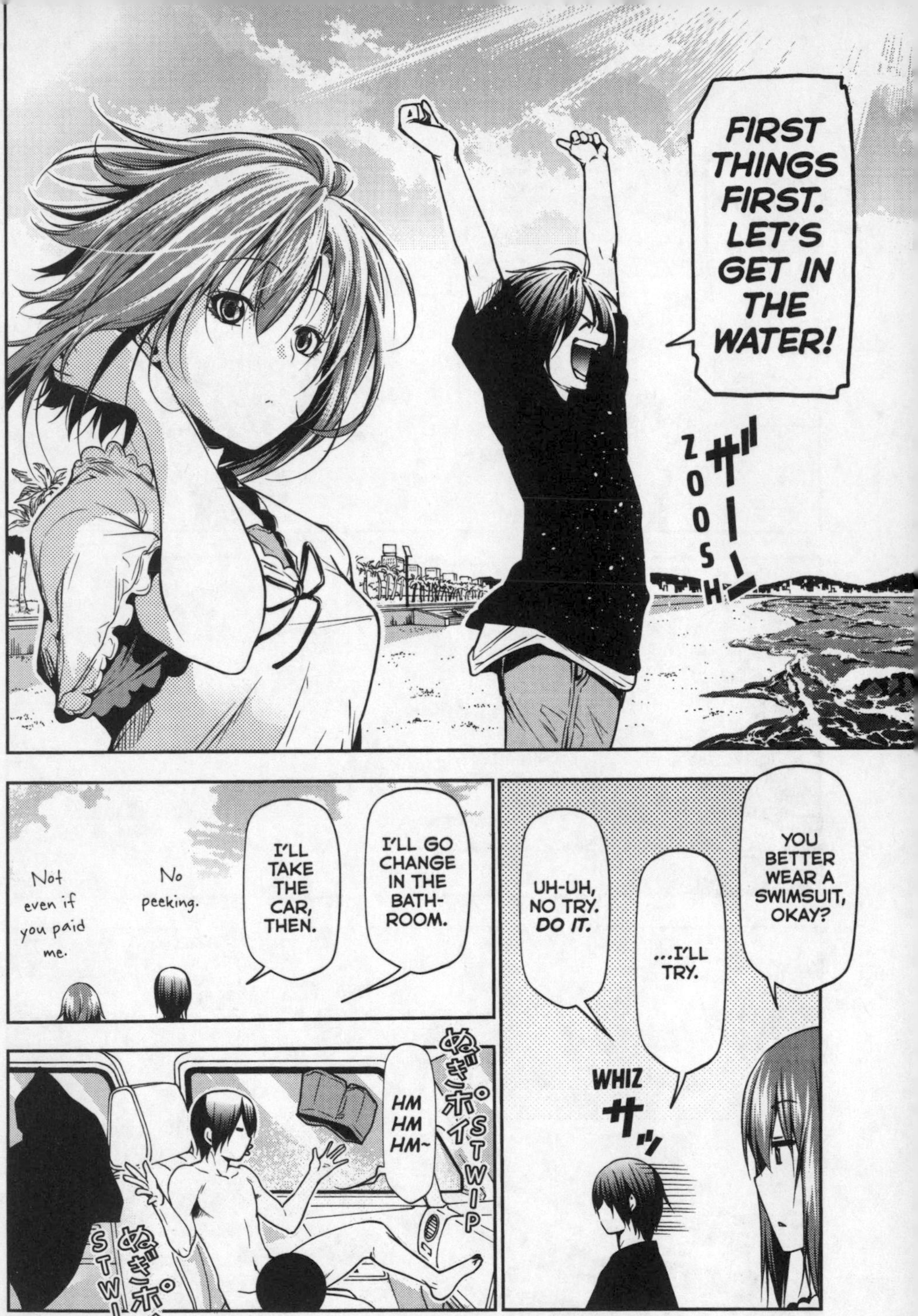
FIRST THINGS FIRST. LET'S GET IN THE WATER!
ZOOSH
ザッー
YOU BETTER WEAR A SWIMSUIT, OKAY?
...I'LL TRY.
UH-UH, NO TRY. *DO IT.*
WHIZ
サッ
I'LL GO CHANGE IN THE BATH-ROOM.
I'LL TAKE THE CAR, THEN.
No peeking.
Not even if you paid me.
ぬぎポイ
STWIP
HM HM HM~
ぬぎポイ
STWIP

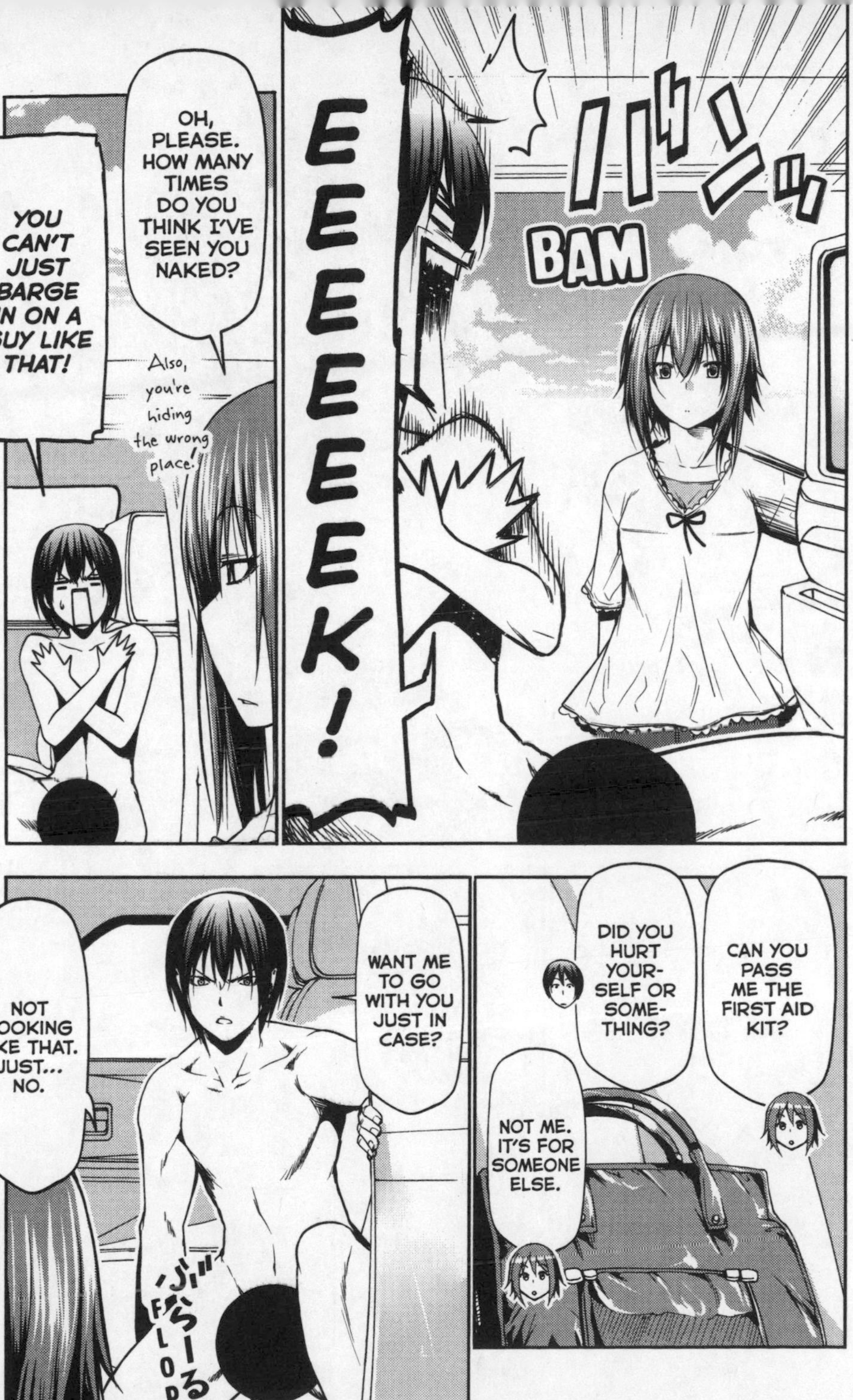

BAM
EEEEK!
OH, PLEASE. HOW MANY TIMES DO YOU THINK I'VE SEEN YOU NAKED?
YOU CAN'T JUST BARGE IN ON A GUY LIKE THAT!
Also, you're hiding the wrong place!
CAN YOU PASS ME THE FIRST AID KIT?
DID YOU HURT YOURSELF OR SOMETHING?
NOT ME. IT'S FOR SOMEONE ELSE.
WANT ME TO GO WITH YOU JUST IN CASE?
NOT LOOKING LIKE THAT. JUST... NO.
FLOP

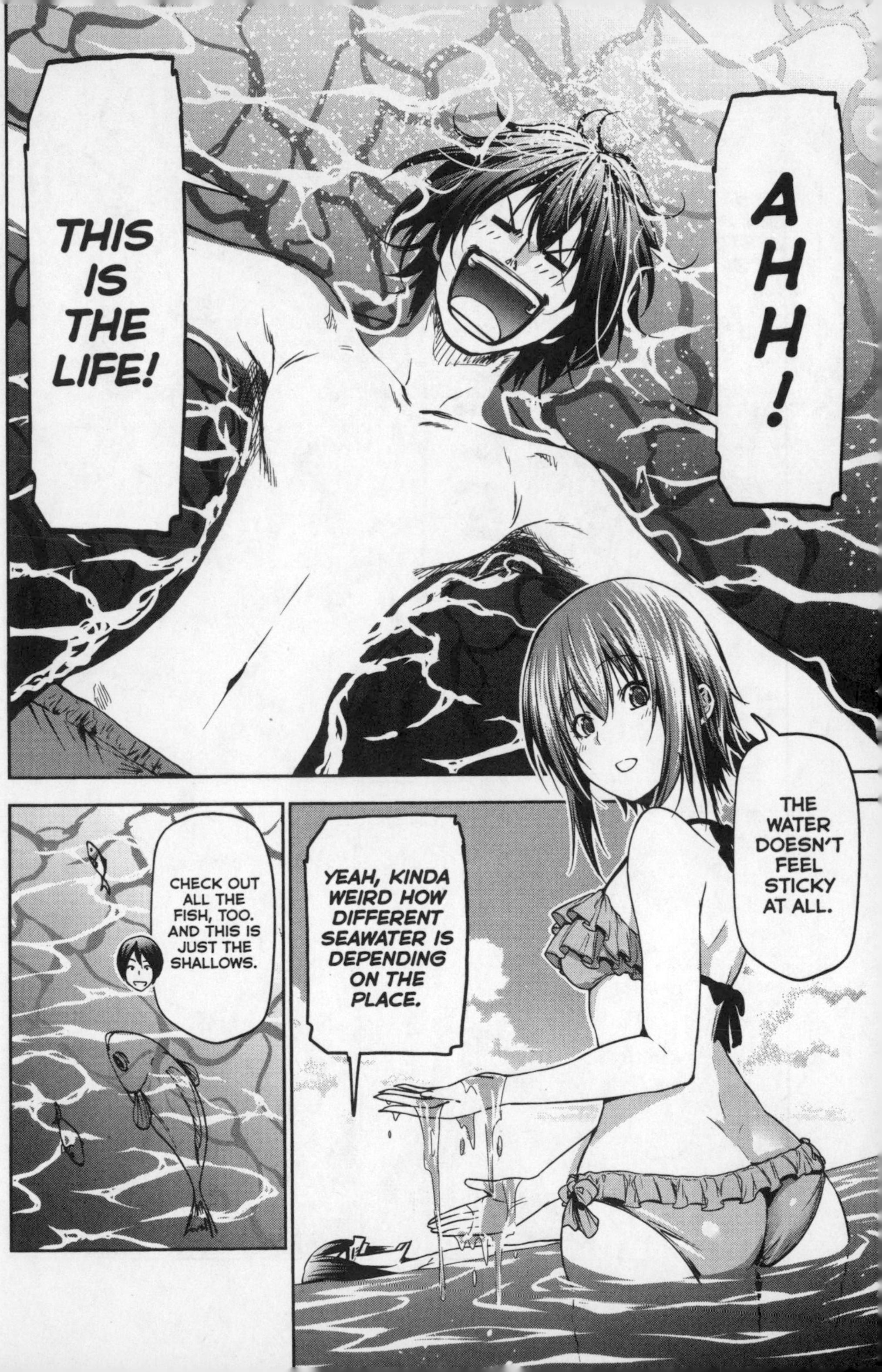
AHH!
THIS IS THE LIFE!
THE WATER DOESN'T FEEL STICKY AT ALL.
YEAH, KINDA WEIRD HOW DIFFERENT SEAWATER IS DEPENDING ON THE PLACE.
CHECK OUT ALL THE FISH, TOO. AND THIS IS JUST THE SHALLOWS.

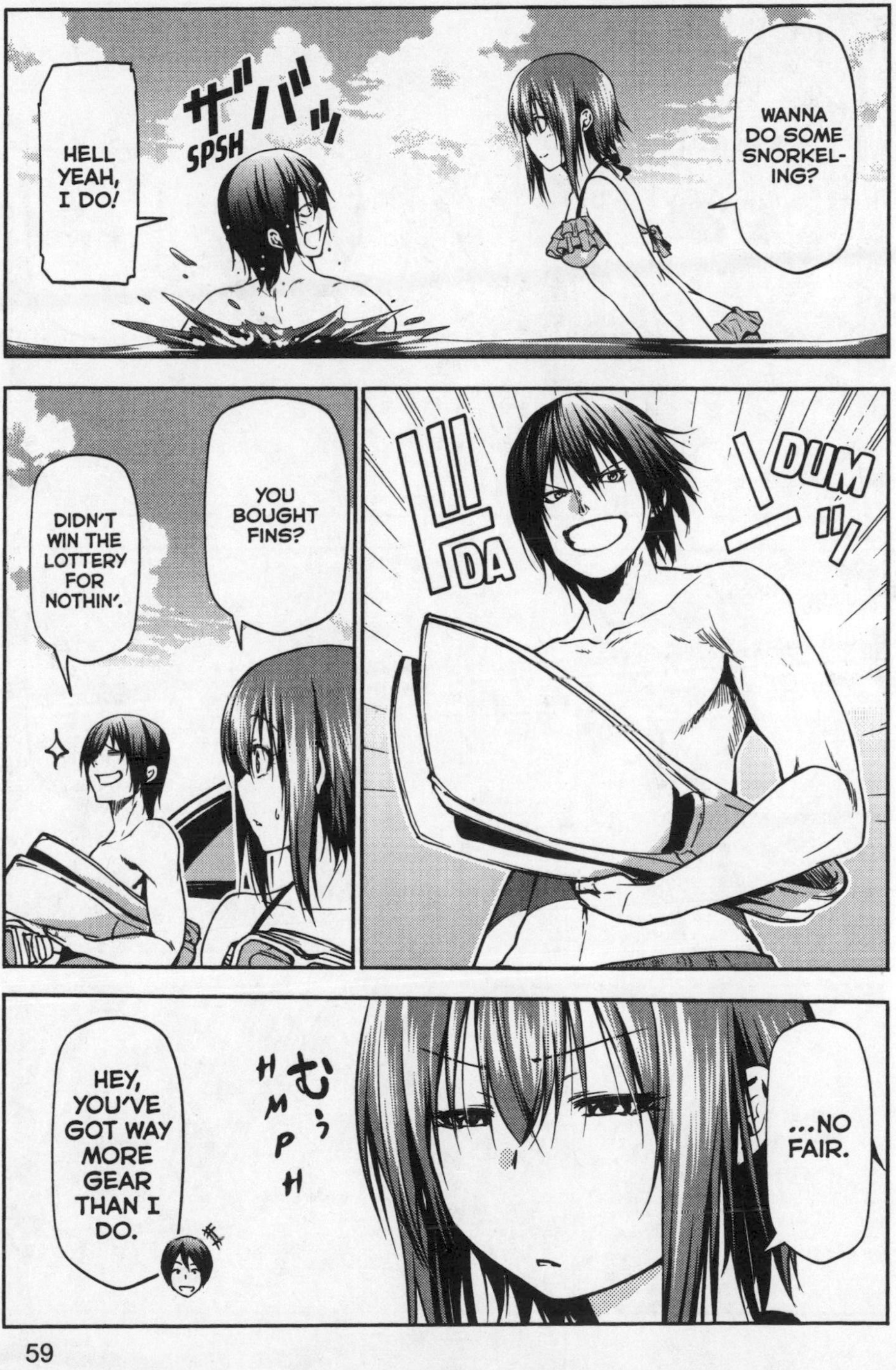

WANNA DO SOME SNORKEL-ING?
SPSH
HELL YEAH, I DO!
DUM
DA
YOU BOUGHT FINS?
DIDN'T WIN THE LOTTERY FOR NOTHIN'.
...NO FAIR.
むぅ
HMPH
HEY, YOU'VE GOT WAY MORE GEAR THAN I DO.

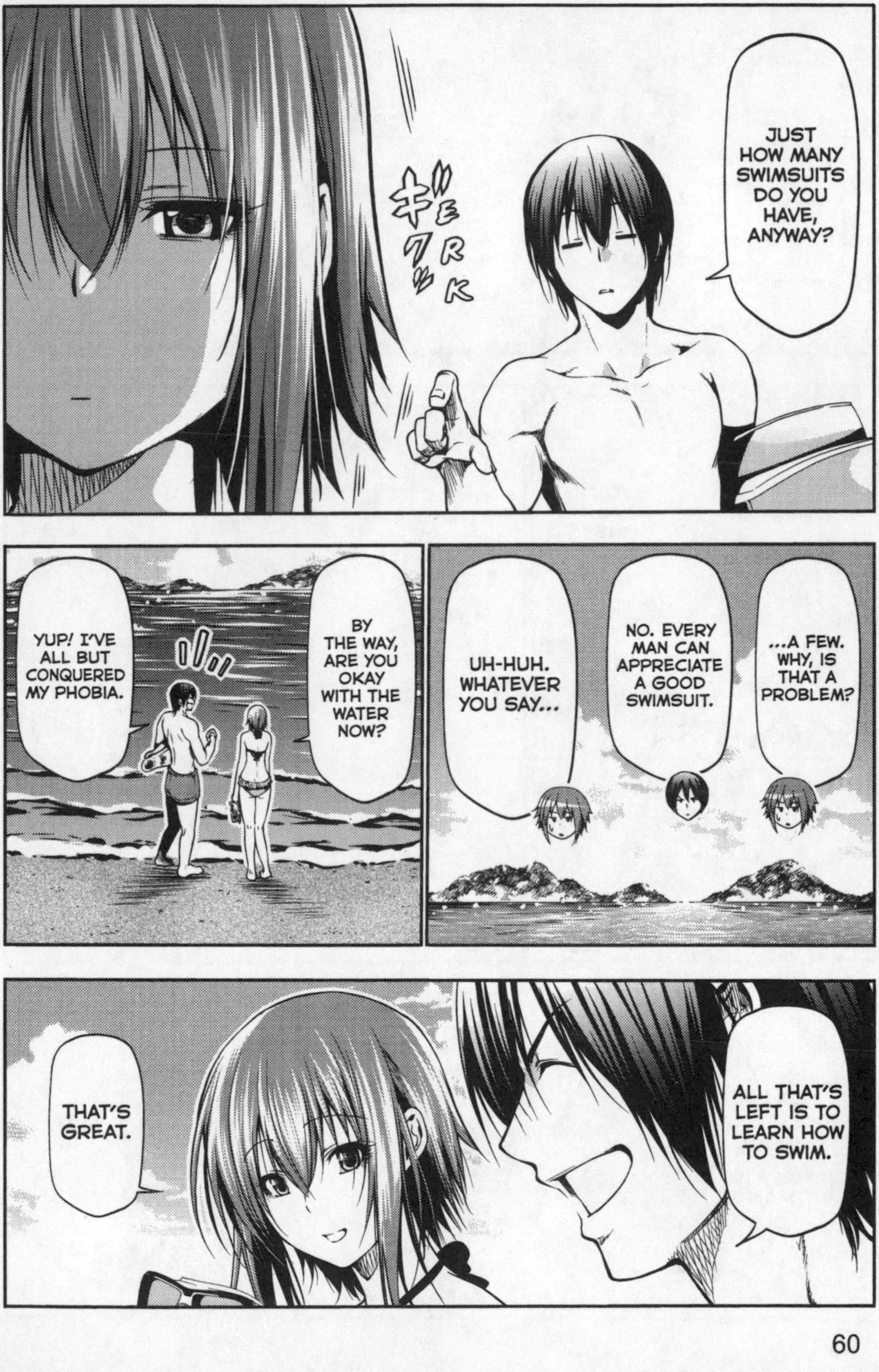
JUST HOW MANY SWIMSUITS DO YOU HAVE, ANYWAY?
ERK
...A FEW. WHY, IS THAT A PROBLEM?
NO. EVERY MAN CAN APPRECIATE A GOOD SWIMSUIT.
UH-HUH. WHATEVER YOU SAY...
BY THE WAY, ARE YOU OKAY WITH THE WATER NOW?
YUP! I'VE ALL BUT CONQUERED MY PHOBIA.
ALL THAT'S LEFT IS TO LEARN HOW TO SWIM.
THAT'S GREAT.

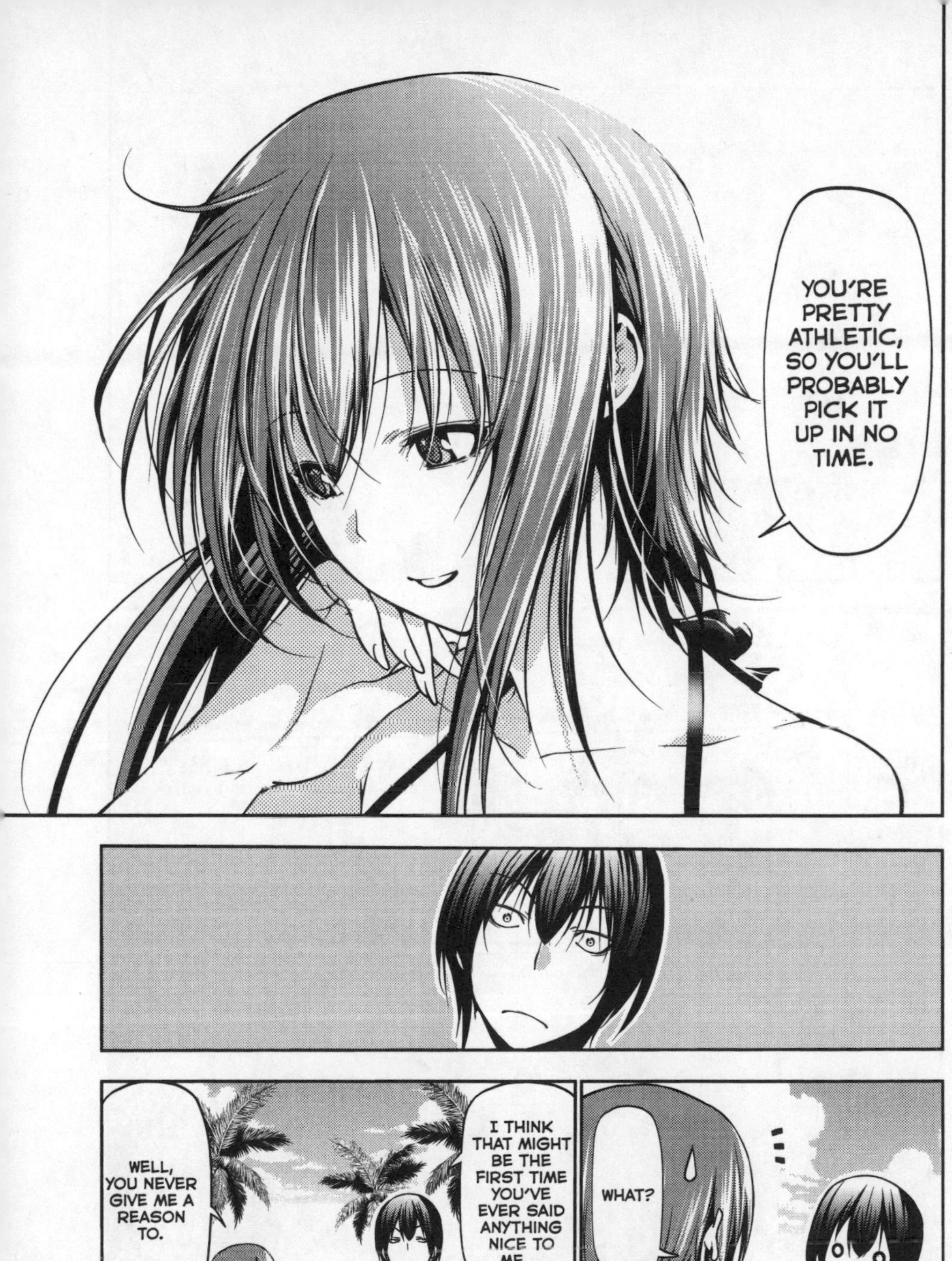
YOU'RE PRETTY ATHLETIC, SO YOU'LL PROBABLY PICK IT UP IN NO TIME.
WHAT?
I THINK THAT MIGHT BE THE FIRST TIME YOU'VE EVER SAID ANYTHING NICE TO ME...
WELL, YOU NEVER GIVE ME A REASON TO.

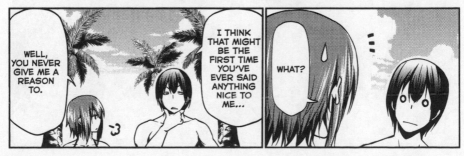

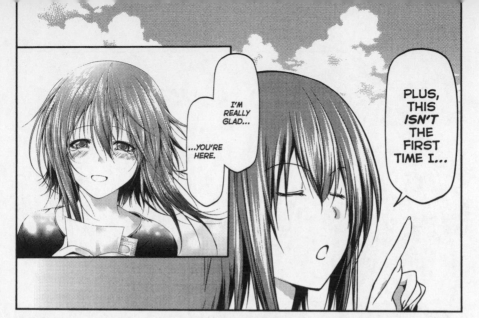

PLUS, THIS *ISN'T* THE FIRST TIME I...
I'M REALLY GLAD...
...YOU'RE HERE.
...
'SUP?
...
FWIP
くるり
NEVER MIND.
パシャッ
SPLISH
SO ANYWAY...
...WANT ME TO TEACH YOU HOW TO SWIM?
REALLY?

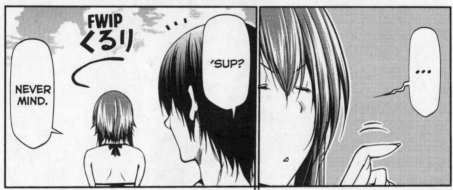

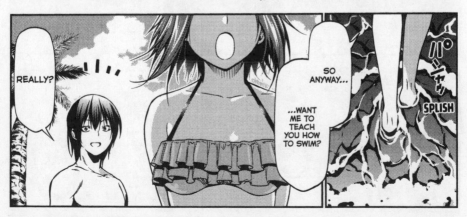

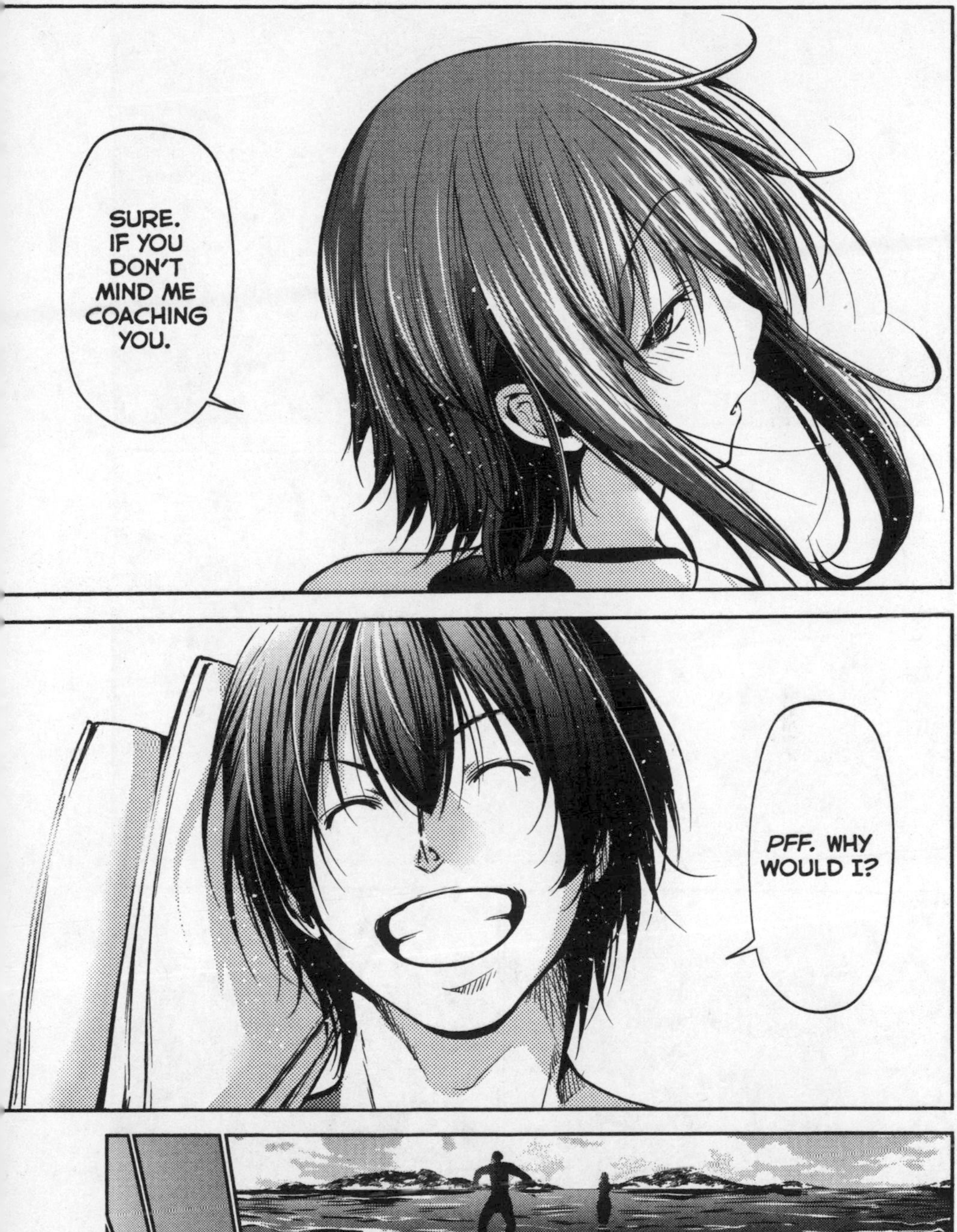
SURE. IF YOU DON'T MIND ME COACHING YOU.
PFF. WHY WOULD I?

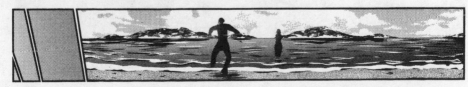

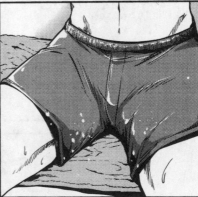

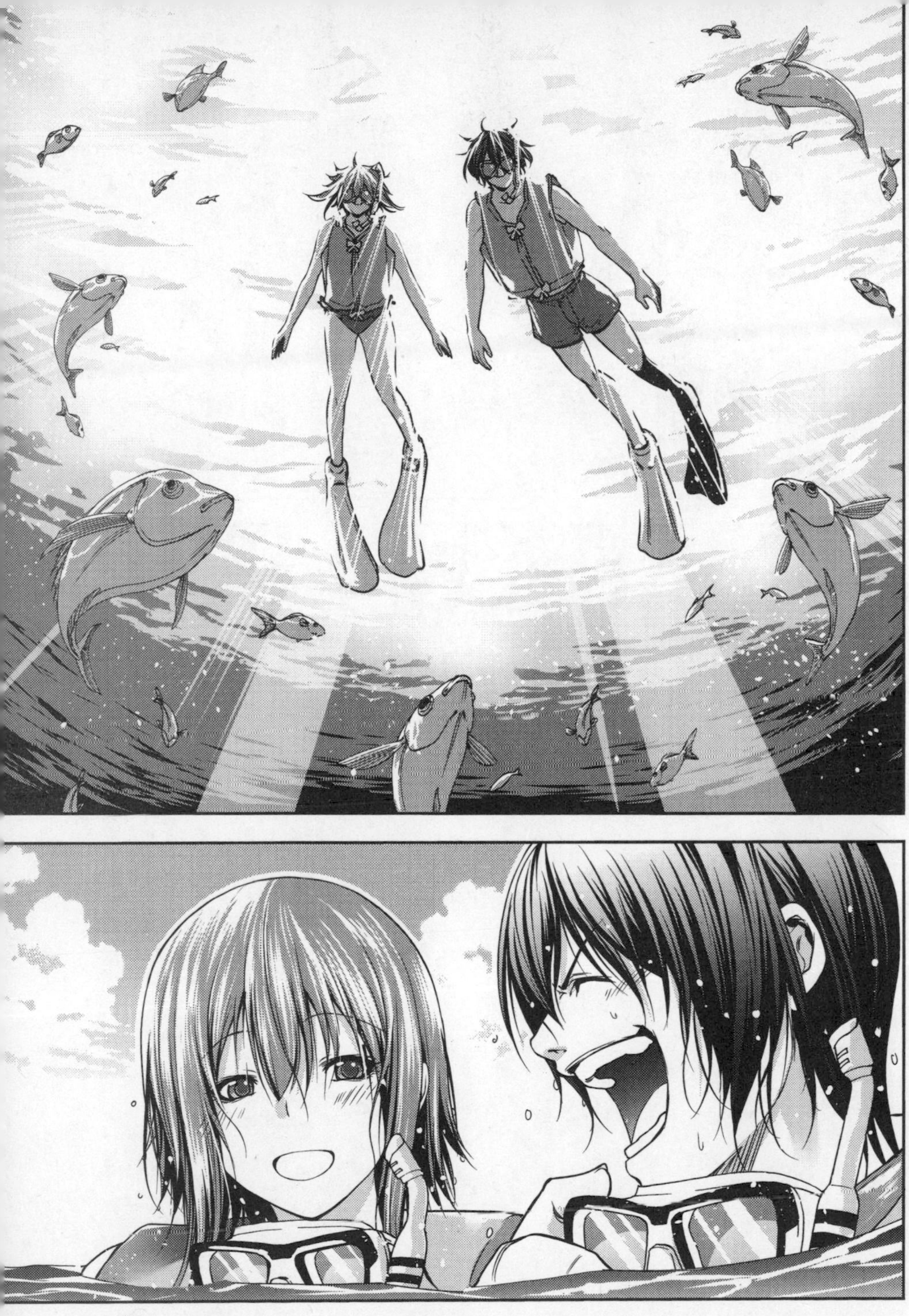

Ahh!
THAT WAS FUN!
MM.
MAN, MY PHONE'S BEEN BLOWING UP ALL DAY.
MAYBE IT'S URGENT.
...
HMM.
CAN'T SAY FOR SURE, BUT I DON'T THINK IT'S ANYTHING MAJOR.
OKAY, THEN.
WANNA STOP SOMEWHERE FOR DINNER SOON?
SURE.

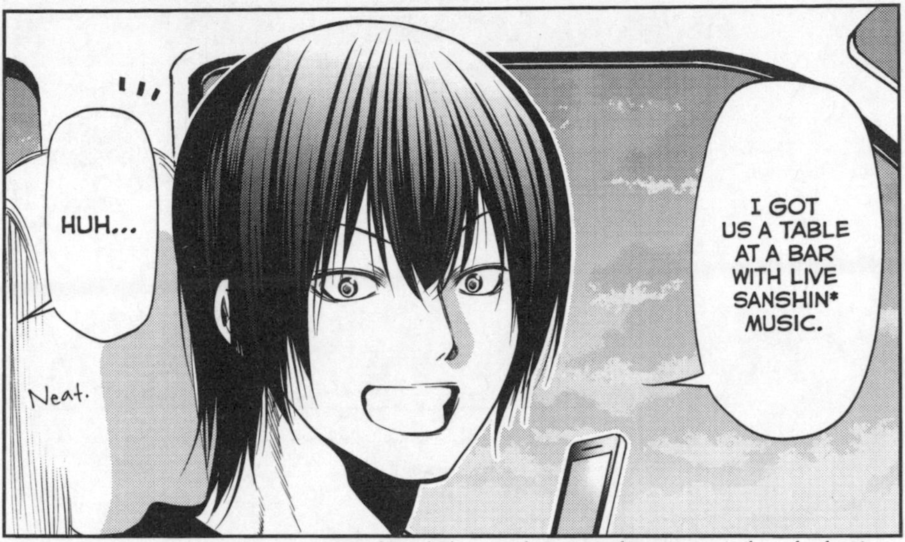
I GOT US A TABLE AT A BAR WITH LIVE SANSHIN* MUSIC.
HUH...
Neat.

*A traditional Okinawan three-stringed instrument similar to the shamisen.

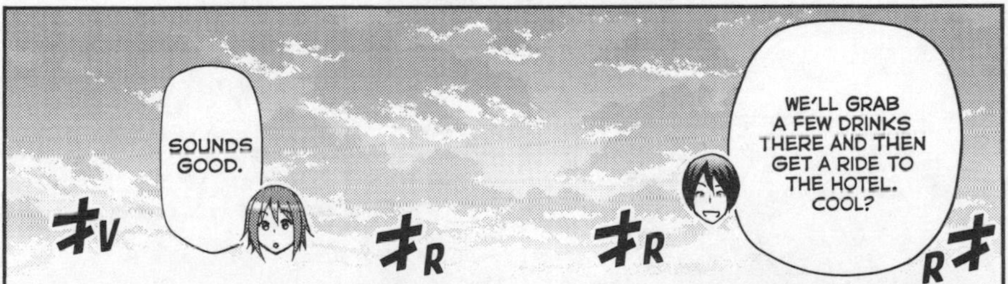
WE'LL GRAB A FEW DRINKS THERE AND THEN GET A RIDE TO THE HOTEL. COOL?
SOUNDS GOOD.

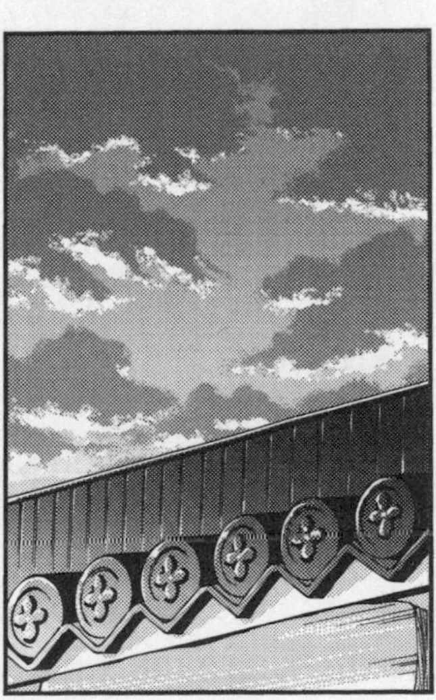

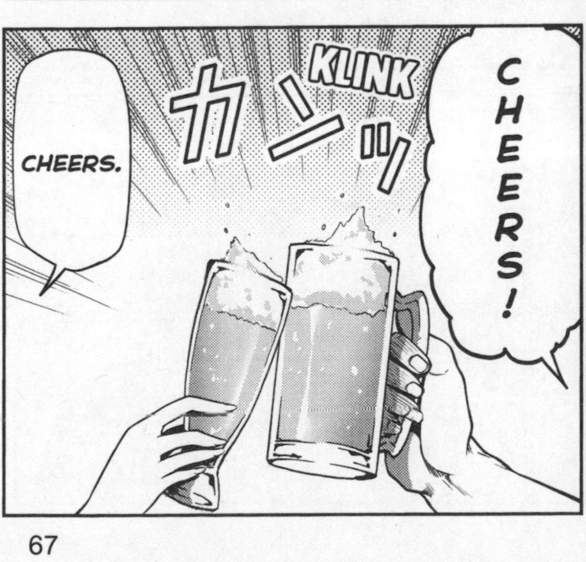
CHEERS!
KLINK
カンッ
CHEERS.

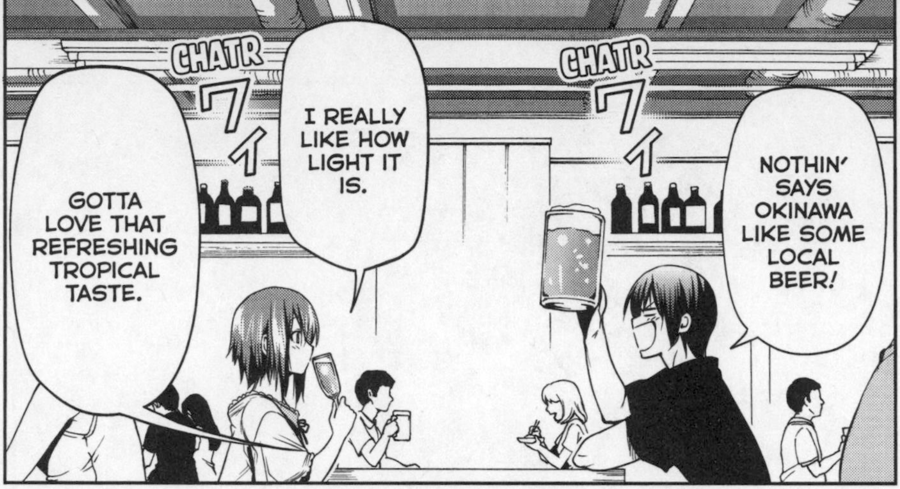
NOTHIN' SAYS OKINAWA LIKE SOME LOCAL BEER!
CHATR
ワイ
I REALLY LIKE HOW LIGHT IT IS.
CHATR
ワイ
GOTTA LOVE THAT REFRESHING TROPICAL TASTE.

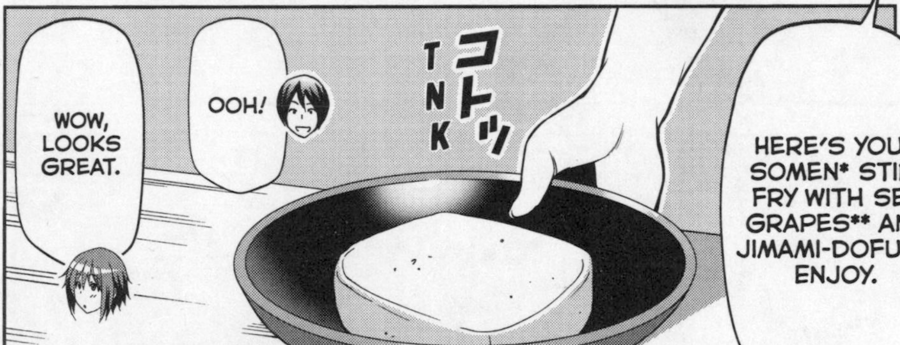
HERE'S YOUR SOMEN* STIR-FRY WITH SEA GRAPES** AND JIMAMI-DOFU***. ENJOY.
TNK
コトッ
OOH!
WOW, LOOKS GREAT.

***Okinawan peanut tofu. **A type of seaweed. *Thin wheat noodles.

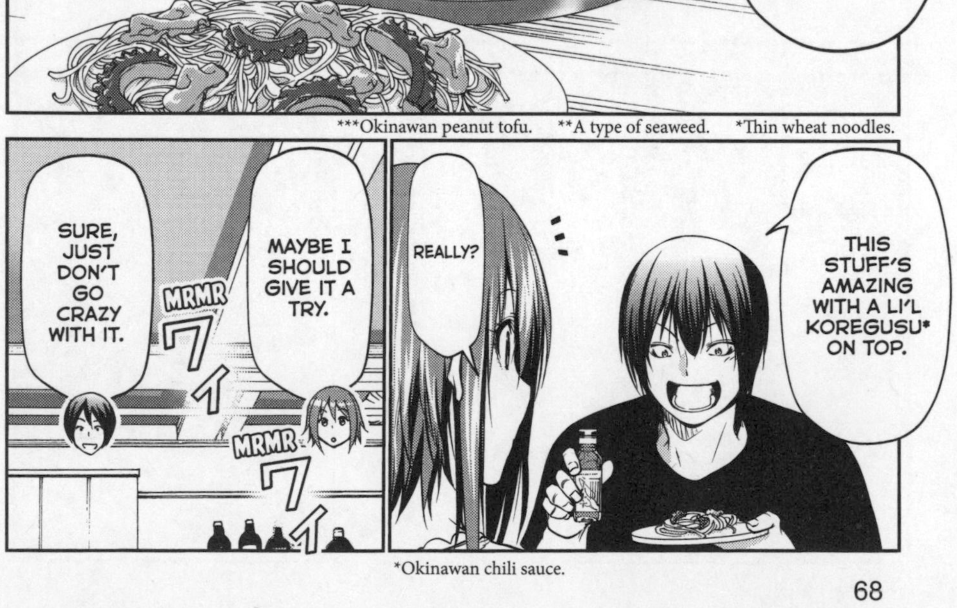
THIS STUFF'S AMAZING WITH A LI'L KOREGUSU* ON TOP.
REALLY?
MAYBE I SHOULD GIVE IT A TRY.
MRMR
ワイ
SURE, JUST DON'T GO CRAZY WITH IT.
MRMR
ワイ

*Okinawan chili sauce.

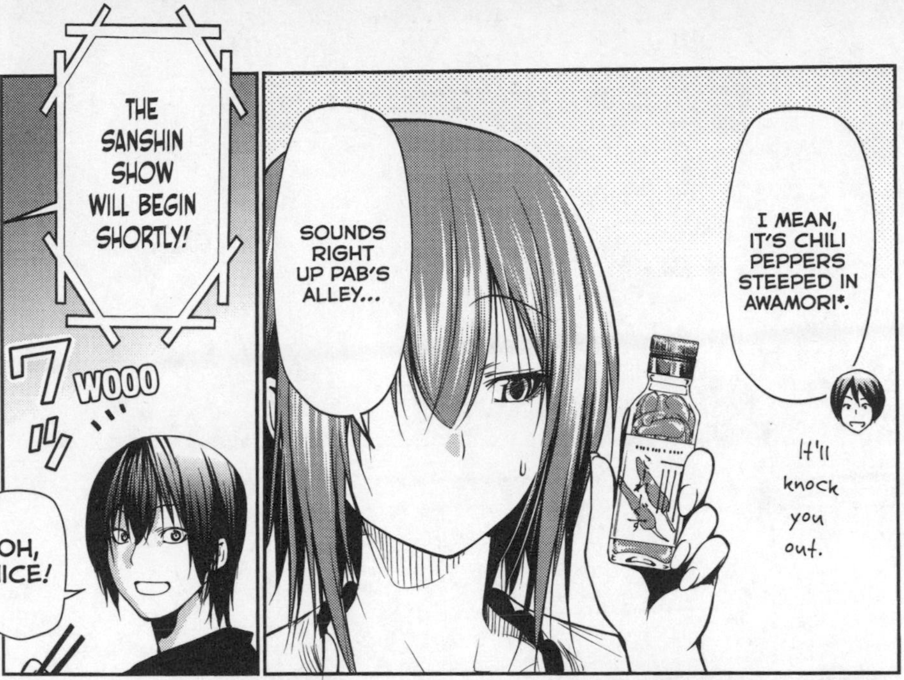
I MEAN, IT'S CHILI PEPPERS STEEPED IN AWAMORI*.
It'll knock you out.
SOUNDS RIGHT UP PAB'S ALLEY...
THE SANSHIN SHOW WILL BEGIN SHORTLY!
WOOO
OH, NICE!

*Distilled rice alcohol indigenous to Okinawa.

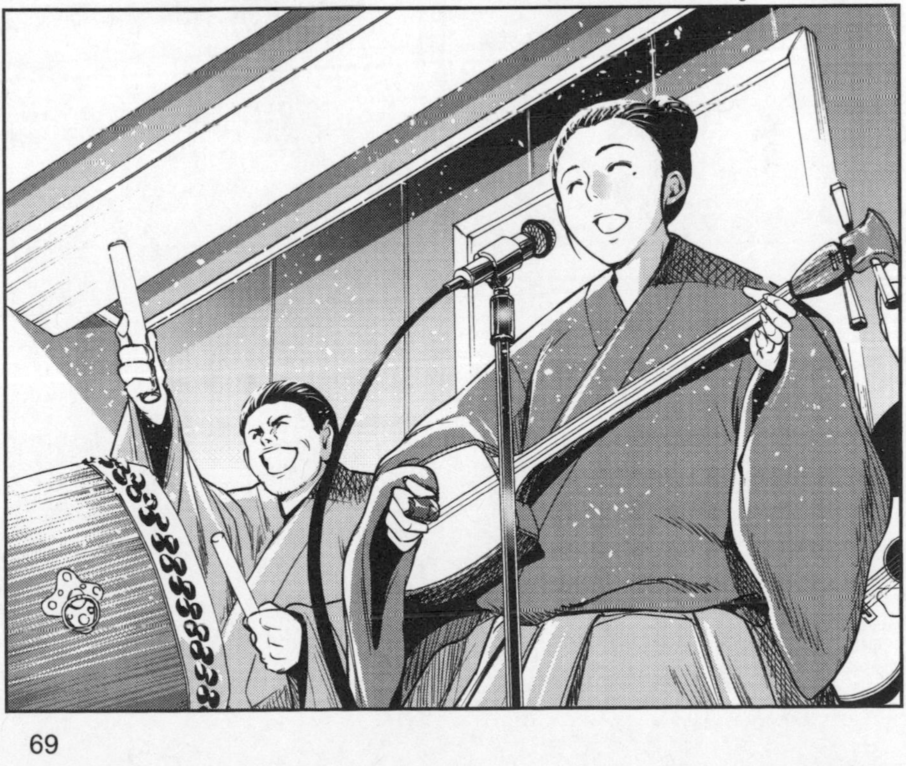

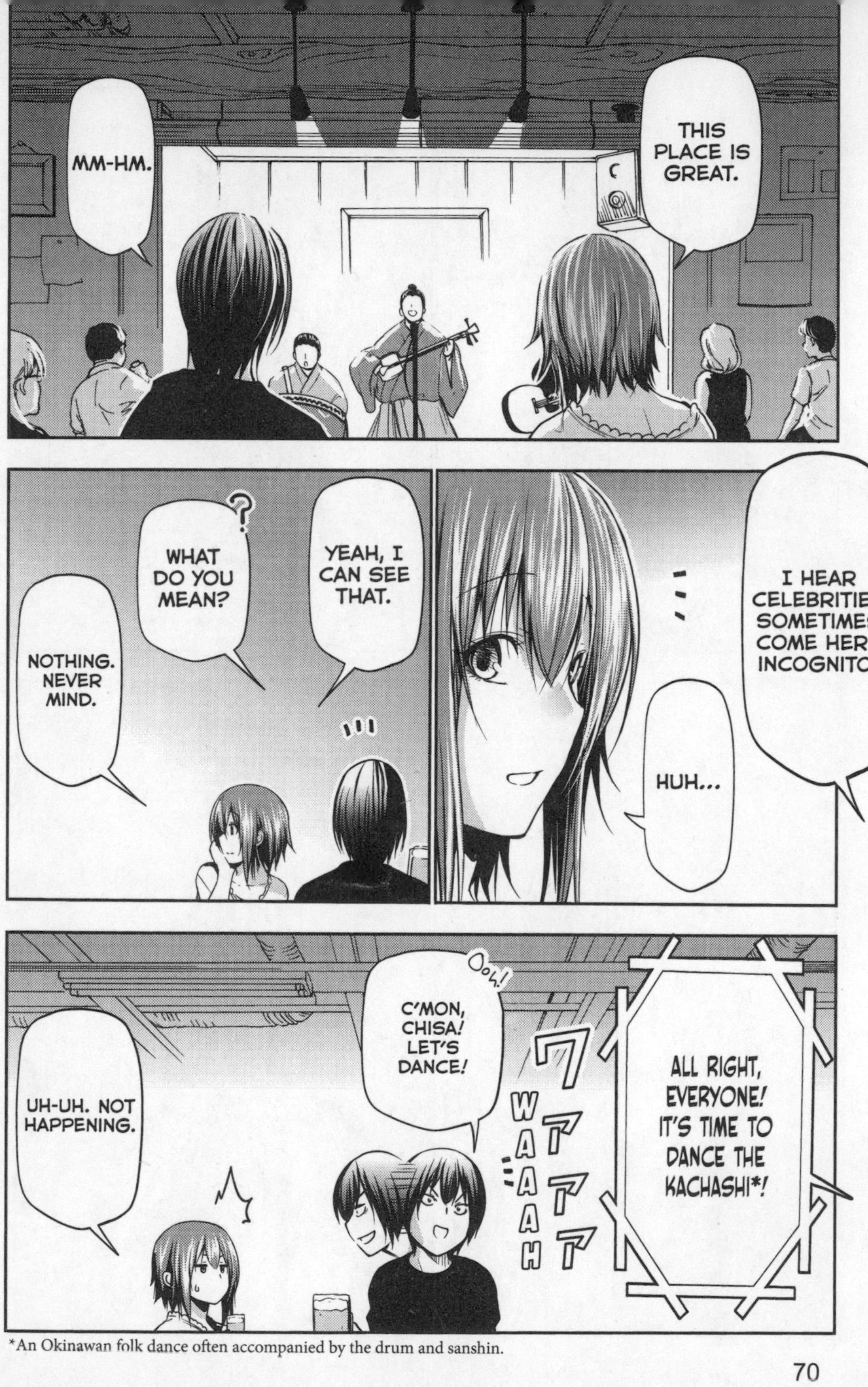
THIS PLACE IS GREAT.
MM-HM.
I HEAR CELEBRITIES SOMETIMES COME HERE INCOGNITO.
HUH...
YEAH, I CAN SEE THAT.
WHAT DO YOU MEAN?
NOTHING. NEVER MIND.
ALL RIGHT, EVERYONE! IT'S TIME TO DANCE THE KACHASHI*!
ワアアア
WAAAH
Ooh!
C'MON, CHISA! LET'S DANCE!
UH-UH. NOT HAPPENING.

*An Okinawan folk dance often accompanied by the drum and sanshin.

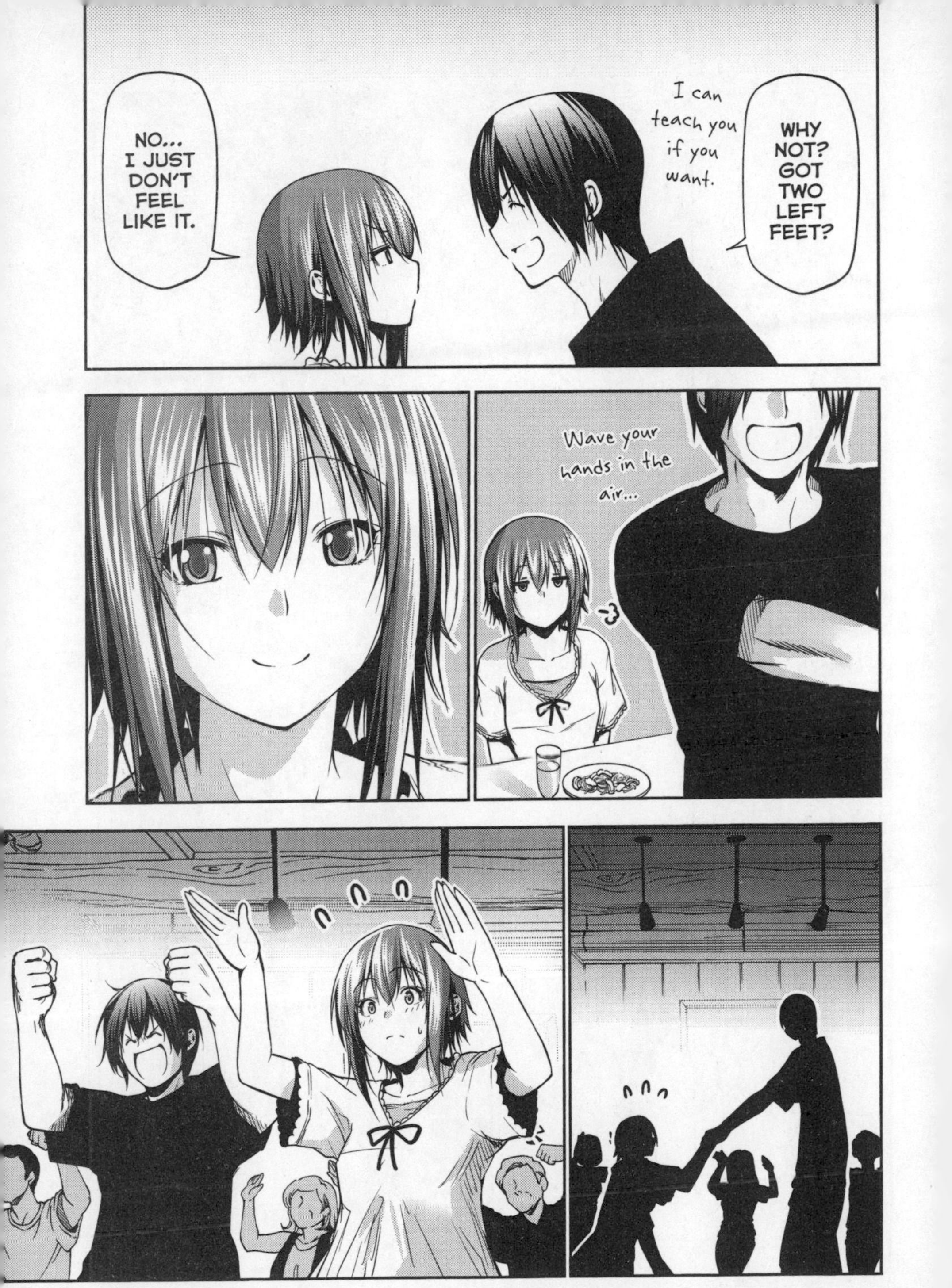
WHY NOT? GOT TWO LEFT FEET?
I can teach you if you want.
NO... I JUST DON'T FEEL LIKE IT.
Wave your hands in the air...

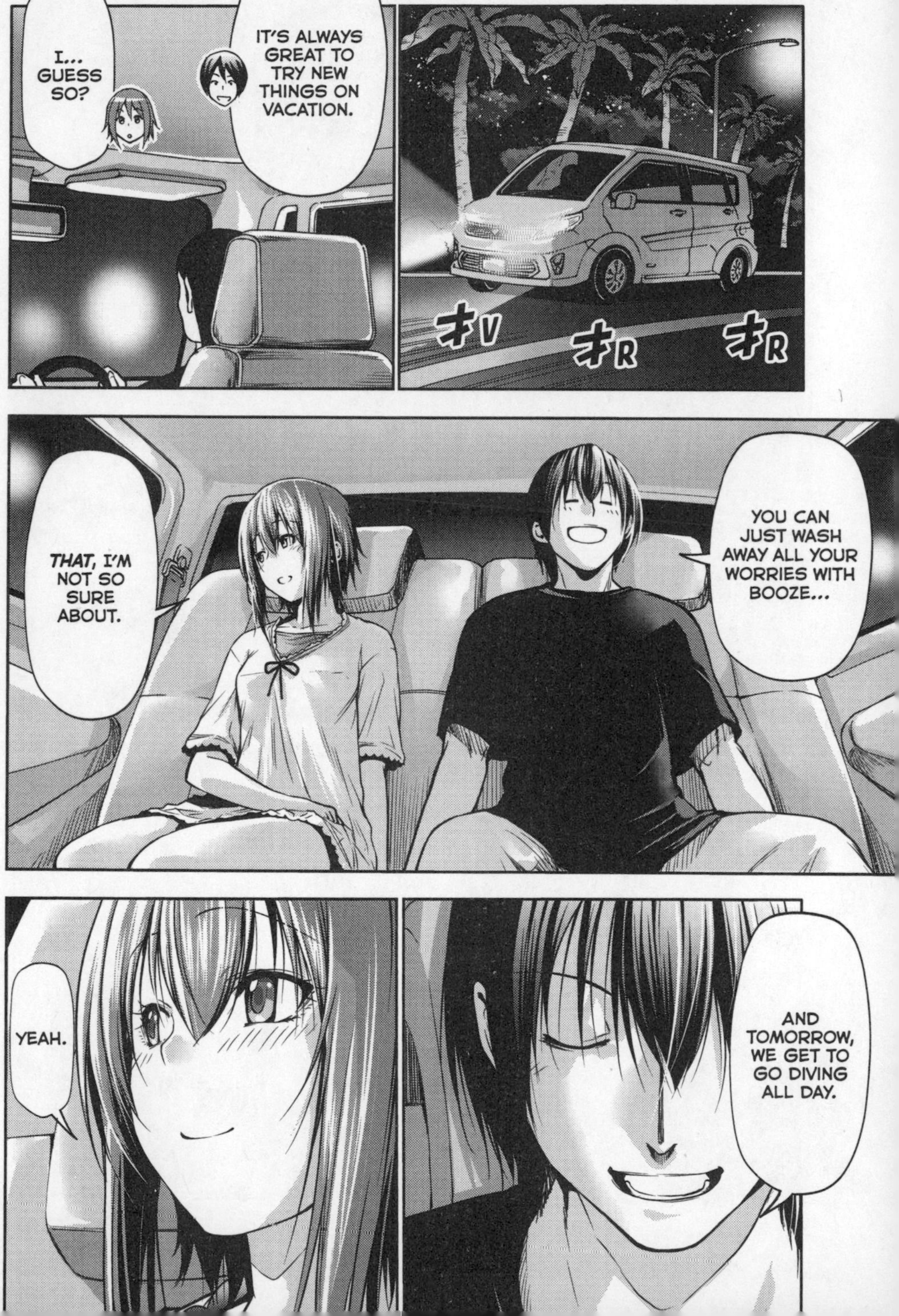
オV オR オR
IT'S ALWAYS GREAT TO TRY NEW THINGS ON VACATION.
I... GUESS SO?
YOU CAN JUST WASH AWAY ALL YOUR WORRIES WITH BOOZE...
THAT, I'M NOT SO SURE ABOUT.
AND TOMORROW, WE GET TO GO DIVING ALL DAY.
YEAH.

MAKE SURE YOU GO TO BED EARLY.
I'LL TRY, BUT I MIGHT BE TOO EXCITED TO SLEEP.
YOU'RE SUCH A WEIRDO...

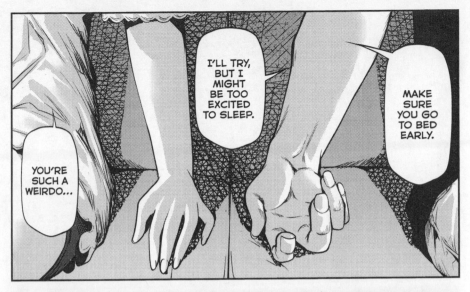

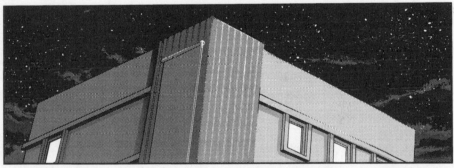

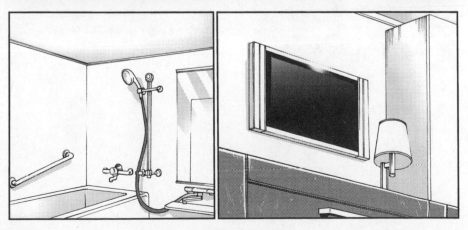

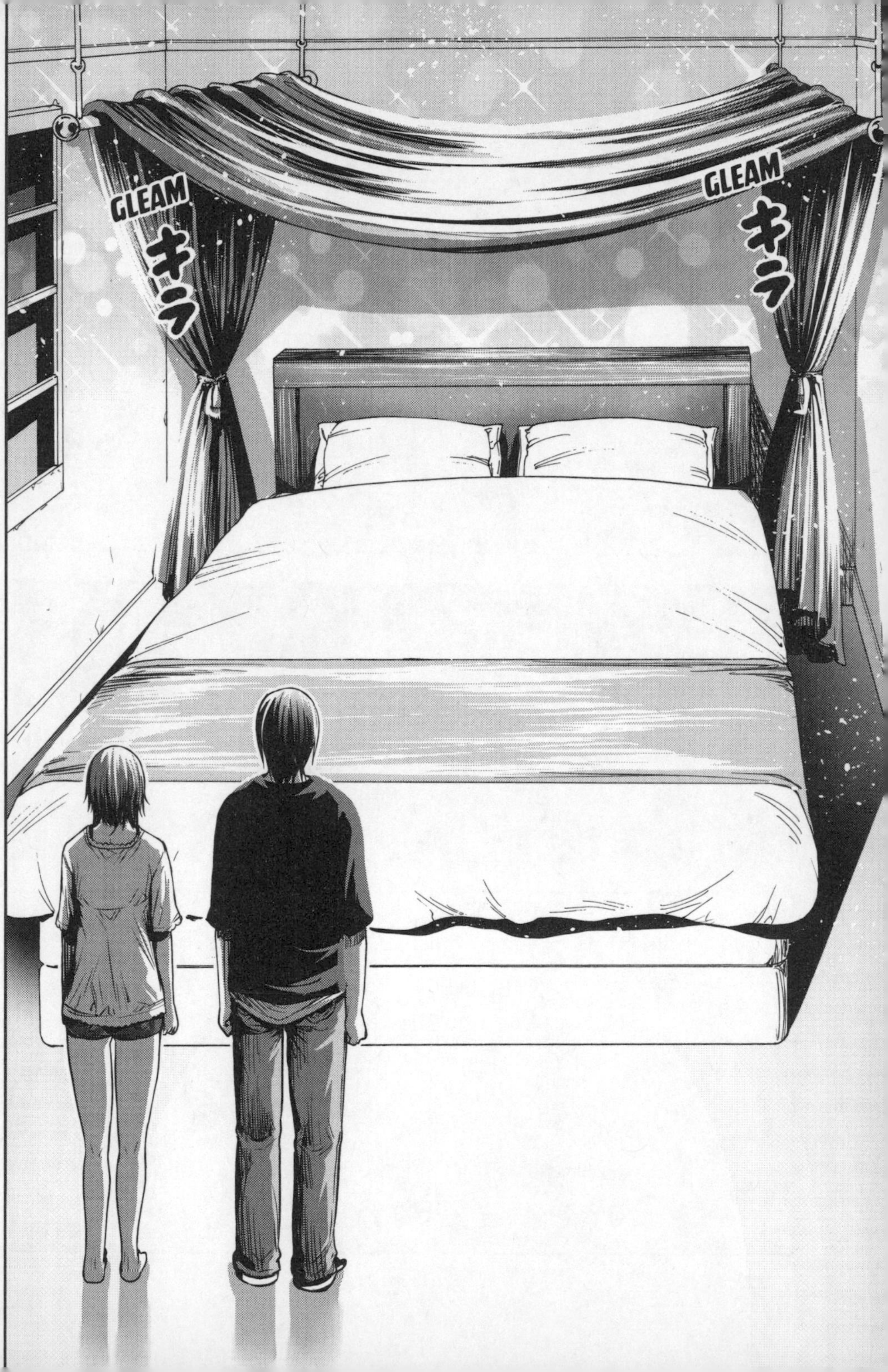
GLEAM
キラ
GLEAM
キラ

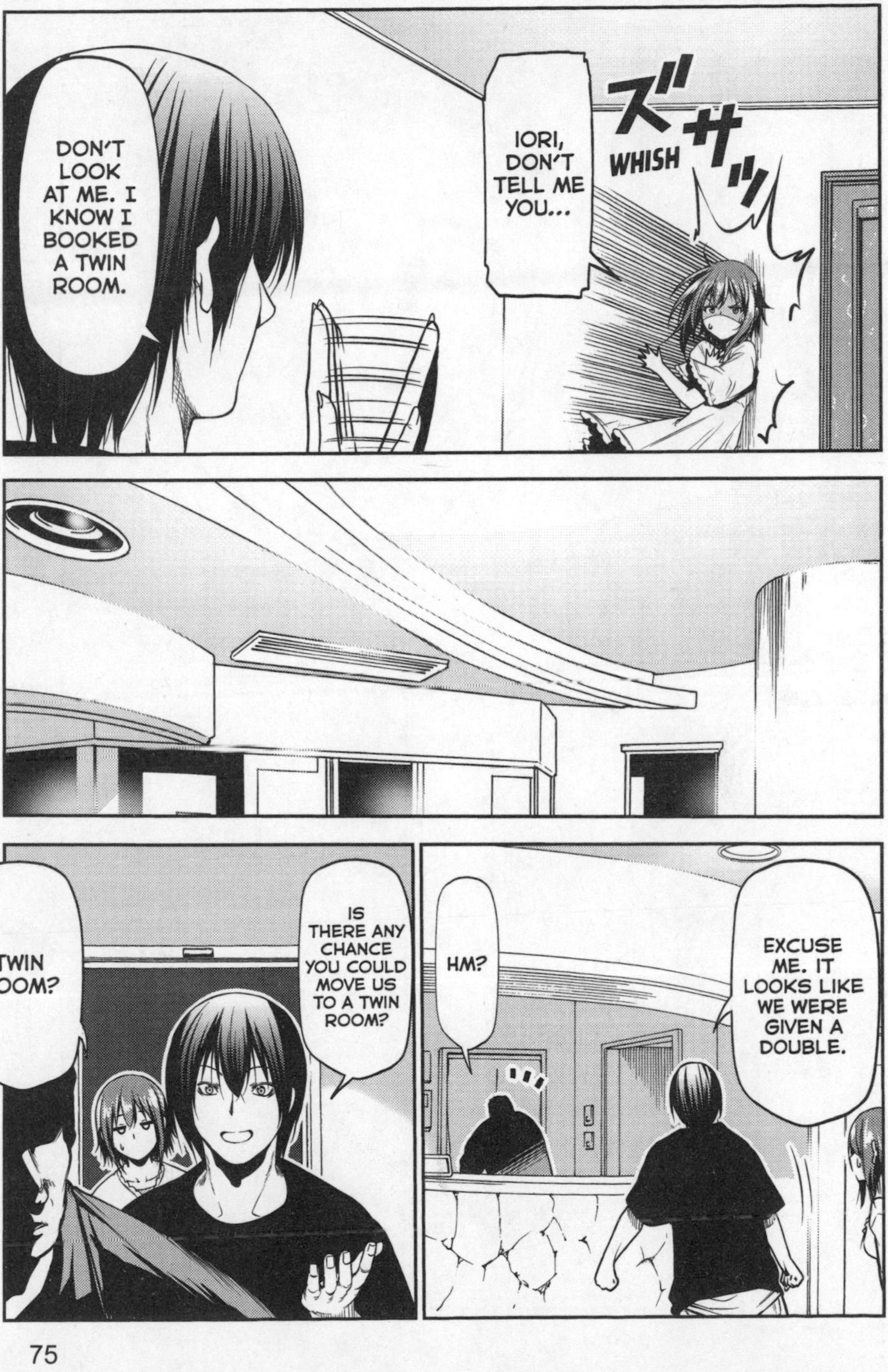
ズザッ
WHISH
IORI, DON'T TELL ME YOU...
DON'T LOOK AT ME. I KNOW I BOOKED A TWIN ROOM.
EXCUSE ME. IT LOOKS LIKE WE WERE GIVEN A DOUBLE.
HM?
IS THERE ANY CHANCE YOU COULD MOVE US TO A TWIN ROOM?
TWIN ROOM?

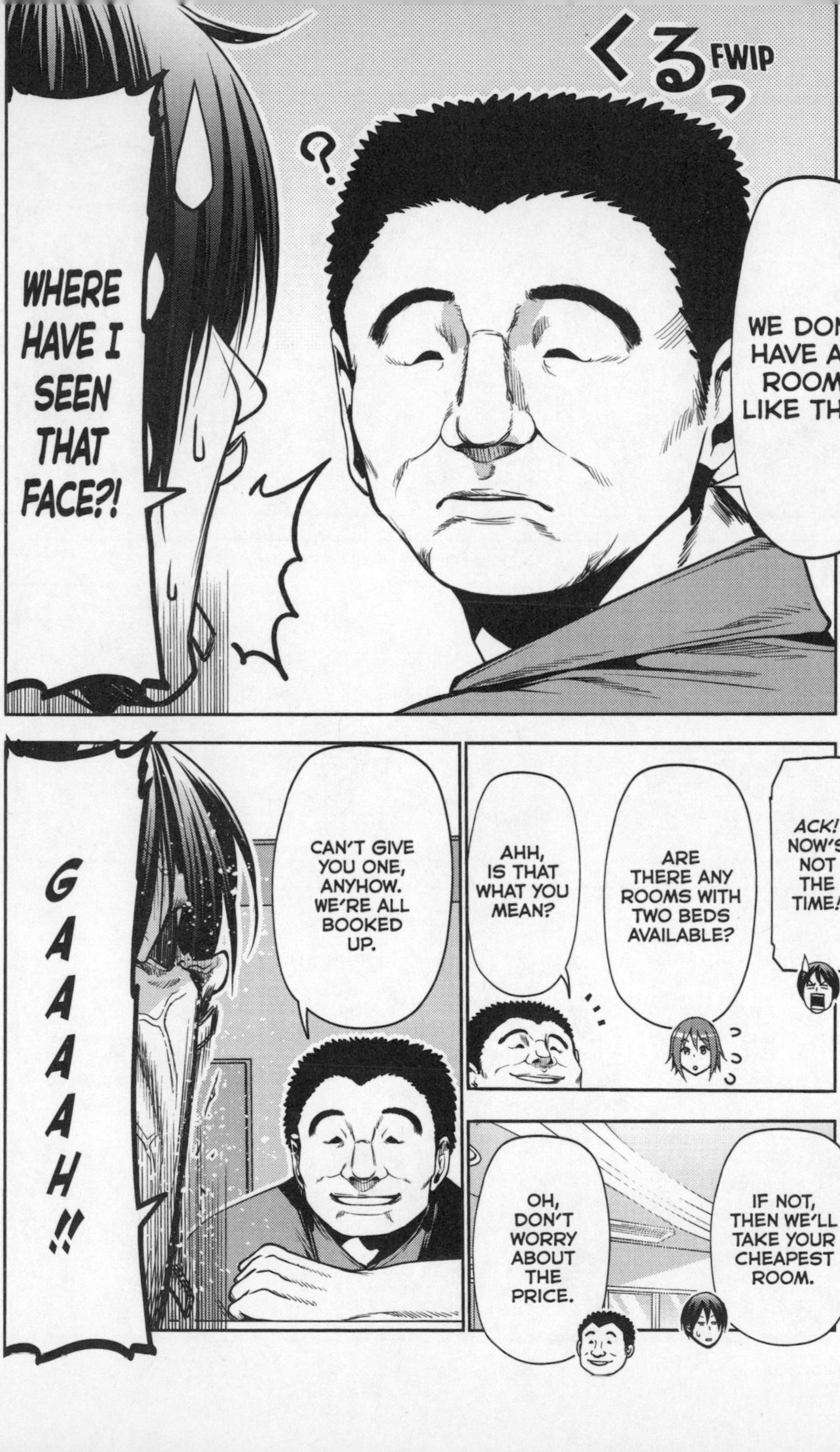
くる FWIP
WE DON'T HAVE ANY ROOMS LIKE THAT.
?
WHERE HAVE I SEEN THAT FACE?!
ACK! NOW'S NOT THE TIME!
ARE THERE ANY ROOMS WITH TWO BEDS AVAILABLE?
AHH, IS THAT WHAT YOU MEAN?
IF NOT, THEN WE'LL TAKE YOUR CHEAPEST ROOM.
OH, DON'T WORRY ABOUT THE PRICE.
CAN'T GIVE YOU ONE, ANYHOW. WE'RE ALL BOOKED UP.
GAAAAAH!!

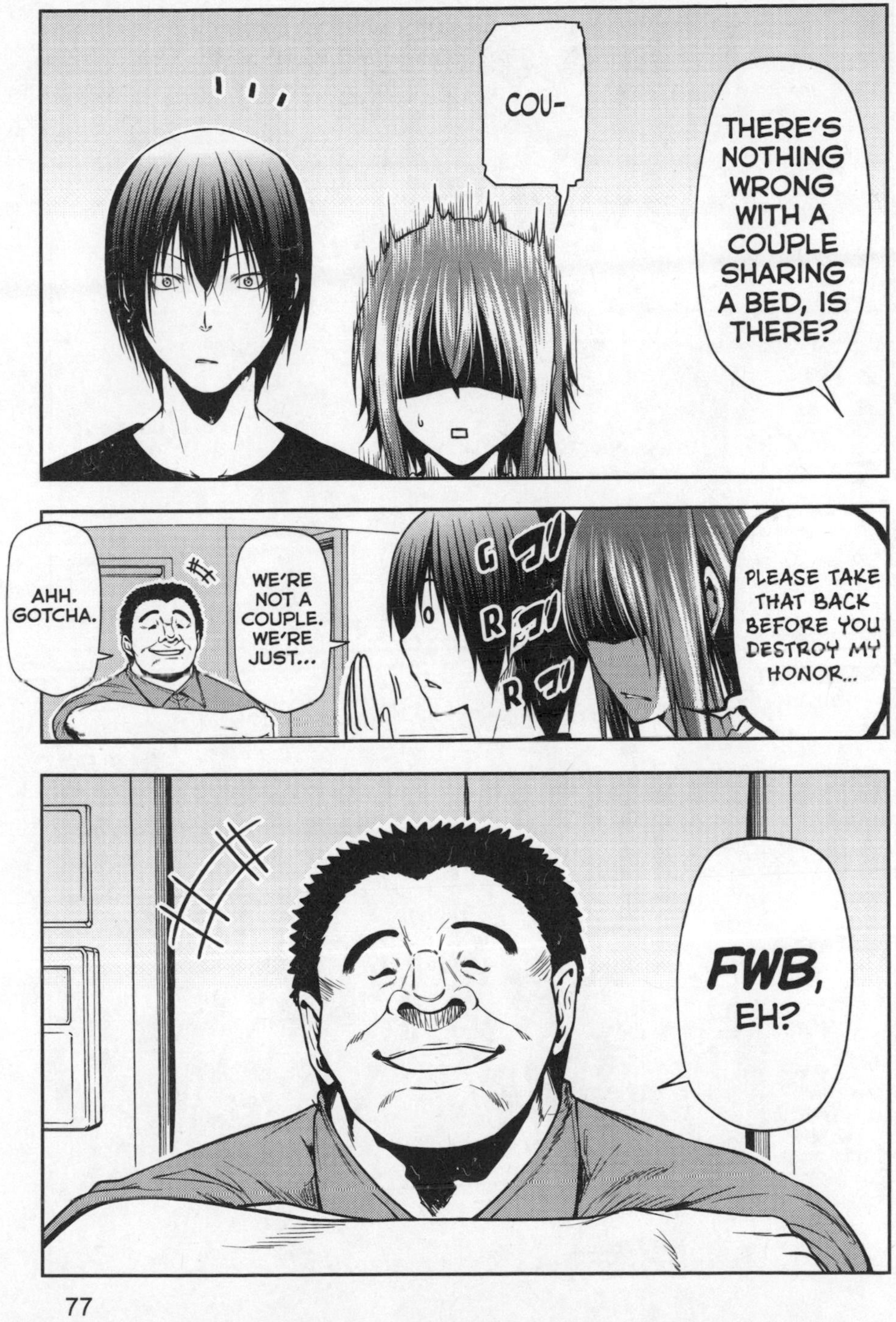
THERE'S NOTHING WRONG WITH A COUPLE SHARING A BED, IS THERE?
COU-
PLEASE TAKE THAT BACK BEFORE YOU DESTROY MY HONOR...
GRRR
WE'RE NOT A COUPLE. WE'RE JUST...
AHH. GOTCHA.
FWB, EH?

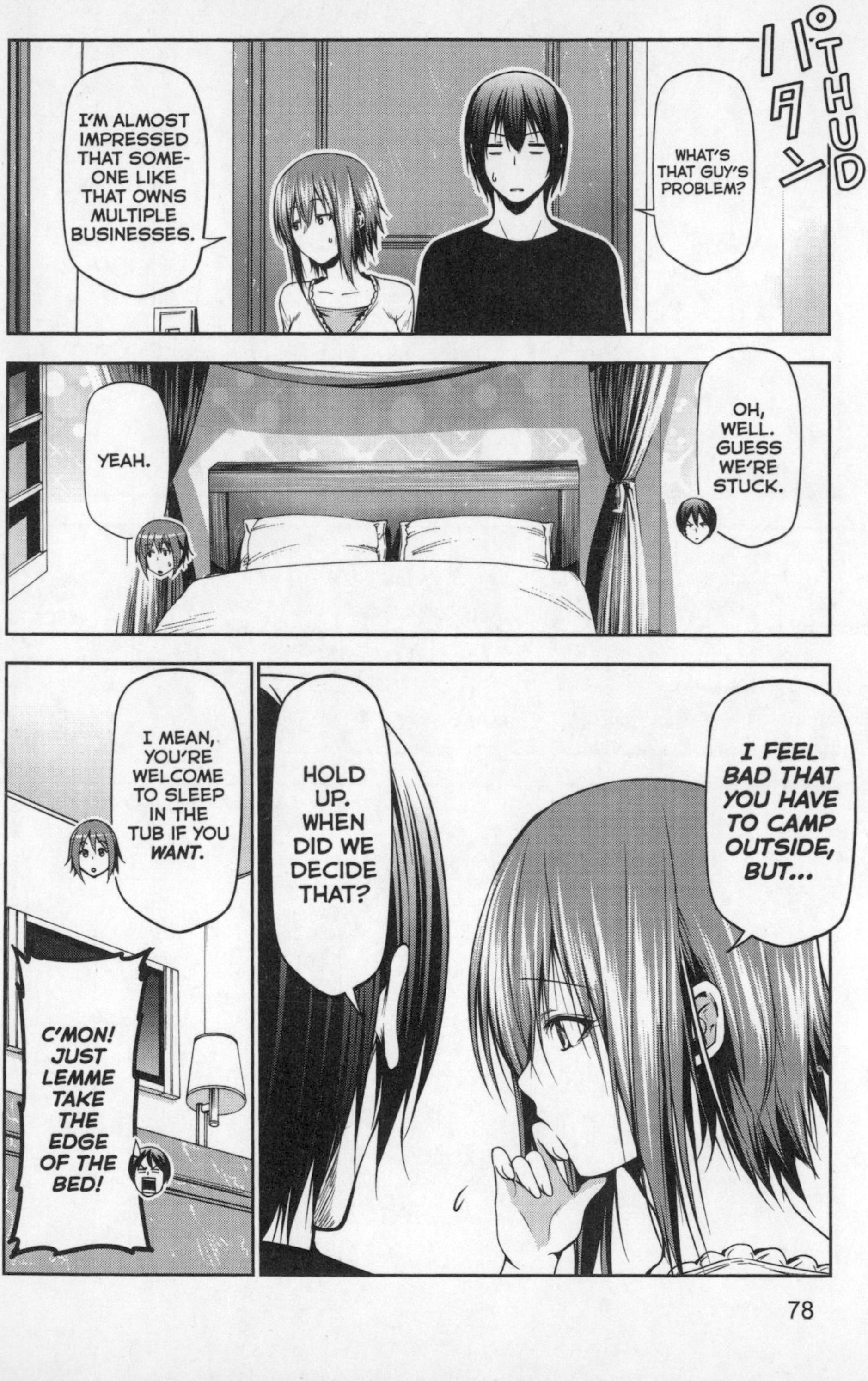
パタン
THUD
WHAT'S THAT GUY'S PROBLEM?
I'M ALMOST IMPRESSED THAT SOME-ONE LIKE THAT OWNS MULTIPLE BUSINESSES.
OH, WELL. GUESS WE'RE STUCK.
YEAH.
I FEEL BAD THAT YOU HAVE TO CAMP OUTSIDE, BUT...
HOLD UP. WHEN DID WE DECIDE THAT?
I MEAN, YOU'RE WELCOME TO SLEEP IN THE TUB IF YOU *WANT*.
C'MON! JUST LEMME TAKE THE EDGE OF THE BED!

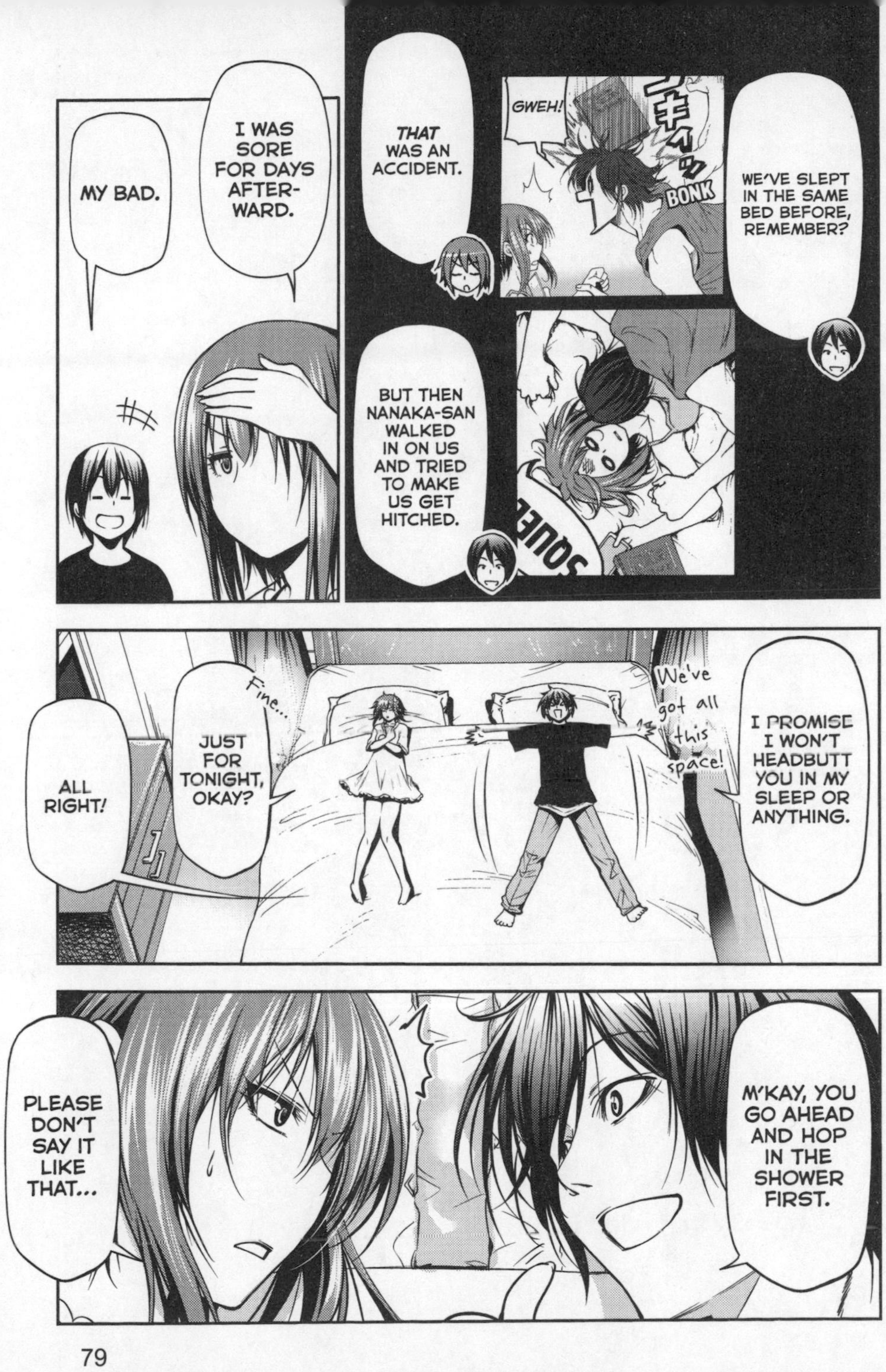
WE'VE SLEPT IN THE SAME BED BEFORE, REMEMBER?
GWEH!
BONK
THAT WAS AN ACCIDENT.
BUT THEN NANAKA-SAN WALKED IN ON US AND TRIED TO MAKE US GET HITCHED.
I WAS SORE FOR DAYS AFTER-WARD.
MY BAD.
I PROMISE I WON'T HEADBUTT YOU IN MY SLEEP OR ANYTHING.
We've got all this space!
Fine...
JUST FOR TONIGHT, OKAY?
ALL RIGHT!
M'KAY, YOU GO AHEAD AND HOP IN THE SHOWER FIRST.
PLEASE DON'T SAY IT LIKE THAT...

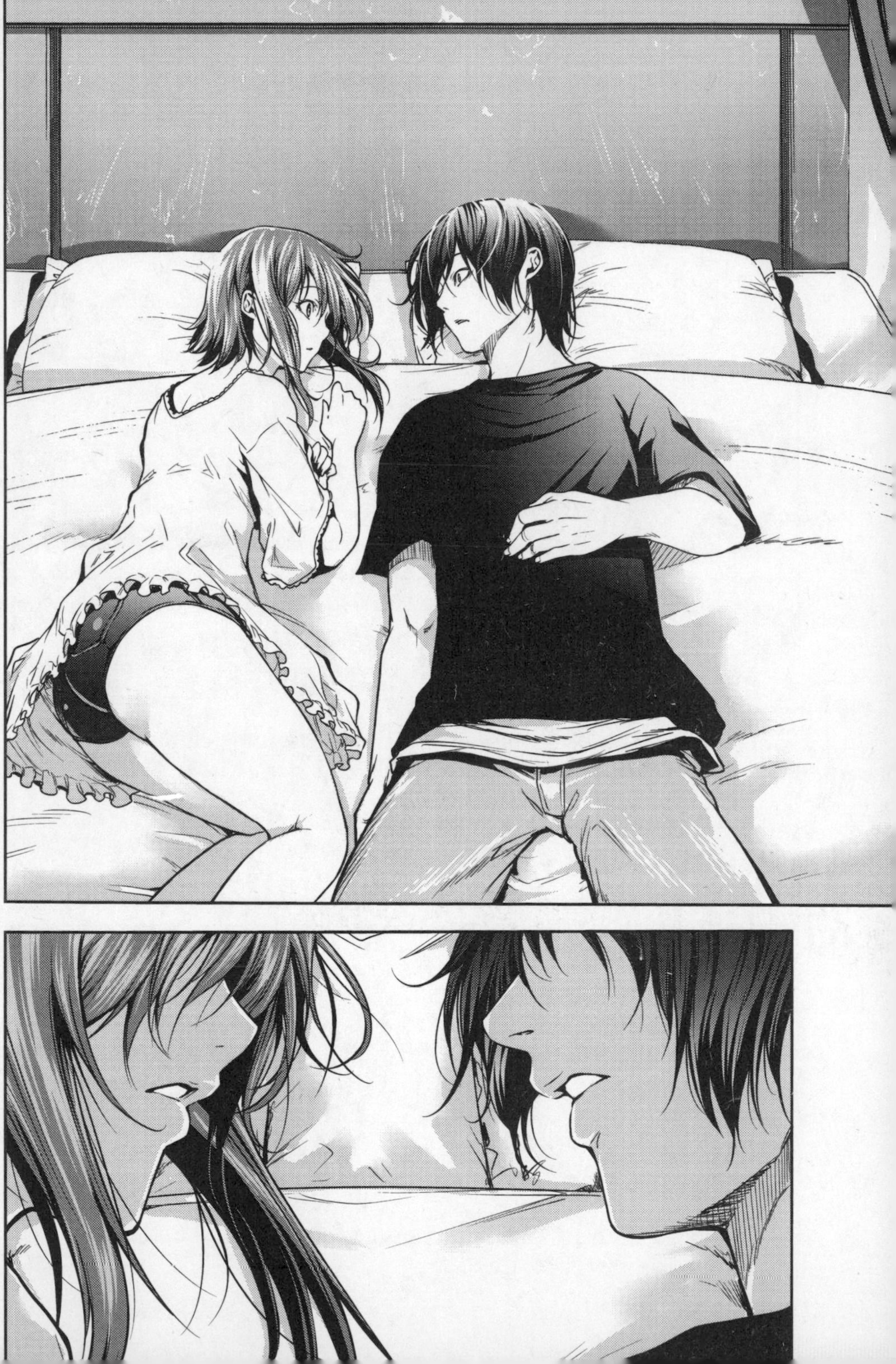

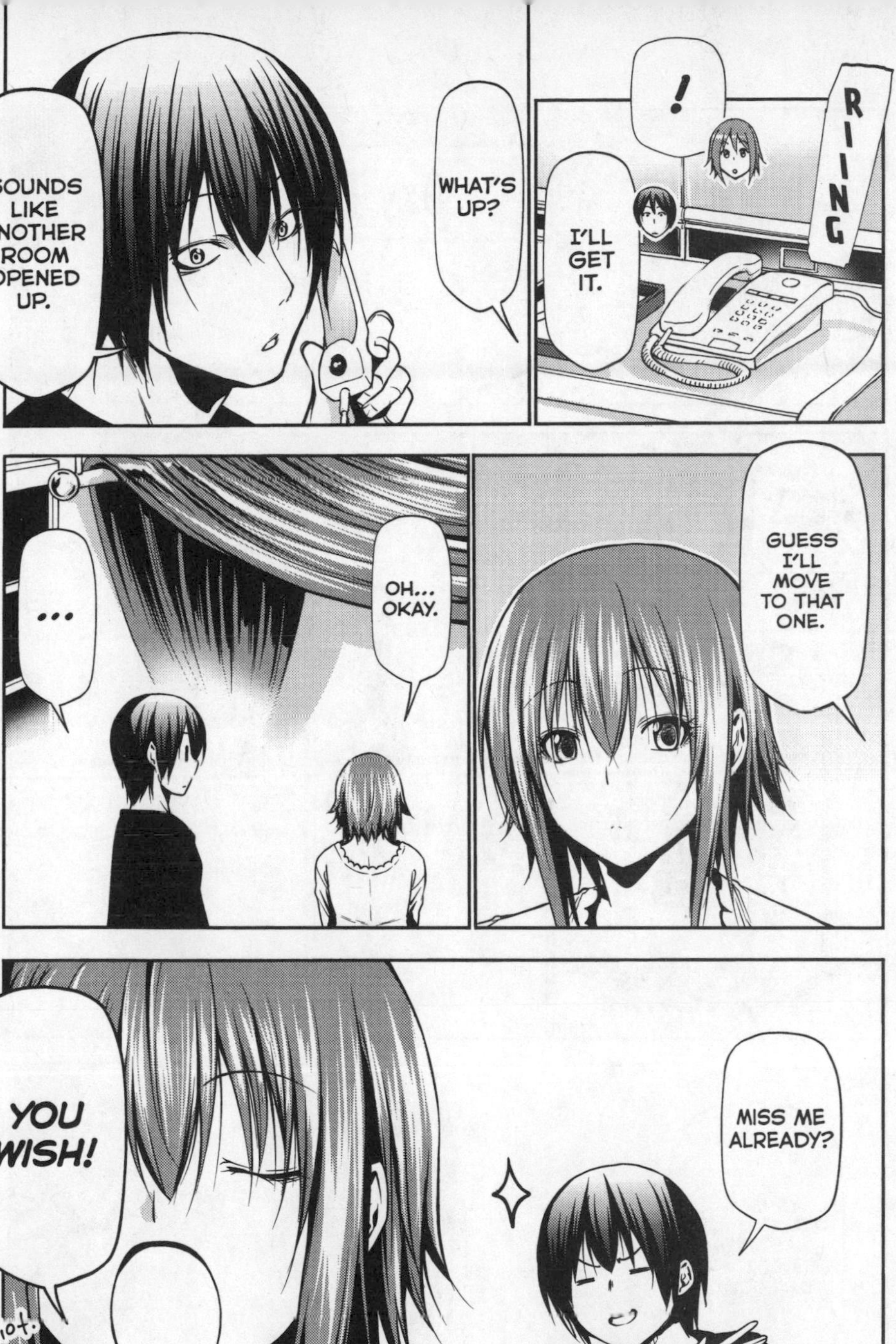
RIIING
!
I'LL GET IT.
WHAT'S UP?
SOUNDS LIKE ANOTHER ROOM OPENED UP.
GUESS I'LL MOVE TO THAT ONE.
OH... OKAY.
...
MISS ME ALREADY?
YOU WISH!
Idiot.

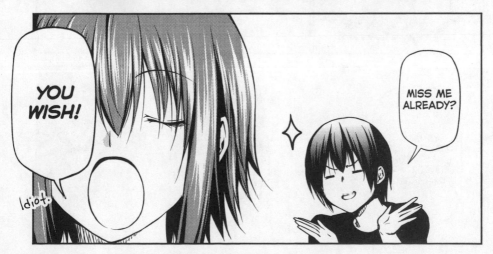

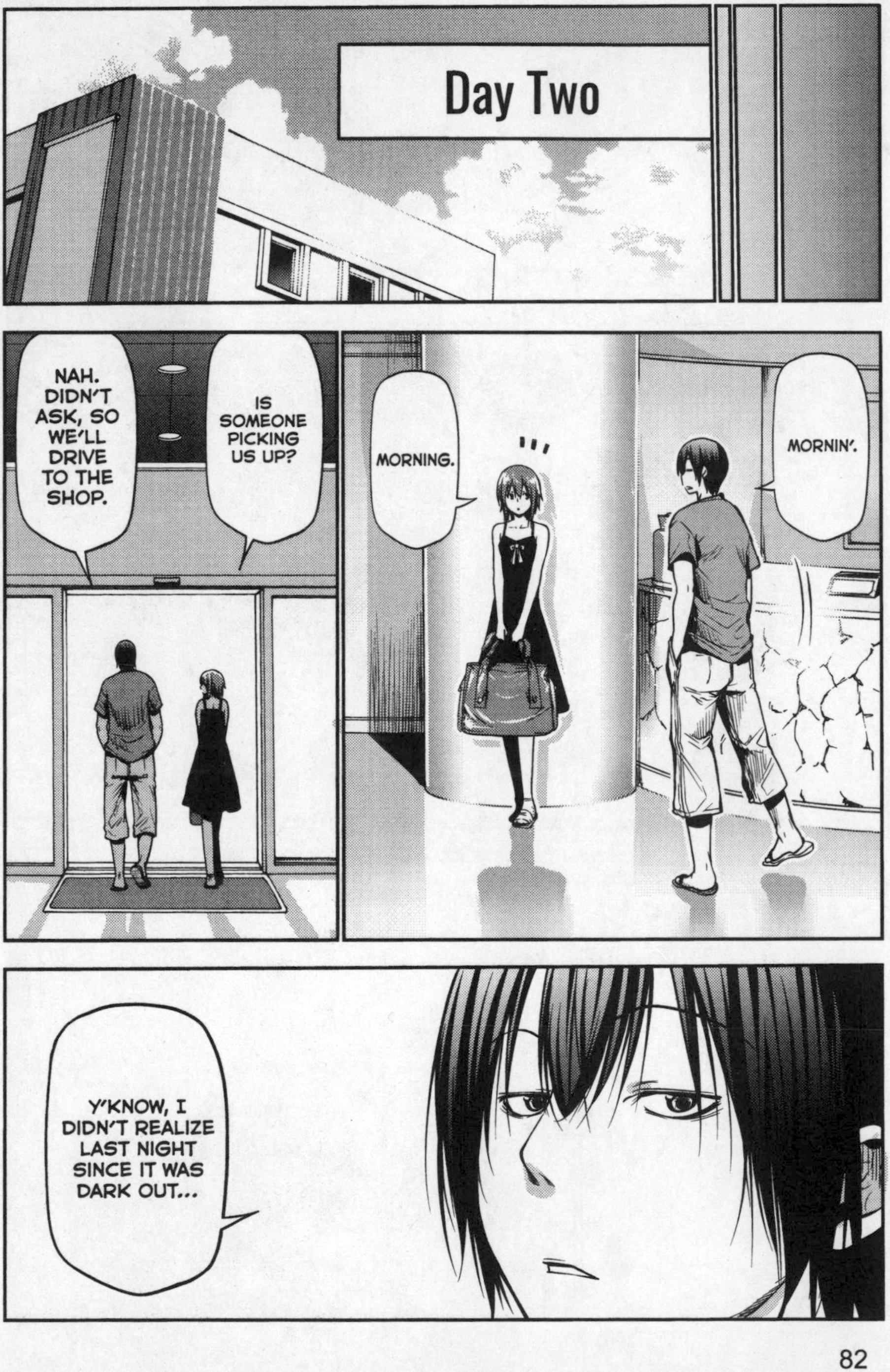
Day Two
MORNIN'.
MORNING.
IS SOMEONE PICKING US UP?
NAH. DIDN'T ASK, SO WE'LL DRIVE TO THE SHOP.
Y'KNOW, I DIDN'T REALIZE LAST NIGHT SINCE IT WAS DARK OUT...

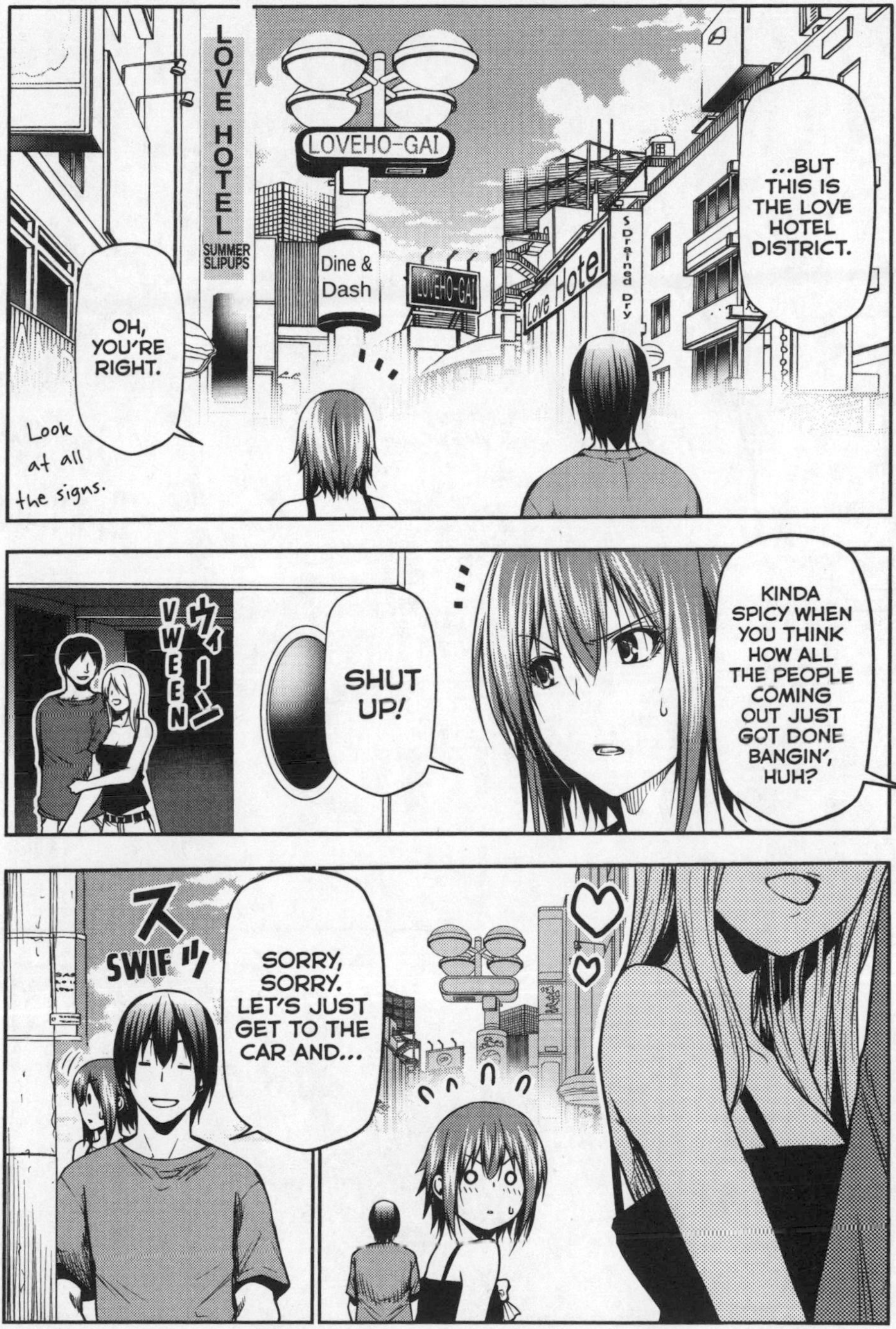
...BUT THIS IS THE LOVE HOTEL DISTRICT.
LOVEHO-GAI
LOVE HOTEL
SUMMER SLIPUPS
Dine & Dash
LOVEHO-GAI
Love Hotel
S Drained Dry
OH, YOU'RE RIGHT.
Look at all the signs.
KINDA SPICY WHEN YOU THINK HOW ALL THE PEOPLE COMING OUT JUST GOT DONE BANGIN', HUH?
SHUT UP!
ウィーン
VWEEN
SORRY, SORRY. LET'S JUST GET TO THE CAR AND...
ス ッ
SWIF

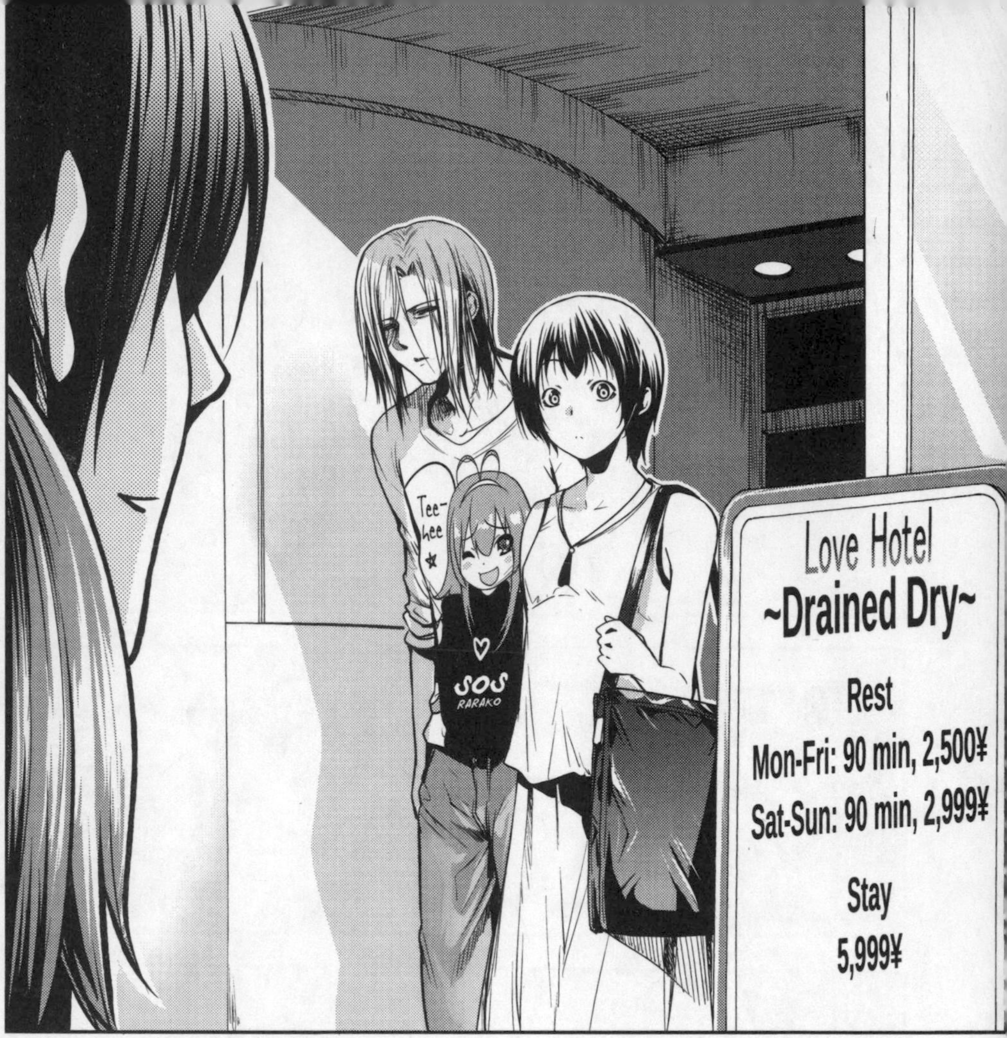
Tee-hee ☆
SOS
RARAKO
Love Hotel
~Drained Dry~
Rest
Mon-Fri: 90 min, 2,500¥
Sat-Sun: 90 min, 2,999¥
Stay
5,999¥

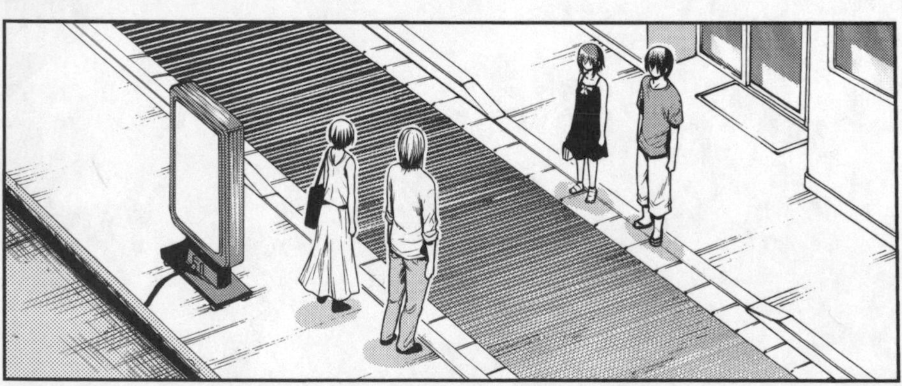

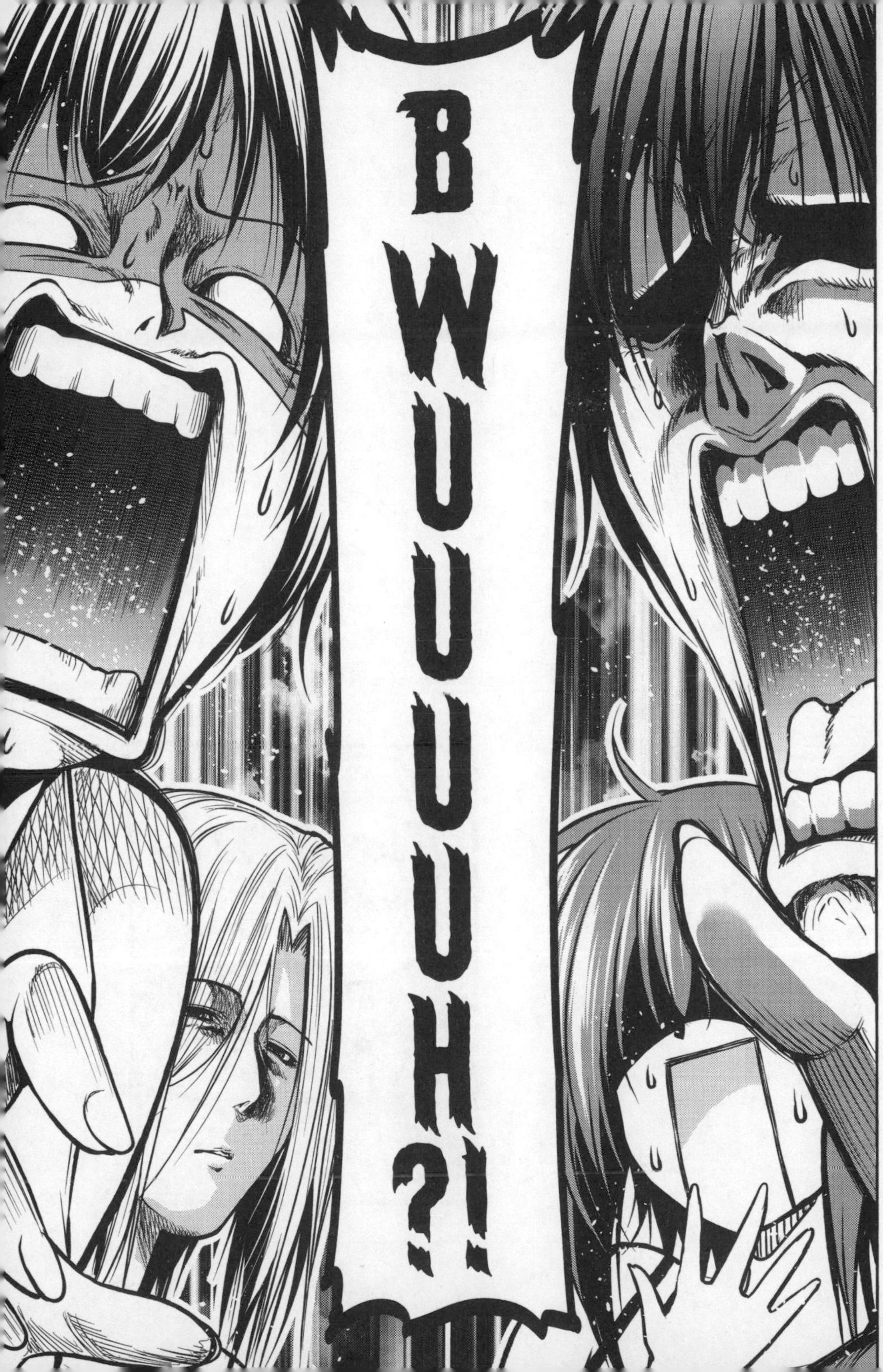
BWUUUUH?!

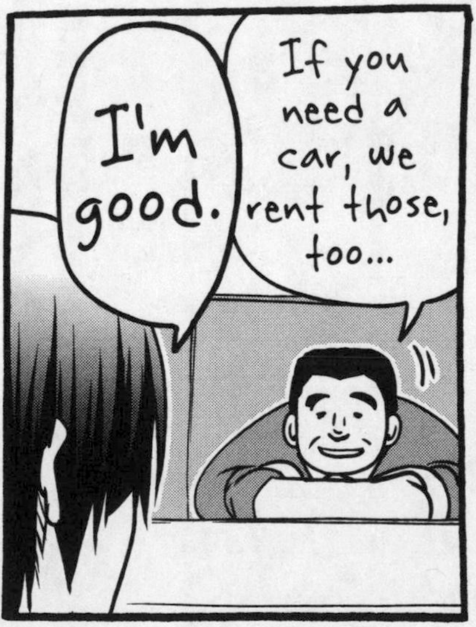
If you need a car, we rent those, too...
I'm good.

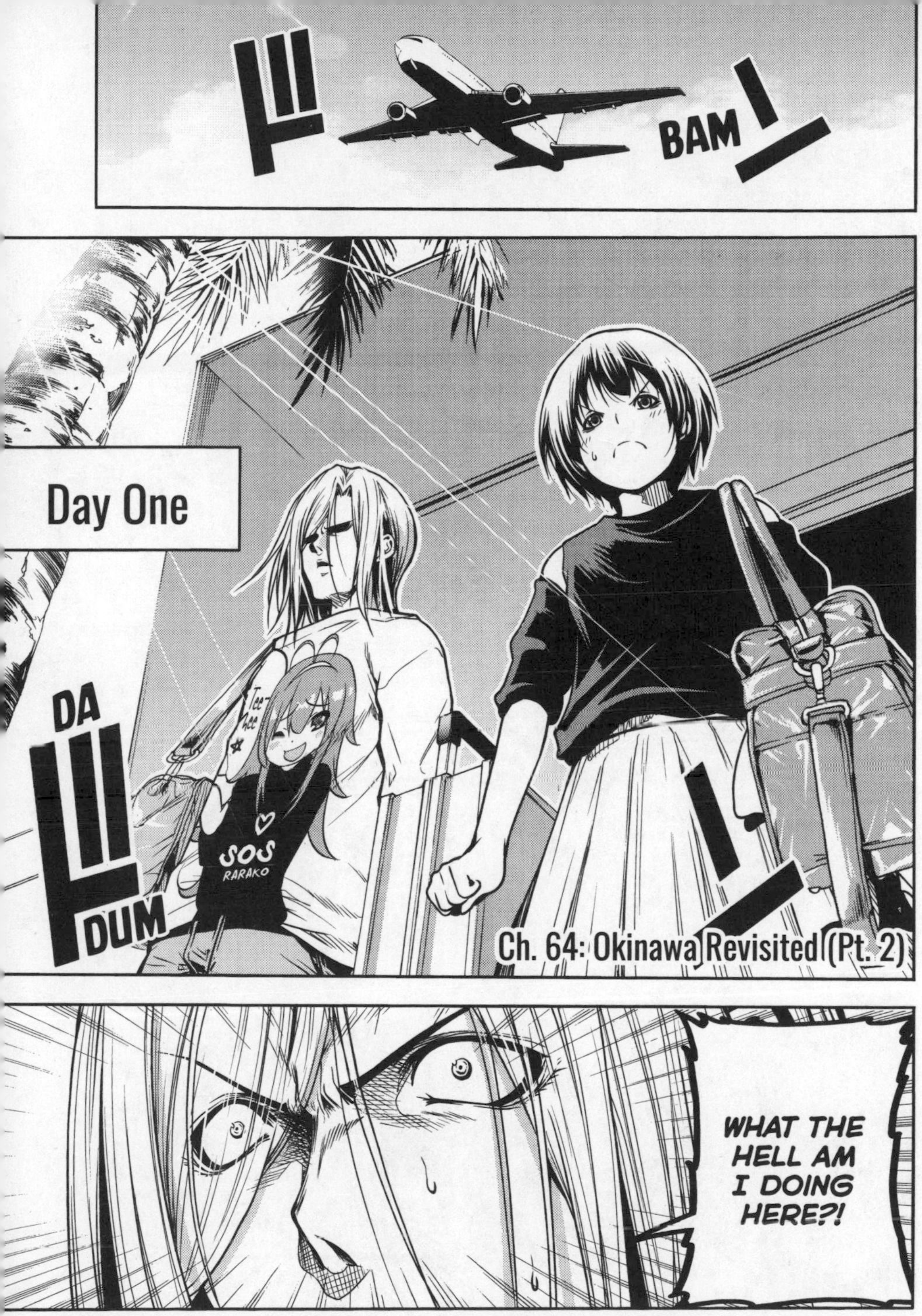
BAM
Day One
Tee hee
SOS
RARAKO
DA
DUM
Ch. 64: Okinawa Revisited (Pt. 2)
WHAT THE HELL AM I DOING HERE?!

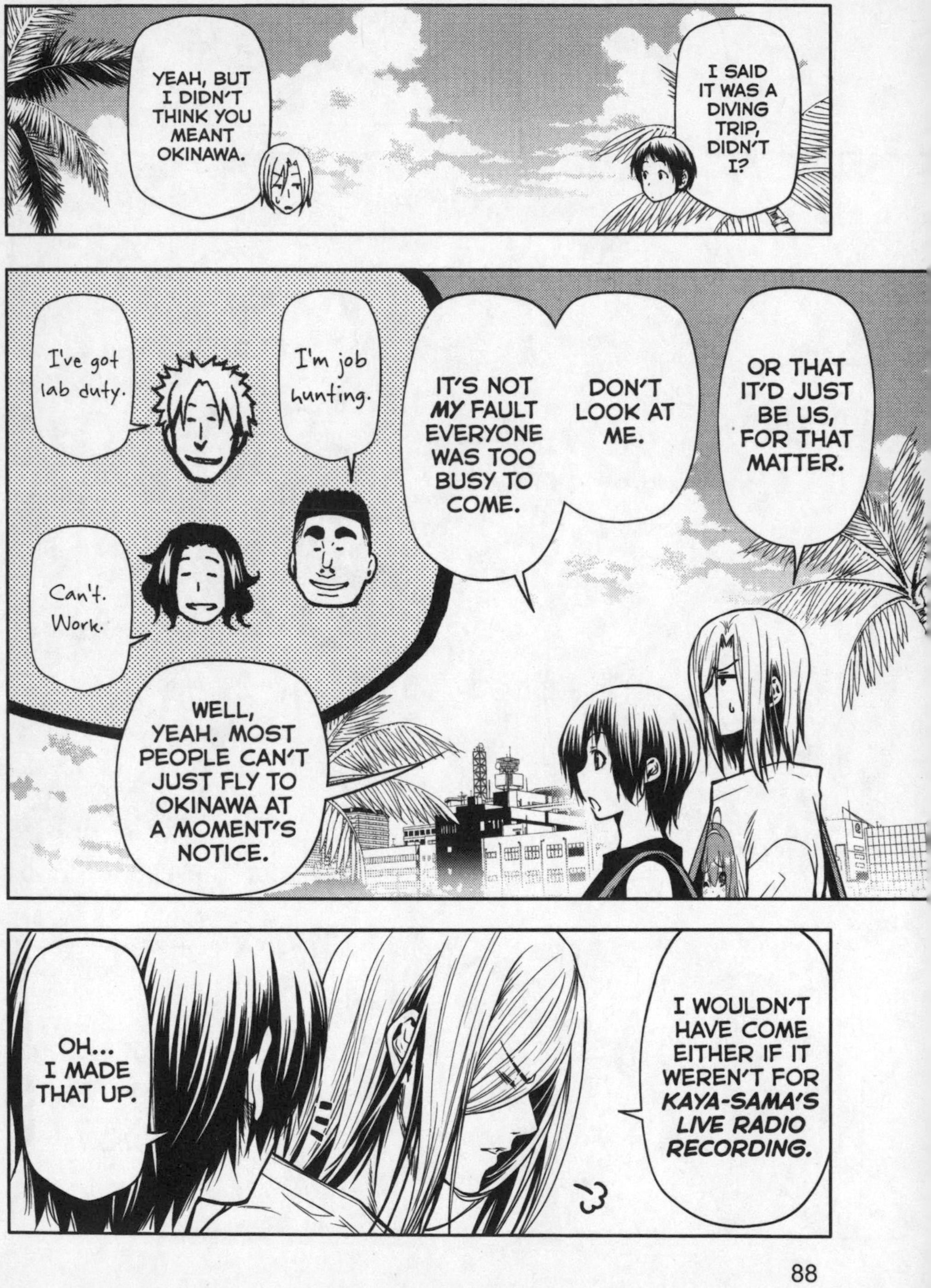
I SAID IT WAS A DIVING TRIP, DIDN'T I?
YEAH, BUT I DIDN'T THINK YOU MEANT OKINAWA.
OR THAT IT'D JUST BE US, FOR THAT MATTER.
DON'T LOOK AT ME.
IT'S NOT MY FAULT EVERYONE WAS TOO BUSY TO COME.
I'm job hunting.
I've got lab duty.
Can't. Work.
WELL, YEAH. MOST PEOPLE CAN'T JUST FLY TO OKINAWA AT A MOMENT'S NOTICE.
I WOULDN'T HAVE COME EITHER IF IT WEREN'T FOR KAYA-SAMA'S LIVE RADIO RECORDING.
OH... I MADE THAT UP.

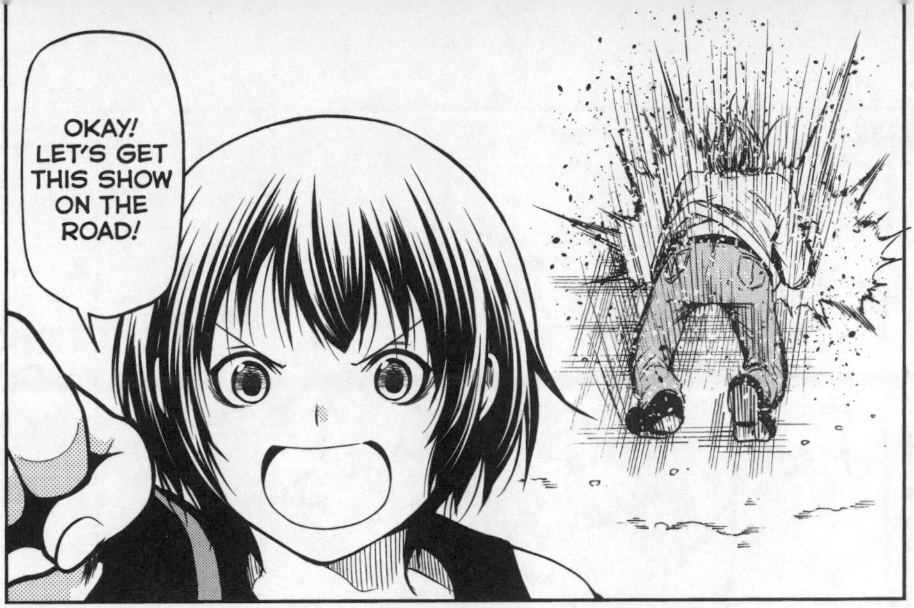
OKAY! LET'S GET THIS SHOW ON THE ROAD!
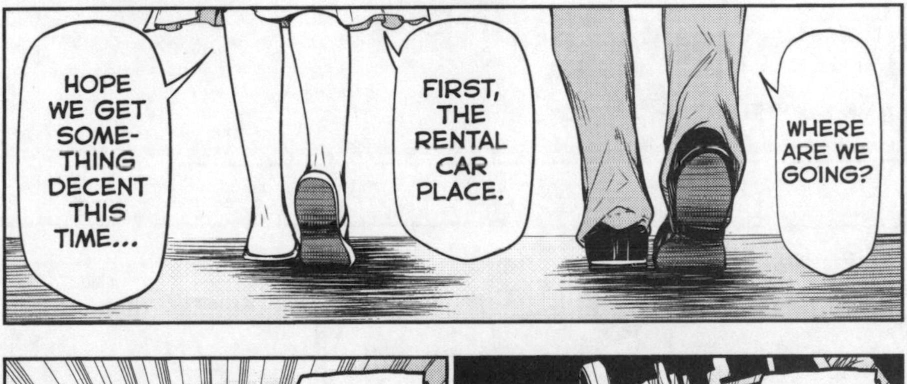
WHERE ARE WE GOING?
FIRST, THE RENTAL CAR PLACE.
HOPE WE GET SOME-THING DECENT THIS TIME...
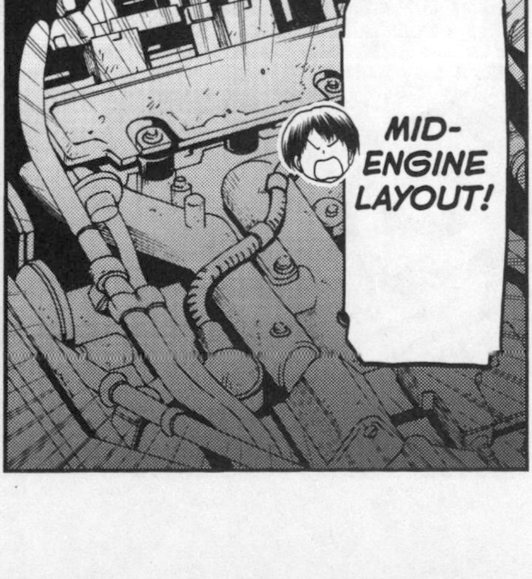
MID-ENGINE LAYOUT!
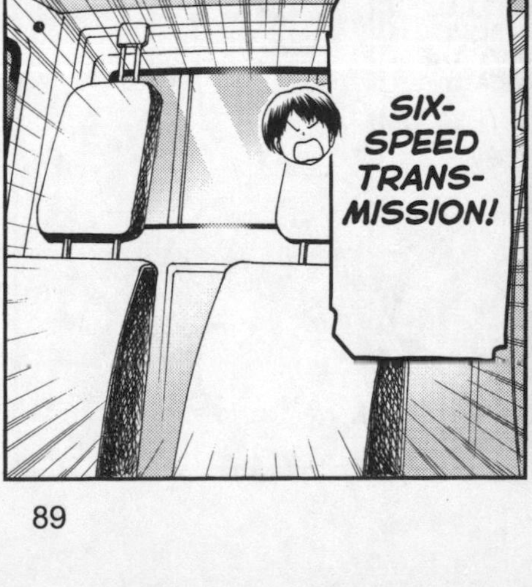
SIX-SPEED TRANS-MISSION!

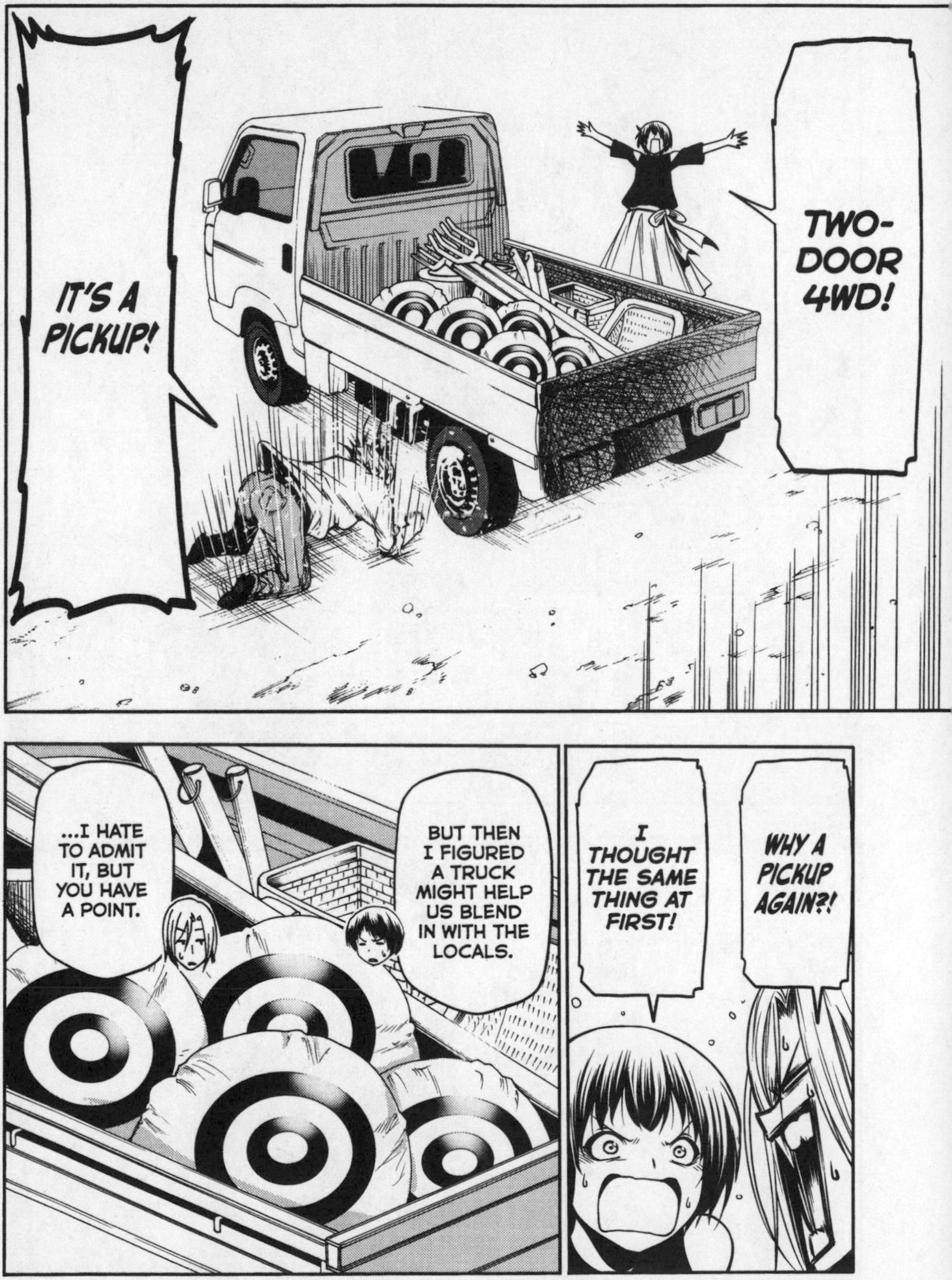
TWO-DOOR 4WD!
IT'S A PICKUP!
WHY A PICKUP AGAIN?!
I THOUGHT THE SAME THING AT FIRST!
BUT THEN I FIGURED A TRUCK MIGHT HELP US BLEND IN WITH THE LOCALS.
...I HATE TO ADMIT IT, BUT YOU HAVE A POINT.

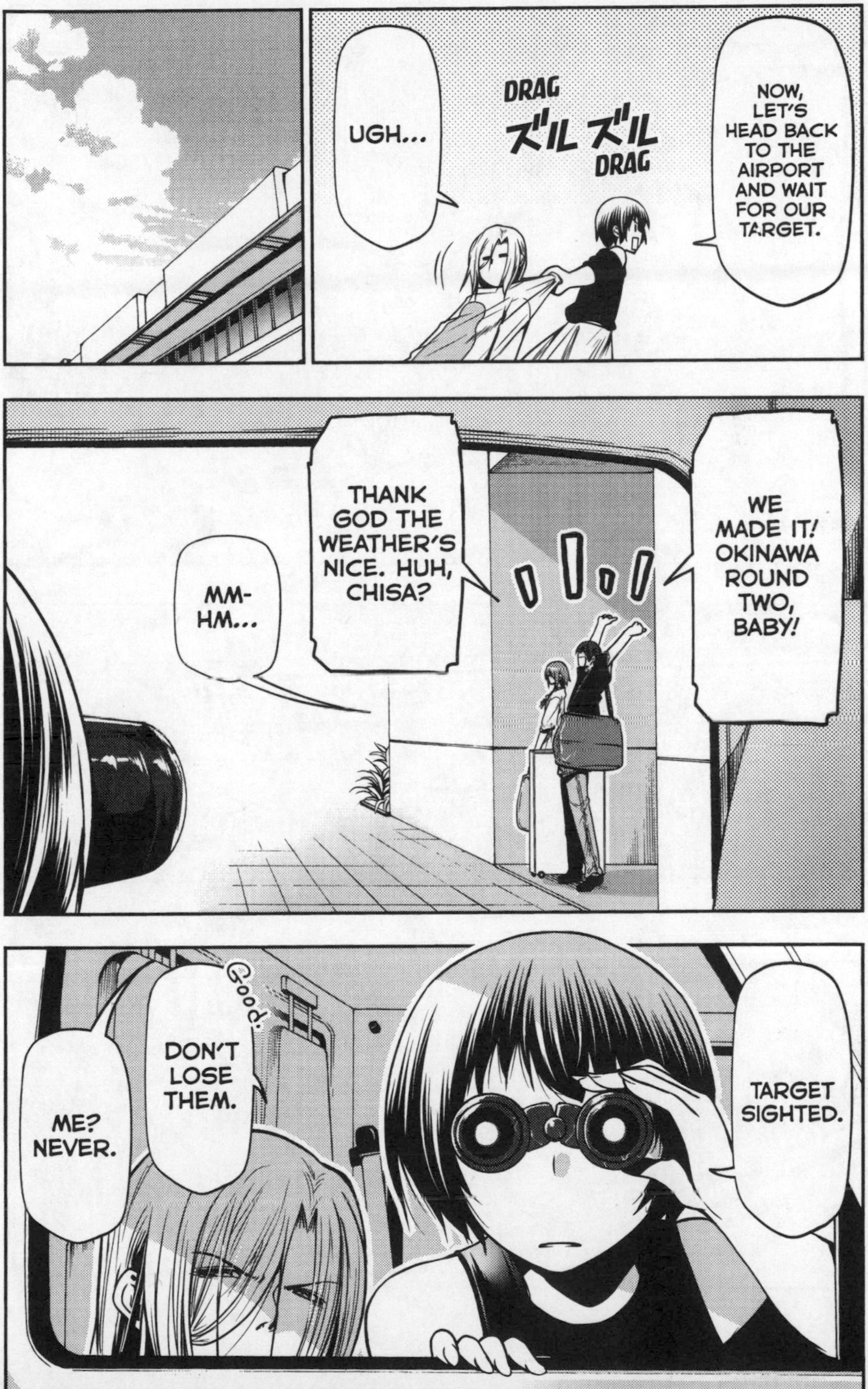
NOW, LET'S HEAD BACK TO THE AIRPORT AND WAIT FOR OUR TARGET.
DRAG
ズルズル
DRAG
UGH...
WE MADE IT! OKINAWA ROUND TWO, BABY!
THANK GOD THE WEATHER'S NICE. HUH, CHISA?
MM-HM...
TARGET SIGHTED.
Good.
DON'T LOSE THEM.
ME? NEVER.

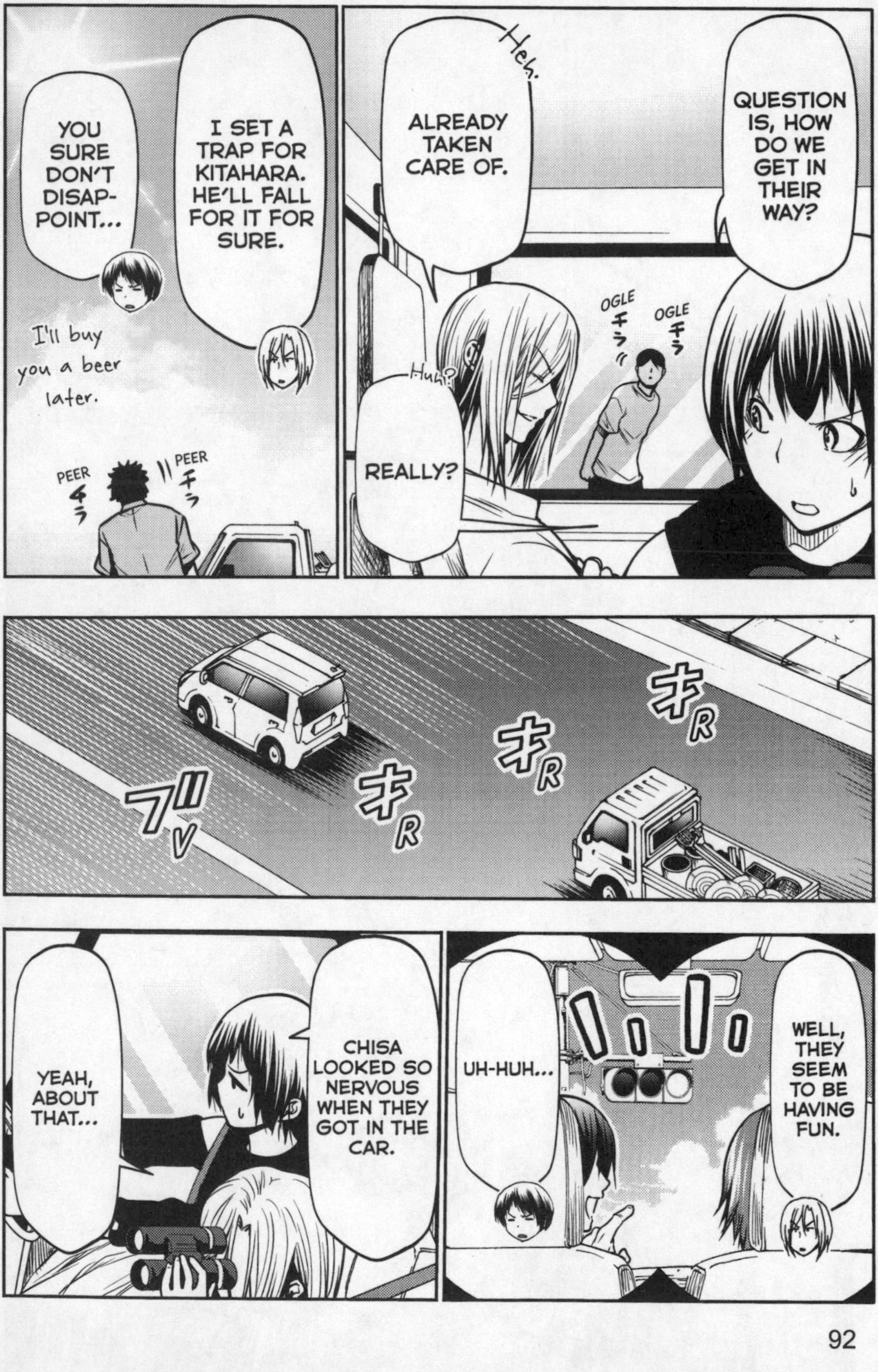
QUESTION IS, HOW DO WE GET IN THEIR WAY?
Heh.
ALREADY TAKEN CARE OF.
OGLE チラ
OGLE チラ
Huh?
REALLY?
I SET A TRAP FOR KITAHARA. HE'LL FALL FOR IT FOR SURE.
YOU SURE DON'T DISAP-POINT...
I'll buy you a beer later.
PEER チラ
PEER チラ
WELL, THEY SEEM TO BE HAVING FUN.
UH-HUH...
CHISA LOOKED SO NERVOUS WHEN THEY GOT IN THE CAR.
YEAH, ABOUT THAT...

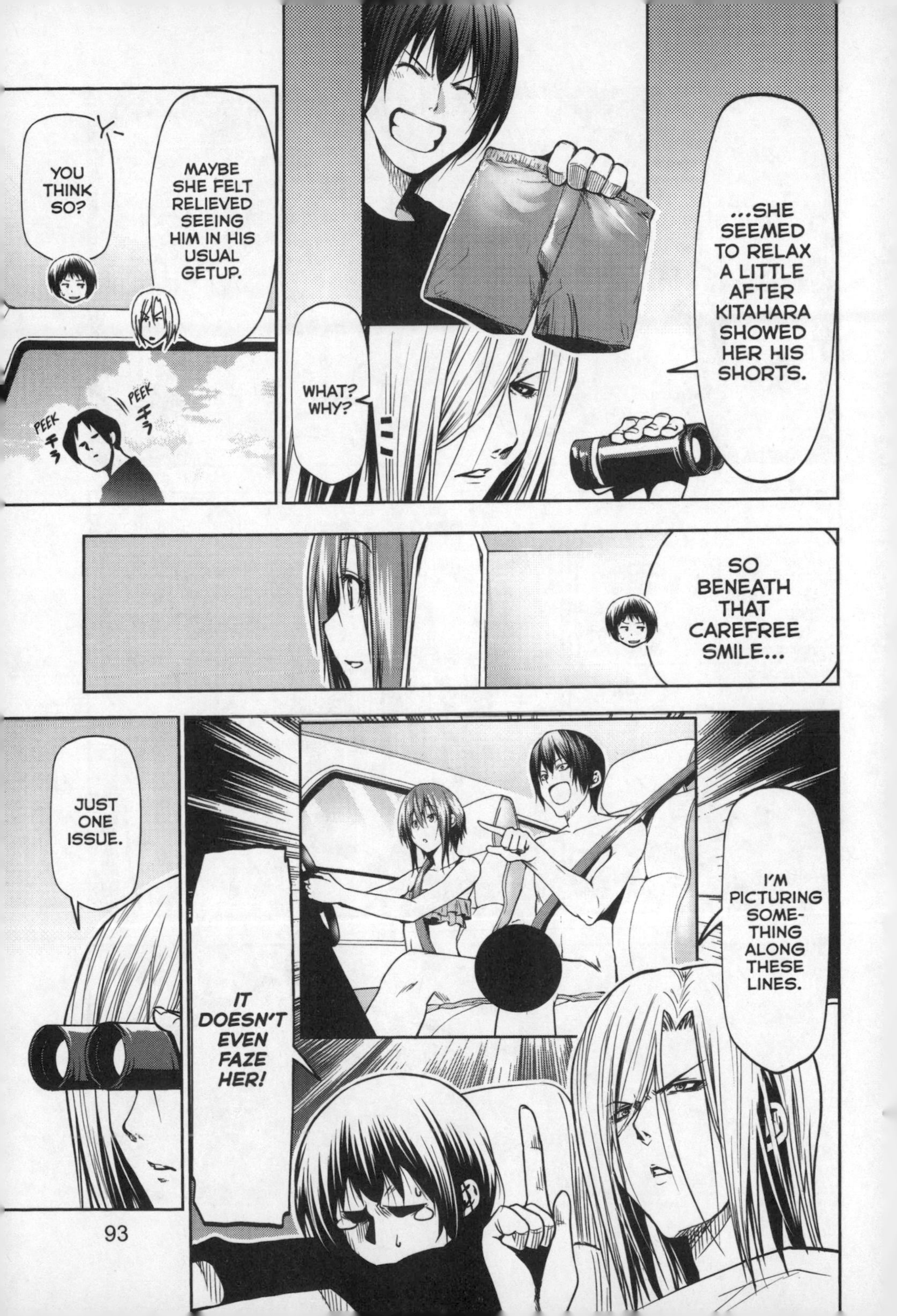
...SHE SEEMED TO RELAX A LITTLE AFTER KITAHARA SHOWED HER HIS SHORTS.
WHAT? WHY?
MAYBE SHE FELT RELIEVED SEEING HIM IN HIS USUAL GETUP.
YOU THINK SO?
PEEK チラ
PEEK チラ
SO BENEATH THAT CAREFREE SMILE...
I'M PICTURING SOME-THING ALONG THESE LINES.
IT DOESN'T EVEN FAZE HER!
JUST ONE ISSUE.

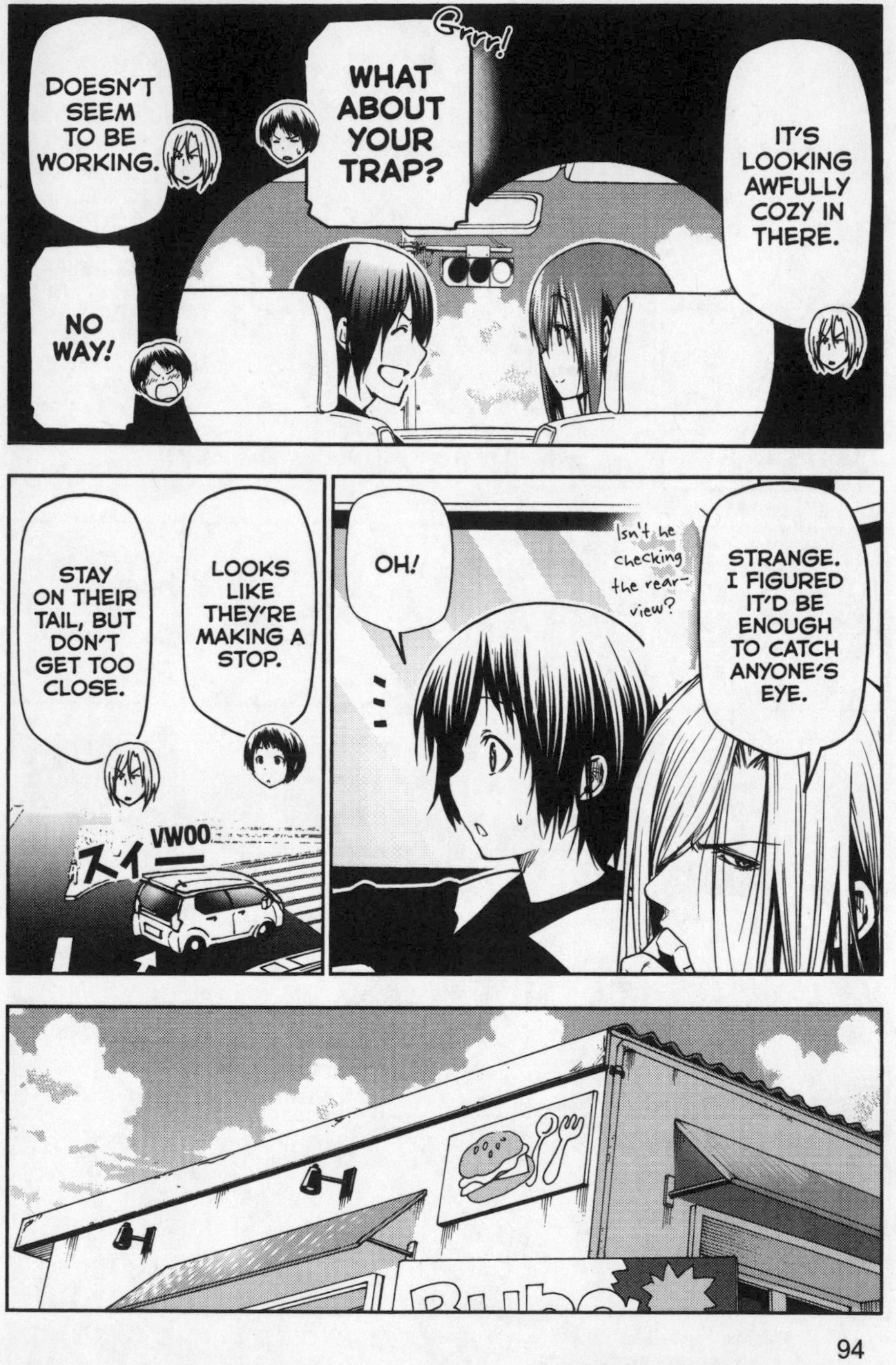
IT'S LOOKING AWFULLY COZY IN THERE.
Grrr!
WHAT ABOUT YOUR TRAP?
DOESN'T SEEM TO BE WORKING.
NO WAY!
STRANGE. I FIGURED IT'D BE ENOUGH TO CATCH ANYONE'S EYE.
Isn't he checking the rear-view?
OH!
LOOKS LIKE THEY'RE MAKING A STOP.
STAY ON THEIR TAIL, BUT DON'T GET TOO CLOSE.
スイー
VWOO

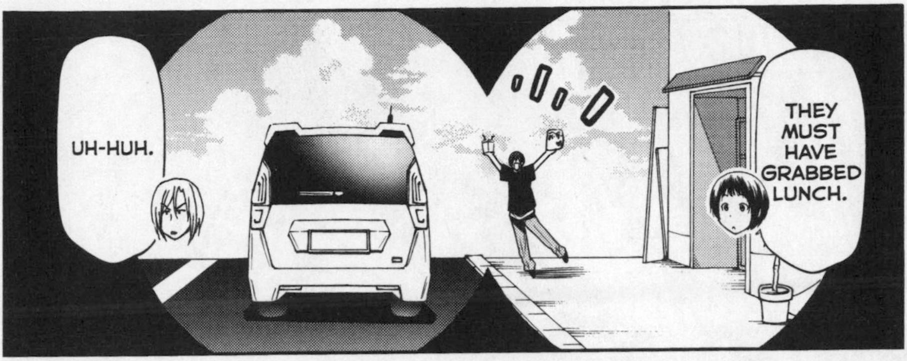
THEY MUST HAVE GRABBED LUNCH.
UH-HUH.
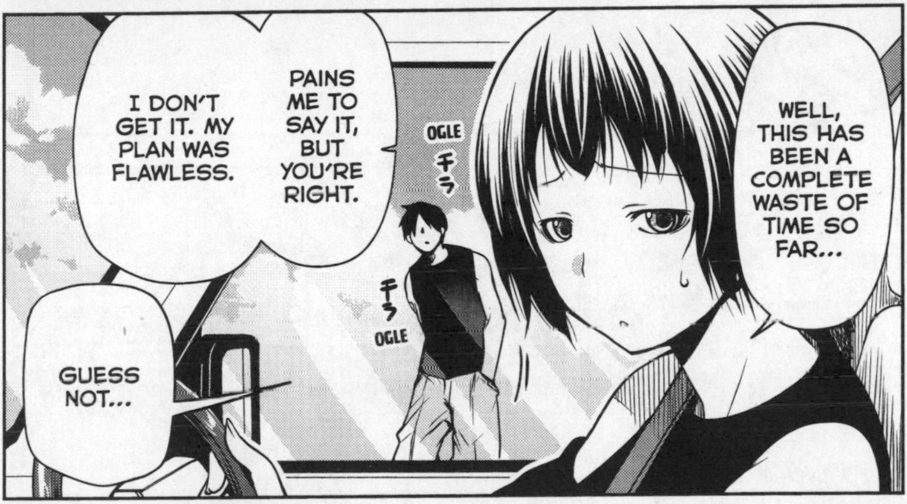
WELL, THIS HAS BEEN A COMPLETE WASTE OF TIME SO FAR...
OGLE
チラ
PAINS ME TO SAY IT, BUT YOU'RE RIGHT.
I DON'T GET IT. MY PLAN WAS FLAWLESS.
チラ
OGLE
GUESS NOT...
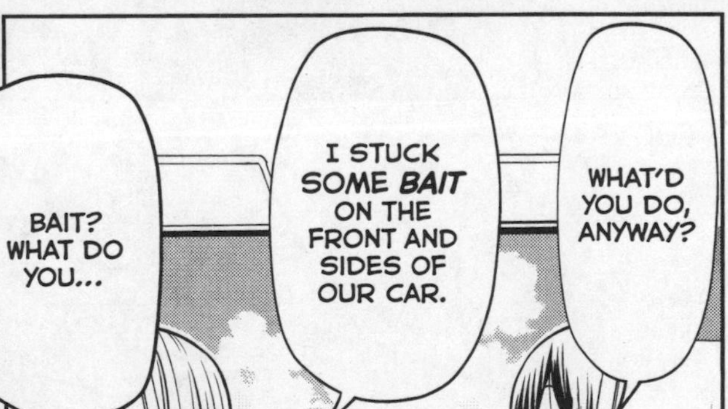
WHAT'D YOU DO, ANYWAY?
I STUCK SOME *BAIT* ON THE FRONT AND SIDES OF OUR CAR.
BAIT? WHAT DO YOU...
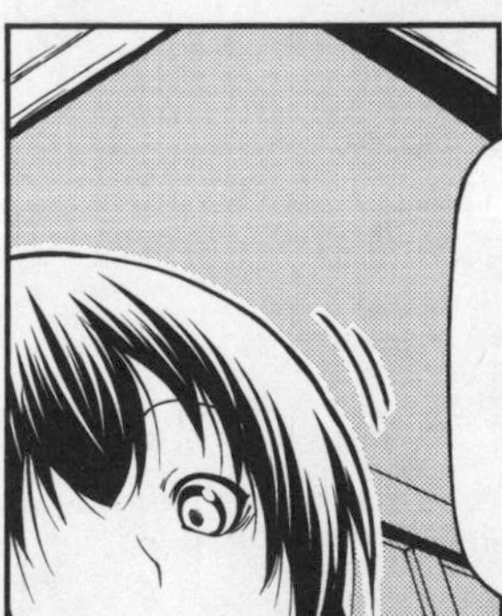

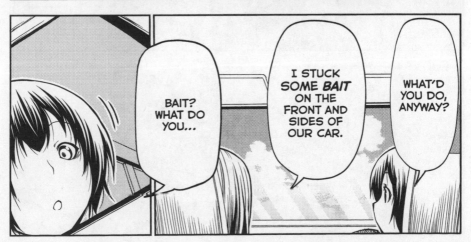

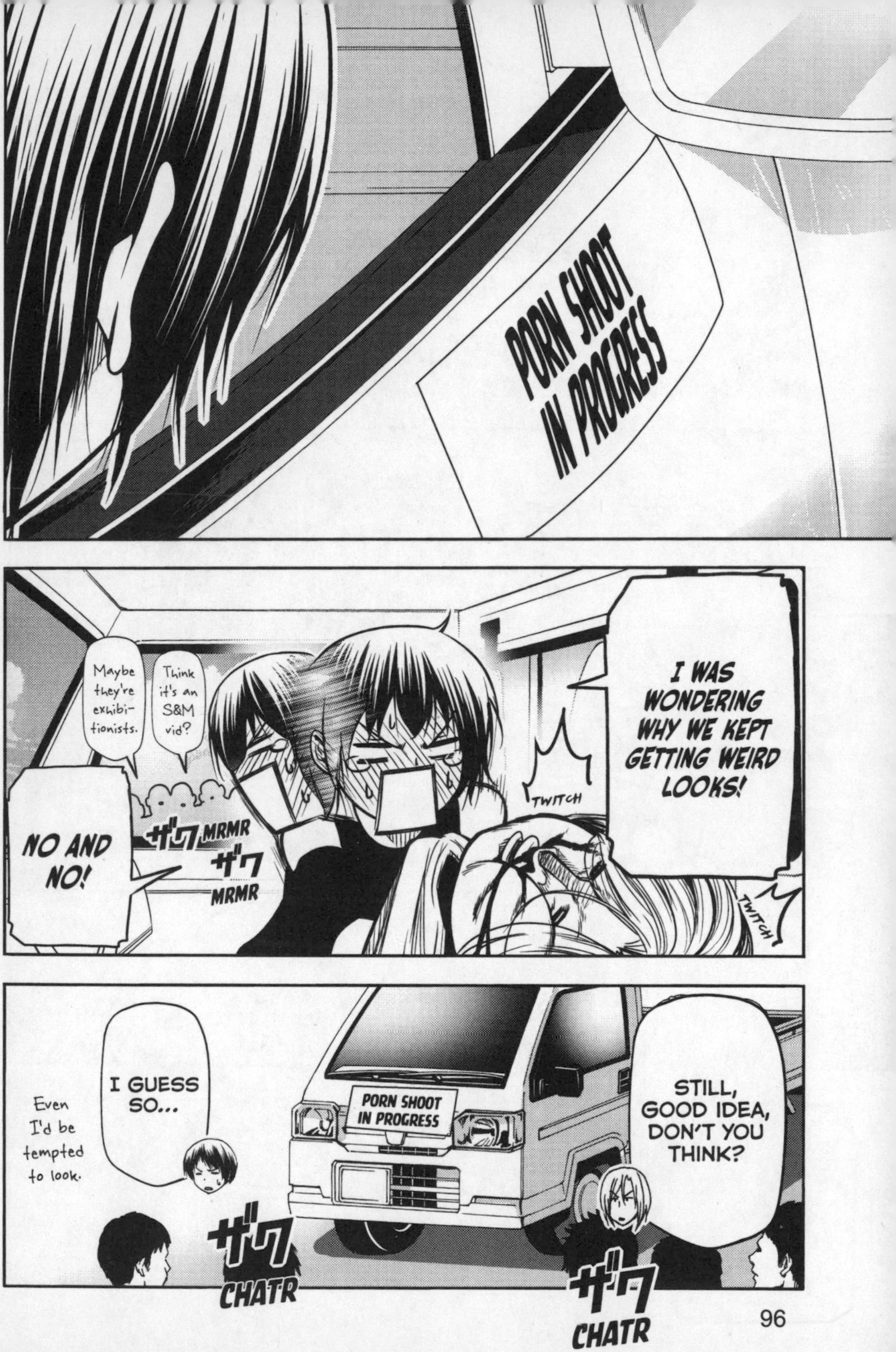
PORN SHOOT IN PROGRESS
I WAS WONDERING WHY WE KEPT GETTING WEIRD LOOKS!
TWITCH
TWITCH
Think it's an S&M vid?
Maybe they're exhibi- tionists.
NO AND NO!
ザワ MRMR
ザワ MRMR
STILL, GOOD IDEA, DON'T YOU THINK?
PORN SHOOT IN PROGRESS
I GUESS SO...
Even I'd be tempted to look.
ザワ CHATR
ザワ CHATR

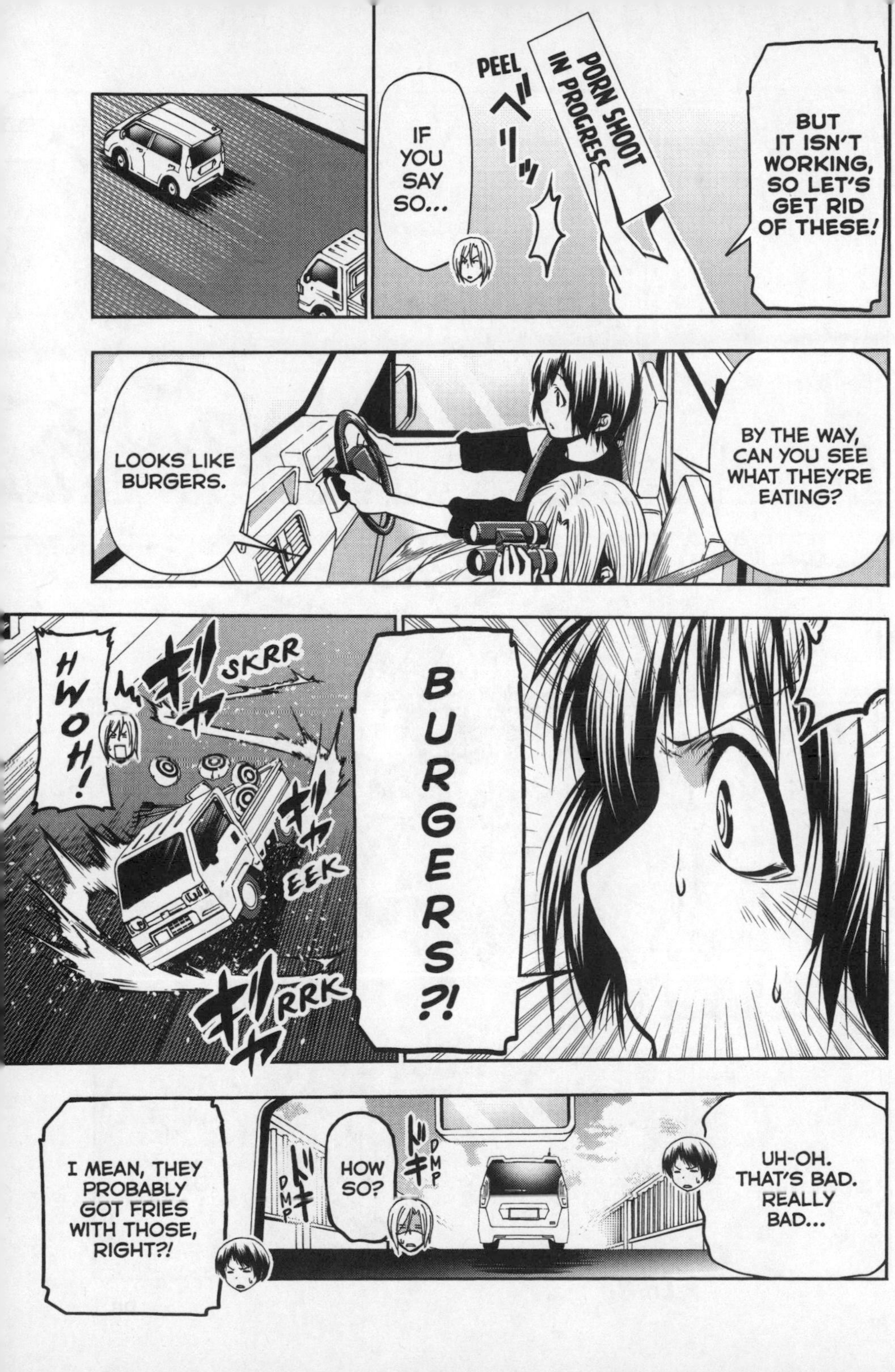
BUT IT ISN'T WORKING, SO LET'S GET RID OF THESE!
PORN SHOOT IN PROGRESS
PEEL
IF YOU SAY SO...
BY THE WAY, CAN YOU SEE WHAT THEY'RE EATING?
LOOKS LIKE BURGERS.
BURGERS?!
SKRR
HWOH!
EEK
RRK
UH-OH. THAT'S BAD. REALLY BAD...
DMP
DMP
HOW SO?
I MEAN, THEY PROBABLY GOT FRIES WITH THOSE, RIGHT?!

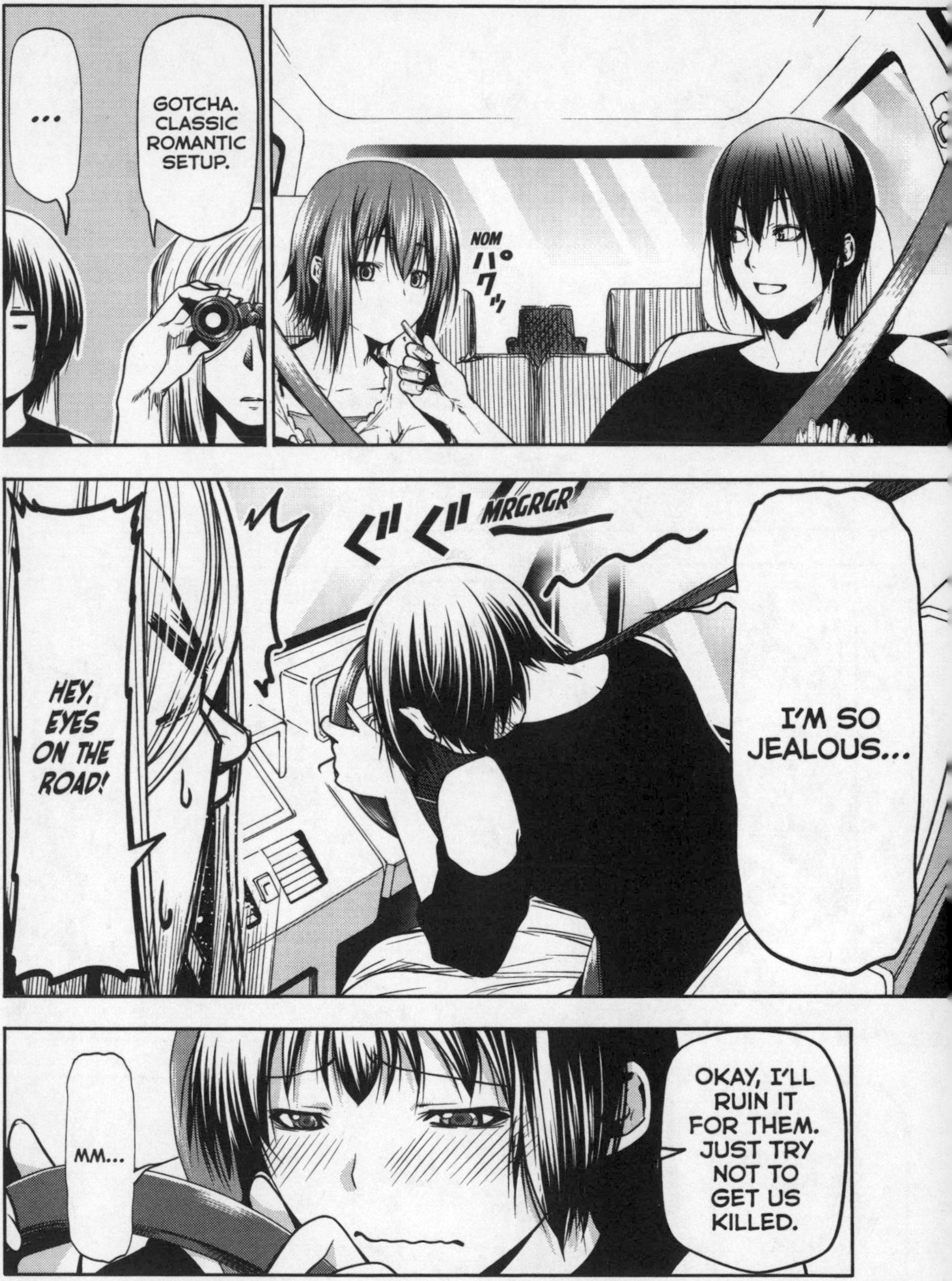
NOM
パクッ
GOTCHA. CLASSIC ROMANTIC SETUP.
...
ぐぐ MRGRGR
I'M SO JEALOUS...
HEY, EYES ON THE ROAD!
OKAY, I'LL RUIN IT FOR THEM. JUST TRY NOT TO GET US KILLED.
MM...

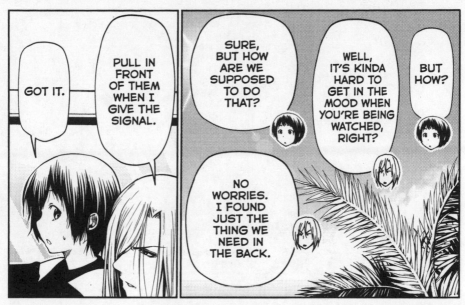

BUT HOW?
WELL, IT'S KINDA HARD TO GET IN THE MOOD WHEN YOU'RE BEING WATCHED, RIGHT?
SURE, BUT HOW ARE WE SUPPOSED TO DO THAT?
NO WORRIES. I FOUND JUST THE THING WE NEED IN THE BACK.
PULL IN FRONT OF THEM WHEN I GIVE THE SIGNAL.
GOT IT.
Scare-Eye Balloons
KUNK
KLA
SHOULD WORK LIKE A CHARM ON A BIRD-BRAIN LIKE KITAHARA.
HOW IS IT THAT *THIS* IS THE MOST PRACTICAL IDEA YOU'VE HAD SO FAR?

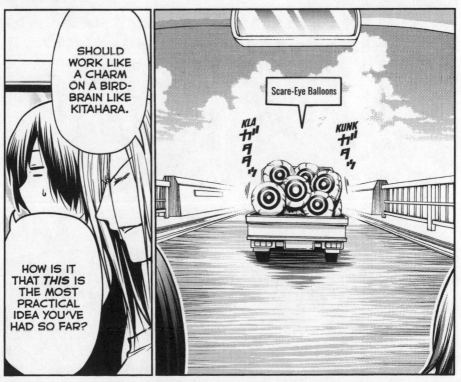

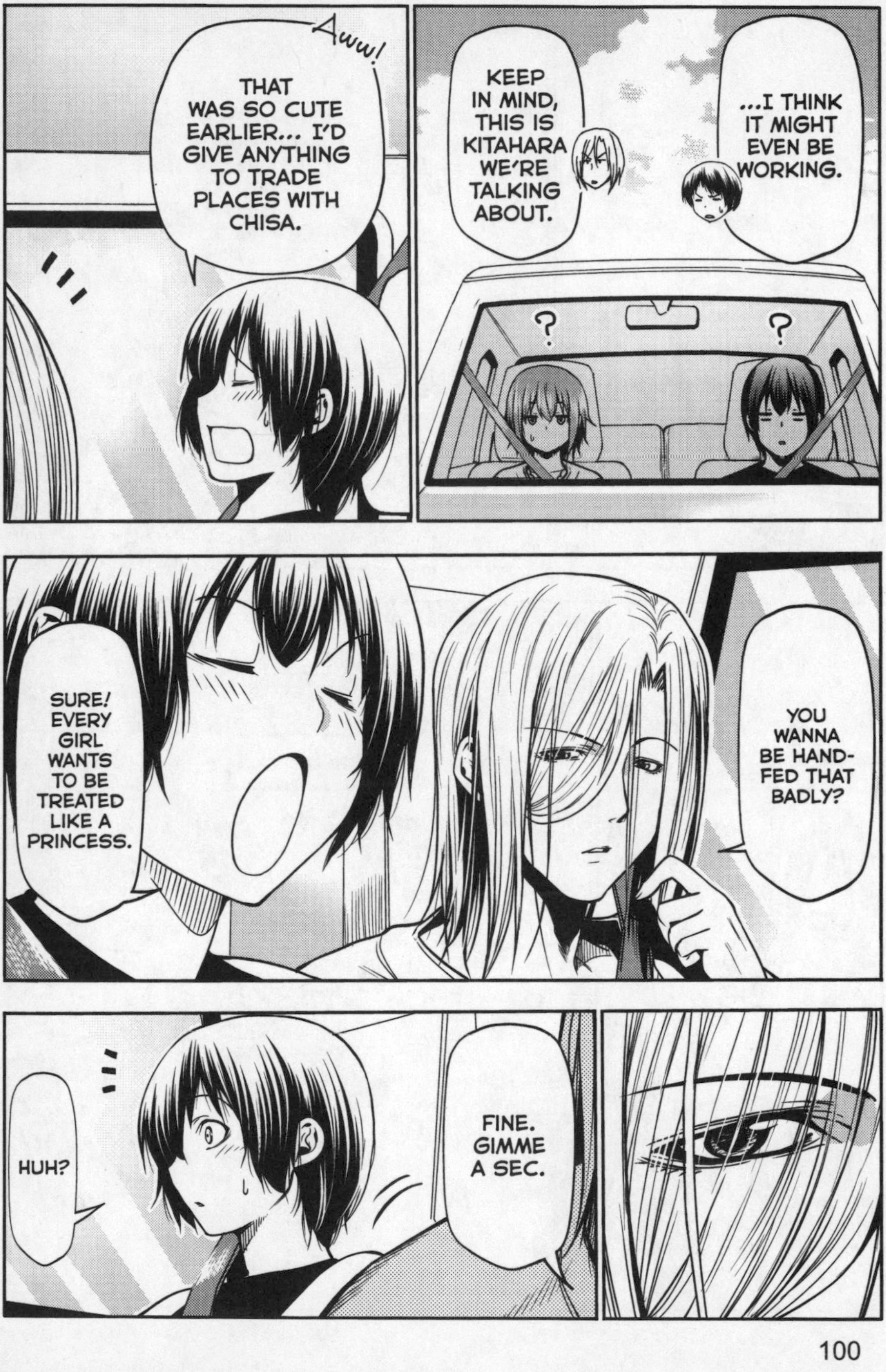
...I THINK IT MIGHT EVEN BE WORKING.
KEEP IN MIND, THIS IS KITAHARA WE'RE TALKING ABOUT.
Aww!
THAT WAS SO CUTE EARLIER... I'D GIVE ANYTHING TO TRADE PLACES WITH CHISA.
YOU WANNA BE HAND-FED THAT BADLY?
SURE! EVERY GIRL WANTS TO BE TREATED LIKE A PRINCESS.
FINE. GIMME A SEC.
HUH?

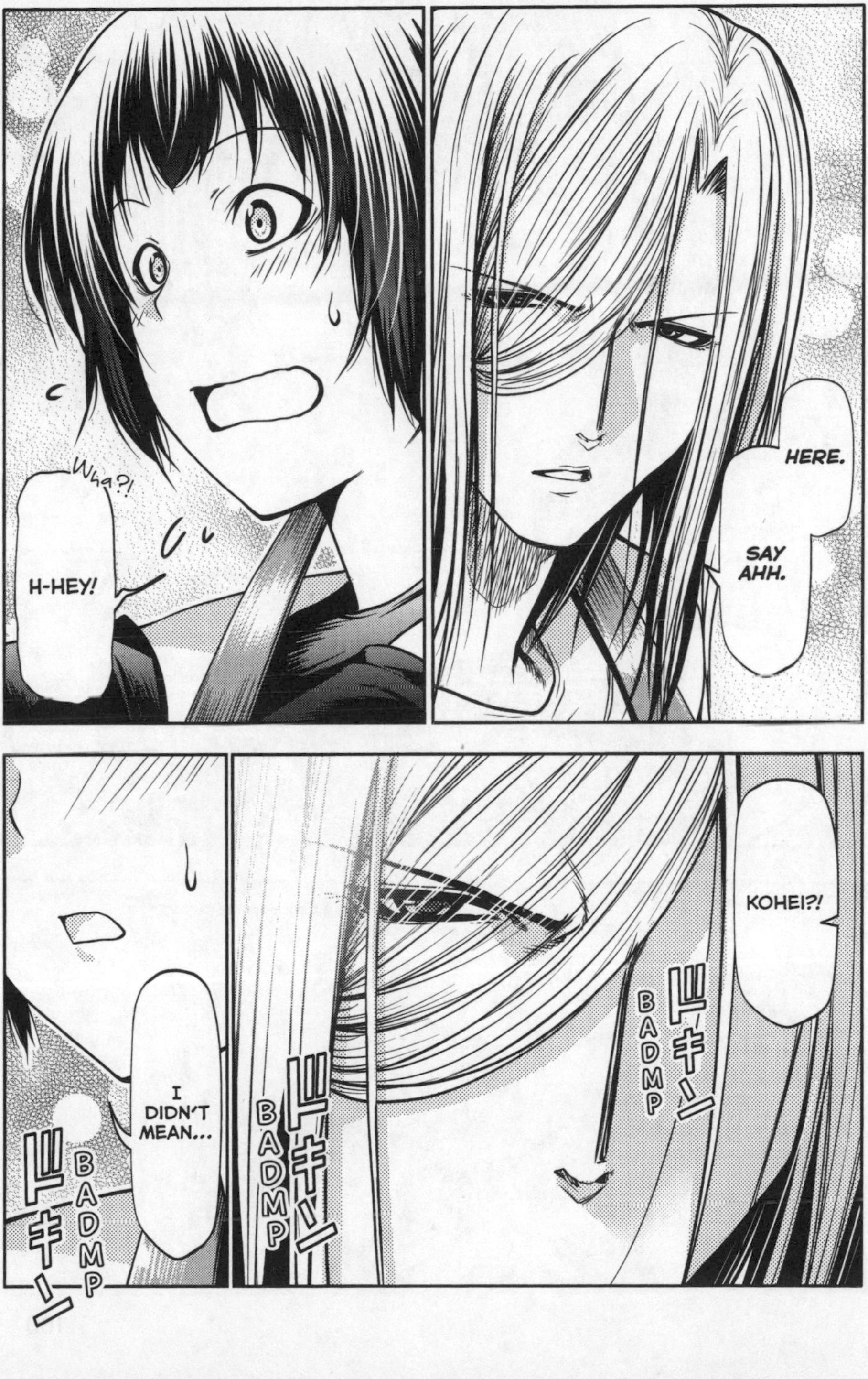
HERE.
SAY AHH.
Wha?!
H-HEY!
KOHEI?!
ドキーン
BADMP
ドキーン
BADMP
I DIDN'T MEAN...
ドキーン
BADMP

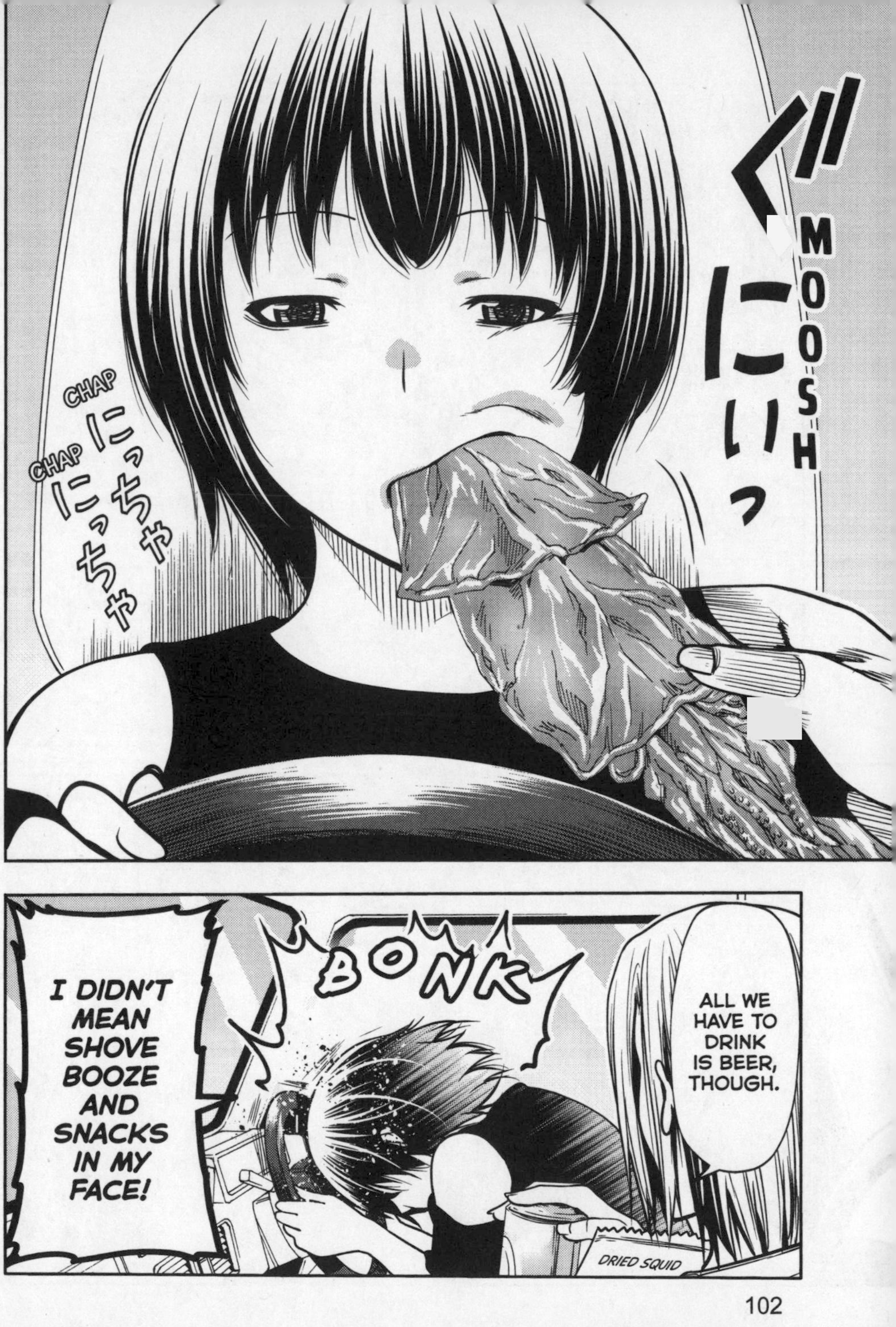
ぐにいっ
MOOSH
CHAP
CHAP
にっちゃ
にっちゃ
ALL WE HAVE TO DRINK IS BEER, THOUGH.
BONK
I DIDN'T MEAN SHOVE BOOZE AND SNACKS IN MY FACE!
DRIED SQUID

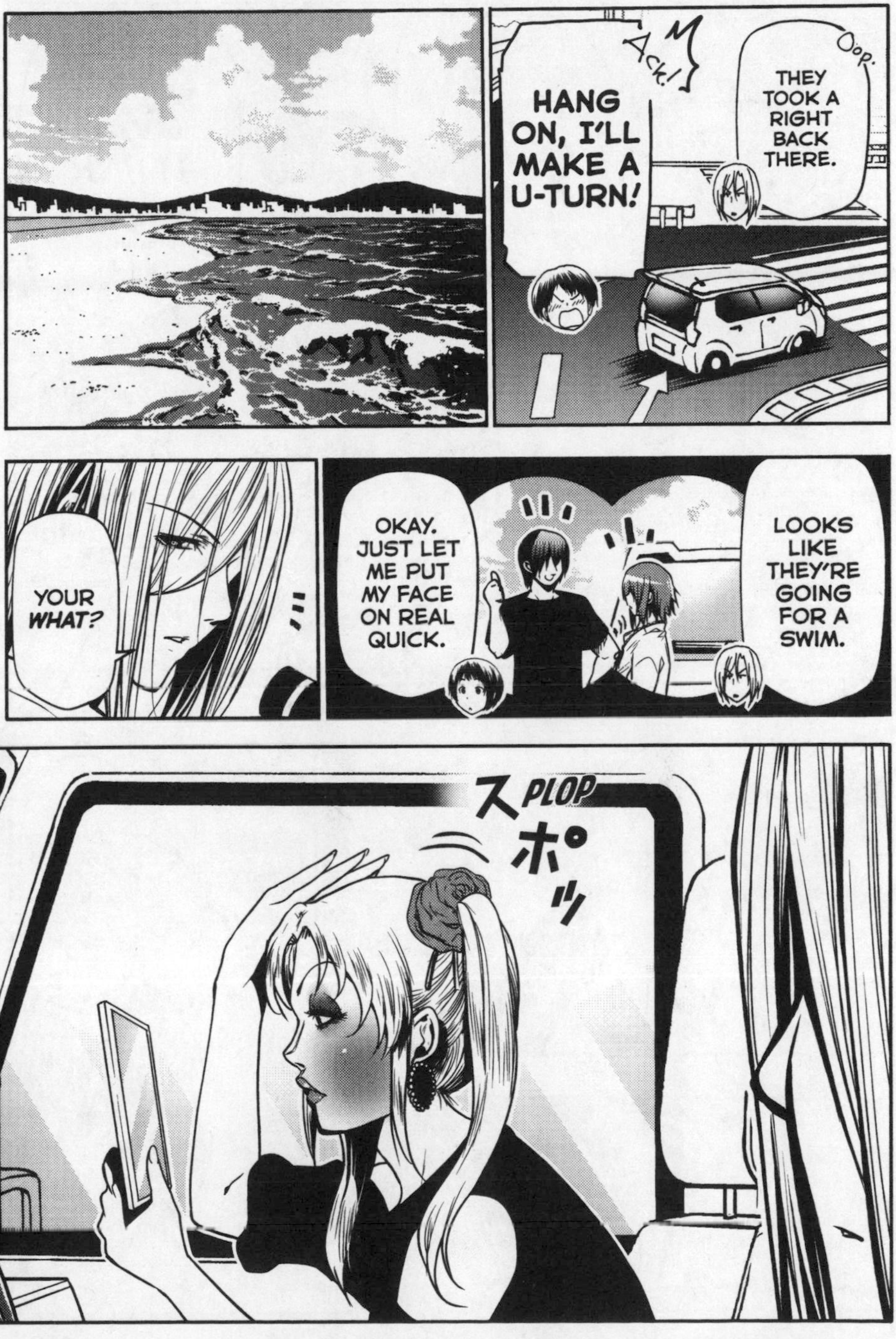
Oop.
THEY TOOK A RIGHT BACK THERE.
Ack!
HANG ON, I'LL MAKE A U-TURN!
LOOKS LIKE THEY'RE GOING FOR A SWIM.
OKAY. JUST LET ME PUT MY FACE ON REAL QUICK.
YOUR *WHAT?*
スポッ
PLOP

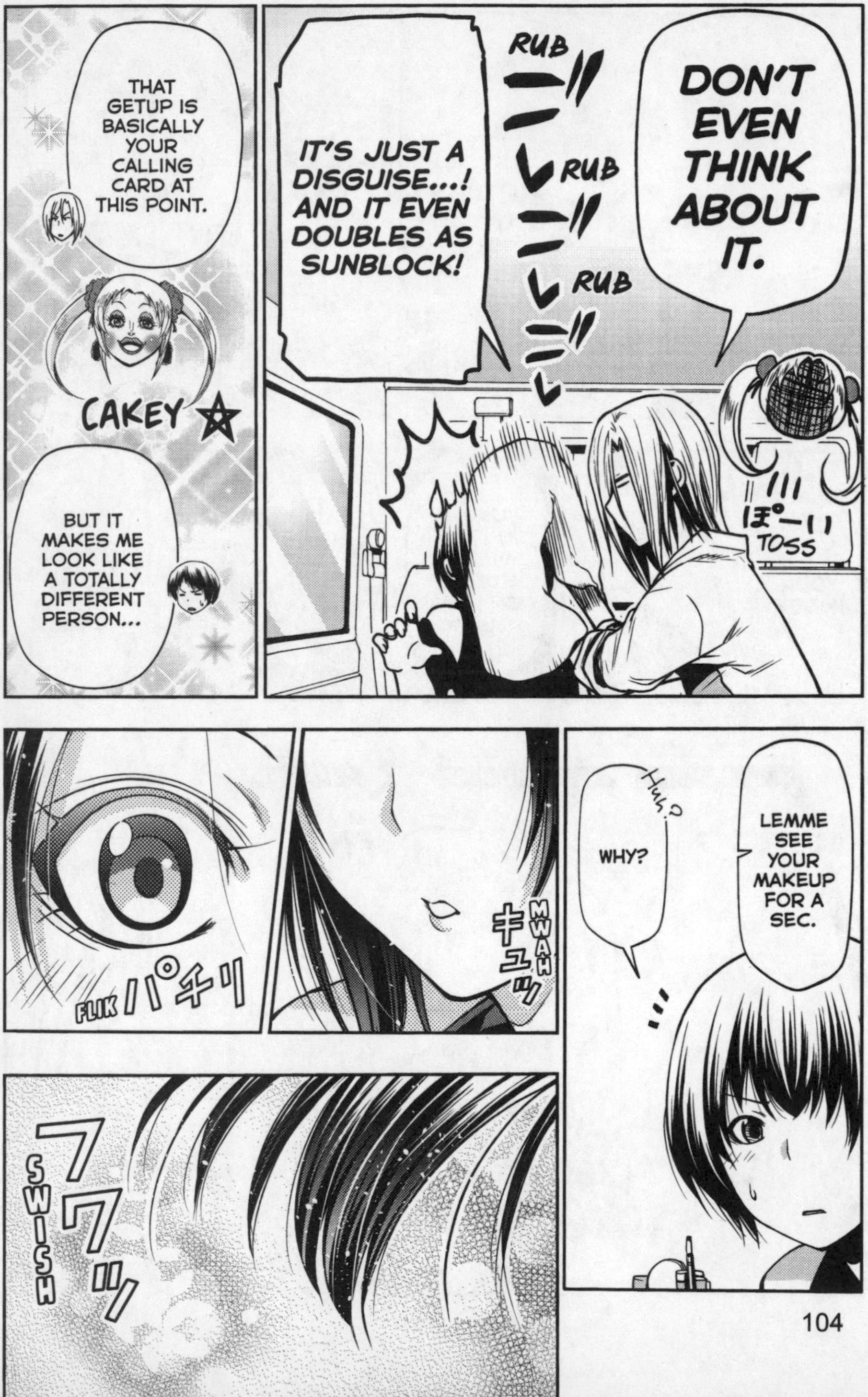
DON'T EVEN THINK ABOUT IT.
RUB
RUB
RUB
IT'S JUST A DISGUISE...! AND IT EVEN DOUBLES AS SUNBLOCK!
ぽーい
TOSS
THAT GETUP IS BASICALLY YOUR CALLING CARD AT THIS POINT.
CAKEY ☆
BUT IT MAKES ME LOOK LIKE A TOTALLY DIFFERENT PERSON...
LEMME SEE YOUR MAKEUP FOR A SEC.
Huh?
WHY?
キュッ
MWAH
パチリ
FLIK
フワッ
SWISH

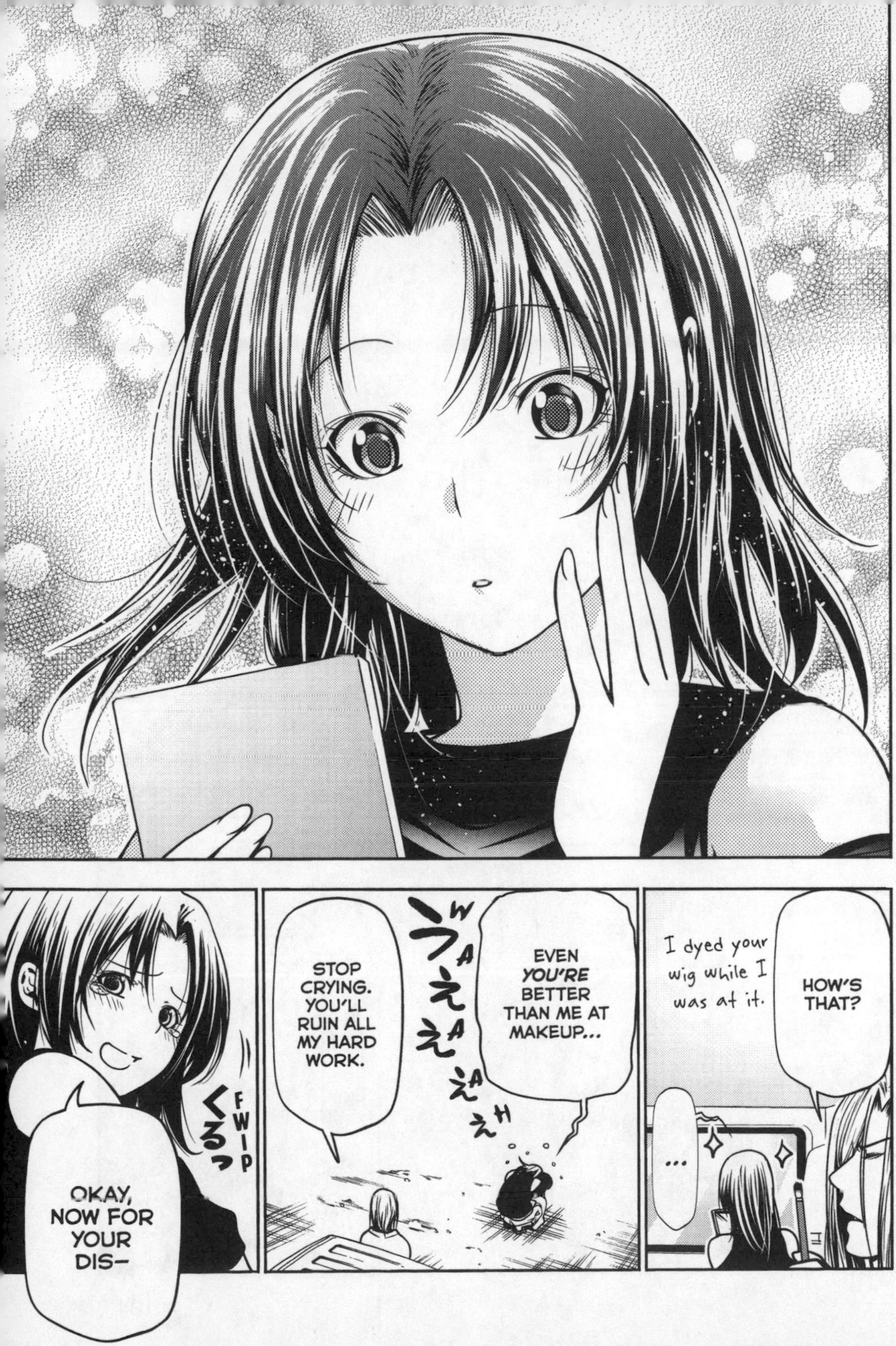
HOW'S THAT?
I dyed your wig while I was at it.
...
EVEN *YOU'RE* BETTER THAN ME AT MAKEUP...
うぇぇぇぇ WAAAH
STOP CRYING. YOU'LL RUIN ALL MY HARD WORK.
くるっ FWIP
OKAY, NOW FOR YOUR DIS–

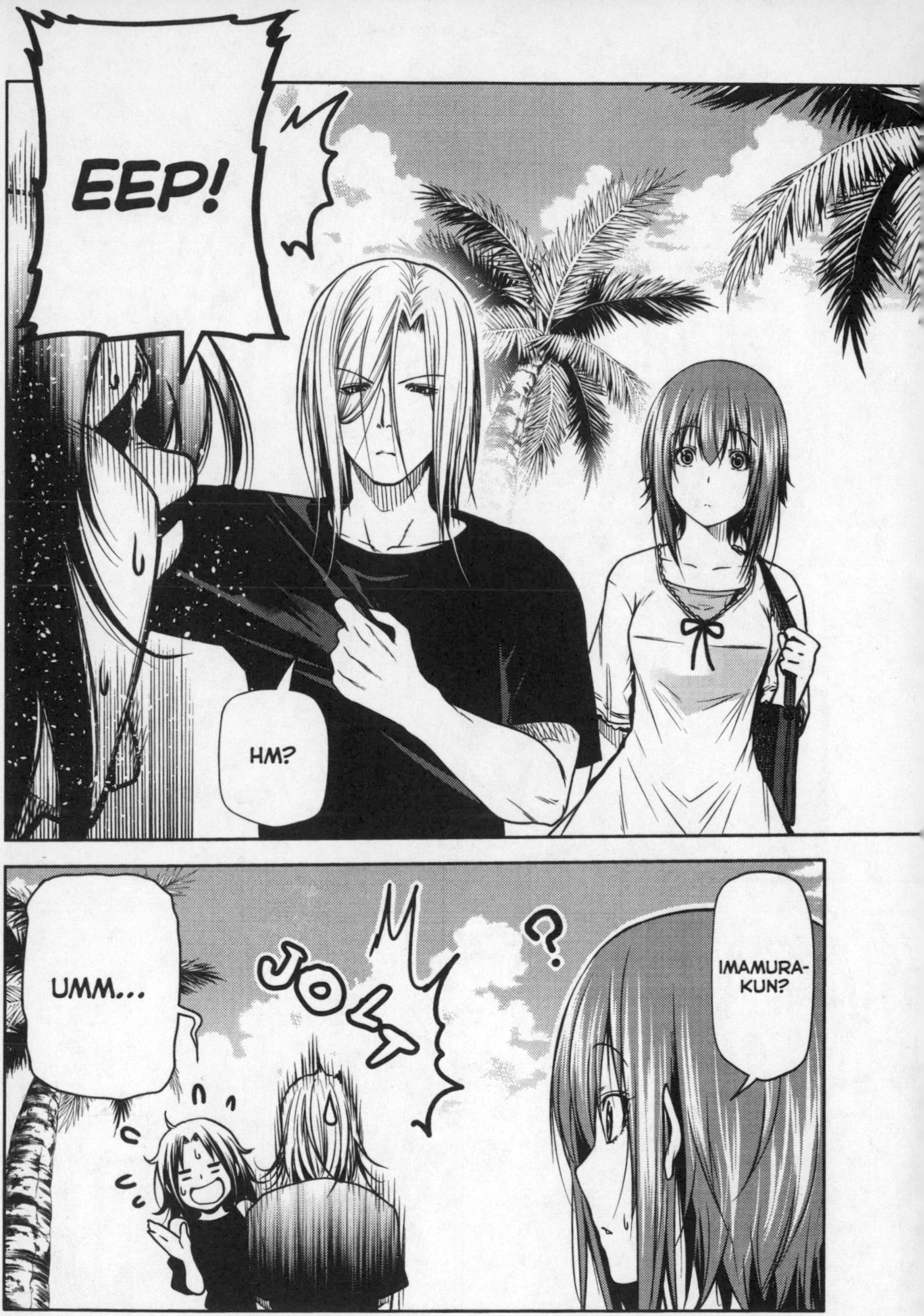
EEP!
HM?
IMAMURA-KUN?
?
JOLT
UMM...

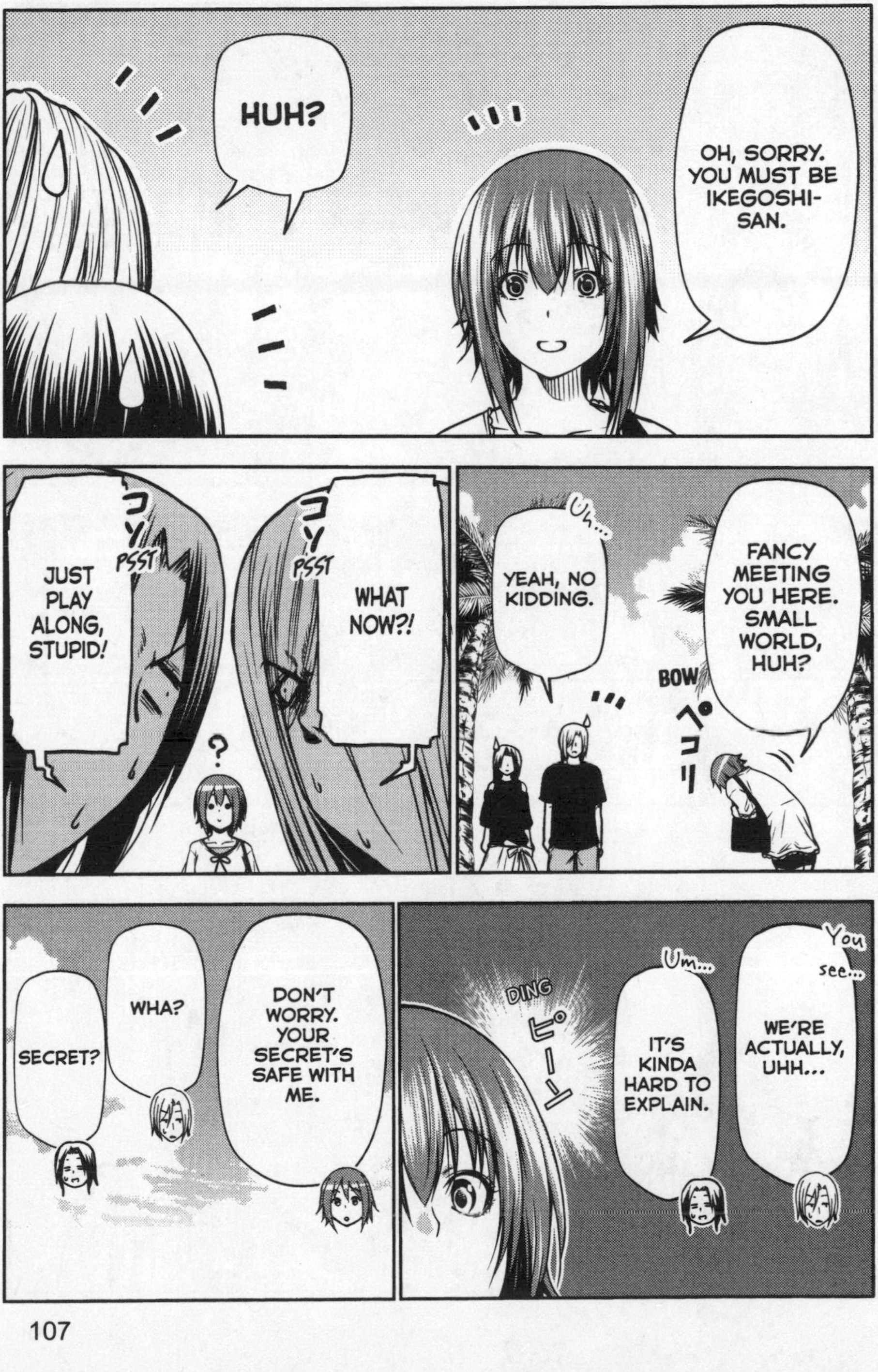
OH, SORRY. YOU MUST BE IKEGOSHI-SAN.
HUH?
FANCY MEETING YOU HERE. SMALL WORLD, HUH?
BOW
ペコリ
Uh...
YEAH, NO KIDDING.
コソ
PSST
WHAT NOW?!
コソ
PSST
JUST PLAY ALONG, STUPID!
You see...
WE'RE ACTUALLY, UHH...
Um...
IT'S KINDA HARD TO EXPLAIN.
DING
ピーン
DON'T WORRY. YOUR SECRET'S SAFE WITH ME.
WHA?
SECRET?

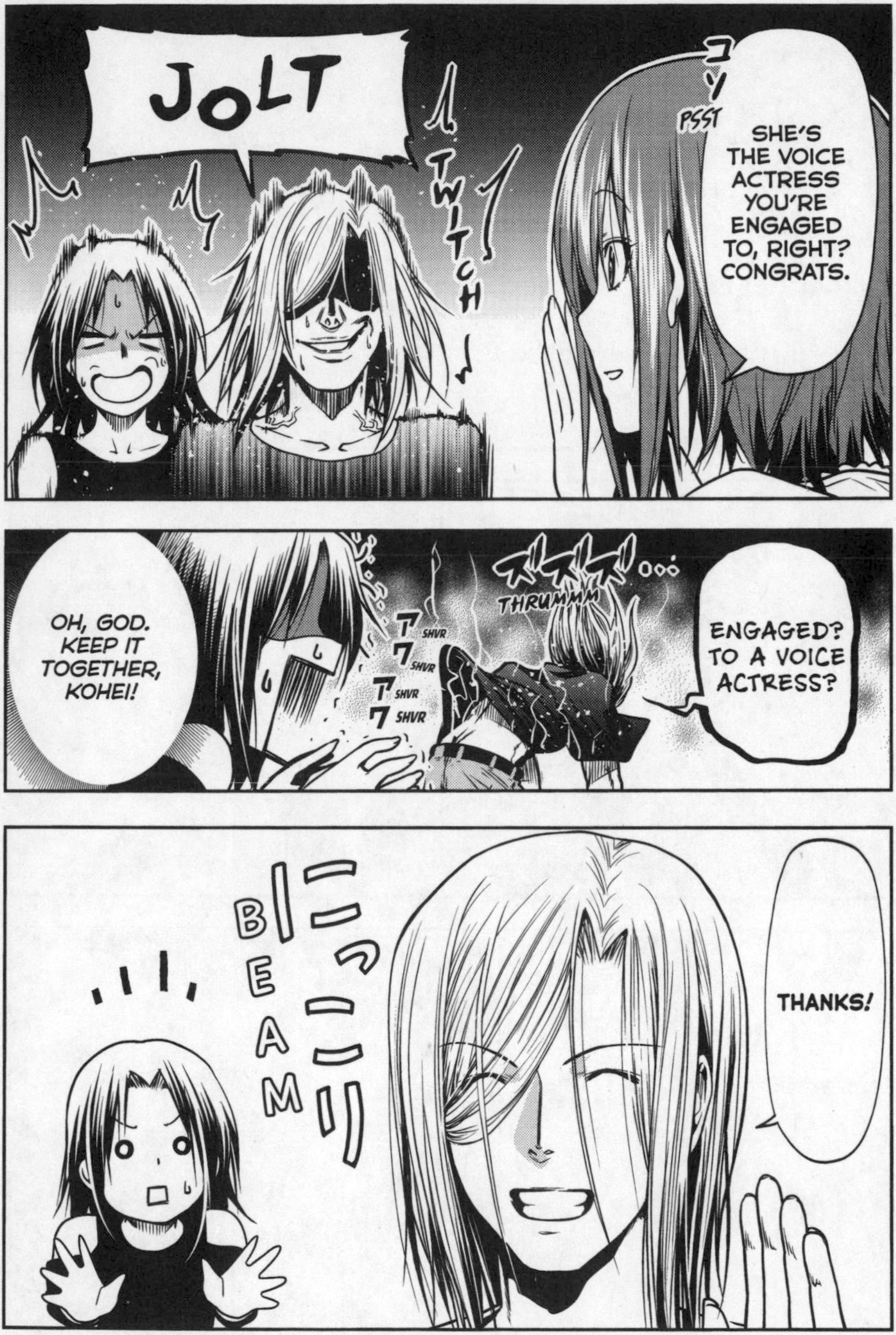
PSST
SHE'S THE VOICE ACTRESS YOU'RE ENGAGED TO, RIGHT? CONGRATS.
TWITCH
JOLT
ENGAGED? TO A VOICE ACTRESS?
THRUMMM
SHVR
SHVR
SHVR
SHVR
OH, GOD. KEEP IT TOGETHER, KOHEI!
THANKS!
BEAM

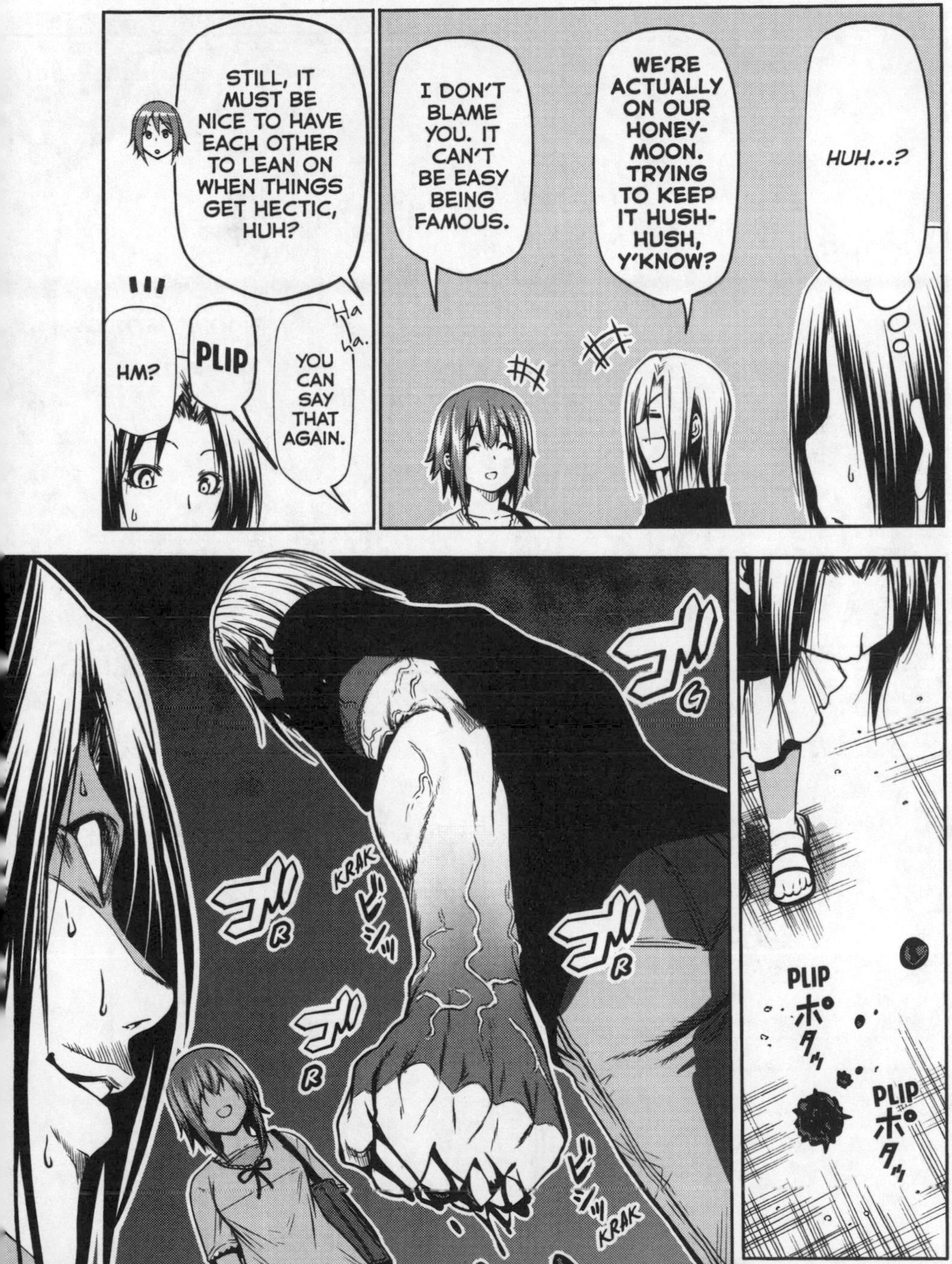
HUH...?
WE'RE ACTUALLY ON OUR HONEY-MOON. TRYING TO KEEP IT HUSH-HUSH, Y'KNOW?
I DON'T BLAME YOU. IT CAN'T BE EASY BEING FAMOUS.
STILL, IT MUST BE NICE TO HAVE EACH OTHER TO LEAN ON WHEN THINGS GET HECTIC, HUH?
Ha ha.
YOU CAN SAY THAT AGAIN.
PLIP
HM?
!!!
PLIP
PLIP
G
R
KRAK
R
R
KRAK

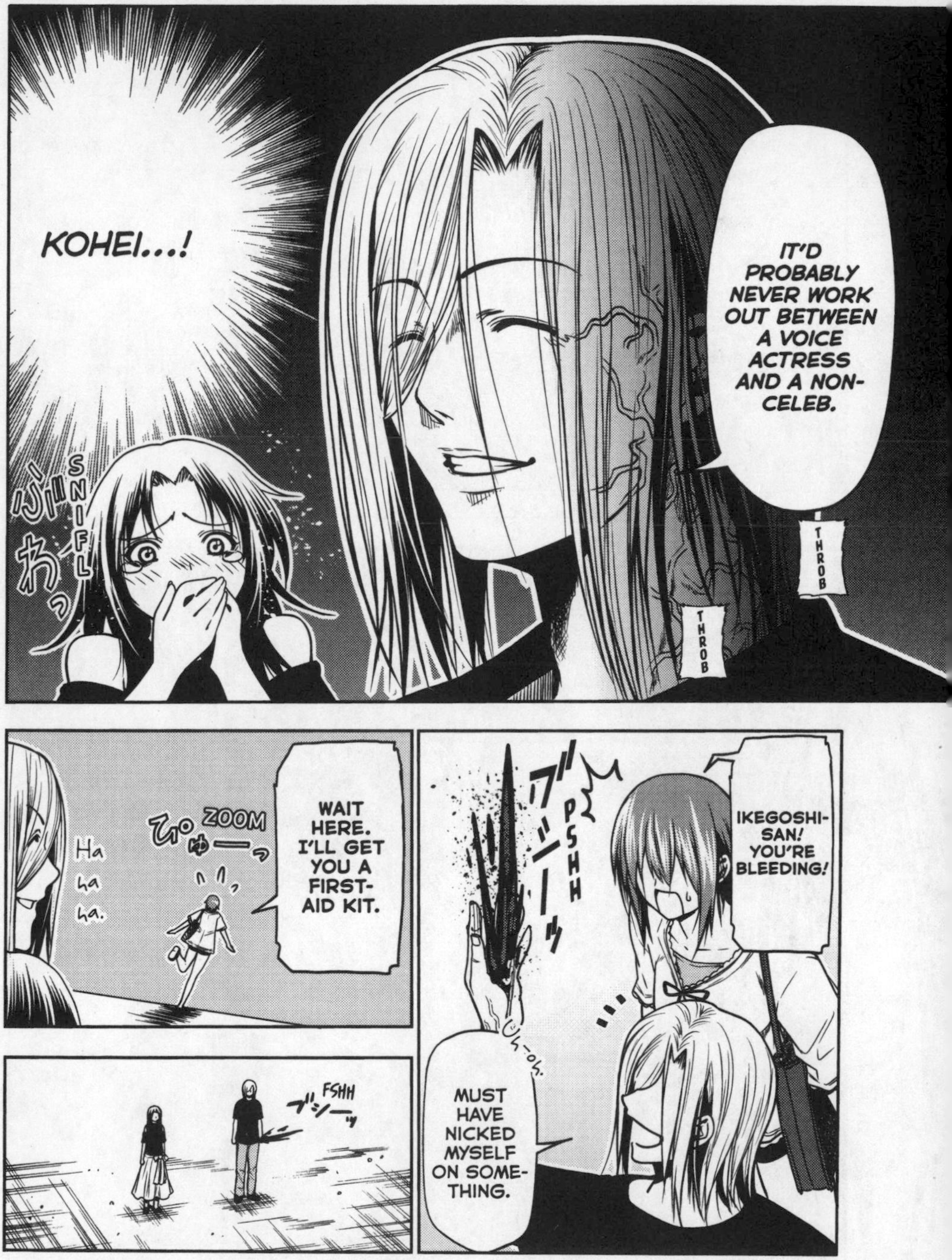
IT'D PROBABLY NEVER WORK OUT BETWEEN A VOICE ACTRESS AND A NON-CELEB.
THROB
THROB
SNIFFL
KOHEI...!
IKEGOSHI-SAN! YOU'RE BLEEDING!
PSHH
Uh-oh.
MUST HAVE NICKED MYSELF ON SOME-THING.
WAIT HERE. I'LL GET YOU A FIRST-AID KIT.
ZOOM
Ha ha ha.
FSHH

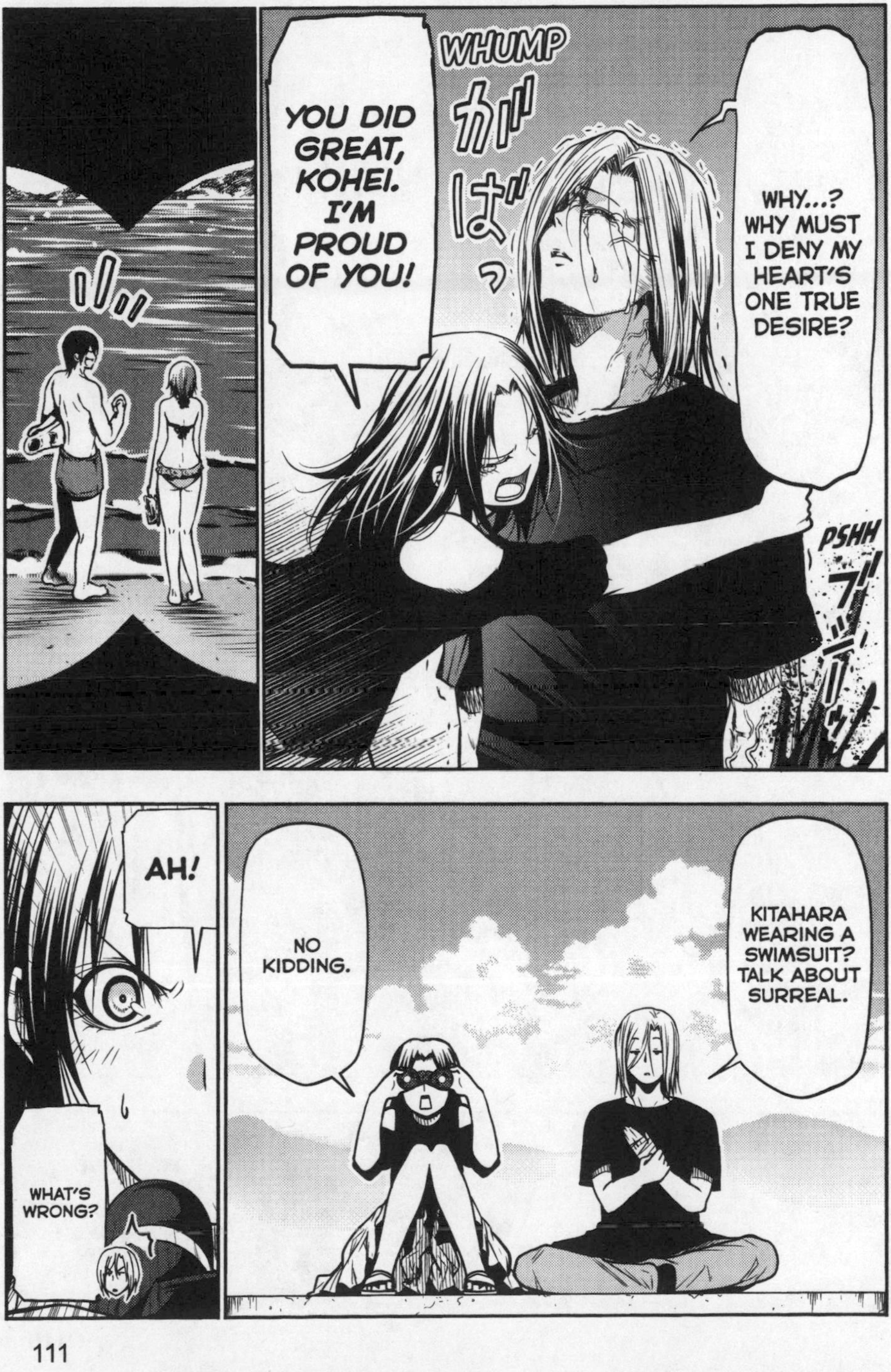

WHY...? WHY MUST I DENY MY HEART'S ONE TRUE DESIRE?
WHUMP
YOU DID GREAT, KOHEI. I'M PROUD OF YOU!
PSHH
KITAHARA WEARING A SWIMSUIT? TALK ABOUT SURREAL.
NO KIDDING.
AH!
WHAT'S WRONG?

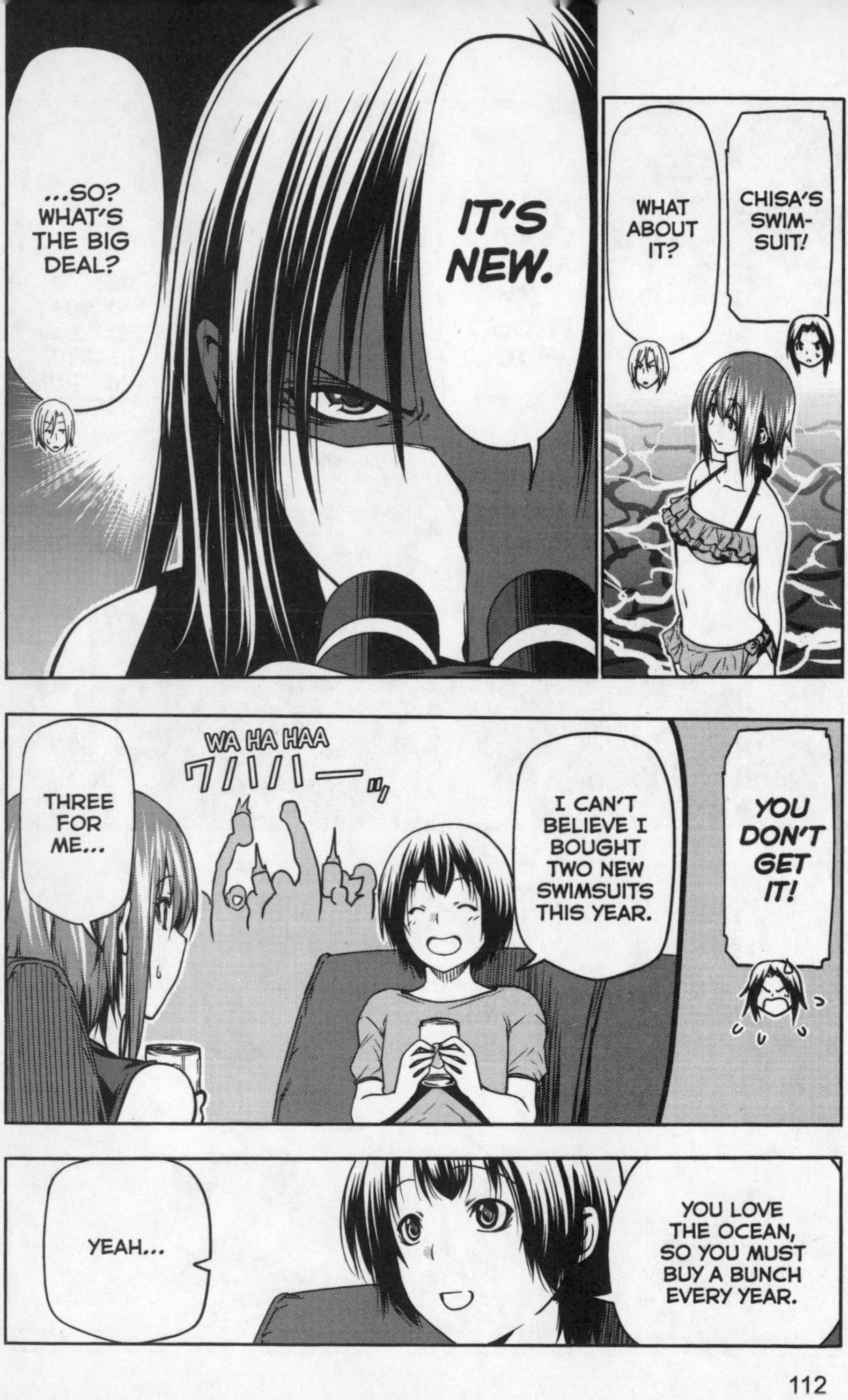
CHISA'S SWIM-SUIT!
WHAT ABOUT IT?
IT'S NEW.
...SO? WHAT'S THE BIG DEAL?
YOU DON'T GET IT!
I CAN'T BELIEVE I BOUGHT TWO NEW SWIMSUITS THIS YEAR.
WA HA HAA
ワハハーッ
THREE FOR ME...
YOU LOVE THE OCEAN, SO YOU MUST BUY A BUNCH EVERY YEAR.
YEAH...

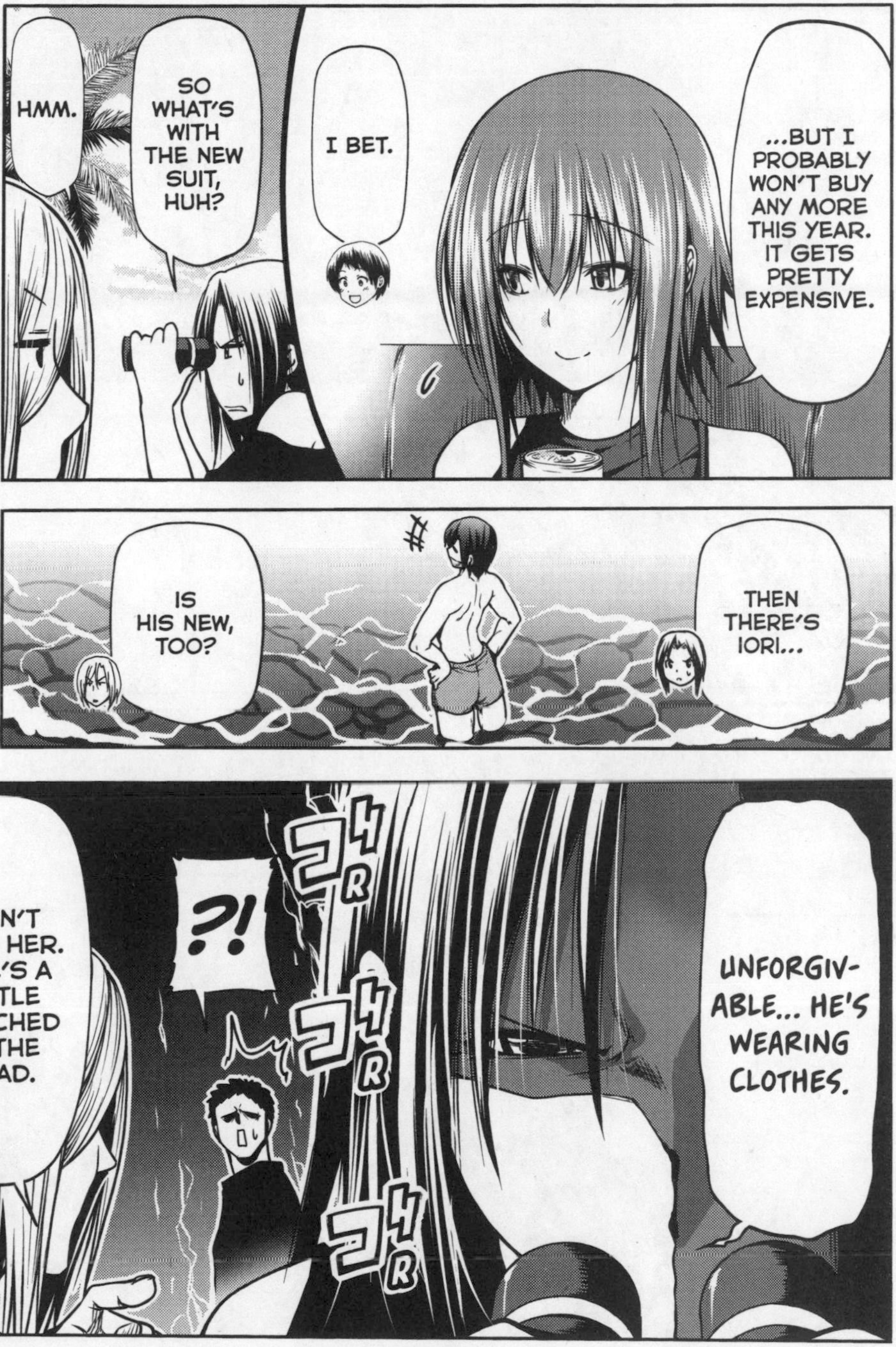
...BUT I PROBABLY WON'T BUY ANY MORE THIS YEAR. IT GETS PRETTY EXPENSIVE.
I BET.
SO WHAT'S WITH THE NEW SUIT, HUH?
HMM.
THEN THERE'S IORI...
IS HIS NEW, TOO?
UNFORGIV-ABLE... HE'S WEARING CLOTHES.
?!
DON'T MIND HER. SHE'S A LITTLE TOUCHED IN THE HEAD.

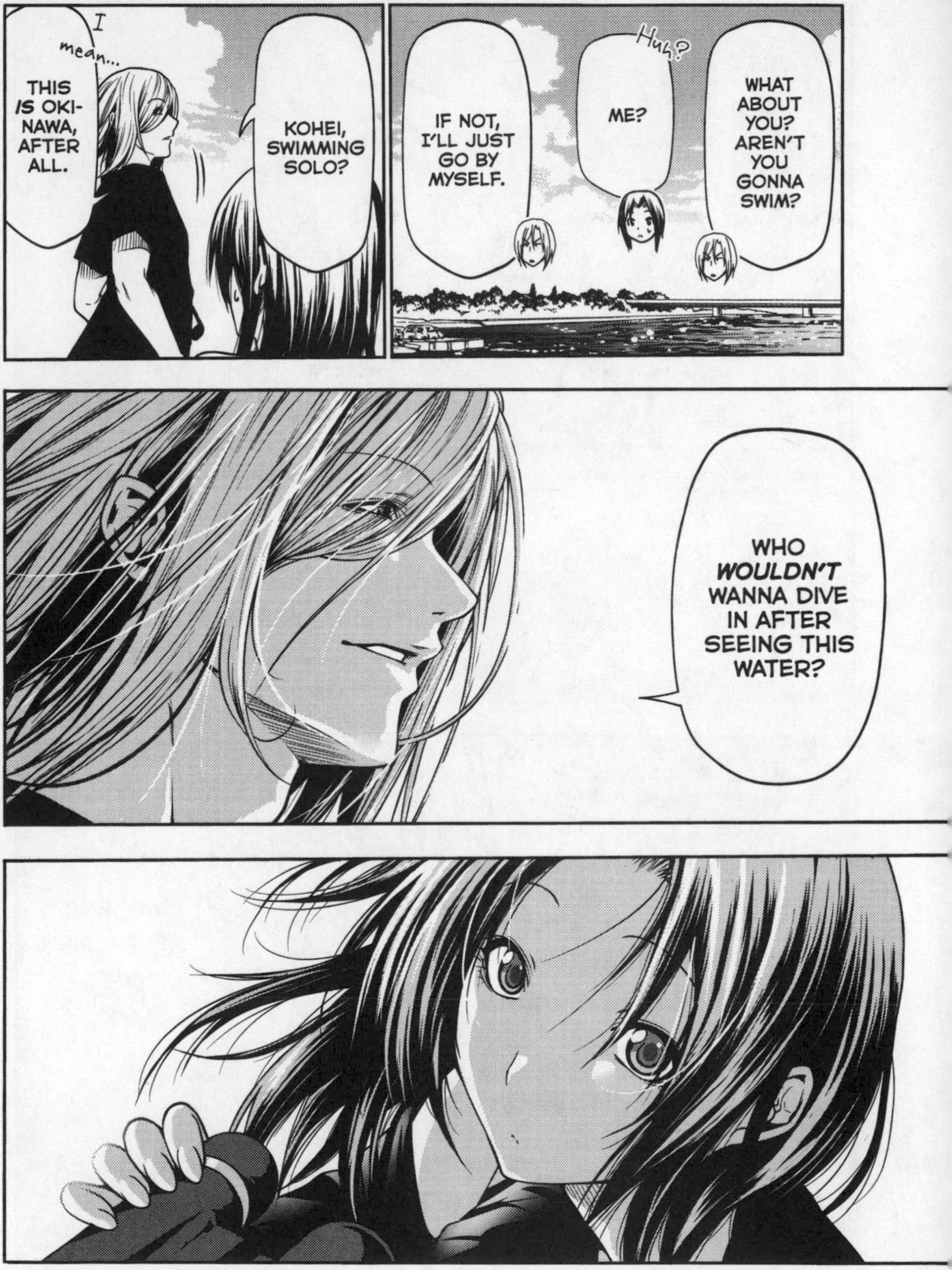
WHAT ABOUT YOU? AREN'T YOU GONNA SWIM?
Huh?
ME?
IF NOT, I'LL JUST GO BY MYSELF.
KOHEI, SWIMMING SOLO?
I mean...
THIS *IS* OKINAWA, AFTER ALL.
WHO *WOULDN'T* WANNA DIVE IN AFTER SEEING THIS WATER?

THAT DOESN'T SOUND LIKE THE KOHEI I KNOW.
CAN IT.
ARE YOU DYING TO SEE MY NEW SWIMSUIT THAT BADLY?
Hmm?
HARDLY.
SEEING YOU IN A SWIMSUIT WOULD DO NOTHING FOR ME. IT'S KIND OF HARD TO BELIEVE, HONESTLY.
UM... RUDE?!

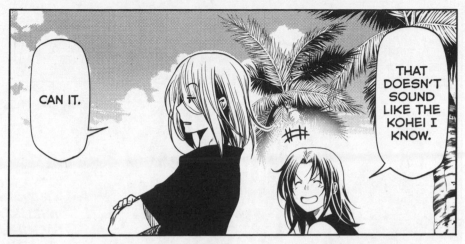

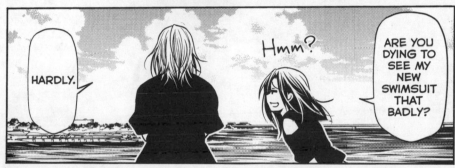

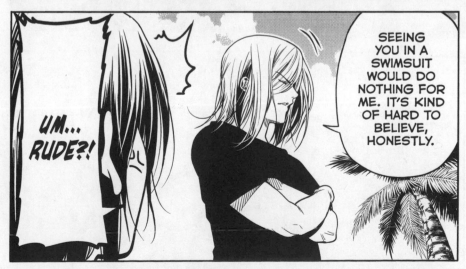

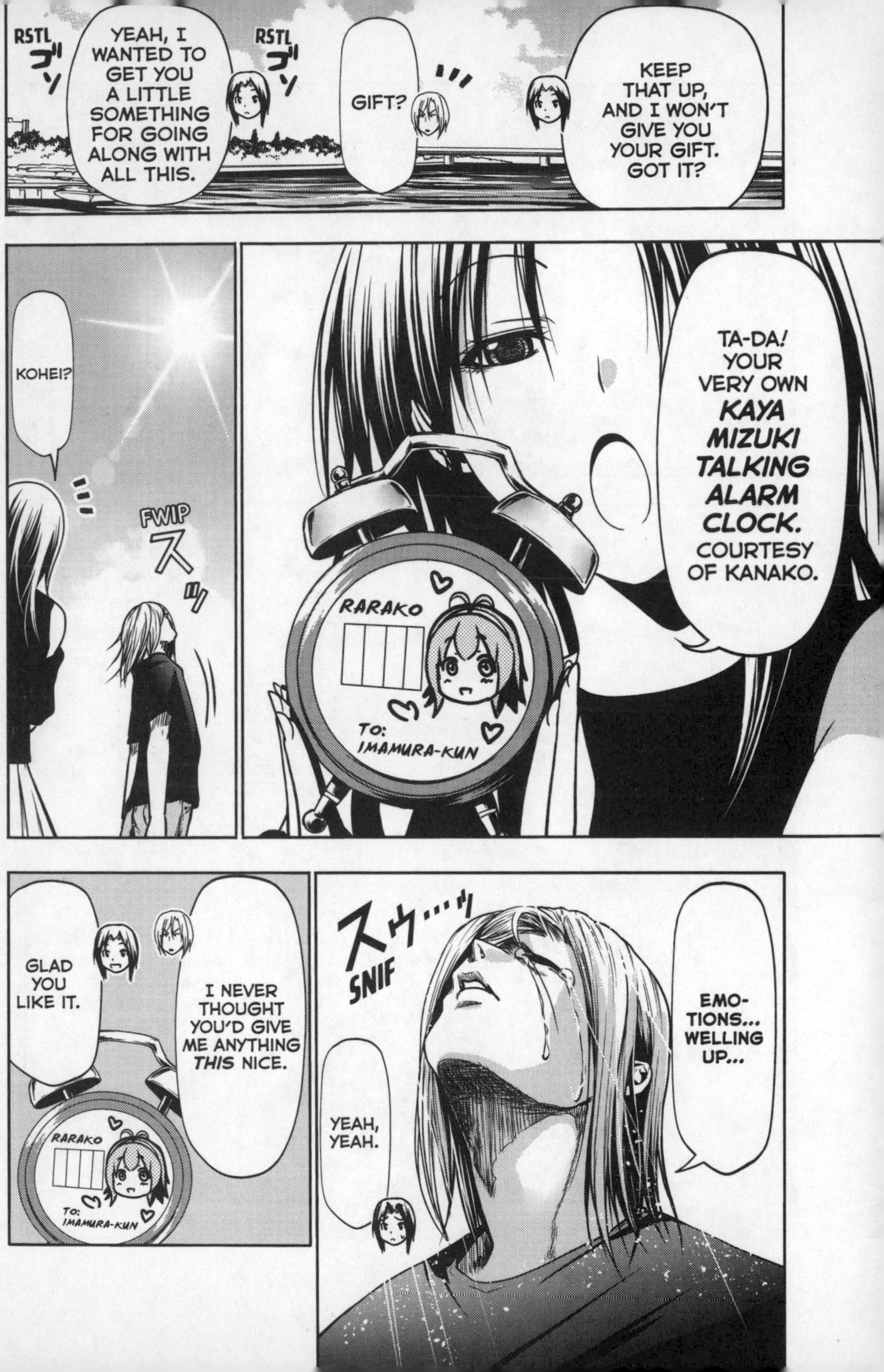
KEEP THAT UP, AND I WON'T GIVE YOU YOUR GIFT. GOT IT?
GIFT?
RSTL
YEAH, I WANTED TO GET YOU A LITTLE SOMETHING FOR GOING ALONG WITH ALL THIS.
RSTL
TA-DA! YOUR VERY OWN ***KAYA MIZUKI TALKING ALARM CLOCK.*** COURTESY OF KANAKO.
RARAKO
TO: IMAMURA-KUN
KOHEI?
FWIP
SNIF
EMO-TIONS... WELLING UP...
YEAH, YEAH.
I NEVER THOUGHT YOU'D GIVE ME ANYTHING *THIS* NICE.
GLAD YOU LIKE IT.
RARAKO
TO: IMAMURA-KUN

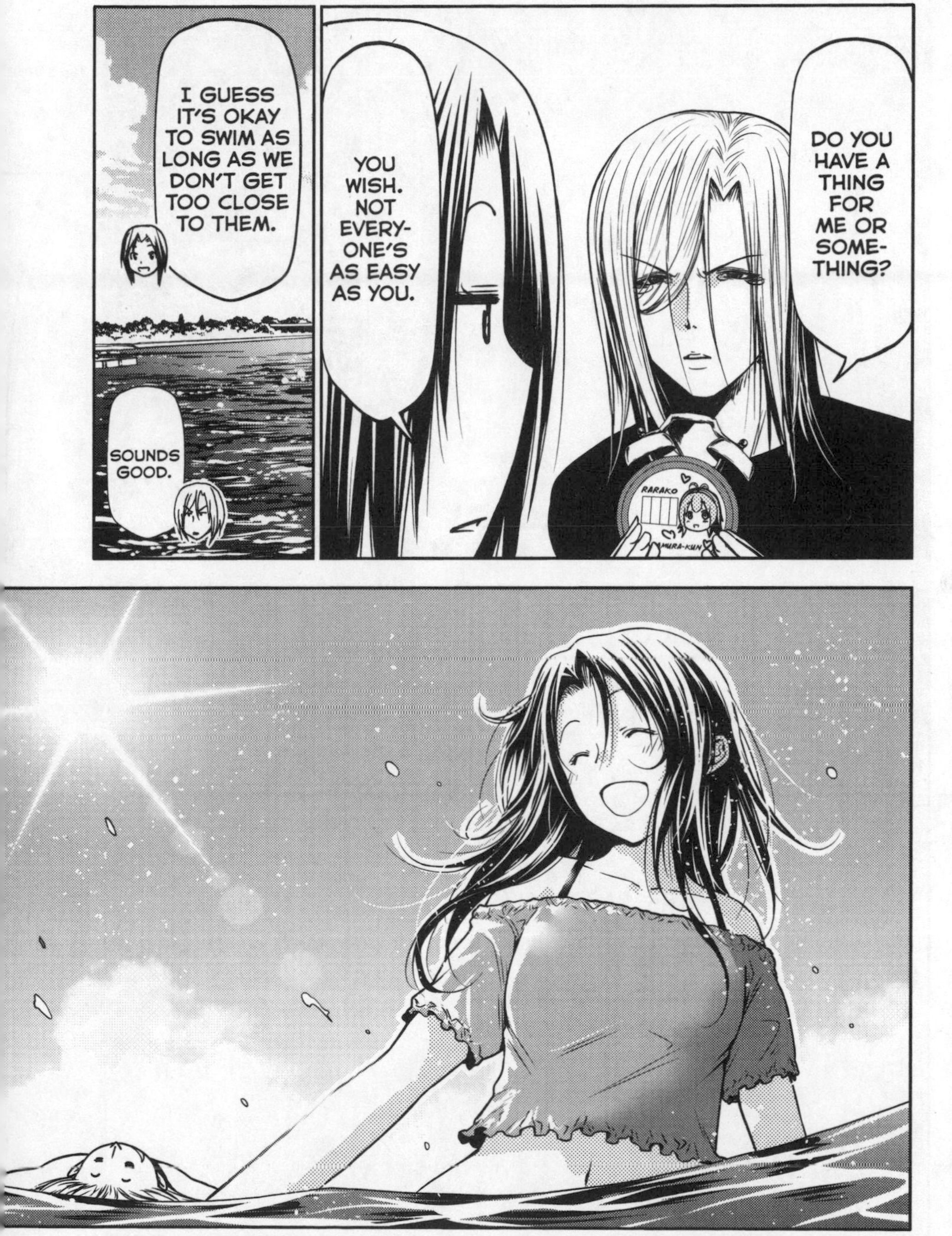

DO YOU HAVE A THING FOR ME OR SOME-THING?
RARAKO
YOU WISH. NOT EVERY-ONE'S AS EASY AS YOU.
I GUESS IT'S OKAY TO SWIM AS LONG AS WE DON'T GET TOO CLOSE TO THEM.
SOUNDS GOOD.

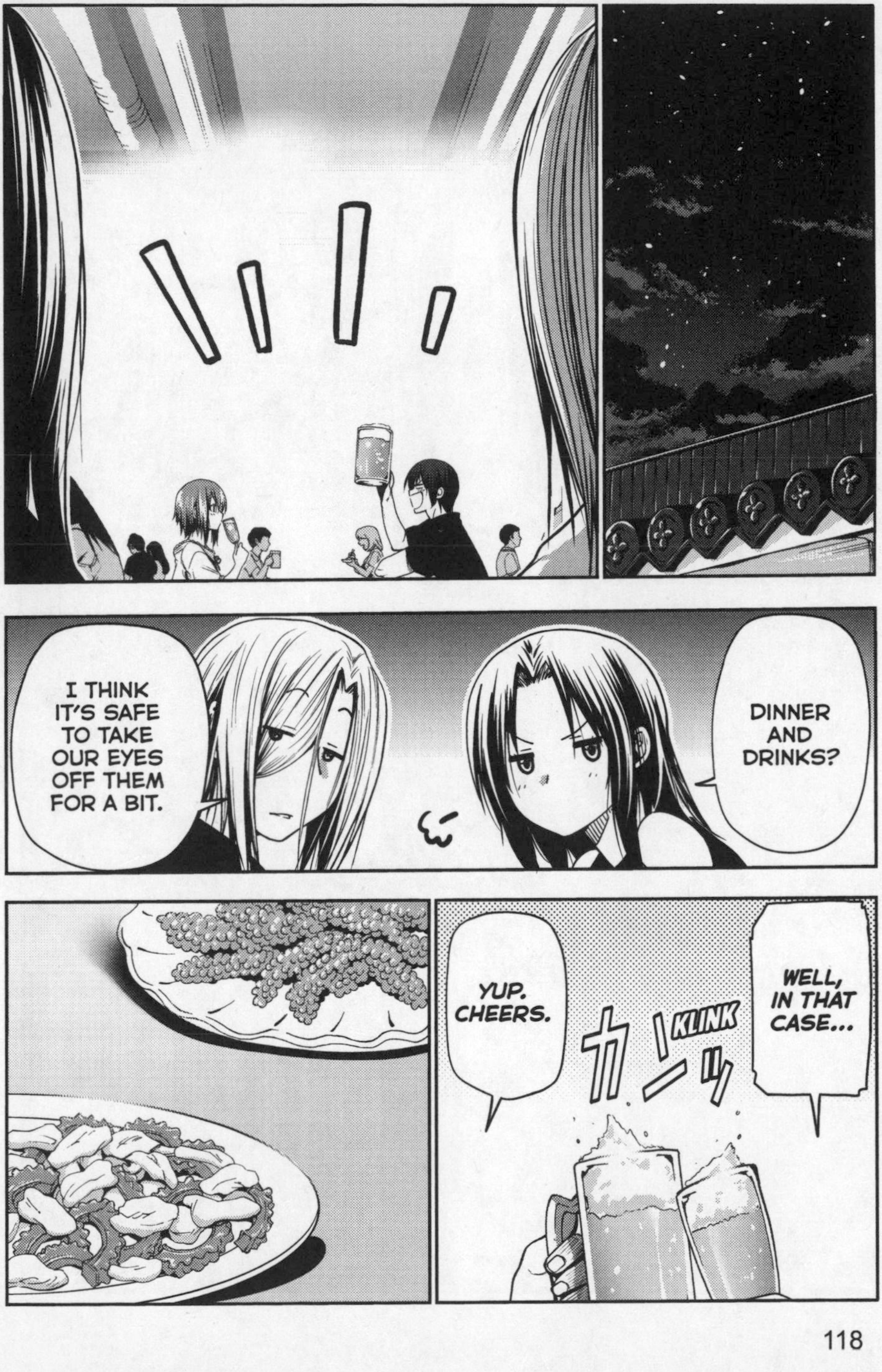
DINNER AND DRINKS?
I THINK IT'S SAFE TO TAKE OUR EYES OFF THEM FOR A BIT.
WELL, IN THAT CASE...
KLINK
カーンッ
YUP. CHEERS.

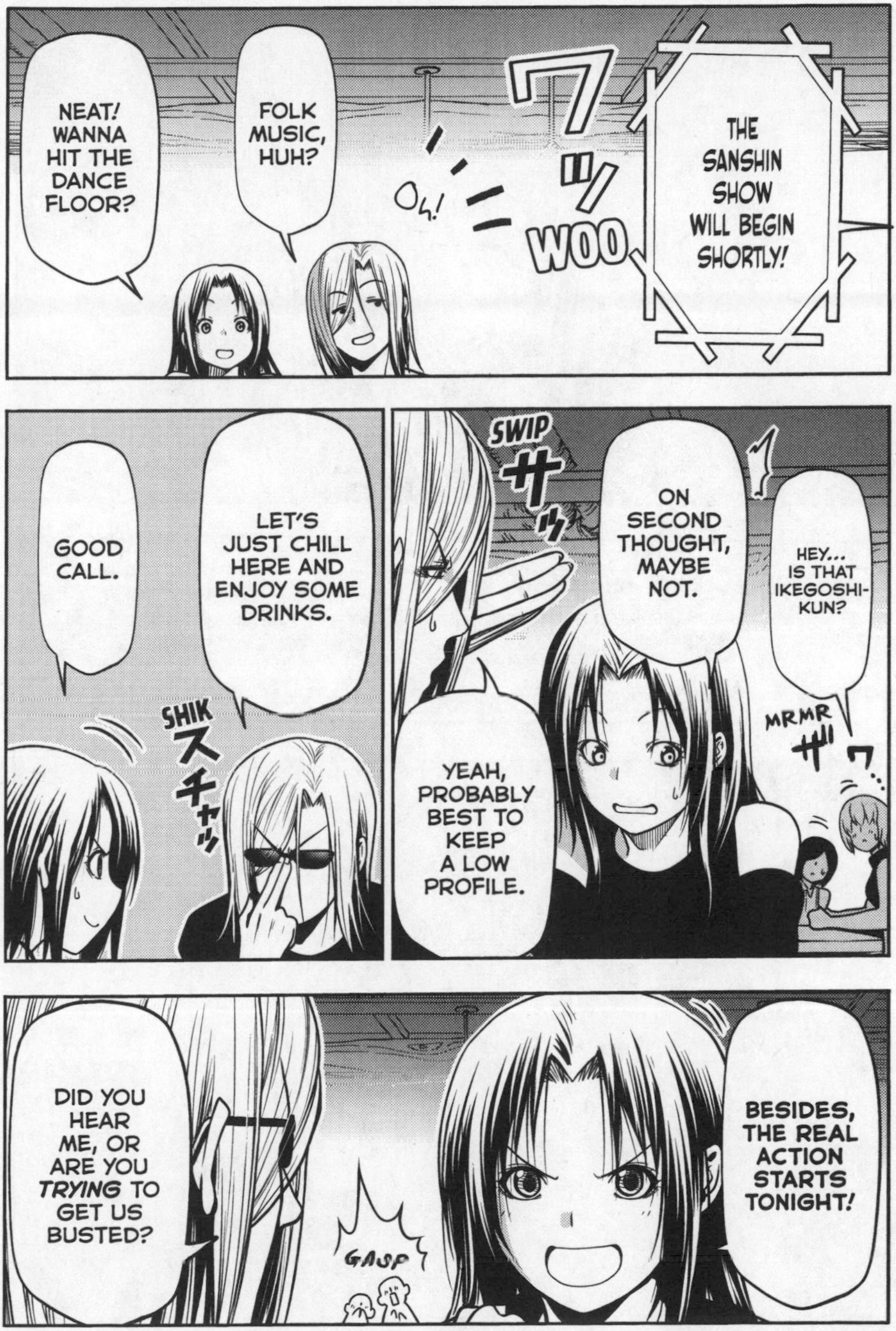
THE SANSHIN SHOW WILL BEGIN SHORTLY!
WOO
Oh!
FOLK MUSIC, HUH?
NEAT! WANNA HIT THE DANCE FLOOR?
HEY... IS THAT IKEGOSHI-KUN?
MRMR
ON SECOND THOUGHT, MAYBE NOT.
SWIP
YEAH, PROBABLY BEST TO KEEP A LOW PROFILE.
LET'S JUST CHILL HERE AND ENJOY SOME DRINKS.
SHIK
GOOD CALL.
BESIDES, THE REAL ACTION STARTS TONIGHT!
GASP
DID YOU HEAR ME, OR ARE YOU *TRYING* TO GET US BUSTED?

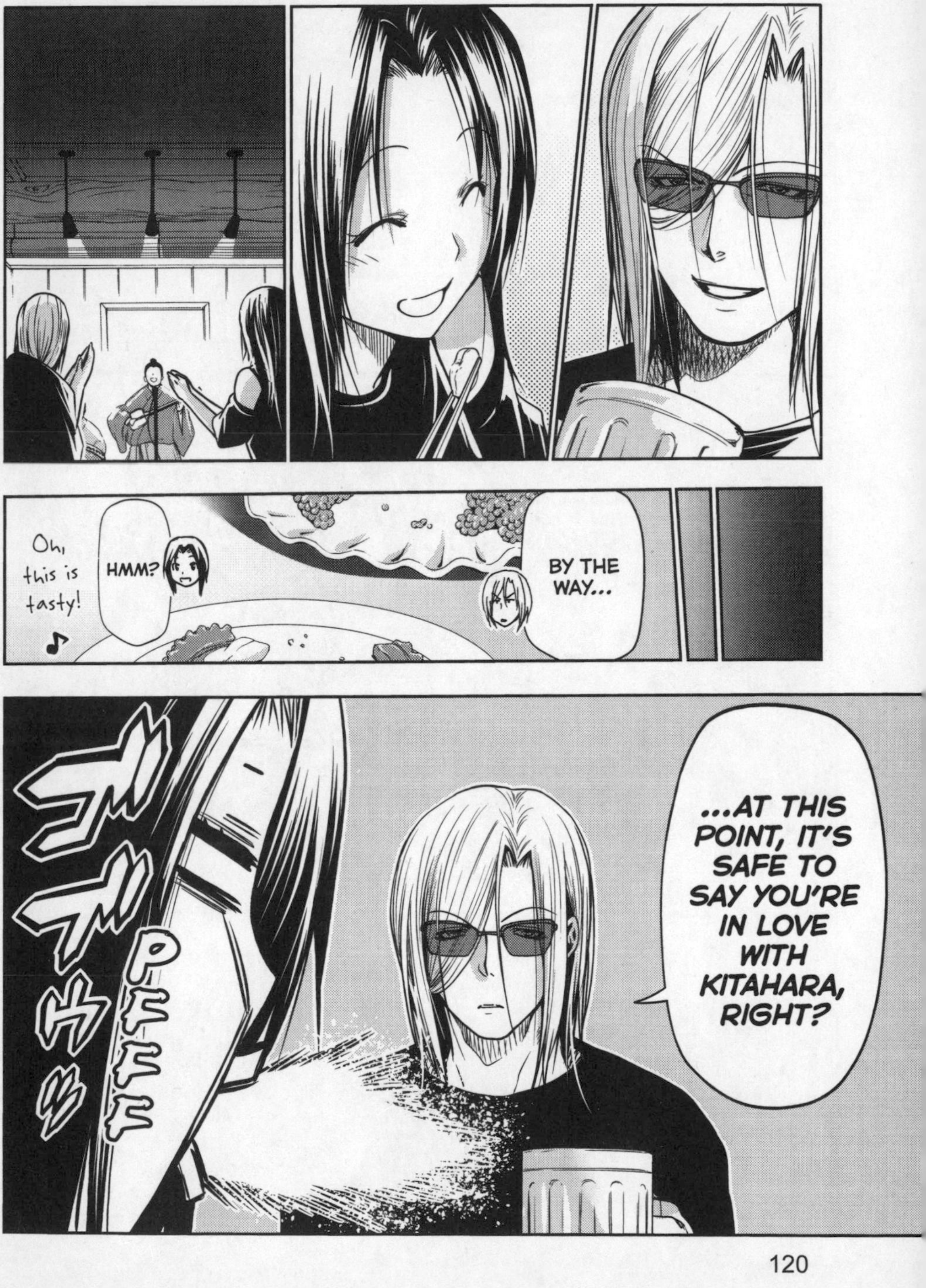
BY THE WAY...
HMM?
Oh, this is tasty! ♪
...AT THIS POINT, IT'S SAFE TO SAY YOU'RE IN LOVE WITH KITAHARA, RIGHT?
PFFF

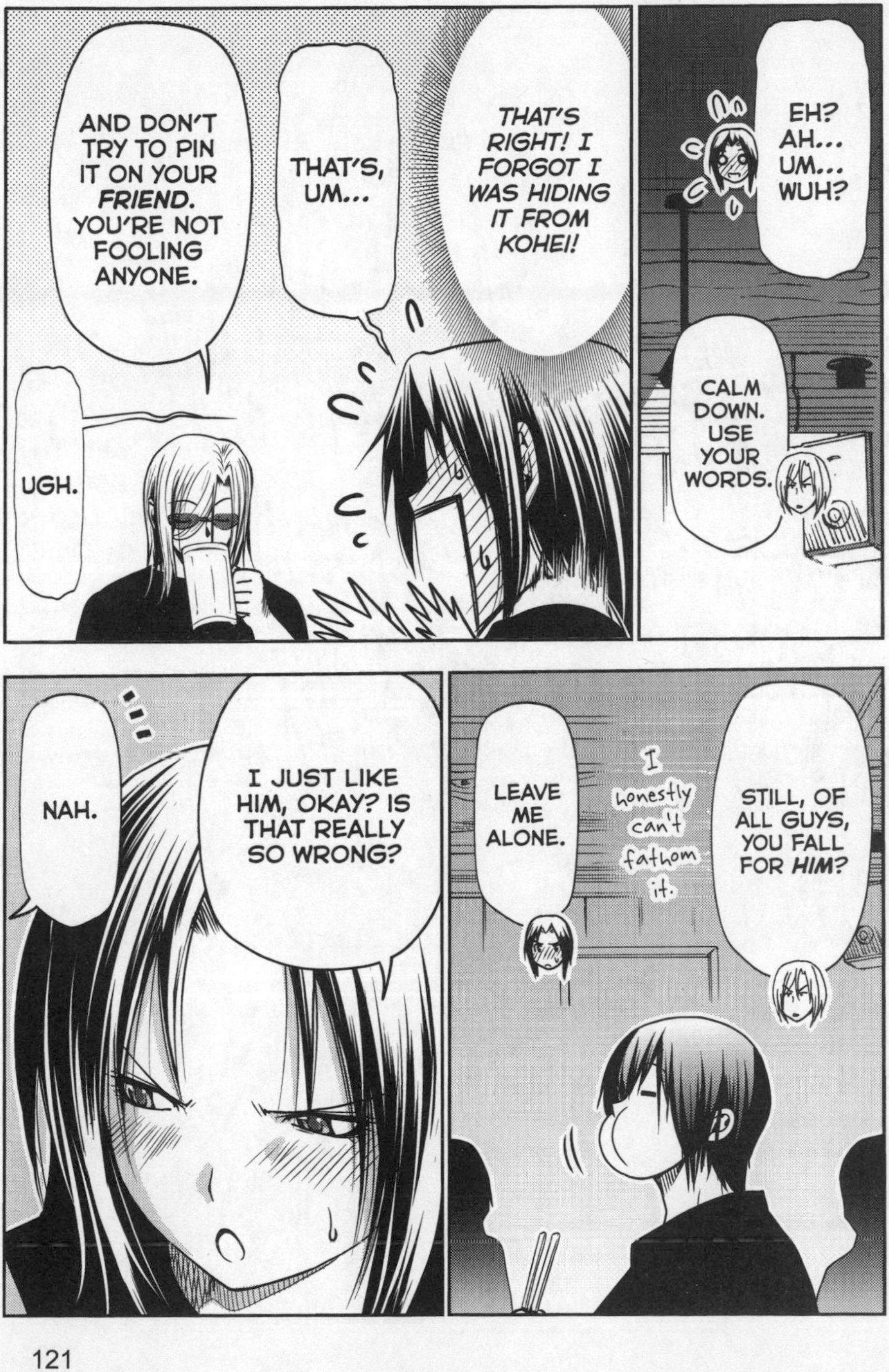
EH? AH... UM... WUH?
CALM DOWN. USE YOUR WORDS.
THAT'S RIGHT! I FORGOT I WAS HIDING IT FROM KOHEI!
THAT'S, UM...
AND DON'T TRY TO PIN IT ON YOUR *FRIEND*. YOU'RE NOT FOOLING ANYONE.
UGH.
STILL, OF ALL GUYS, YOU FALL FOR *HIM*?
I honestly can't fathom it.
LEAVE ME ALONE.
I JUST LIKE HIM, OKAY? IS THAT REALLY SO WRONG?
NAH.

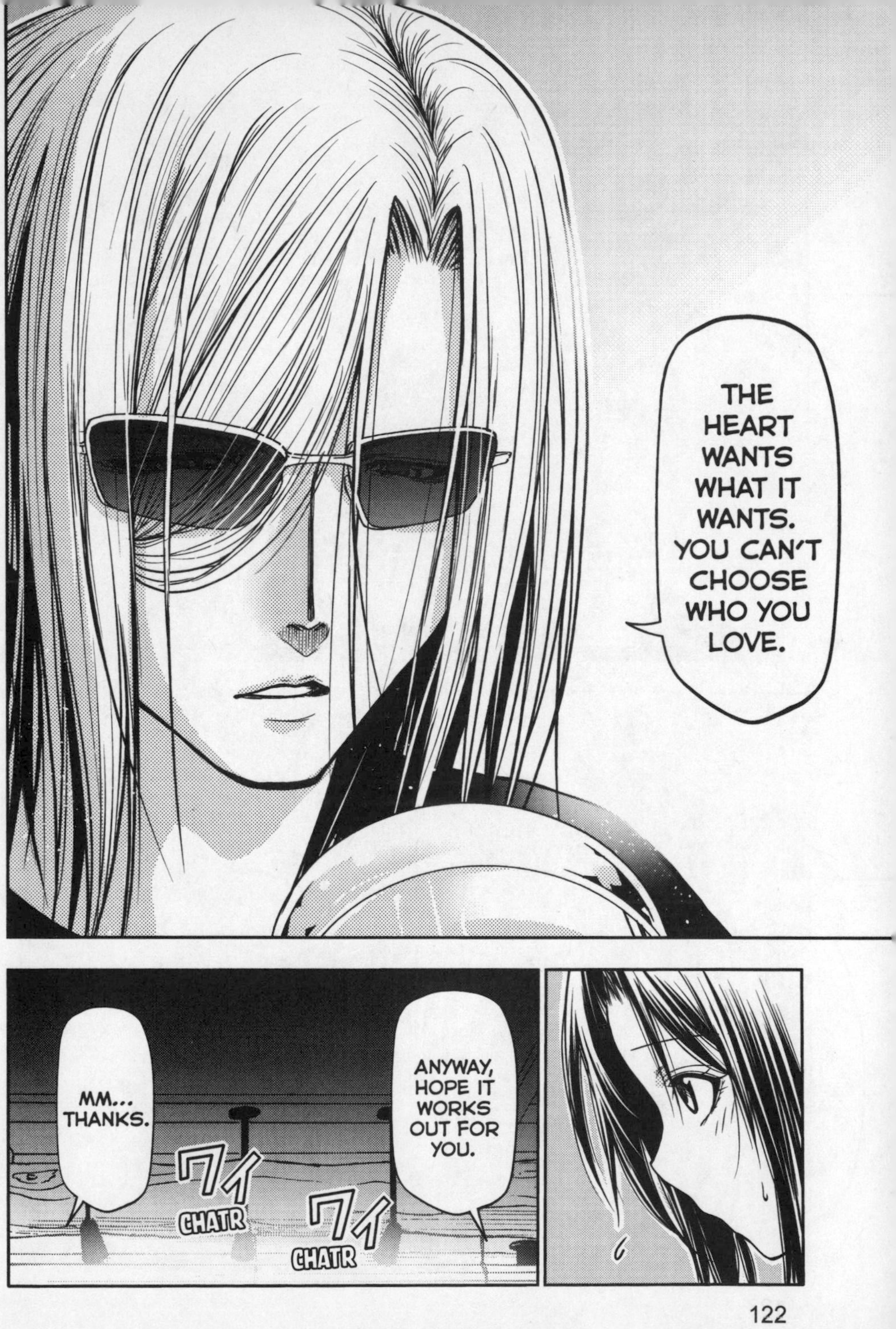
THE HEART WANTS WHAT IT WANTS. YOU CAN'T CHOOSE WHO YOU LOVE.
ANYWAY, HOPE IT WORKS OUT FOR YOU.
ワイ
CHATR
MM... THANKS.
ワイ
CHATR

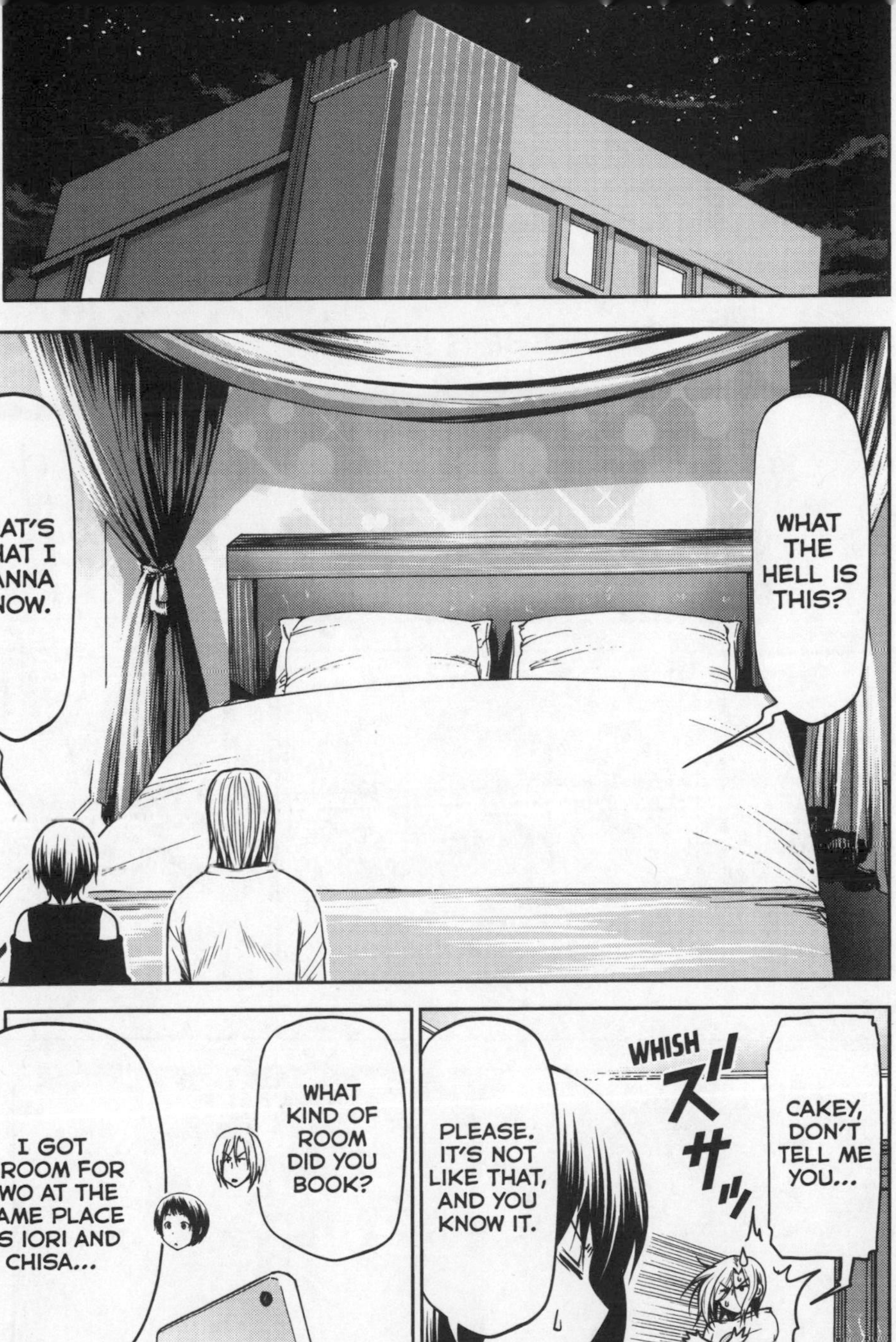
WHAT THE HELL IS THIS?
THAT'S WHAT I WANNA KNOW.
CAKEY, DON'T TELL ME YOU...
WHISH
ズザッ
PLEASE. IT'S NOT LIKE THAT, AND YOU KNOW IT.
WHAT KIND OF ROOM DID YOU BOOK?
I GOT A ROOM FOR TWO AT THE SAME PLACE AS IORI AND CHISA...

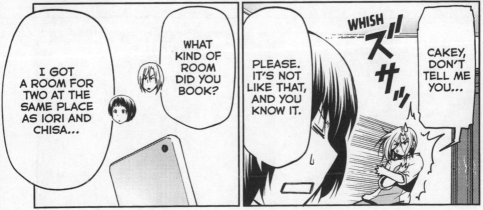

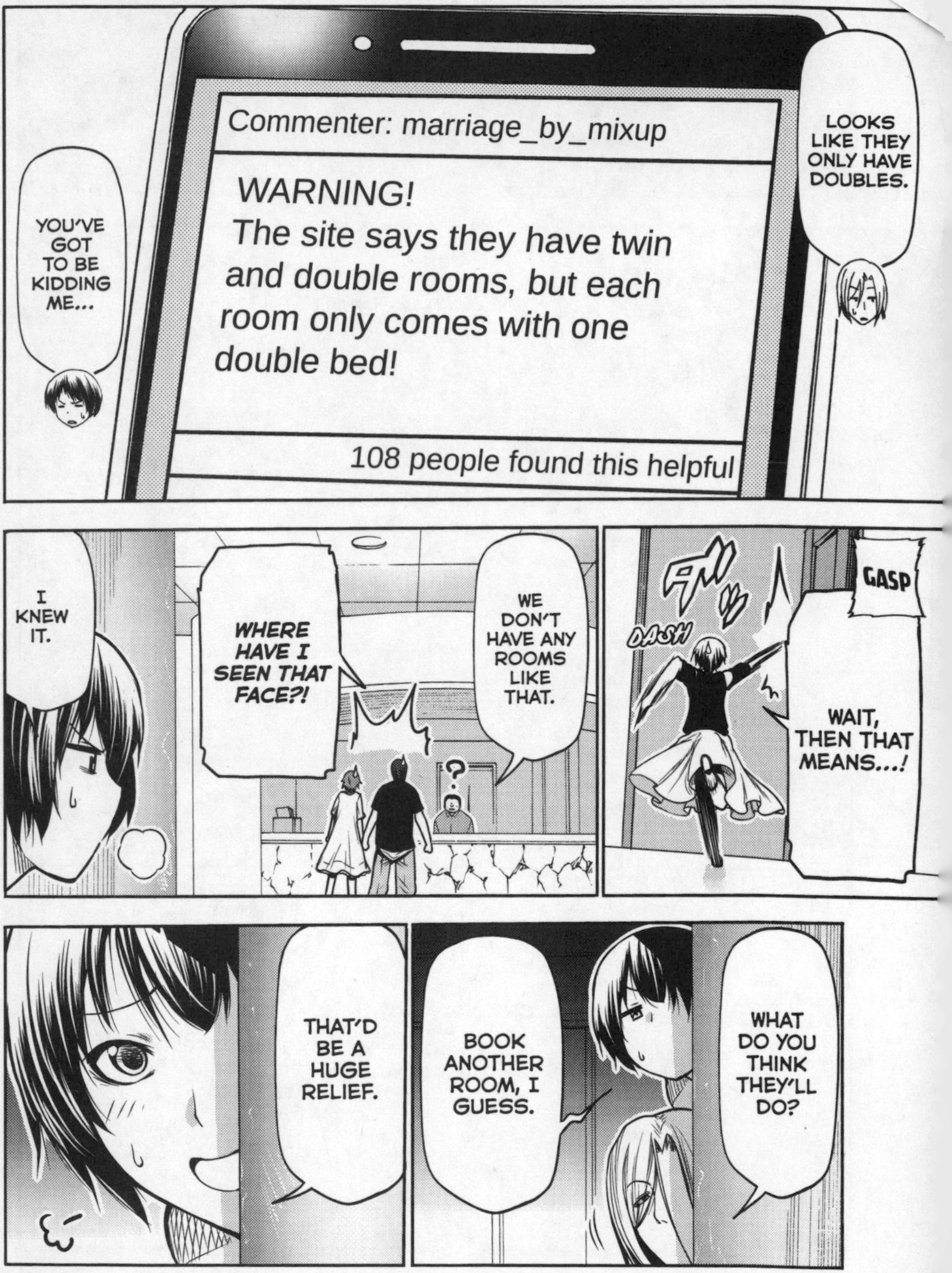
LOOKS LIKE THEY ONLY HAVE DOUBLES.
Commenter: marriage_by_mixup
WARNING!
The site says they have twin and double rooms, but each room only comes with one double bed!
108 people found this helpful
YOU'VE GOT TO BE KIDDING ME...
GASP
DASH
WAIT, THEN THAT MEANS...!
WE DON'T HAVE ANY ROOMS LIKE THAT.
WHERE HAVE I SEEN THAT FACE?!
I KNEW IT.
WHAT DO YOU THINK THEY'LL DO?
BOOK ANOTHER ROOM, I GUESS.
THAT'D BE A HUGE RELIEF.

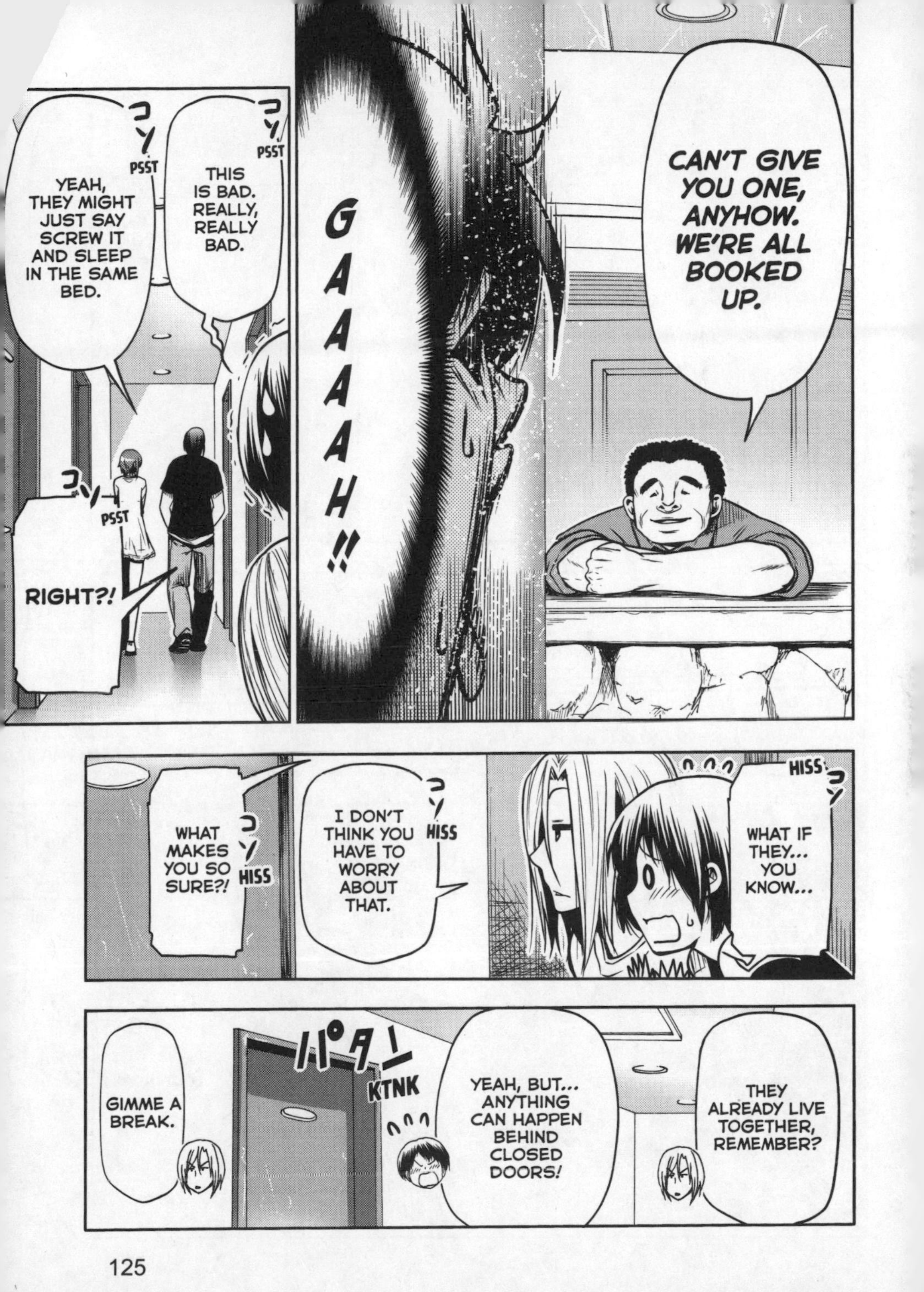
CAN'T GIVE YOU ONE, ANYHOW. WE'RE ALL BOOKED UP.
GAAAAAH!!
PSST
THIS IS BAD. REALLY, REALLY BAD.
PSST
YEAH, THEY MIGHT JUST SAY SCREW IT AND SLEEP IN THE SAME BED.
PSST
RIGHT?!
HISS
WHAT IF THEY... YOU KNOW...
HISS
I DON'T THINK YOU HAVE TO WORRY ABOUT THAT.
HISS
WHAT MAKES YOU SO SURE?!
THEY ALREADY LIVE TOGETHER, REMEMBER?
YEAH, BUT... ANYTHING CAN HAPPEN BEHIND CLOSED DOORS!
KTNK
GIMME A BREAK.

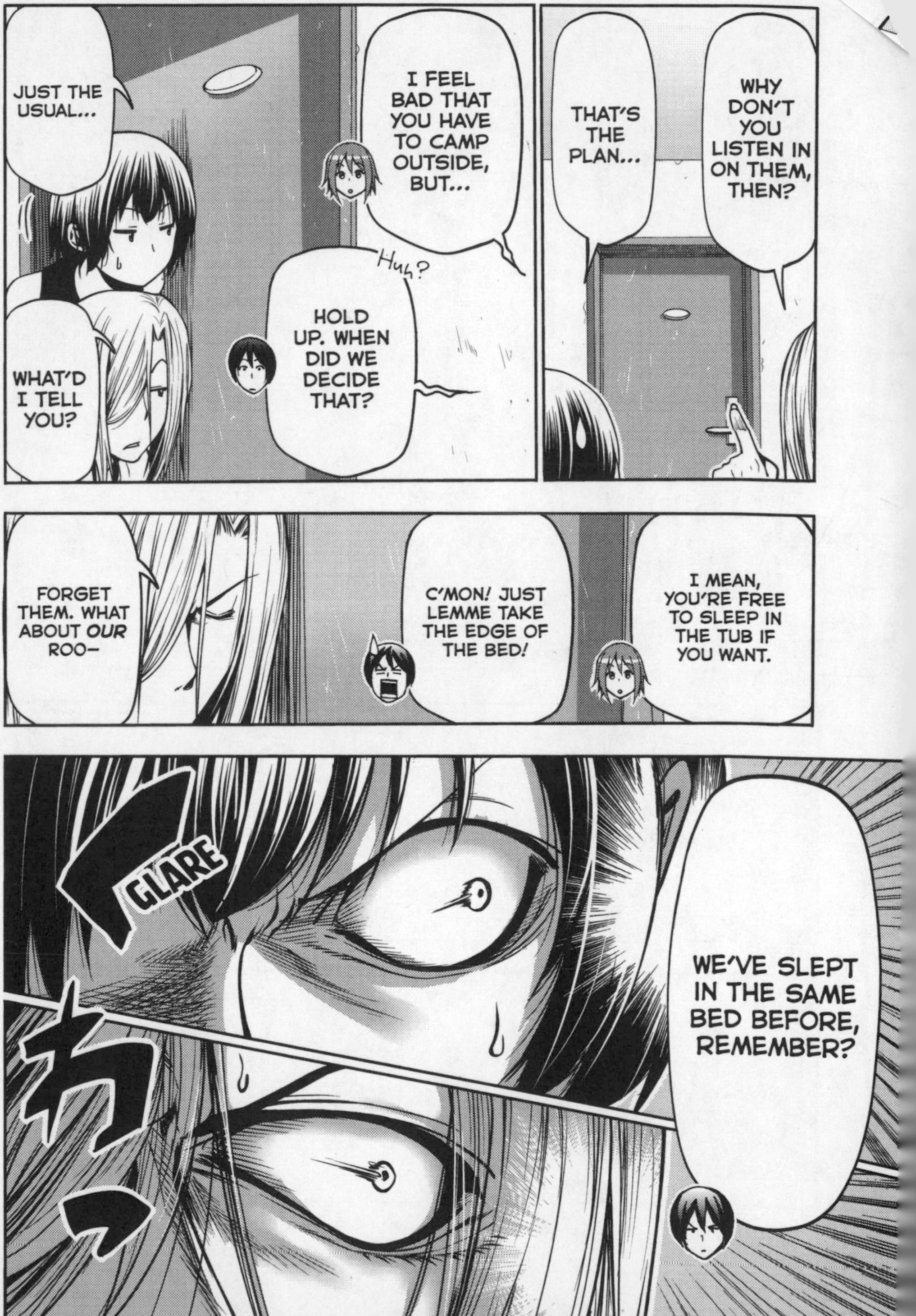
WHY DON'T YOU LISTEN IN ON THEM, THEN?
THAT'S THE PLAN...
I FEEL BAD THAT YOU HAVE TO CAMP OUTSIDE, BUT...
JUST THE USUAL...
Huh?
HOLD UP. WHEN DID WE DECIDE THAT?
WHAT'D I TELL YOU?
I MEAN, YOU'RE FREE TO SLEEP IN THE TUB IF YOU WANT.
C'MON! JUST LEMME TAKE THE EDGE OF THE BED!
FORGET THEM. WHAT ABOUT *OUR* ROO—
WE'VE SLEPT IN THE SAME BED BEFORE, REMEMBER?
GLARE

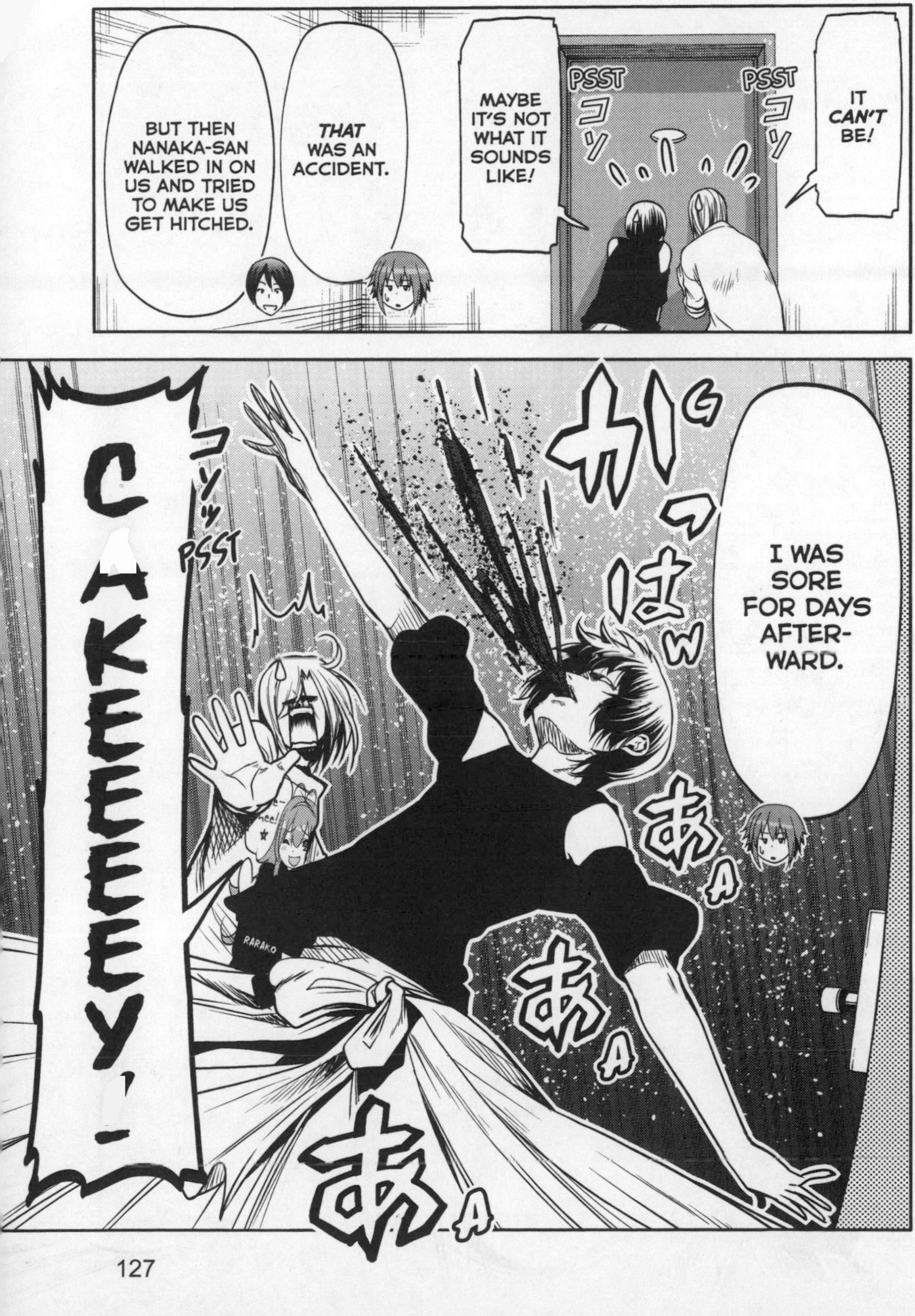
IT *CAN'T* BE!
PSST
コツ
MAYBE IT'S NOT WHAT IT SOUNDS LIKE!
PSST
コツ
THAT WAS AN ACCIDENT.
BUT THEN NANAKA-SAN WALKED IN ON US AND TRIED TO MAKE US GET HITCHED.
I WAS SORE FOR DAYS AFTER-WARD.
カっはあああ
G W A A A
コツッ
PSST
CAKEEEEY!!
RARAKO

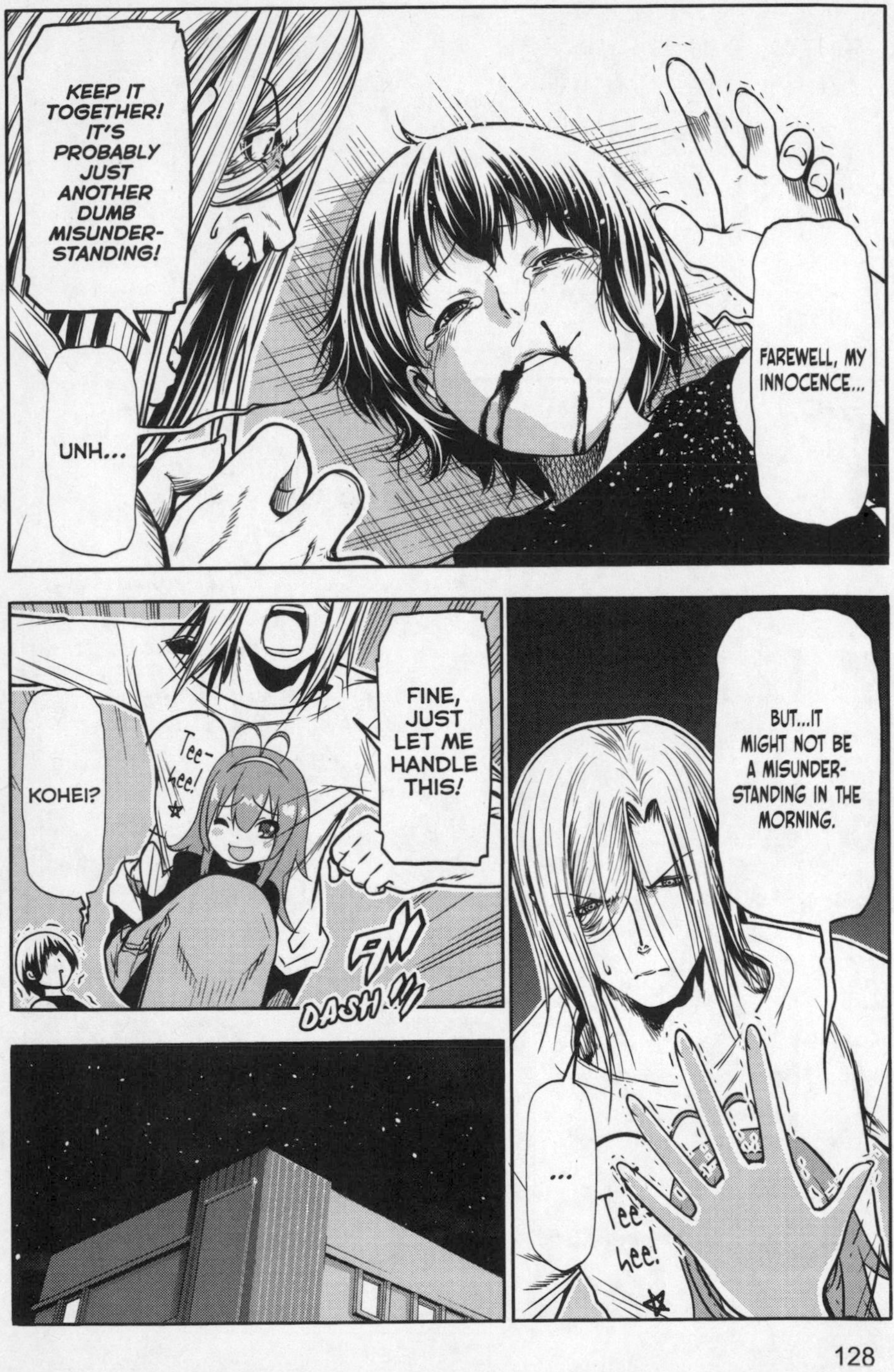
FAREWELL, MY INNOCENCE...
KEEP IT TOGETHER! IT'S PROBABLY JUST ANOTHER DUMB MISUNDER-STANDING!
UNH...
BUT...IT MIGHT NOT BE A MISUNDER-STANDING IN THE MORNING.
...
Tee-hee!
FINE, JUST LET ME HANDLE THIS!
Tee-hee!
KOHEI?
DASH

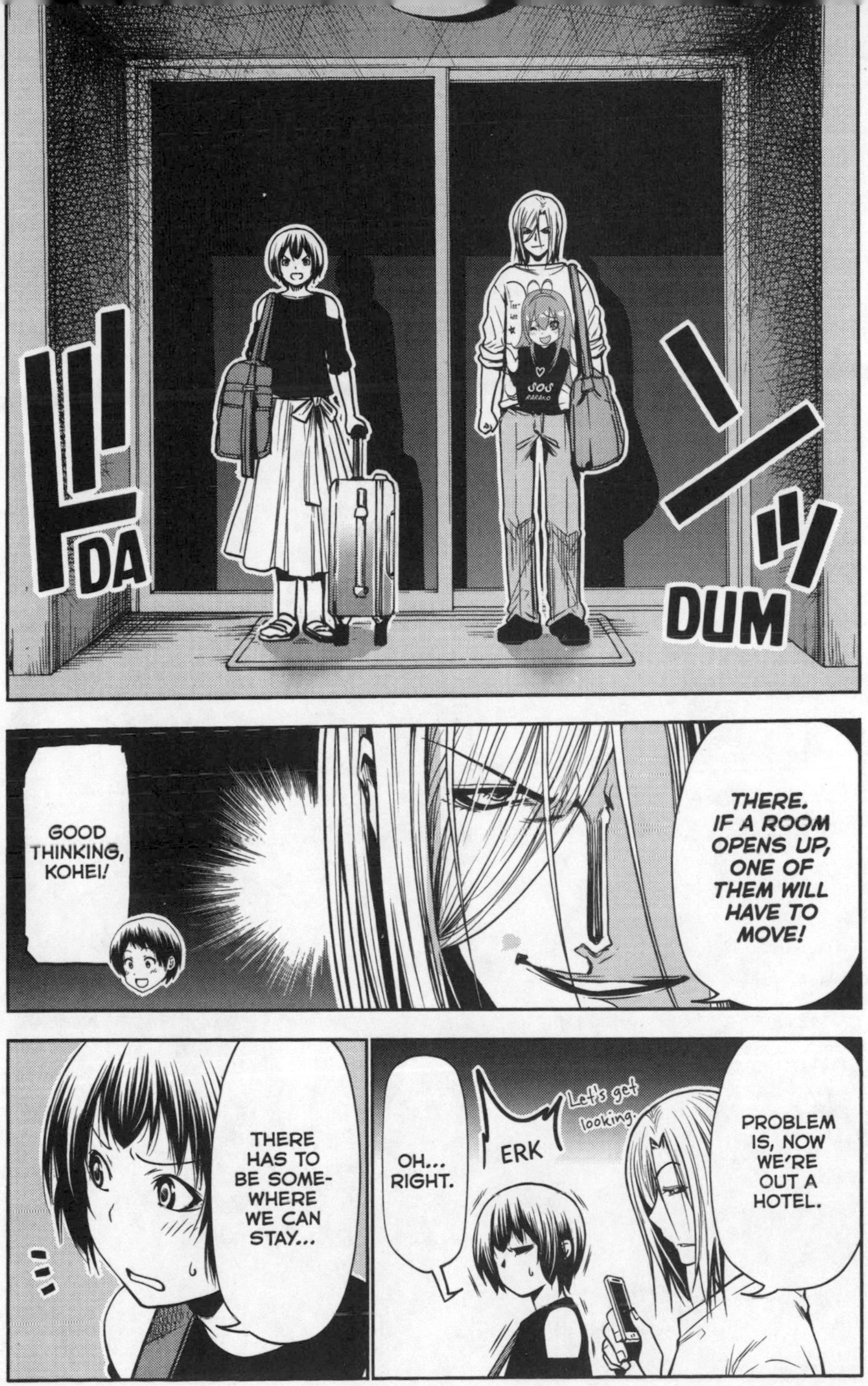
DA
DUM
THERE. IF A ROOM OPENS UP, ONE OF THEM WILL HAVE TO MOVE!
GOOD THINKING, KOHEI!
PROBLEM IS, NOW WE'RE OUT A HOTEL.
Let's get looking.
ERK
OH... RIGHT.
THERE HAS TO BE SOME-WHERE WE CAN STAY...

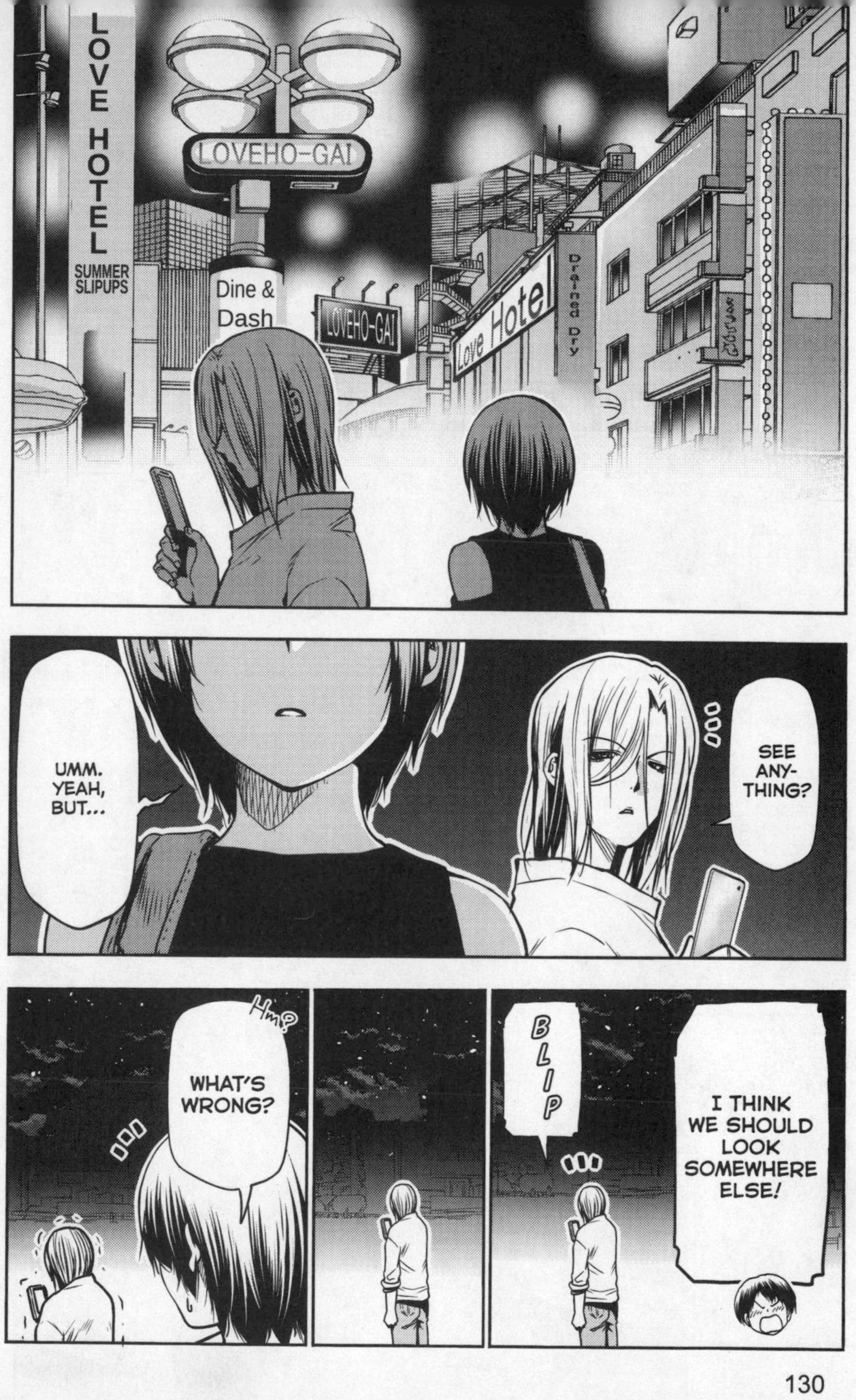
Love Hotel
Drained Dry
LOVEHO-GAI
Dine & Dash
LOVEHO-GAI
LOVE HOTEL
SUMMER SLIPUPS
SEE ANY-THING?
UMM. YEAH, BUT...
BLIP
I THINK WE SHOULD LOOK SOMEWHERE ELSE!
Hm?
WHAT'S WRONG?

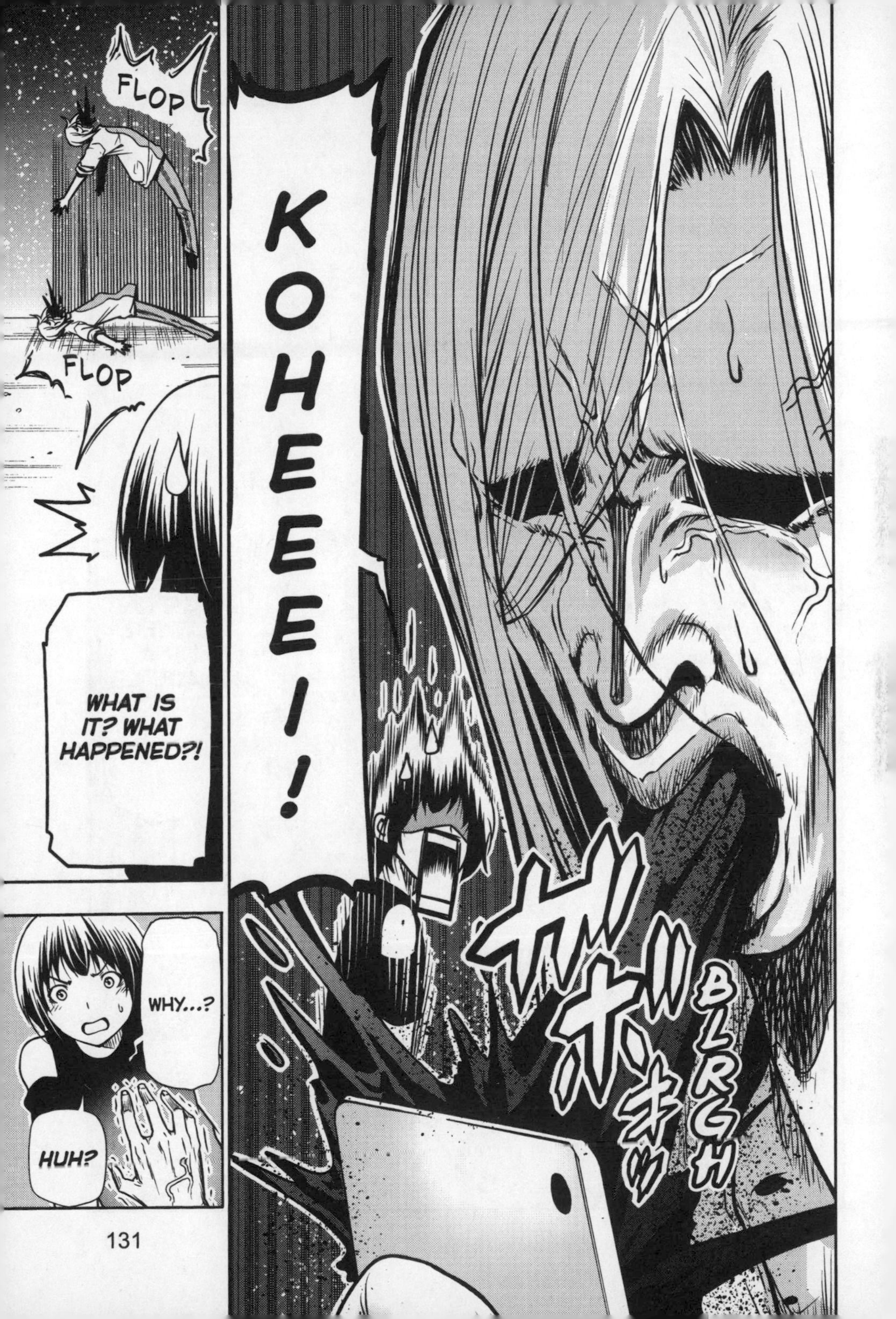
KOHEEEI!!
BLRGH
FLOP
FLOP
WHAT IS IT? WHAT HAPPENED?!
WHY...?
HUH?

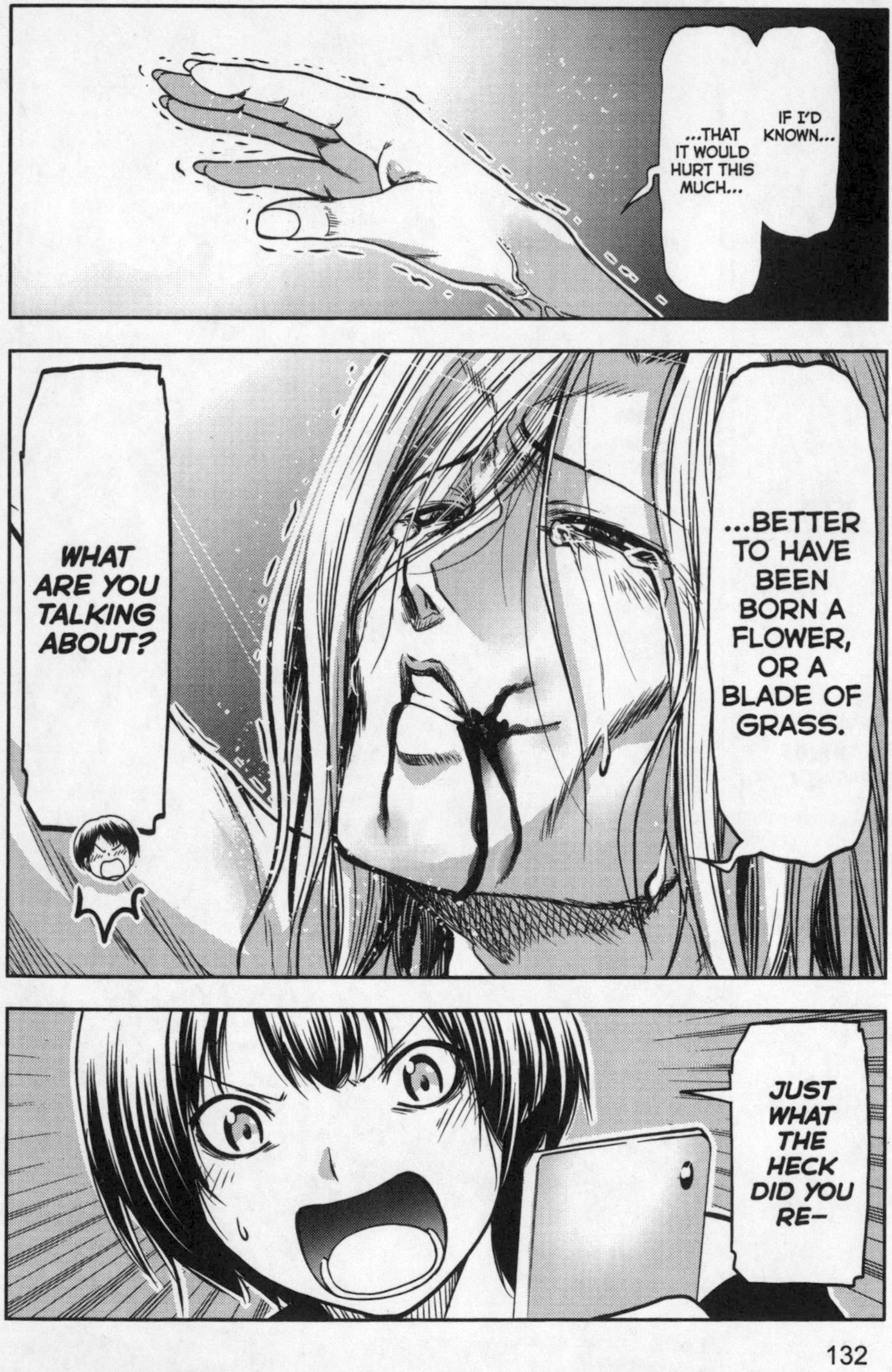
IF I'D KNOWN...
...THAT IT WOULD HURT THIS MUCH...
...BETTER TO HAVE BEEN BORN A FLOWER, OR A BLADE OF GRASS.
WHAT ARE YOU TALKING ABOUT?
JUST WHAT THE HECK DID YOU RE–

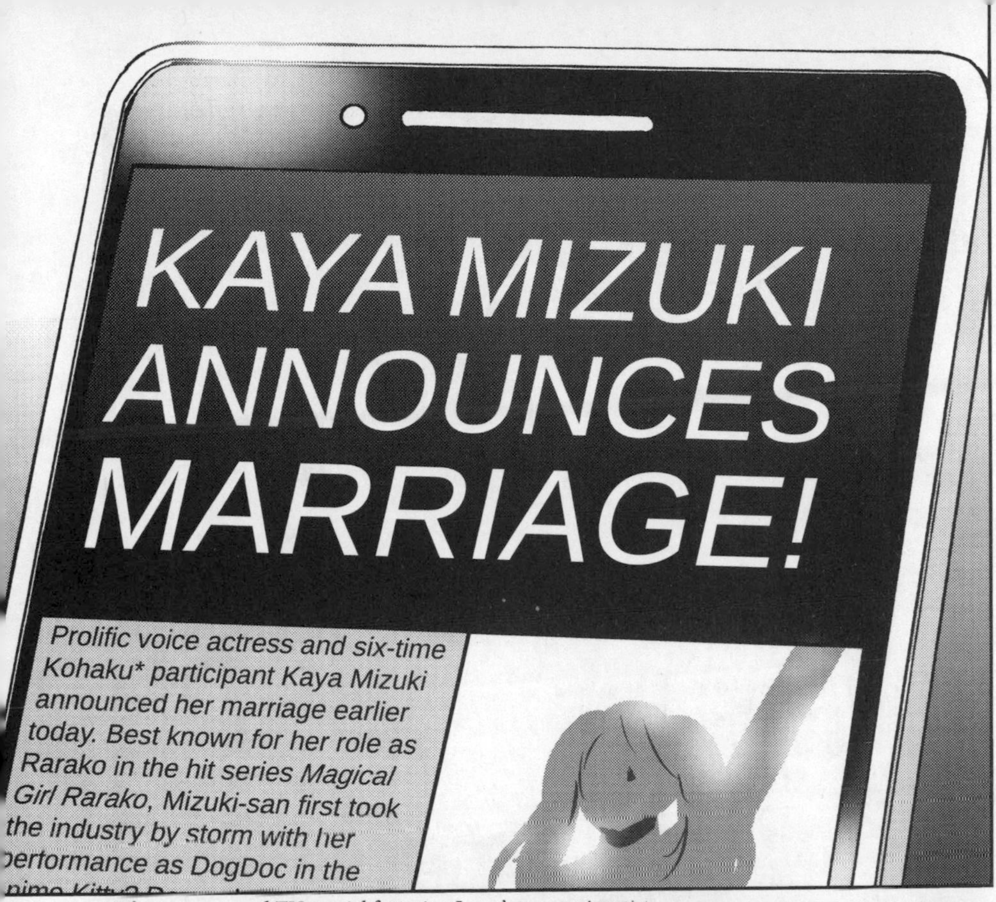
KAYA MIZUKI ANNOUNCES MARRIAGE!
Prolific voice actress and six-time Kohaku* participant Kaya Mizuki announced her marriage earlier today. Best known for her role as Rarako in the hit series Magical Girl Rarako, Mizuki-san first took the industry by storm with her performance as DogDoc in the

*A famous year-end TV special featuring Japan's top music artists.

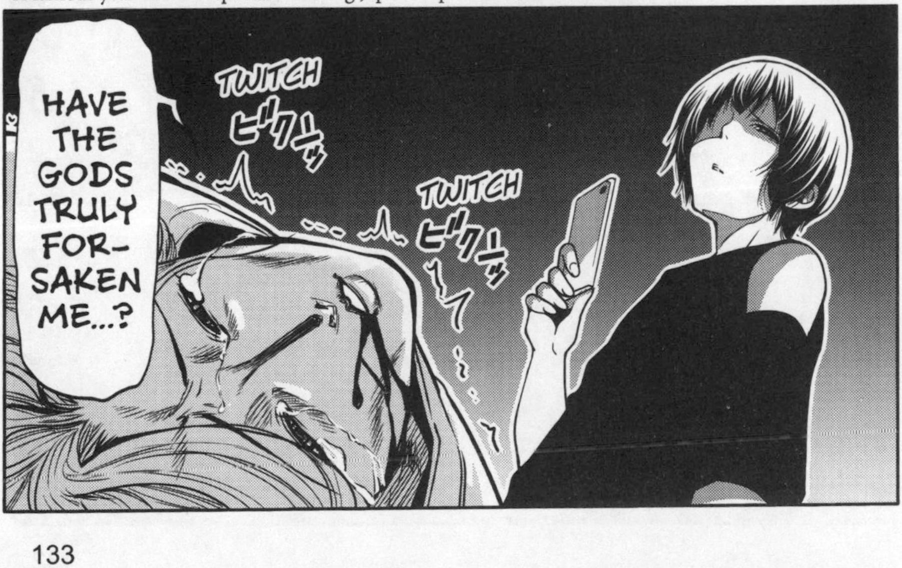
HAVE THE GODS TRULY FOR-SAKEN ME...?
TWITCH
ビクッ
TWITCH
ビクッ

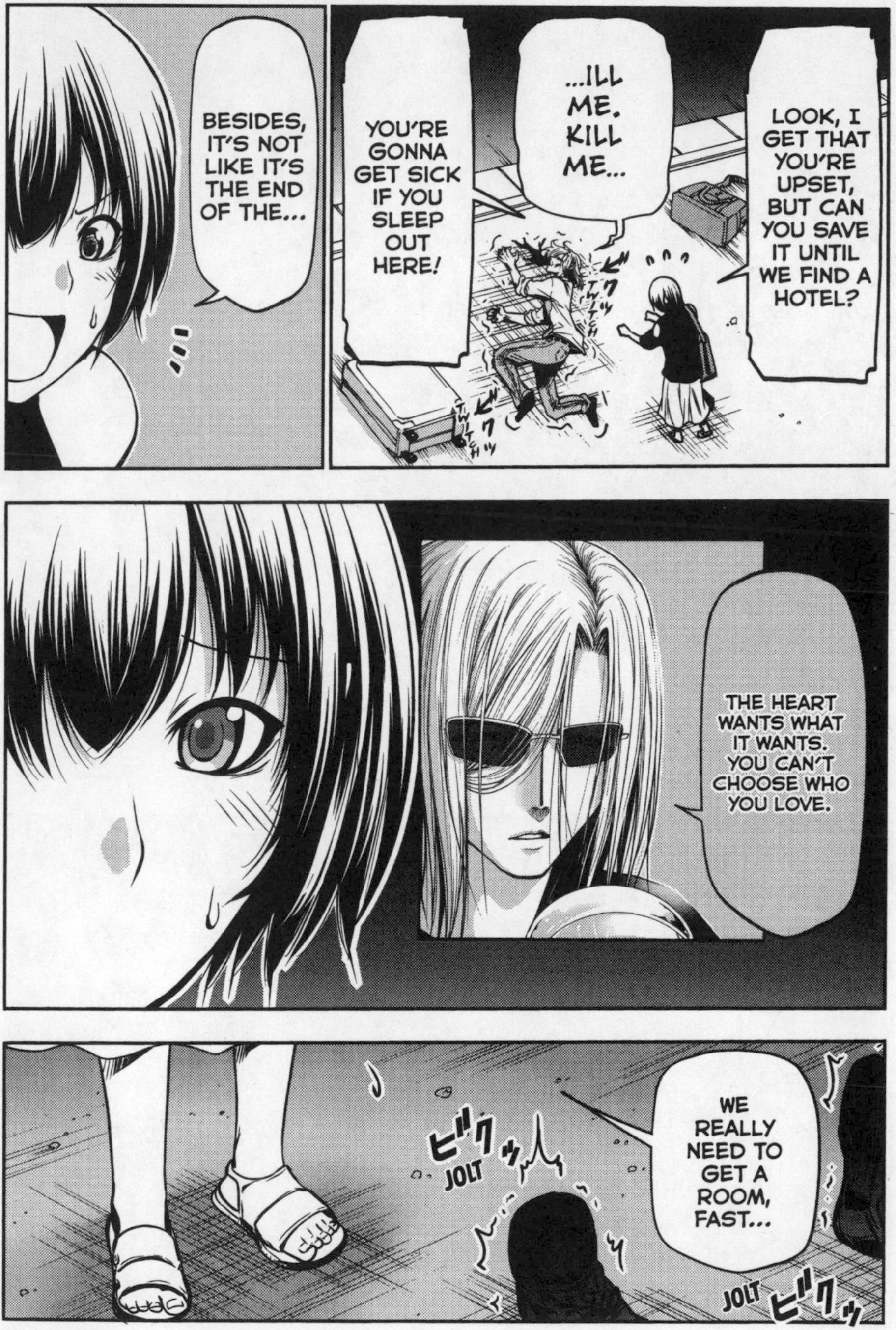
LOOK, I GET THAT YOU'RE UPSET, BUT CAN YOU SAVE IT UNTIL WE FIND A HOTEL?
...ILL ME. KILL ME. KILL ME...
TWITCH
YOU'RE GONNA GET SICK IF YOU SLEEP OUT HERE!
TWITCH
BESIDES, IT'S NOT LIKE IT'S THE END OF THE...
THE HEART WANTS WHAT IT WANTS. YOU CAN'T CHOOSE WHO YOU LOVE.
WE REALLY NEED TO GET A ROOM, FAST...
JOLT
JOLT

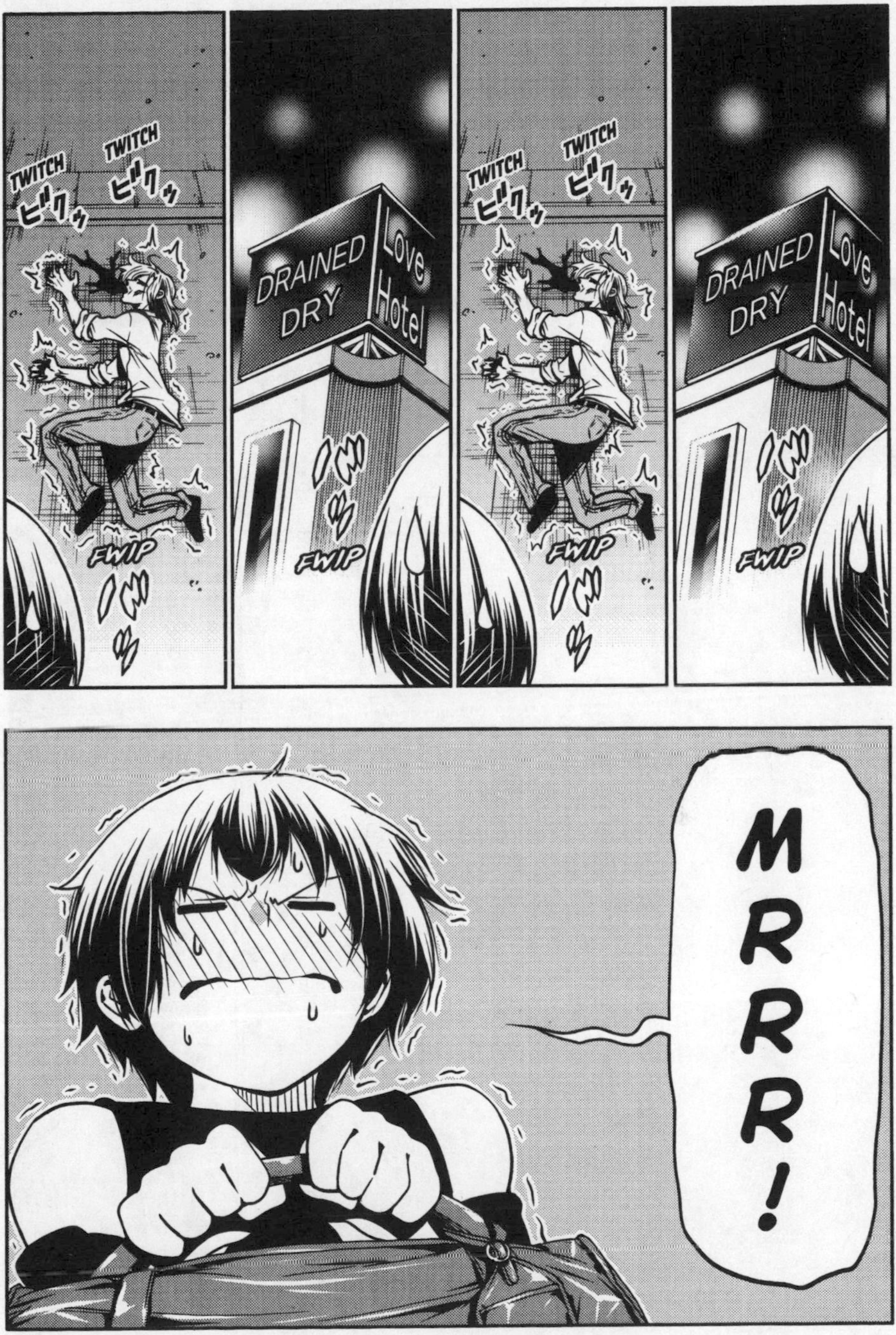
DRAINED DRY
Love Hotel
FWIP
TWITCH ビクッ
TWITCH ビクッ
FWIP
DRAINED DRY
Love Hotel
FWIP
TWITCH ビクッ
TWITCH ビクッ
FWIP
MRRR!

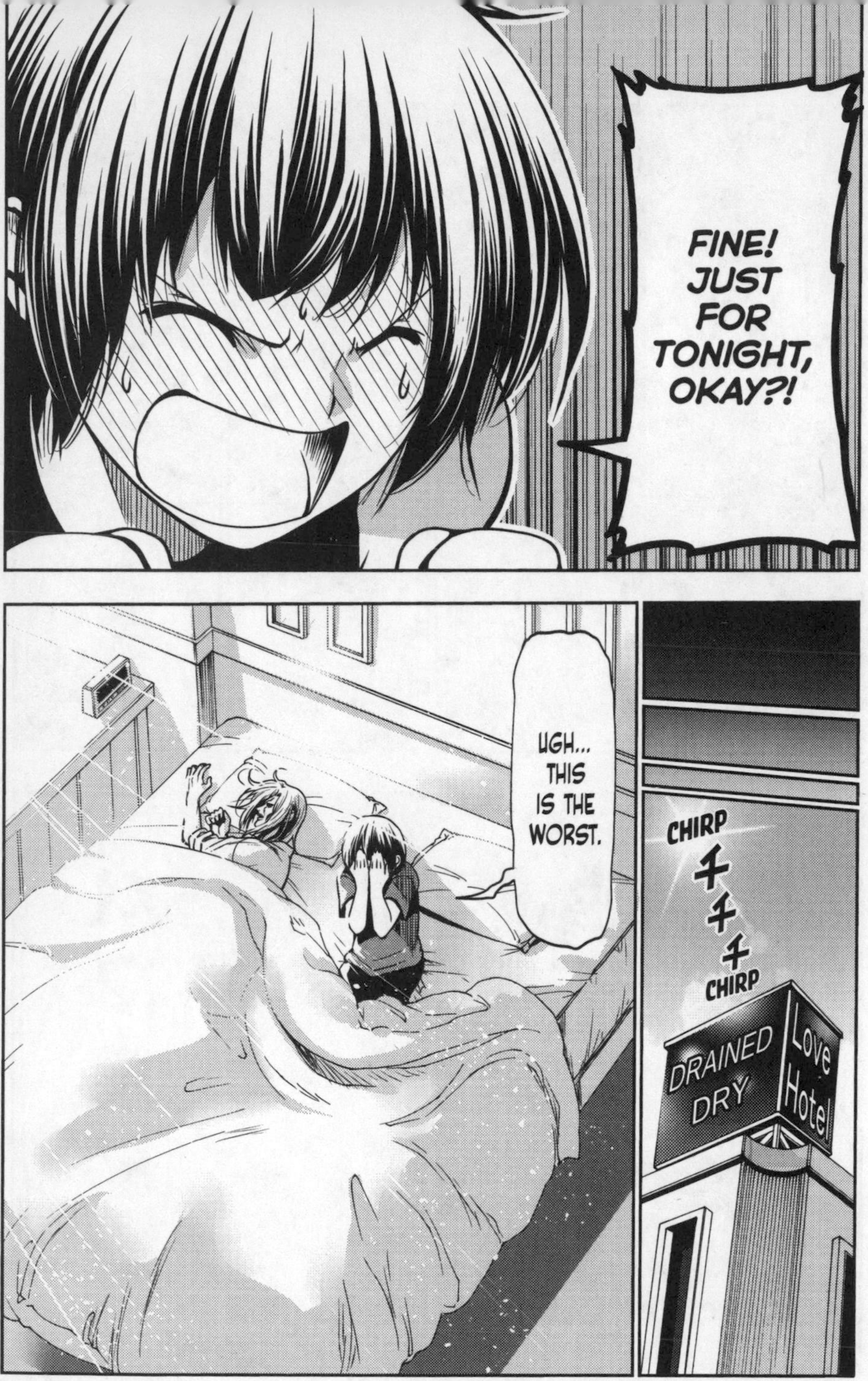
FINE! JUST FOR TONIGHT, OKAY?!
CHIRP
CHIRP
DRAINED DRY
Love Hotel
UGH... THIS IS THE WORST.

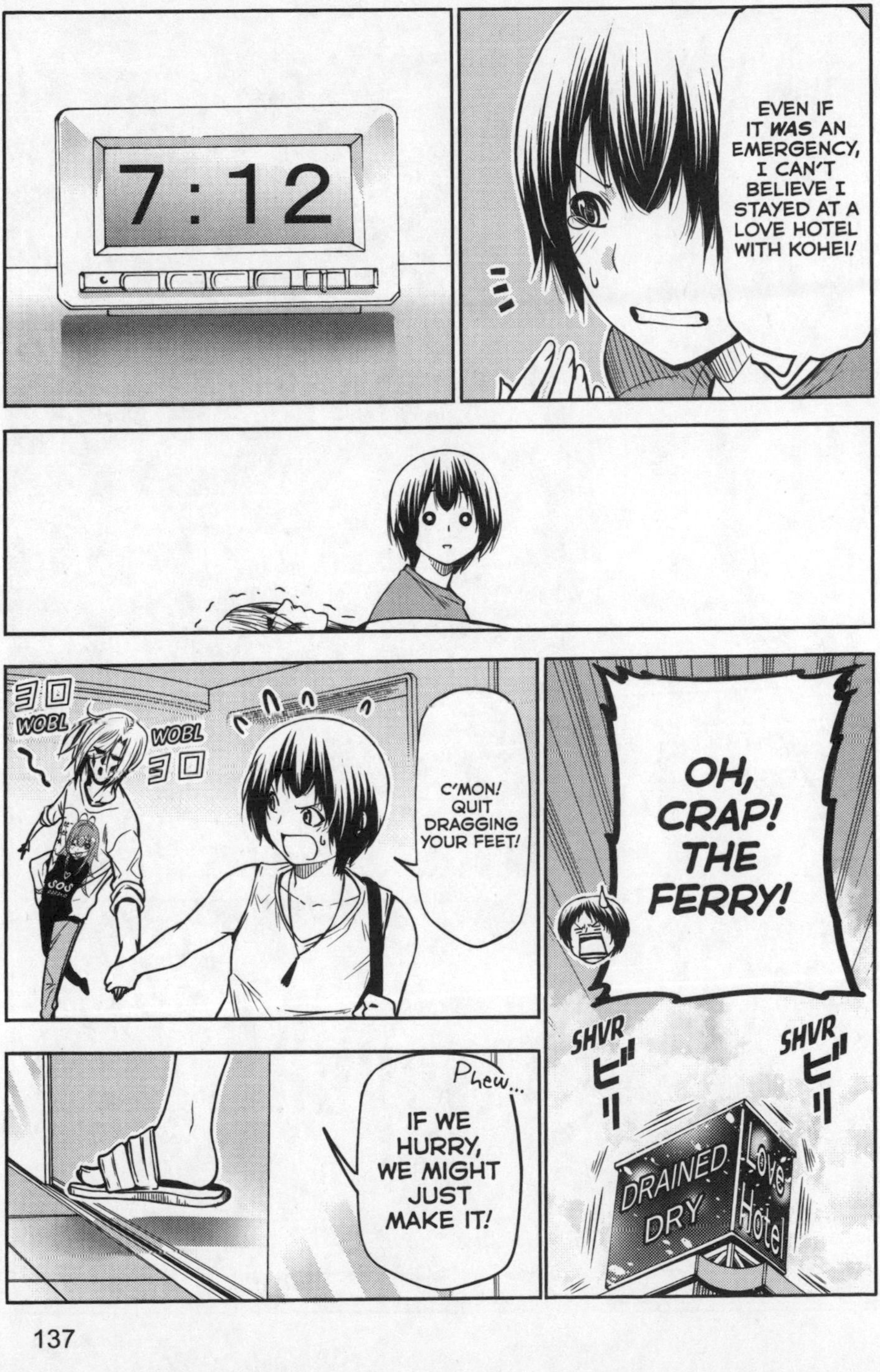
EVEN IF IT WAS AN EMERGENCY, I CAN'T BELIEVE I STAYED AT A LOVE HOTEL WITH KOHEI!
7:12
OH, CRAP! THE FERRY!
SHVR ビリ
SHVR ビリ
Love Hotel
DRAINED DRY
C'MON! QUIT DRAGGING YOUR FEET!
WOBL ヨロ
WOBL ヨロ
Phew...
IF WE HURRY, WE MIGHT JUST MAKE IT!

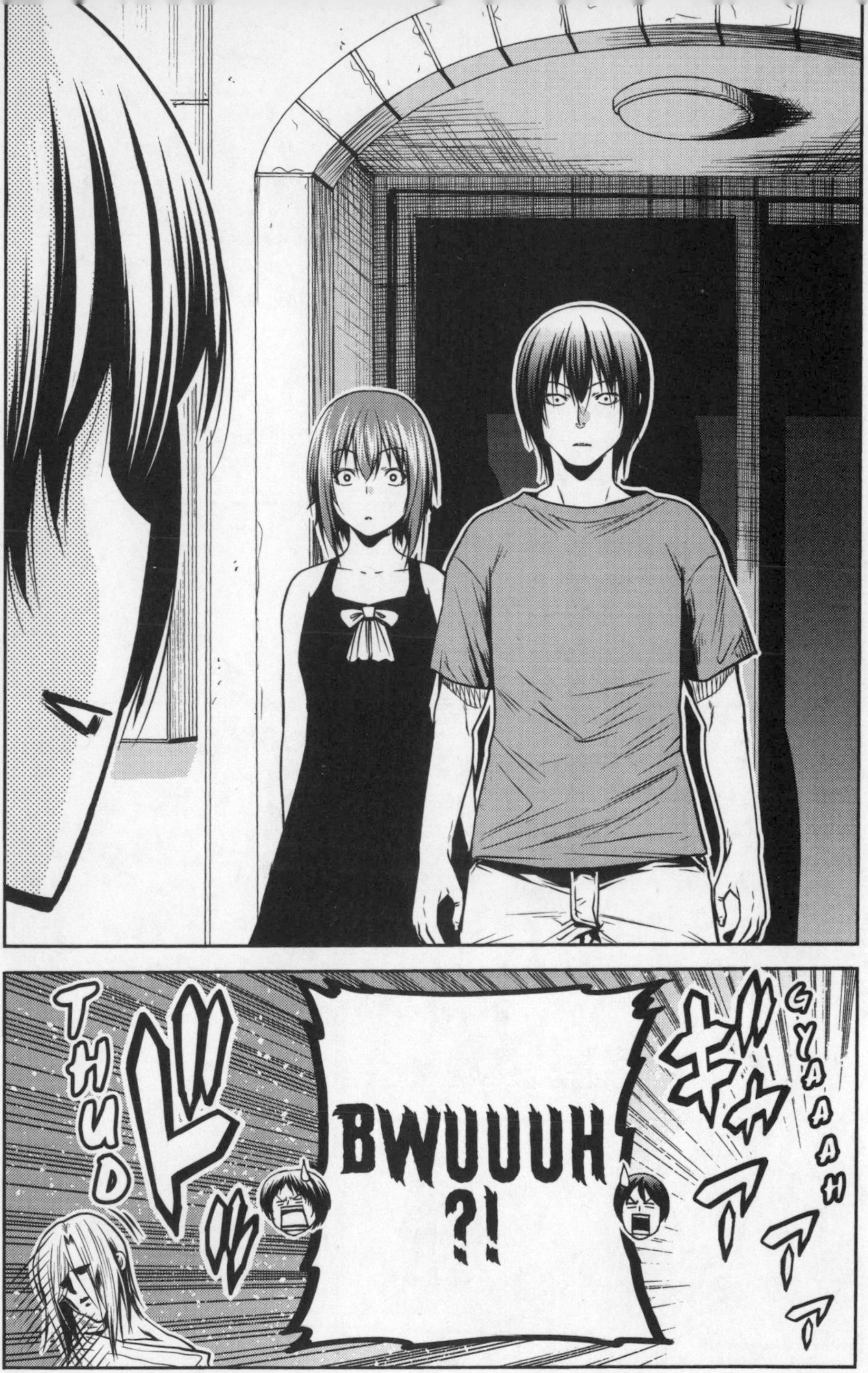
GYAAAH
BWUUUH?!
THUD

IKEGOSHI TRENDING ON SNS
IKEGOSHI
Did I do some-thing ...?
RANKING
1. IKEGOSHI-KUN
2. OKINAWA
3. YUICHI IKEGOSHI
4. PORN SHOOT

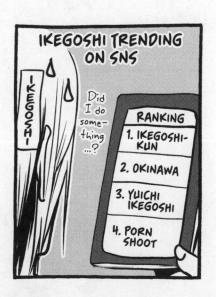

Grand Blue Dreaming

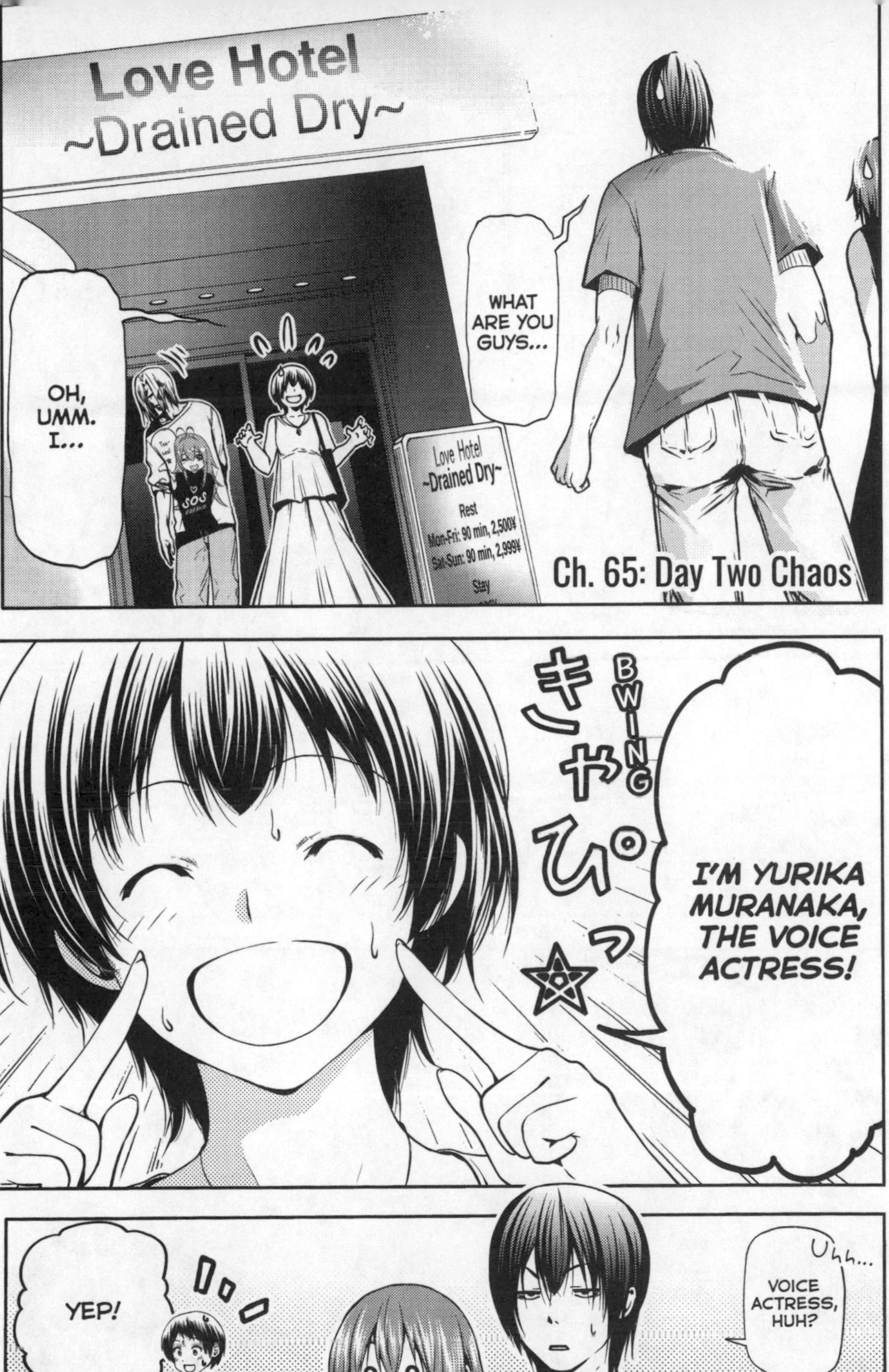
Love Hotel
~Drained Dry~
Ch. 65: Day Two Chaos
WHAT ARE YOU GUYS...
Love Hotel
~Drained Dry~
Rest
Mon-Fri: 90 min, 2,500¥
Sat-Sun: 90 min, 2,999¥
Stay
OH, UMM. I...
きゃぴっ☆
BWING
I'M YURIKA MURANAKA, THE VOICE ACTRESS!
Uhh...
VOICE ACTRESS, HUH?
YEP!

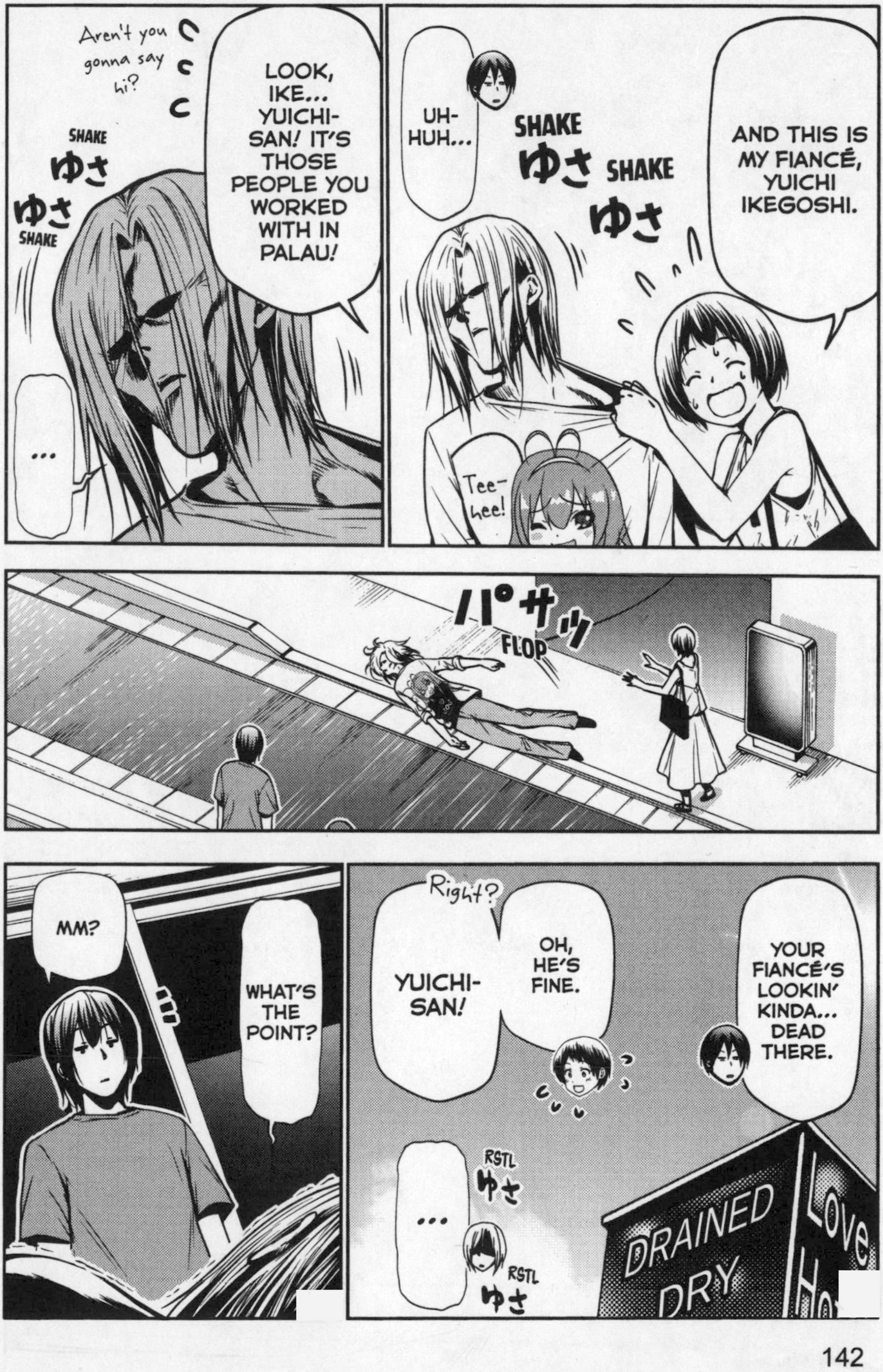
AND THIS IS MY FIANCÉ, YUICHI IKEGOSHI.
SHAKE ゆさ SHAKE ゆさ
UH-HUH...
Tee-hee!
LOOK, IKE... YUICHI-SAN! IT'S THOSE PEOPLE YOU WORKED WITH IN PALAU!
Aren't you gonna say hi?
SHAKE ゆさ ゆさ SHAKE
...
パサッ FLOP
YOUR FIANCÉ'S LOOKIN' KINDA... DEAD THERE.
OH, HE'S FINE.
YUICHI-SAN!
Right?
...
RSTL ゆさ RSTL ゆさ
DRAINED DRY
Love Ho
MM?
WHAT'S THE POINT?

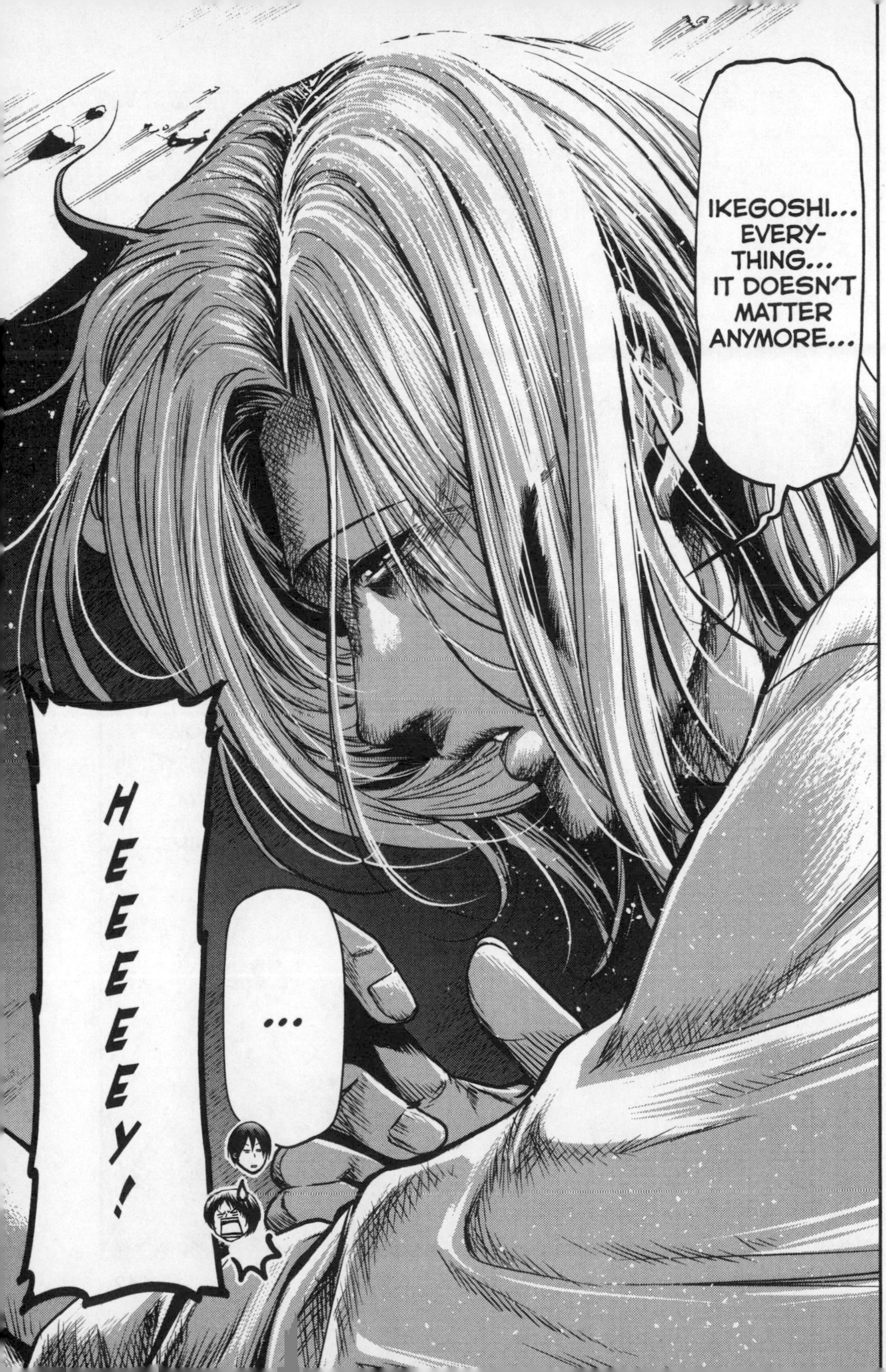
IKEGOSHI... EVERY-THING... IT DOESN'T MATTER ANYMORE...
...
HEEEEEEY!

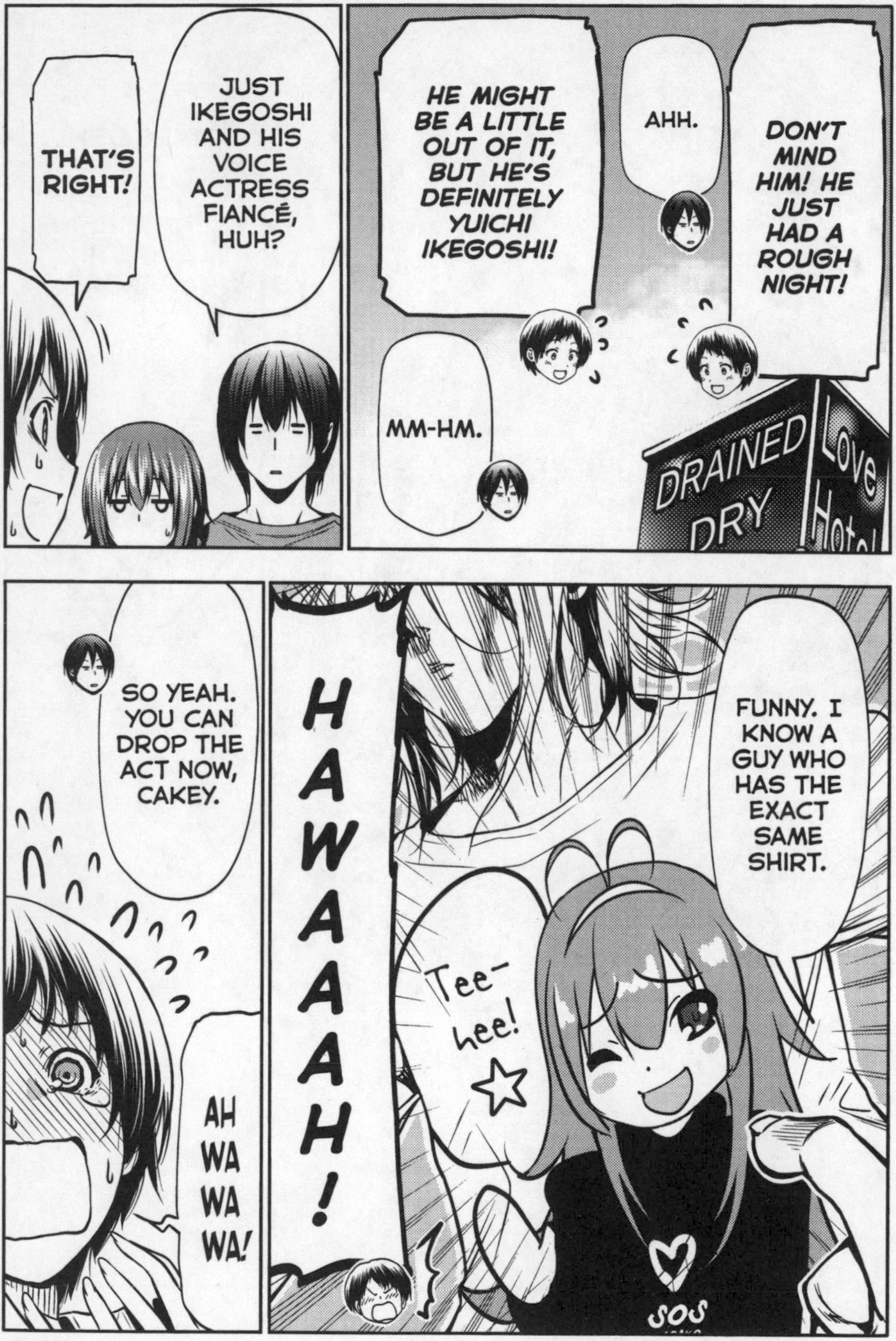

DON'T MIND HIM! HE JUST HAD A ROUGH NIGHT!
AHH.
HE MIGHT BE A LITTLE OUT OF IT, BUT HE'S DEFINITELY YUICHI IKEGOSHI!
MM-HM.
DRAINED DRY
Love
JUST IKEGOSHI AND HIS VOICE ACTRESS FIANCÉ, HUH?
THAT'S RIGHT!
FUNNY. I KNOW A GUY WHO HAS THE EXACT SAME SHIRT.
Tee-hee! ☆
SOS
HAWAAAAH!
SO YEAH. YOU CAN DROP THE ACT NOW, CAKEY.
AH WA WA WA WA!

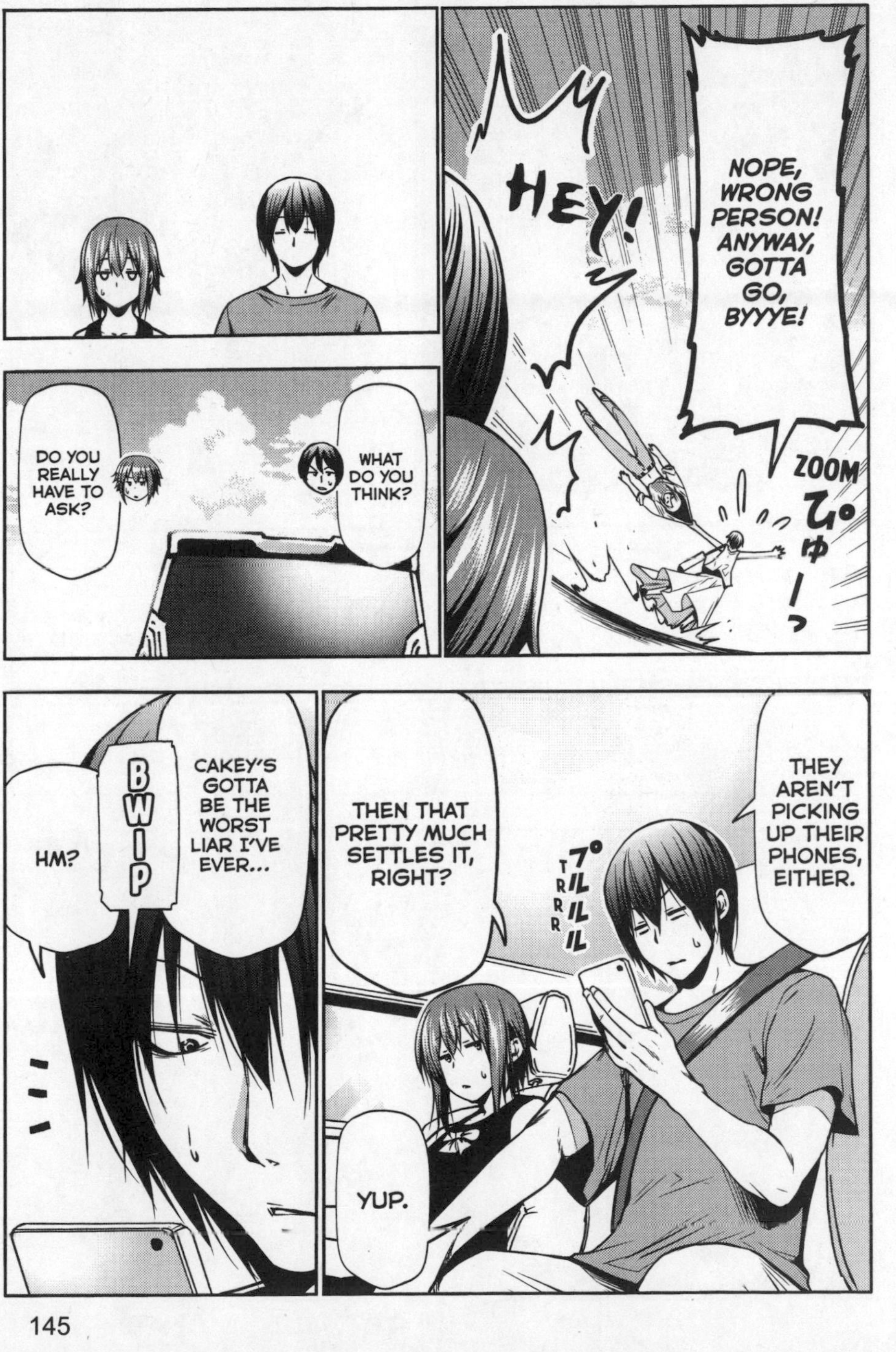

NOPE, WRONG PERSON! ANYWAY, GOTTA GO, BYYYE!
HEY!
ZOOM
ぴゅーっ
WHAT DO YOU THINK?
DO YOU REALLY HAVE TO ASK?
THEY AREN'T PICKING UP THEIR PHONES, EITHER.
TRRR
プルルル
THEN THAT PRETTY MUCH SETTLES IT, RIGHT?
YUP.
CAKEY'S GOTTA BE THE WORST LIAR I'VE EVER...
BWIP
HM?

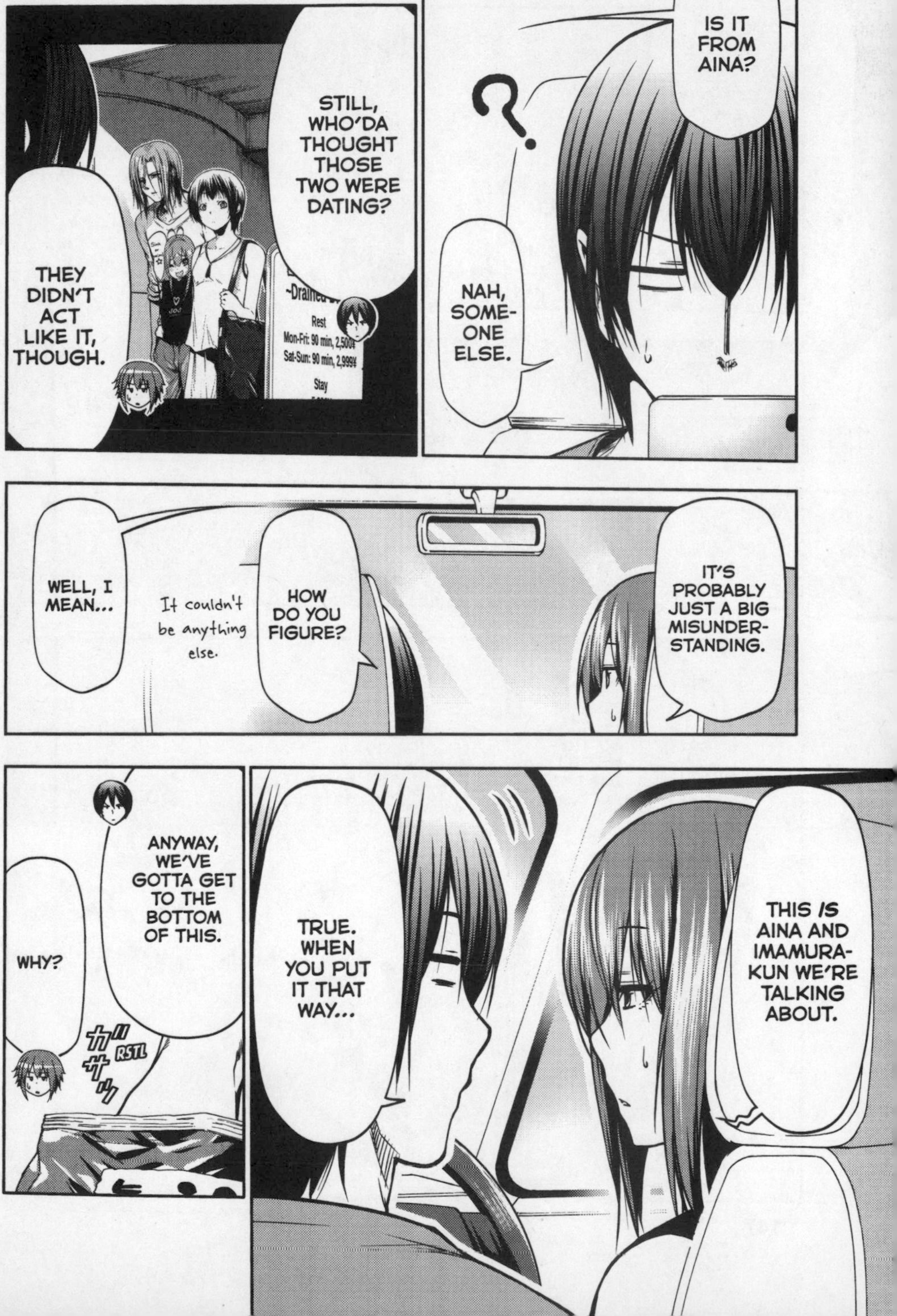
IS IT FROM AINA?
?
NAH, SOME-ONE ELSE.
STILL, WHO'DA THOUGHT THOSE TWO WERE DATING?
THEY DIDN'T ACT LIKE IT, THOUGH.
Rest
Mon-Fri: 90 min, 2,500¥
Sat-Sun: 90 min, 2,999¥
Stay
IT'S PROBABLY JUST A BIG MISUNDER-STANDING.
HOW DO YOU FIGURE?
It couldn't be anything else.
WELL, I MEAN...
THIS *IS* AINA AND IMAMURA-KUN WE'RE TALKING ABOUT.
TRUE. WHEN YOU PUT IT THAT WAY...
ANYWAY, WE'VE GOTTA GET TO THE BOTTOM OF THIS.
WHY?
RSTL

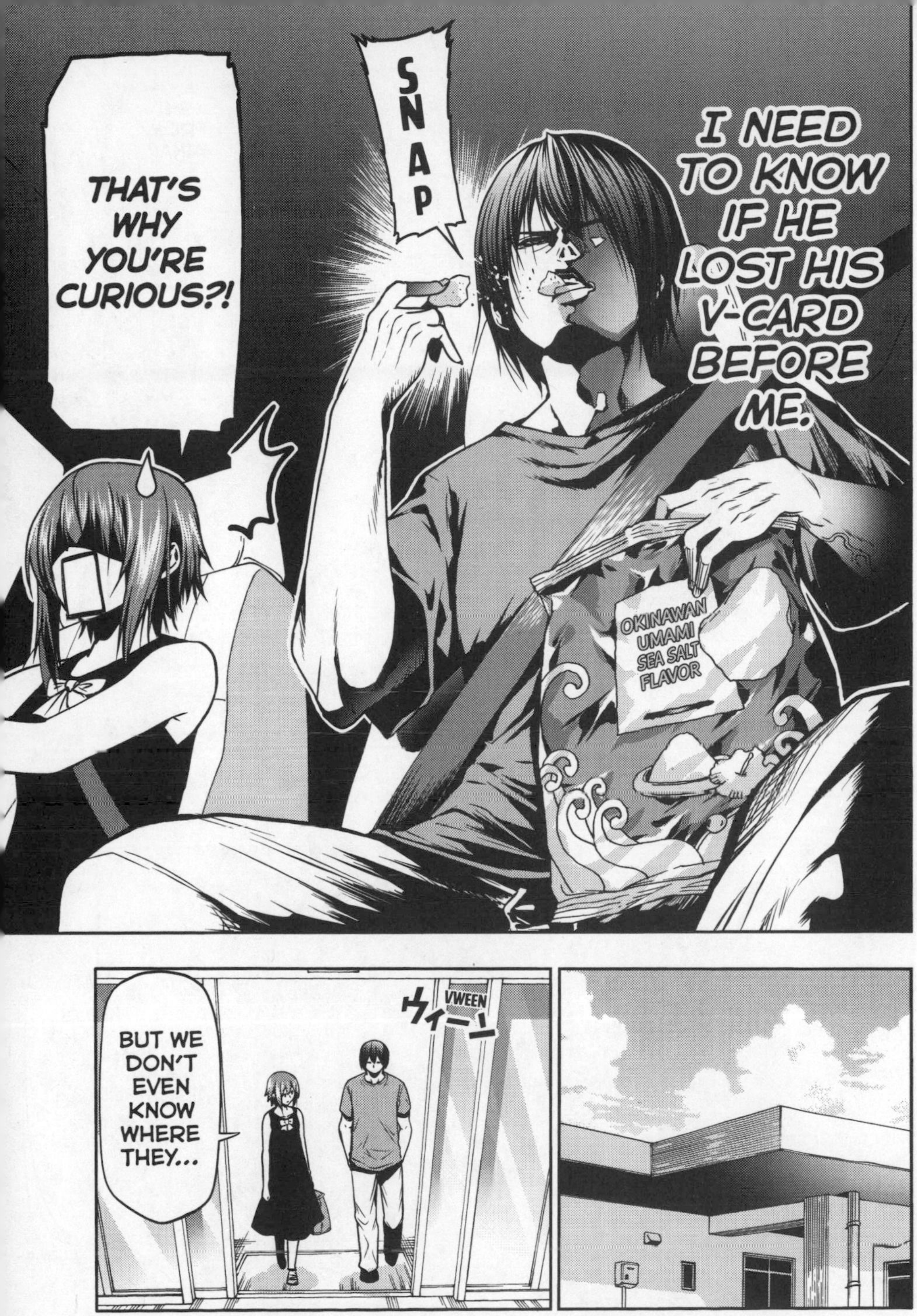
I NEED TO KNOW IF HE LOST HIS V-CARD BEFORE ME.
SNAP
THAT'S WHY YOU'RE CURIOUS?!
OKINAWAN UMAMI SEA SALT FLAVOR
ウィーン
VWEEN
BUT WE DON'T EVEN KNOW WHERE THEY...

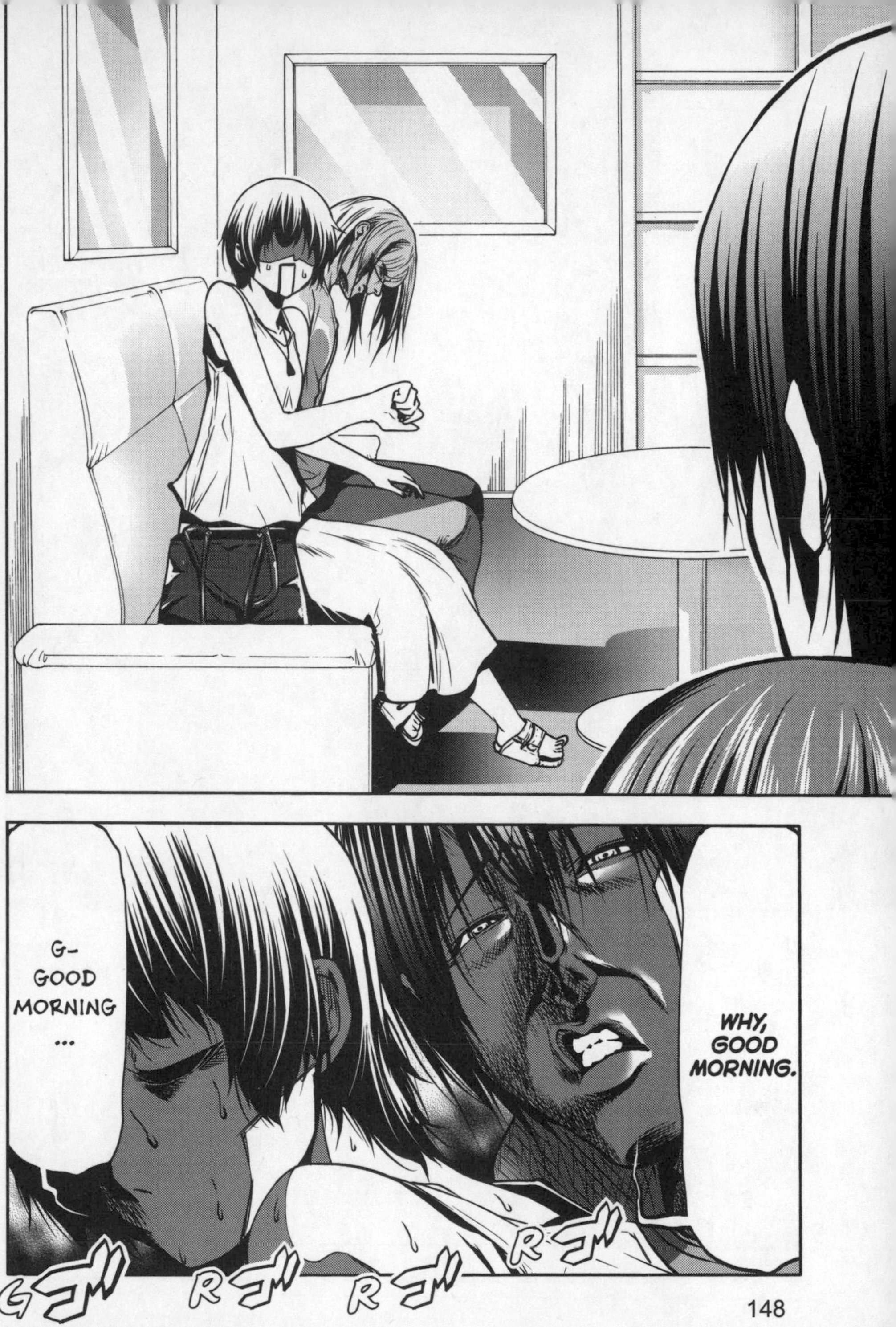
WHY, GOOD MORNING.
G- GOOD MORNING ...
GRRR

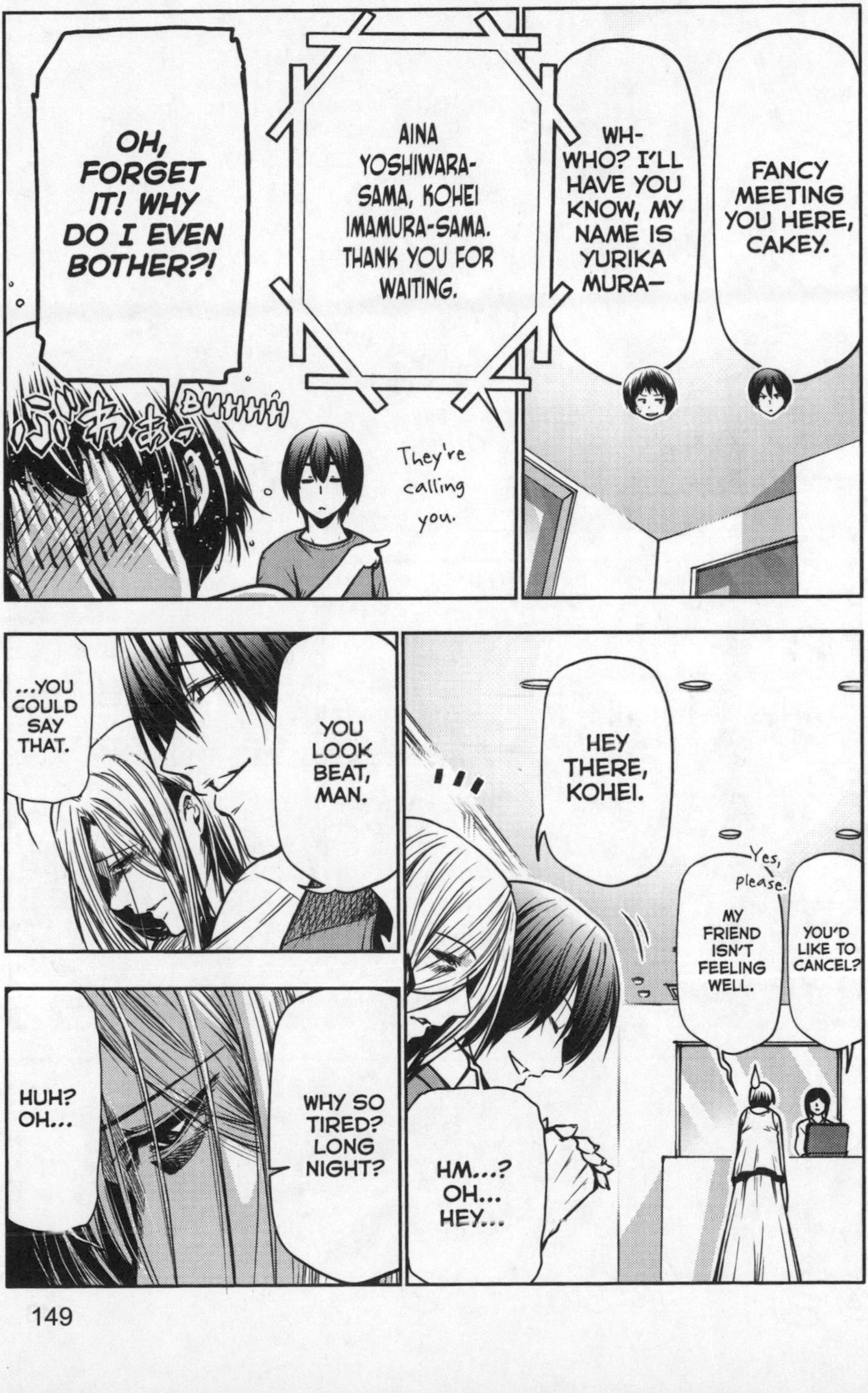
FANCY MEETING YOU HERE, CAKEY.
WH-WHO? I'LL HAVE YOU KNOW, MY NAME IS YURIKA MURA—
AINA YOSHIWARA-SAMA, KOHEI IMAMURA-SAMA. THANK YOU FOR WAITING.
They're calling you.
OH, FORGET IT! WHY DO I EVEN BOTHER?!
ぶわぁっ BUHHH
HEY THERE, KOHEI.
YOU'D LIKE TO CANCEL?
Yes, please.
MY FRIEND ISN'T FEELING WELL.
...
HM...? OH... HEY...
YOU LOOK BEAT, MAN.
...YOU COULD SAY THAT.
WHY SO TIRED? LONG NIGHT?
HUH? OH...

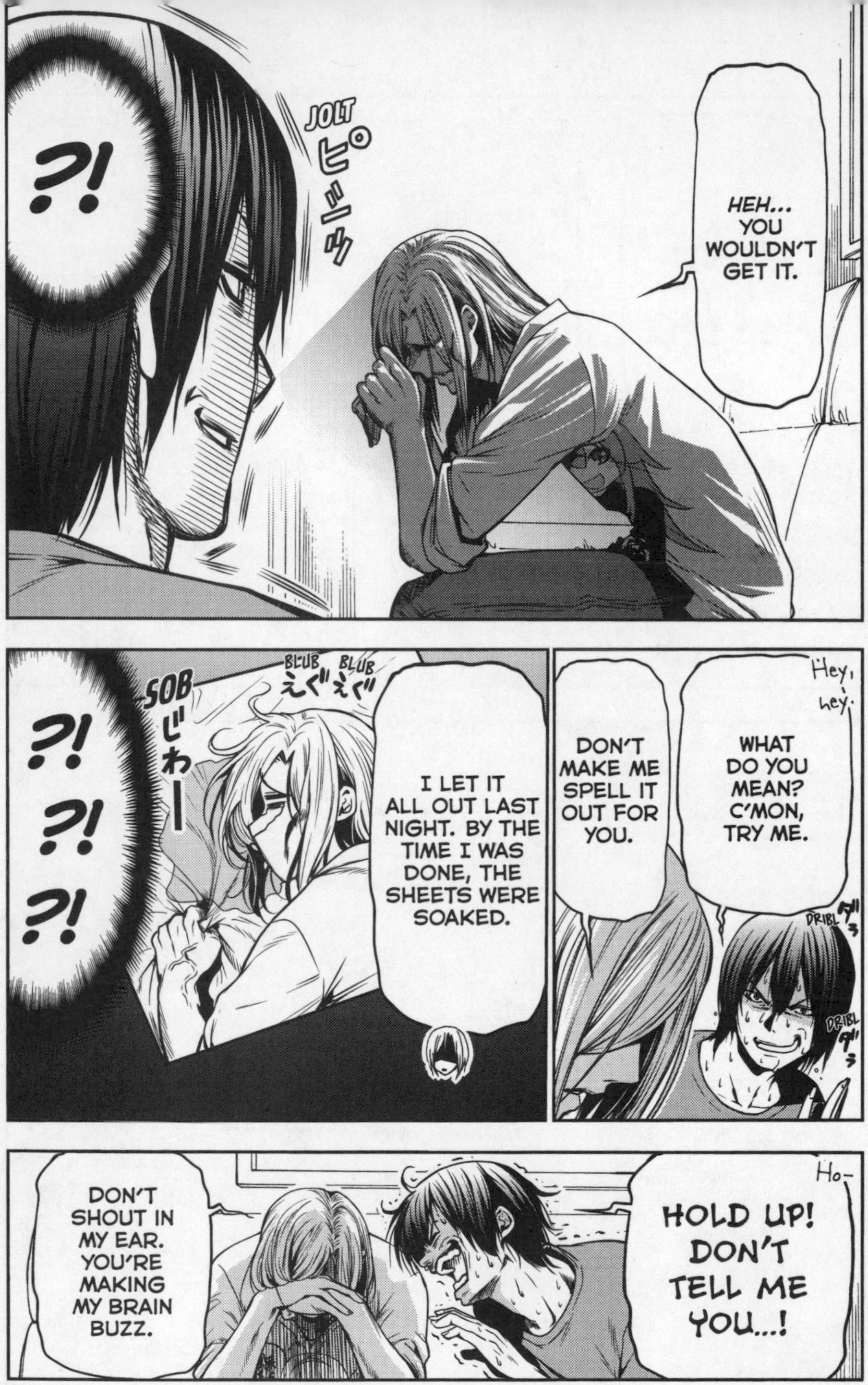
HEH... YOU WOULDN'T GET IT.
JOLT
?!
Hey, hey.
WHAT DO YOU MEAN? C'MON, TRY ME.
DON'T MAKE ME SPELL IT OUT FOR YOU.
DRIBL
DRIBL
I LET IT ALL OUT LAST NIGHT. BY THE TIME I WAS DONE, THE SHEETS WERE SOAKED.
BLUB えぐ BLUB えぐ
SOB じわー
?! ?! ?!
Ho-
HOLD UP! DON'T TELL ME YOU...!
DON'T SHOUT IN MY EAR. YOU'RE MAKING MY BRAIN BUZZ.

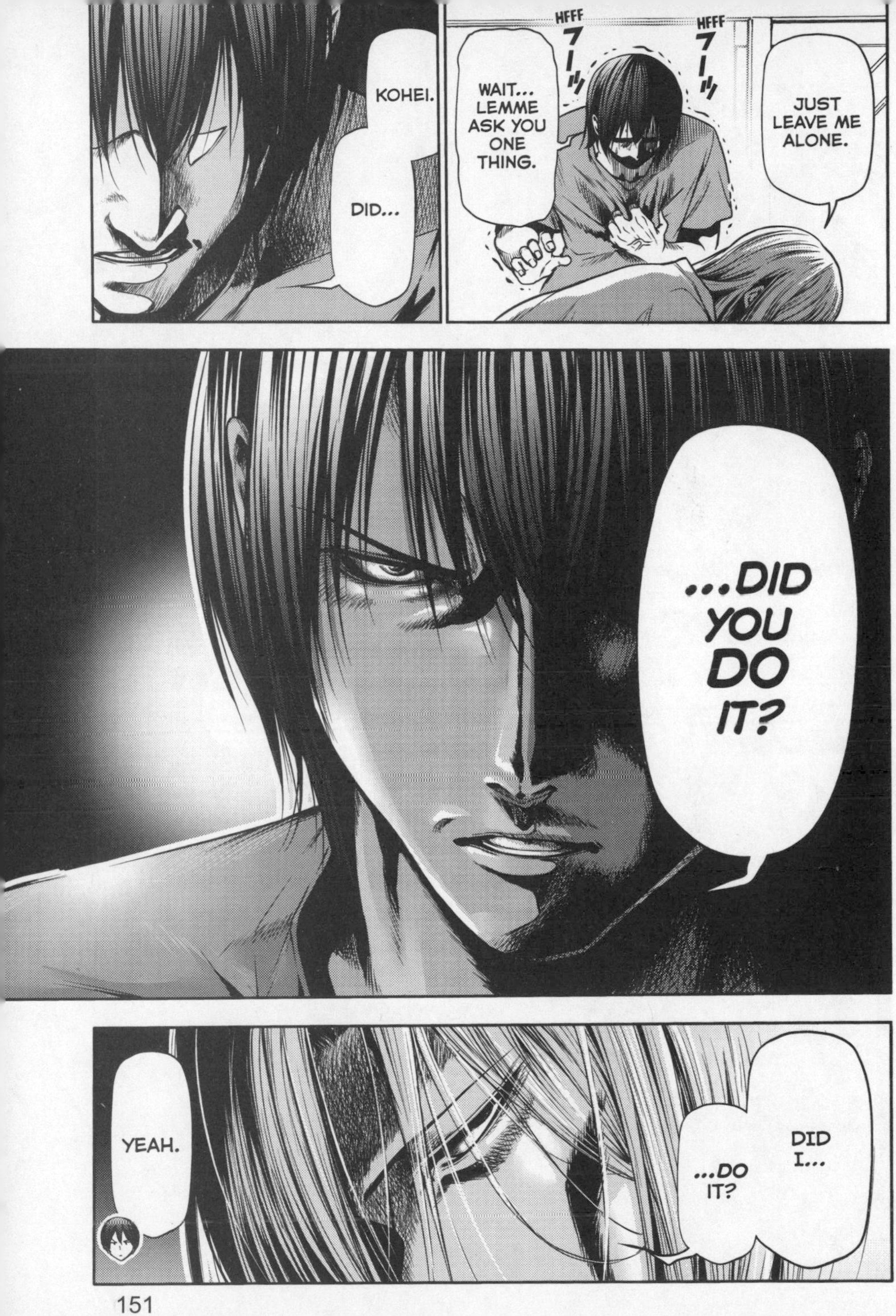
HFFF
JUST LEAVE ME ALONE.
HFFF
WAIT... LEMME ASK YOU ONE THING.
KOHEI.
DID...
...DID YOU DO IT?
DID I...
...DO IT?
YEAH.

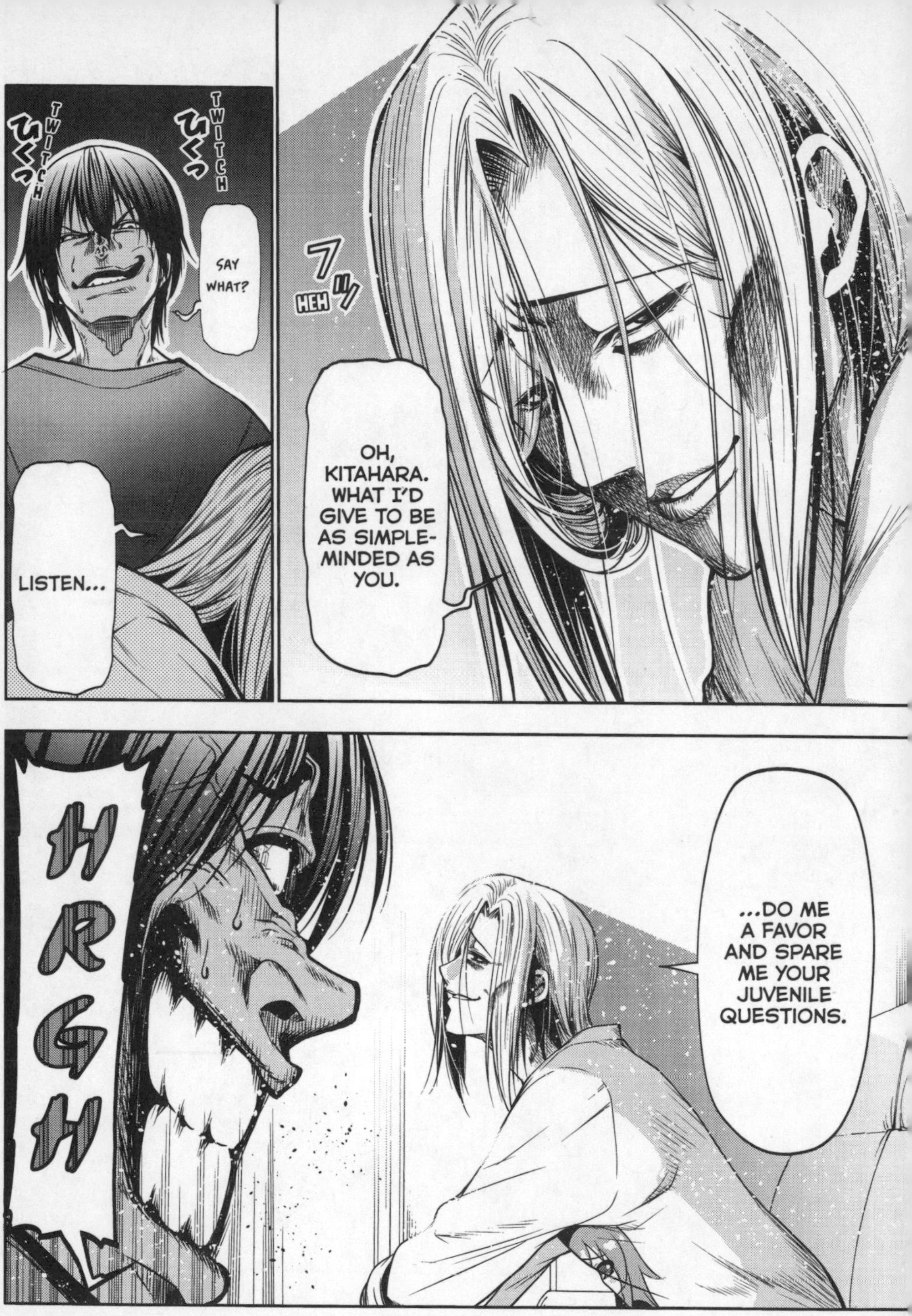
フッ
HEH
OH, KITAHARA. WHAT I'D GIVE TO BE AS SIMPLE-MINDED AS YOU.
ひくっ
TWITCH
ひくっ
TWITCH
SAY WHAT?
LISTEN...
...DO ME A FAVOR AND SPARE ME YOUR JUVENILE QUESTIONS.
HRGH

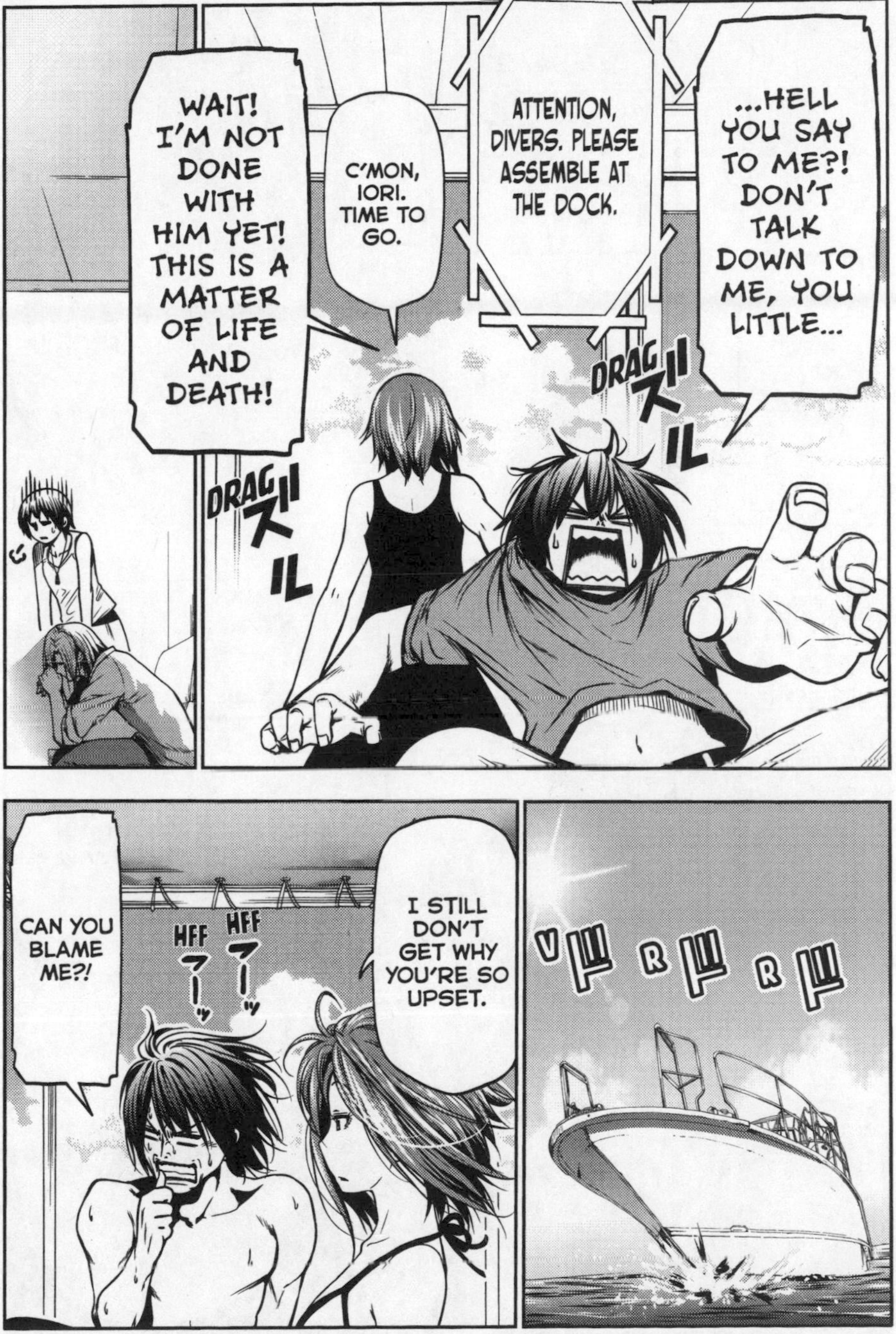
...HELL YOU SAY TO ME?! DON'T TALK DOWN TO ME, YOU LITTLE...
ATTENTION, DIVERS. PLEASE ASSEMBLE AT THE DOCK.
DRAG
C'MON, IORI. TIME TO GO.
WAIT! I'M NOT DONE WITH HIM YET! THIS IS A MATTER OF LIFE AND DEATH!
DRAG
V R R
I STILL DON'T GET WHY YOU'RE SO UPSET.
HFF
HFF
CAN YOU BLAME ME?!

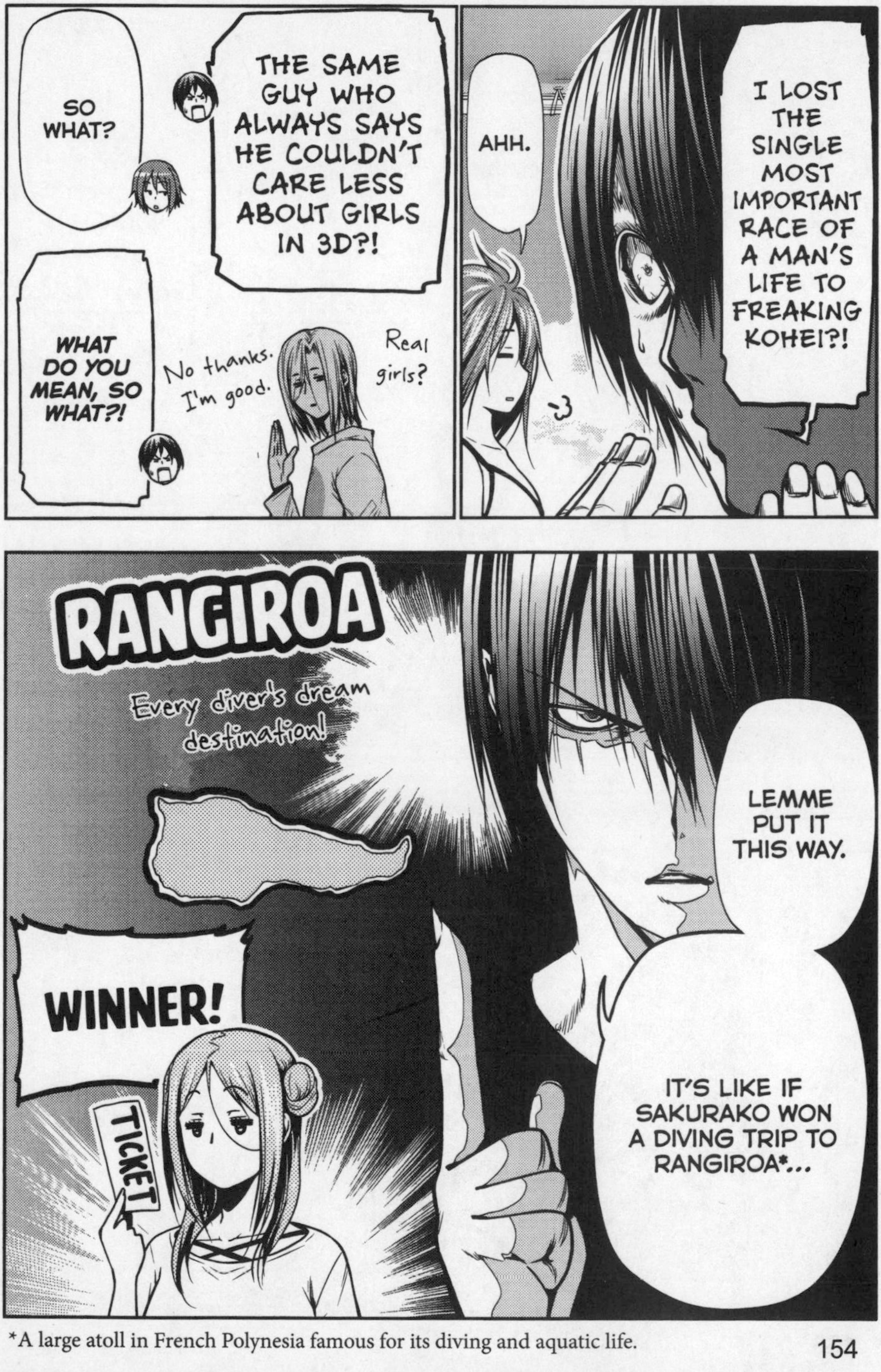
I LOST THE SINGLE MOST IMPORTANT RACE OF A MAN'S LIFE TO FREAKING KOHEI?!
AHH.
THE SAME GUY WHO ALWAYS SAYS HE COULDN'T CARE LESS ABOUT GIRLS IN 3D?!
SO WHAT?
Real girls?
No thanks. I'm good.
WHAT DO YOU MEAN, SO WHAT?!
LEMME PUT IT THIS WAY.
IT'S LIKE IF SAKURAKO WON A DIVING TRIP TO RANGIROA*...
RANGIROA
Every diver's dream destination!
WINNER!
TICKET

*A large atoll in French Polynesia famous for its diving and aquatic life.

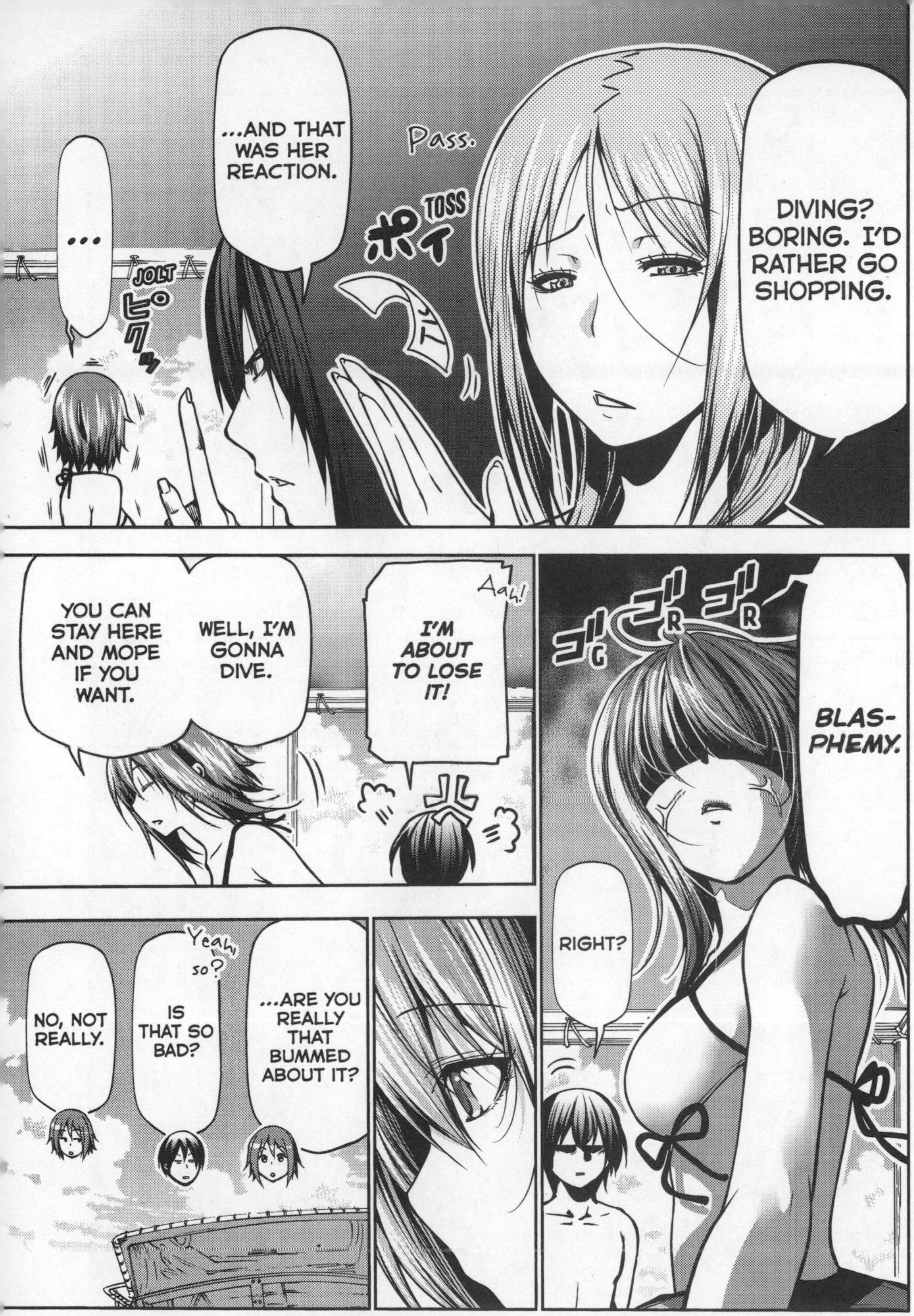
DIVING? BORING. I'D RATHER GO SHOPPING.
Pass.
TOSS
ポイ
...AND THAT WAS HER REACTION.
JOLT
ピクッ
...
ゴ G ゴ R ゴ R
BLAS-PHEMY.
RIGHT?
Aah!
I'M ABOUT TO LOSE IT!
WELL, I'M GONNA DIVE.
YOU CAN STAY HERE AND MOPE IF YOU WANT.
...ARE YOU REALLY THAT BUMMED ABOUT IT?
Yeah, so?
IS THAT SO BAD?
NO, NOT REALLY.

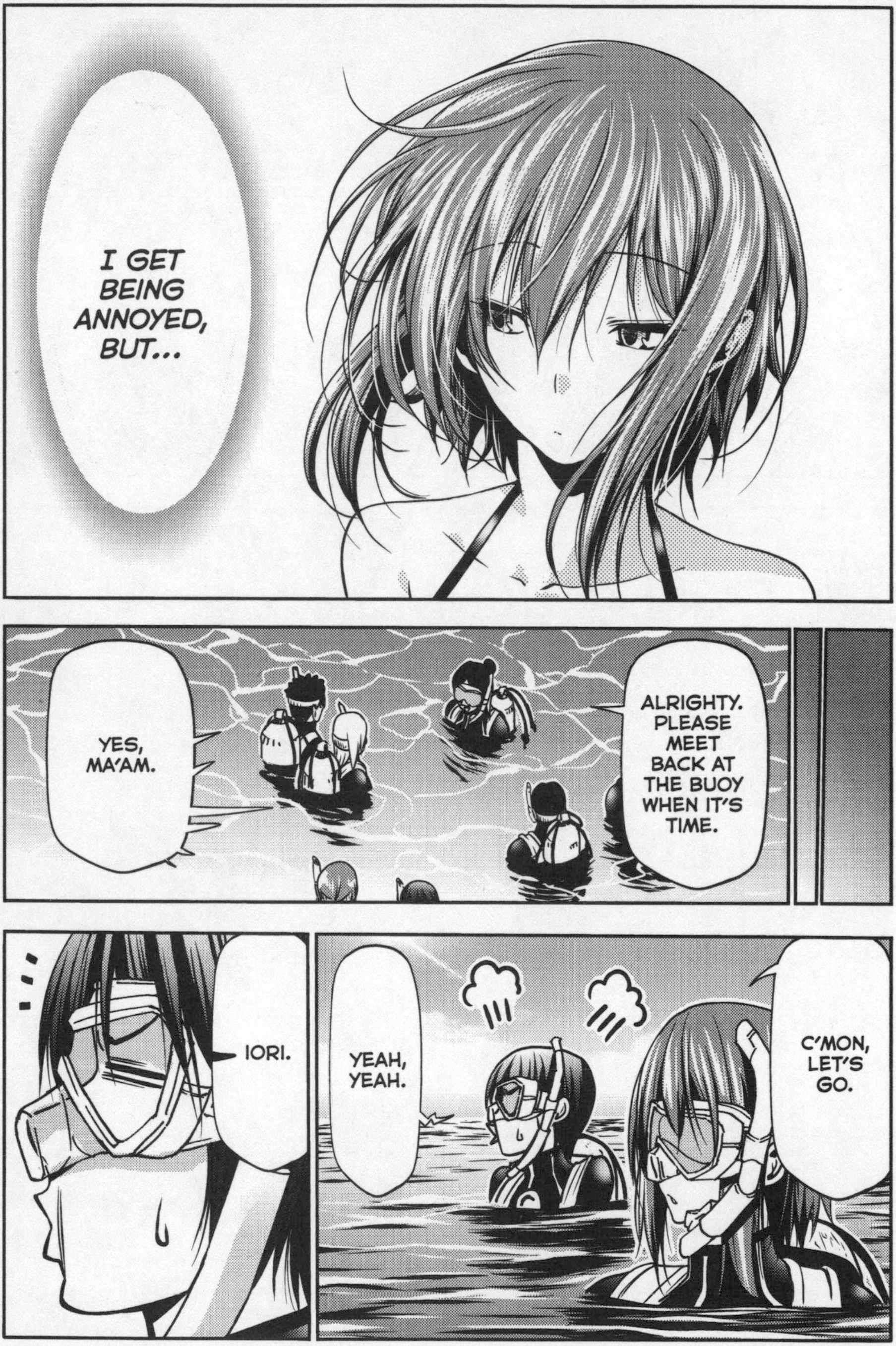
I GET BEING ANNOYED, BUT...
ALRIGHTY. PLEASE MEET BACK AT THE BUOY WHEN IT'S TIME.
YES, MA'AM.
C'MON, LET'S GO.
YEAH, YEAH.
IORI.

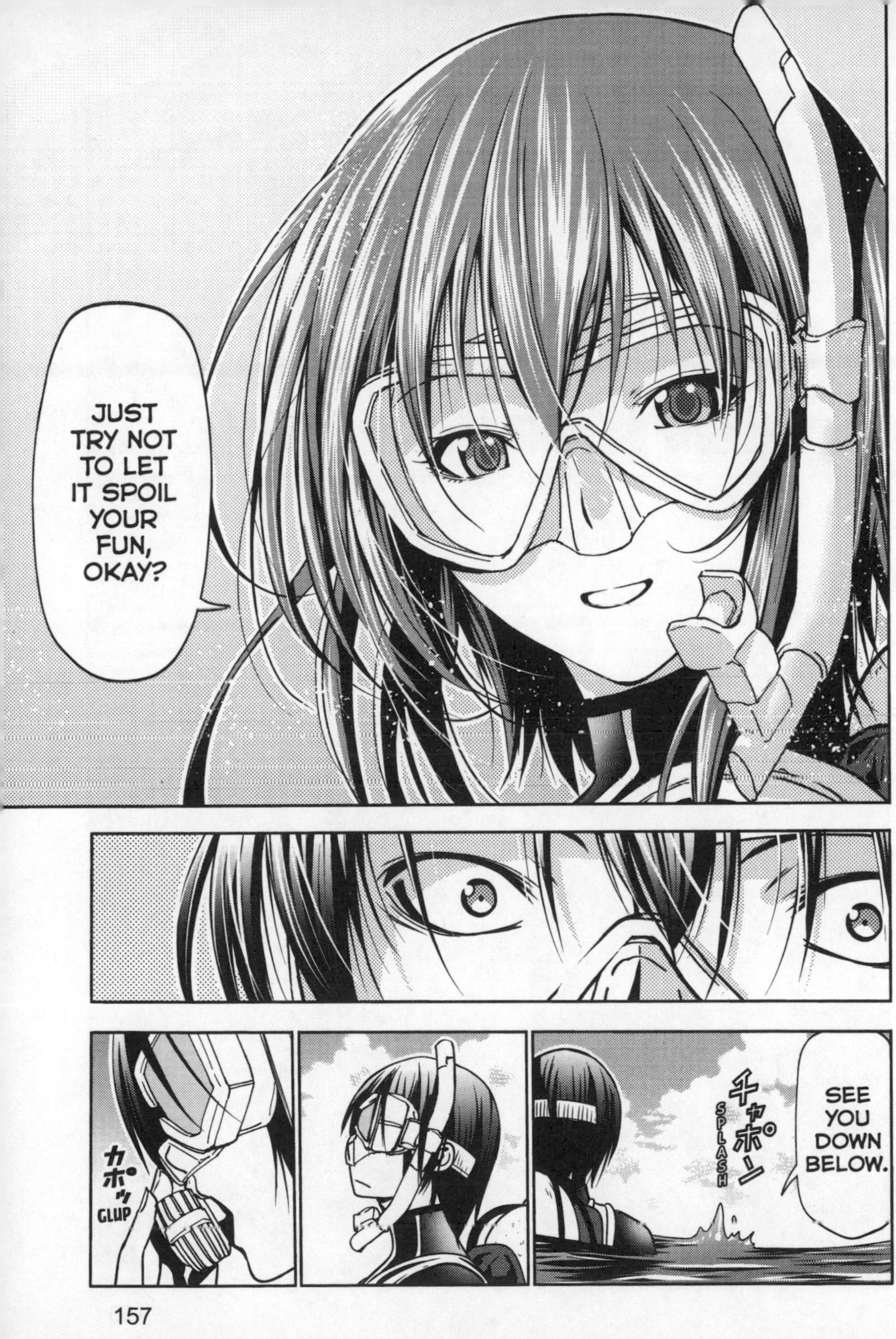
JUST TRY NOT TO LET IT SPOIL YOUR FUN, OKAY?
SEE YOU DOWN BELOW.
チャポーン
SPLASH
カポッ
GLUP

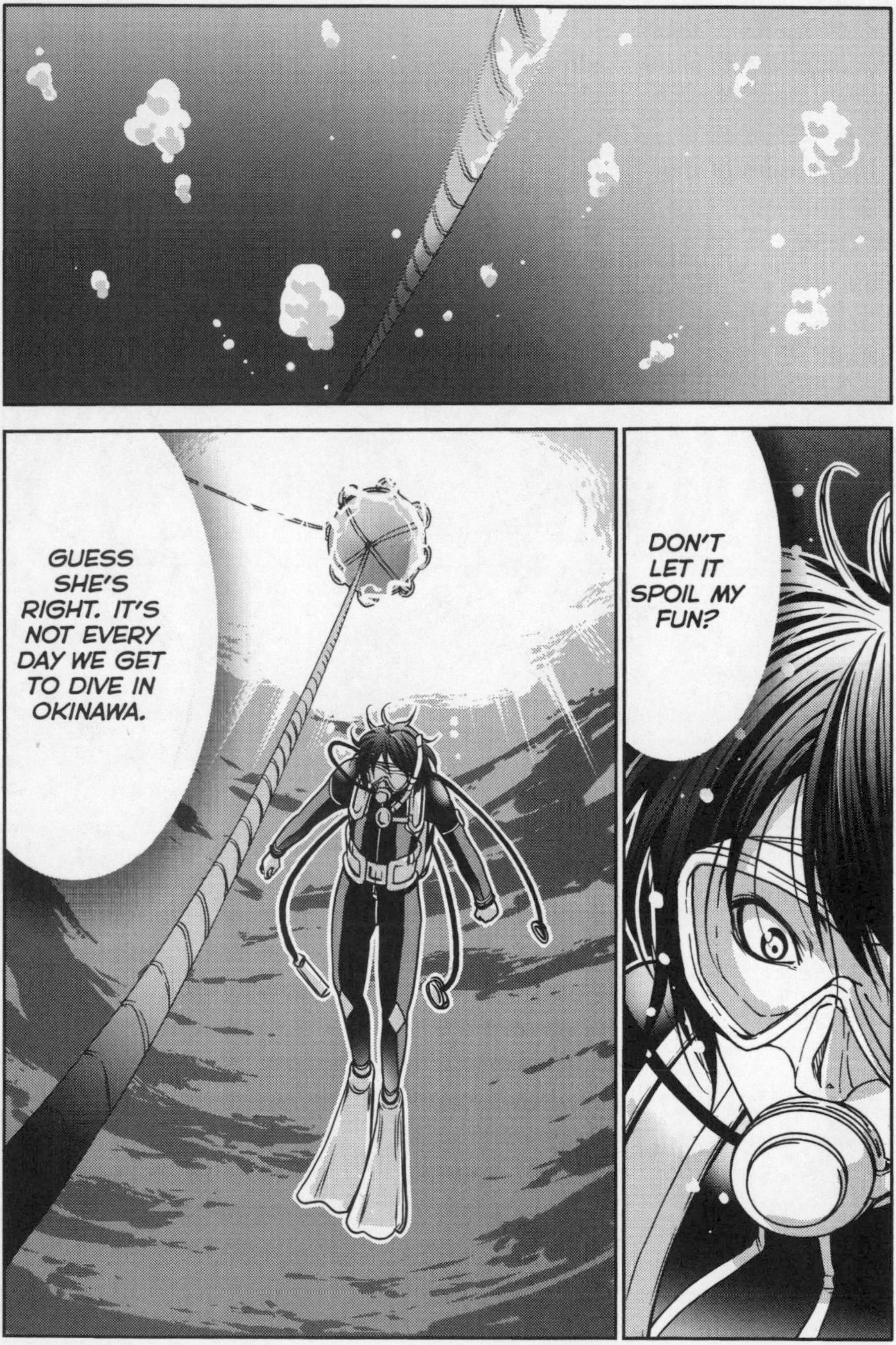
DON'T LET IT SPOIL MY FUN?
GUESS SHE'S RIGHT. IT'S NOT EVERY DAY WE GET TO DIVE IN OKINAWA.

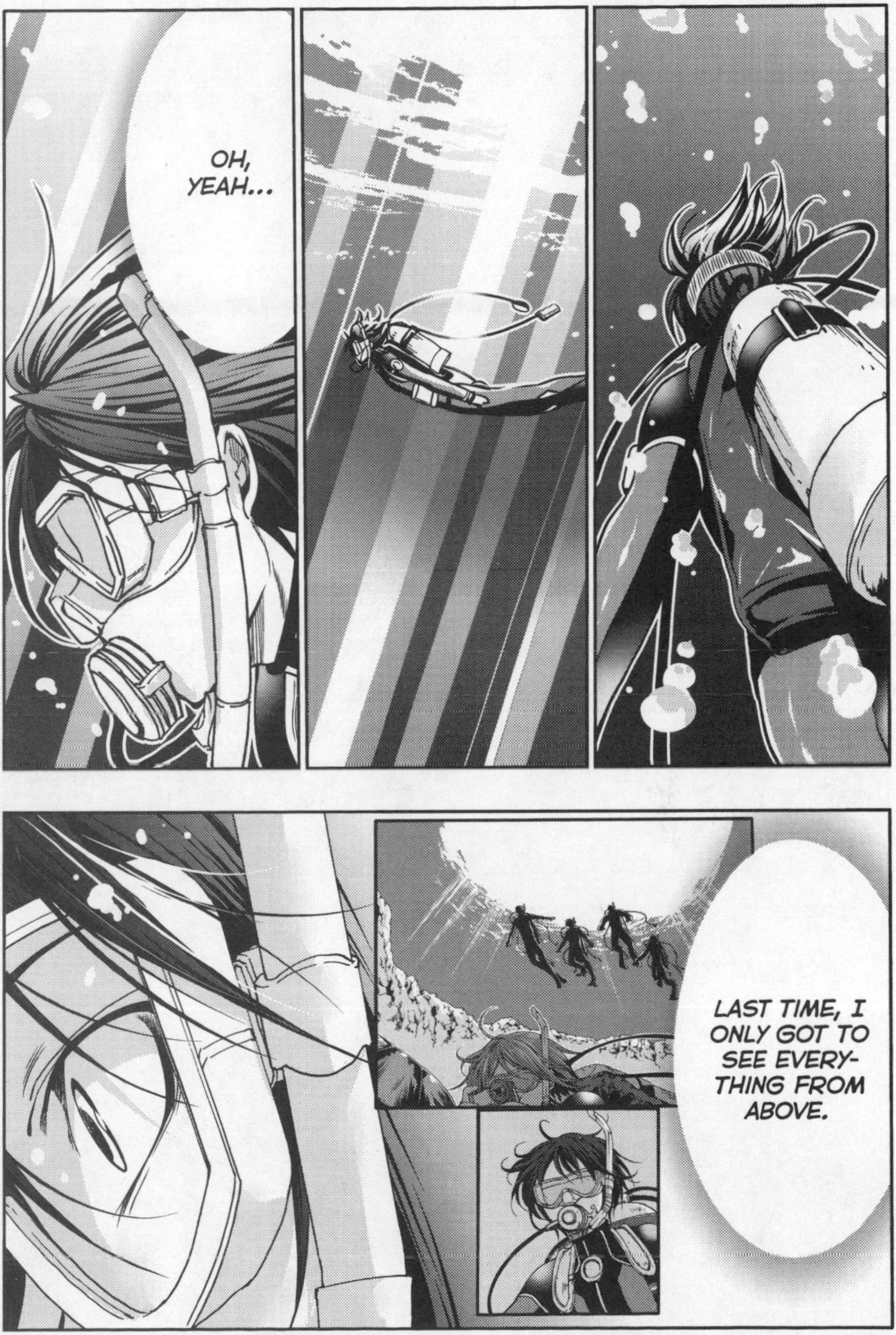
OH, YEAH...
LAST TIME, I ONLY GOT TO SEE EVERY-THING FROM ABOVE.

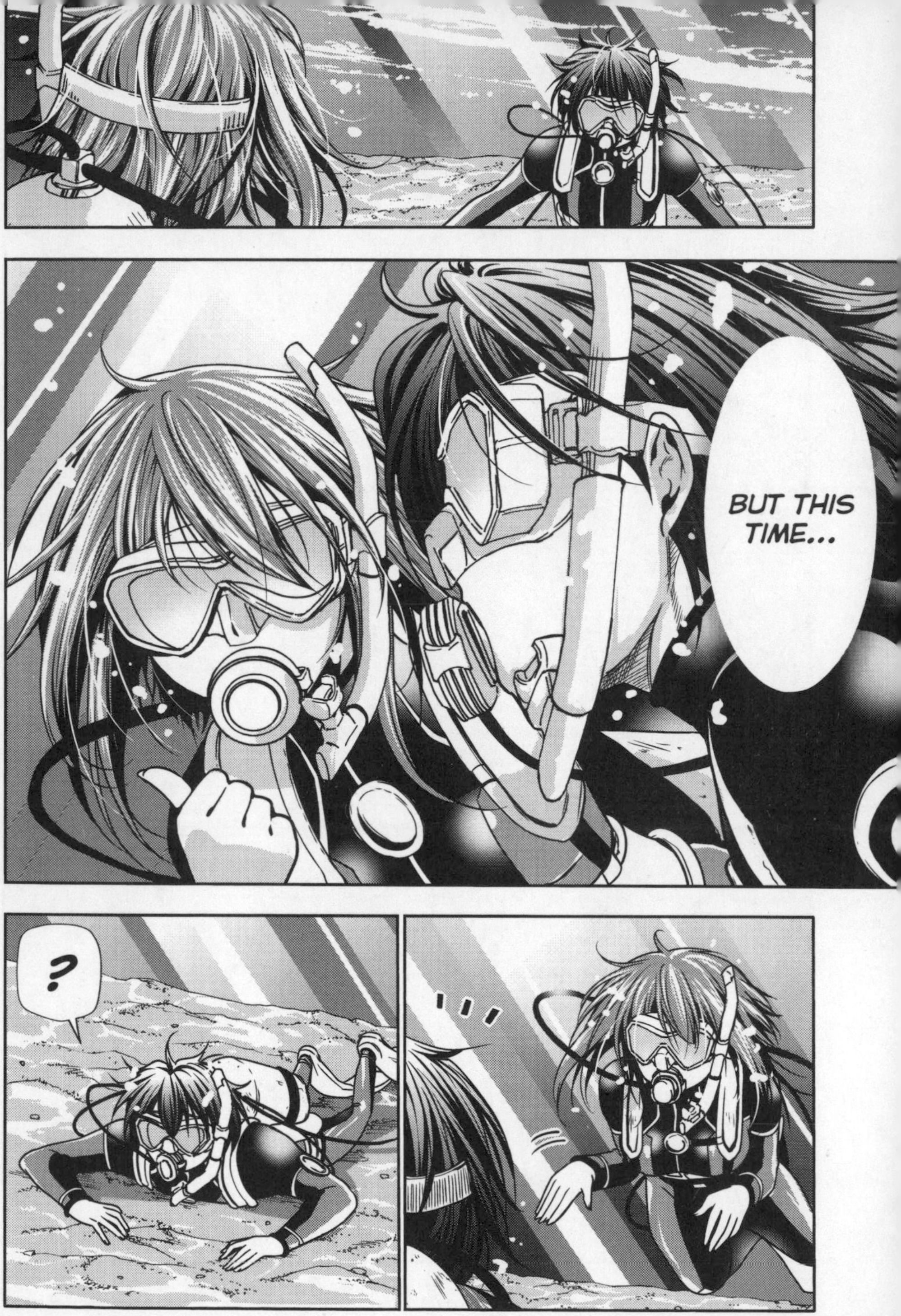
BUT THIS TIME...
?

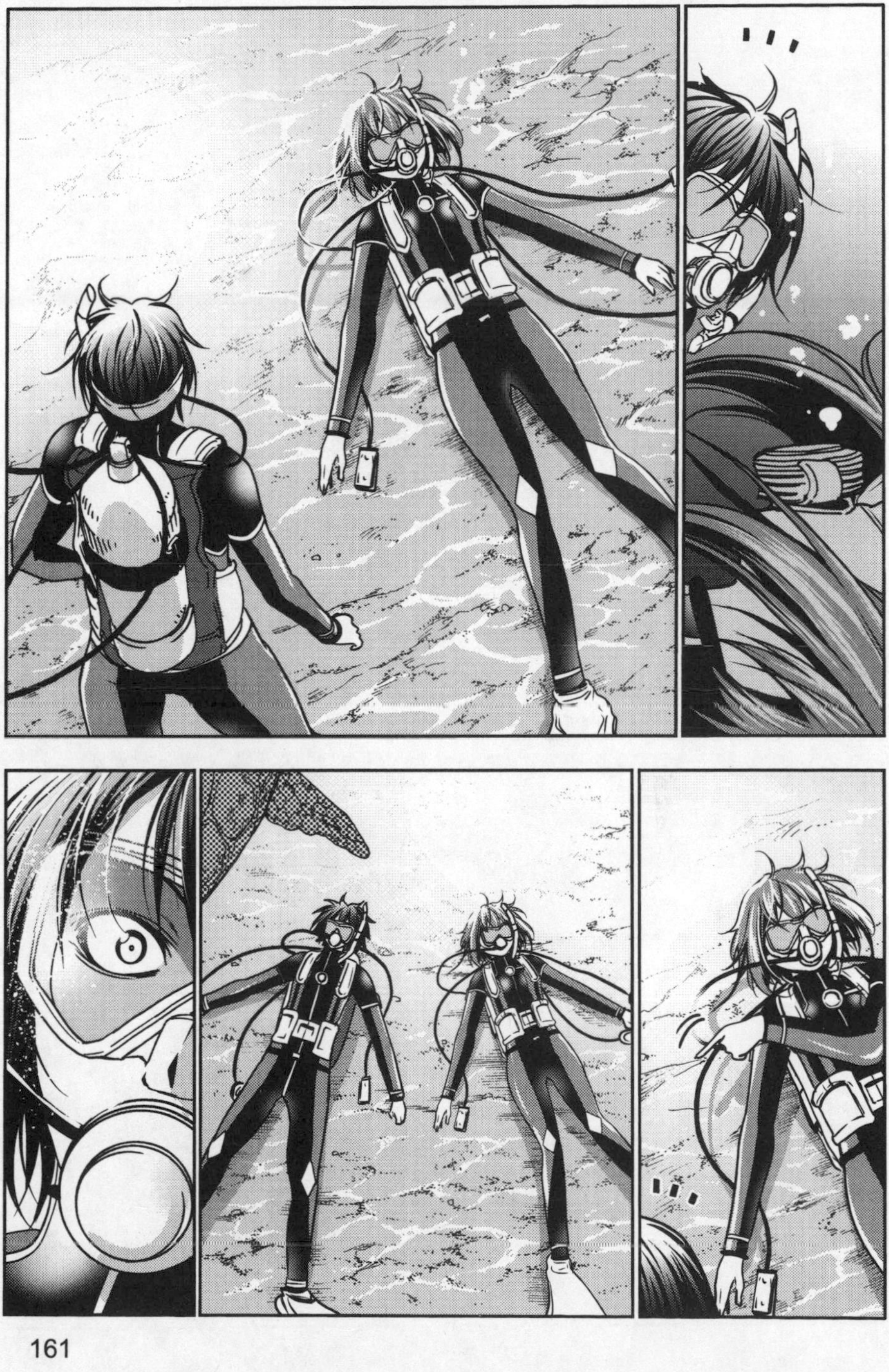

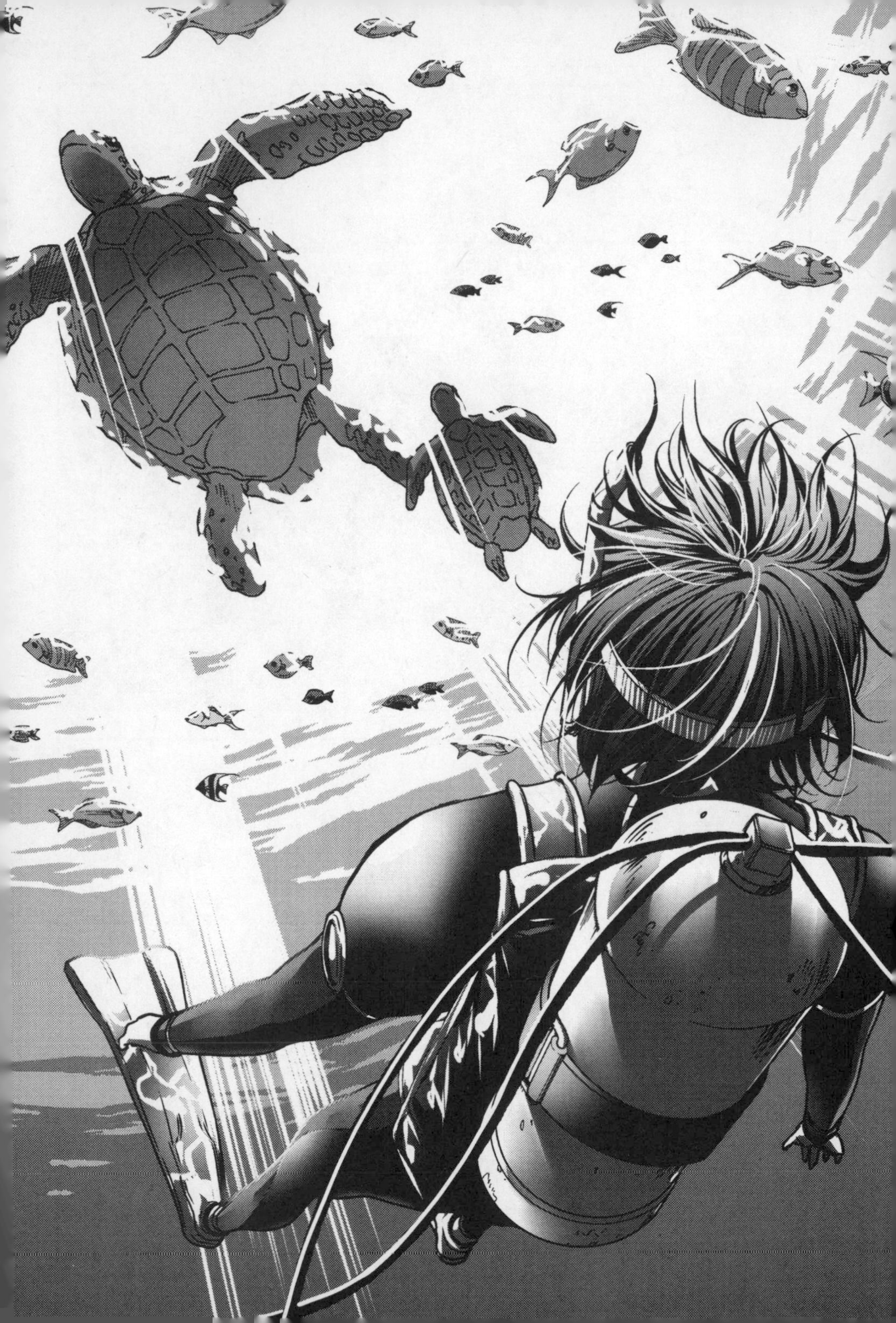

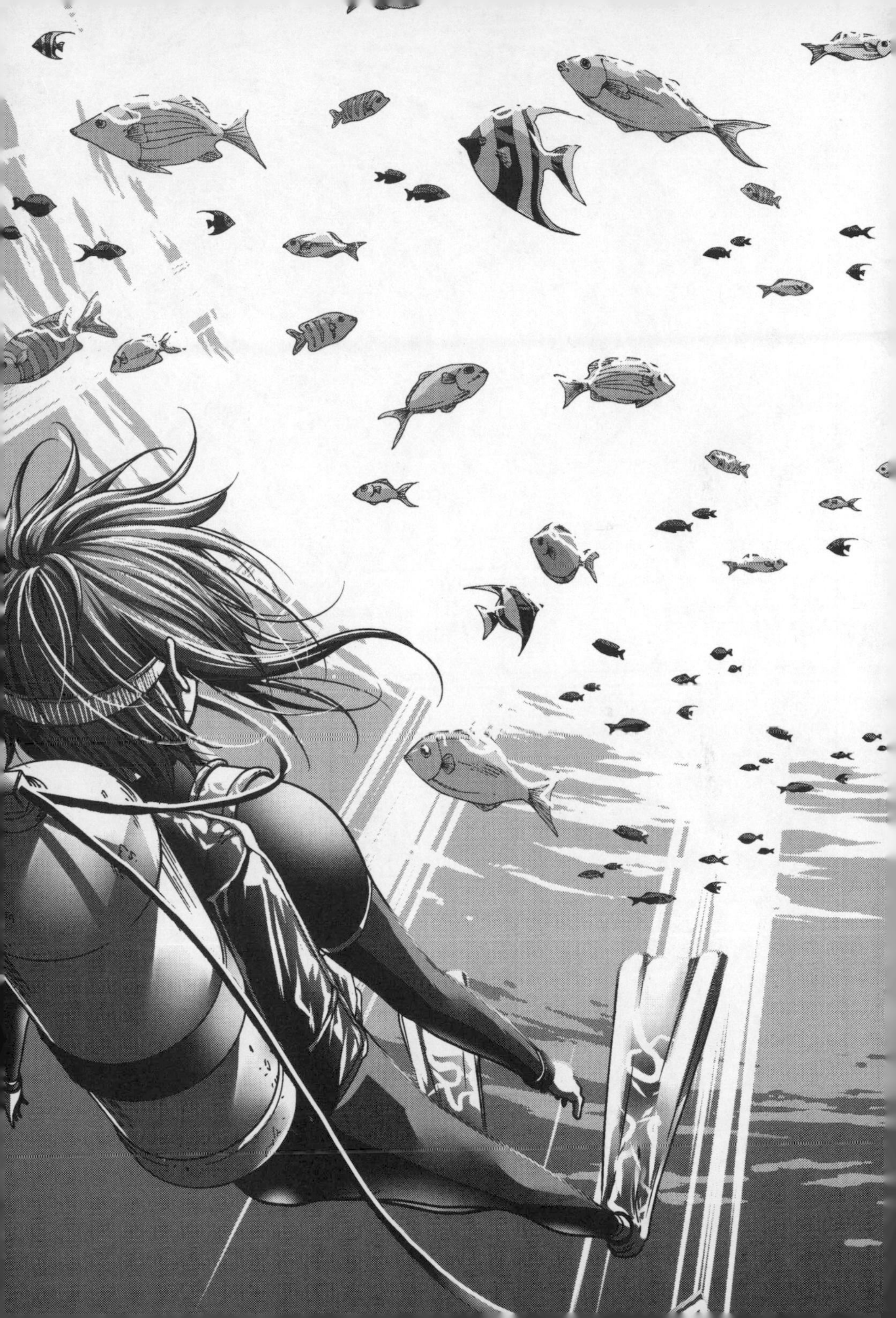

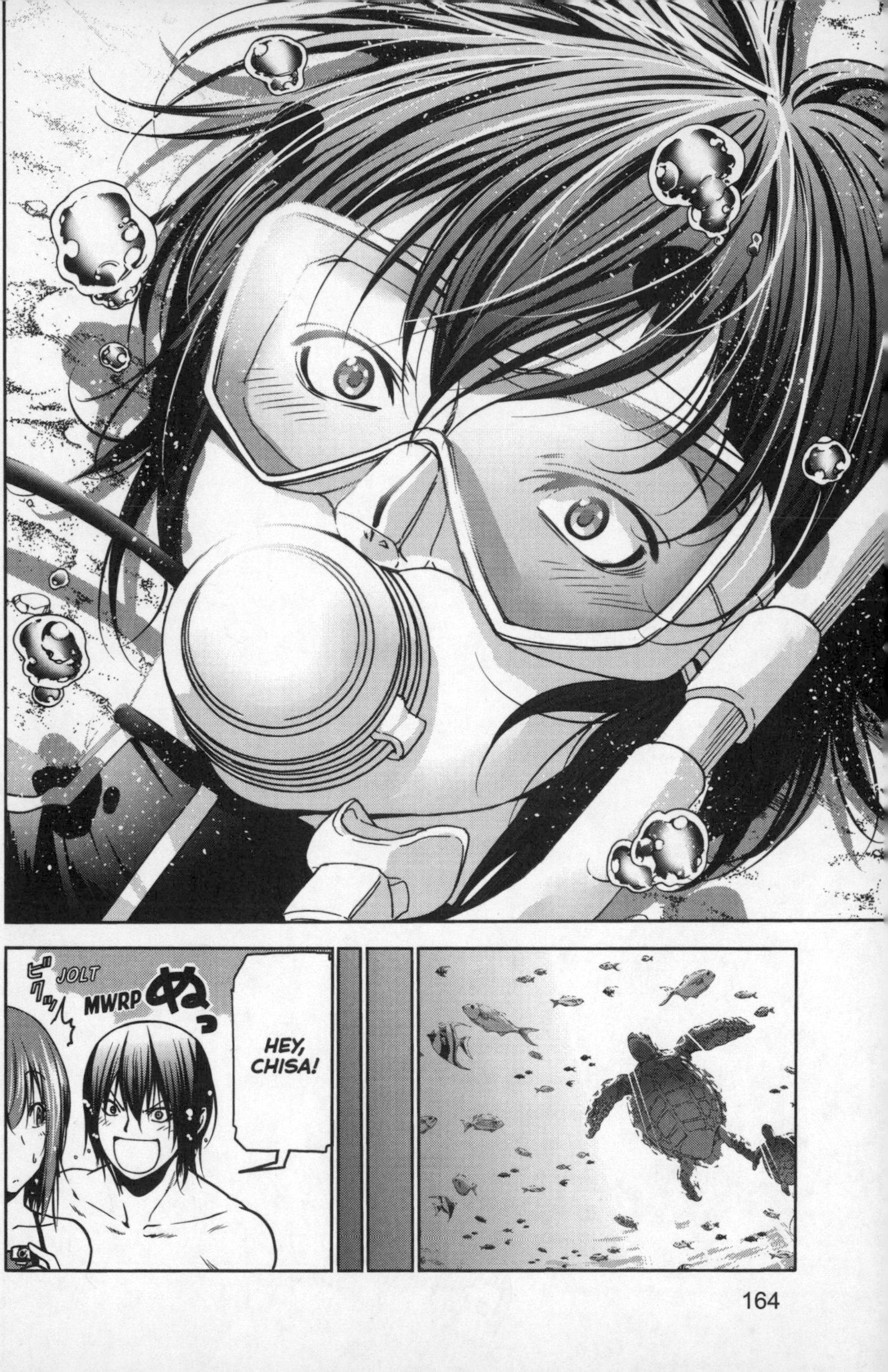
HEY, CHISA!
ぬっ
MWRP
ビクッ
JOLT

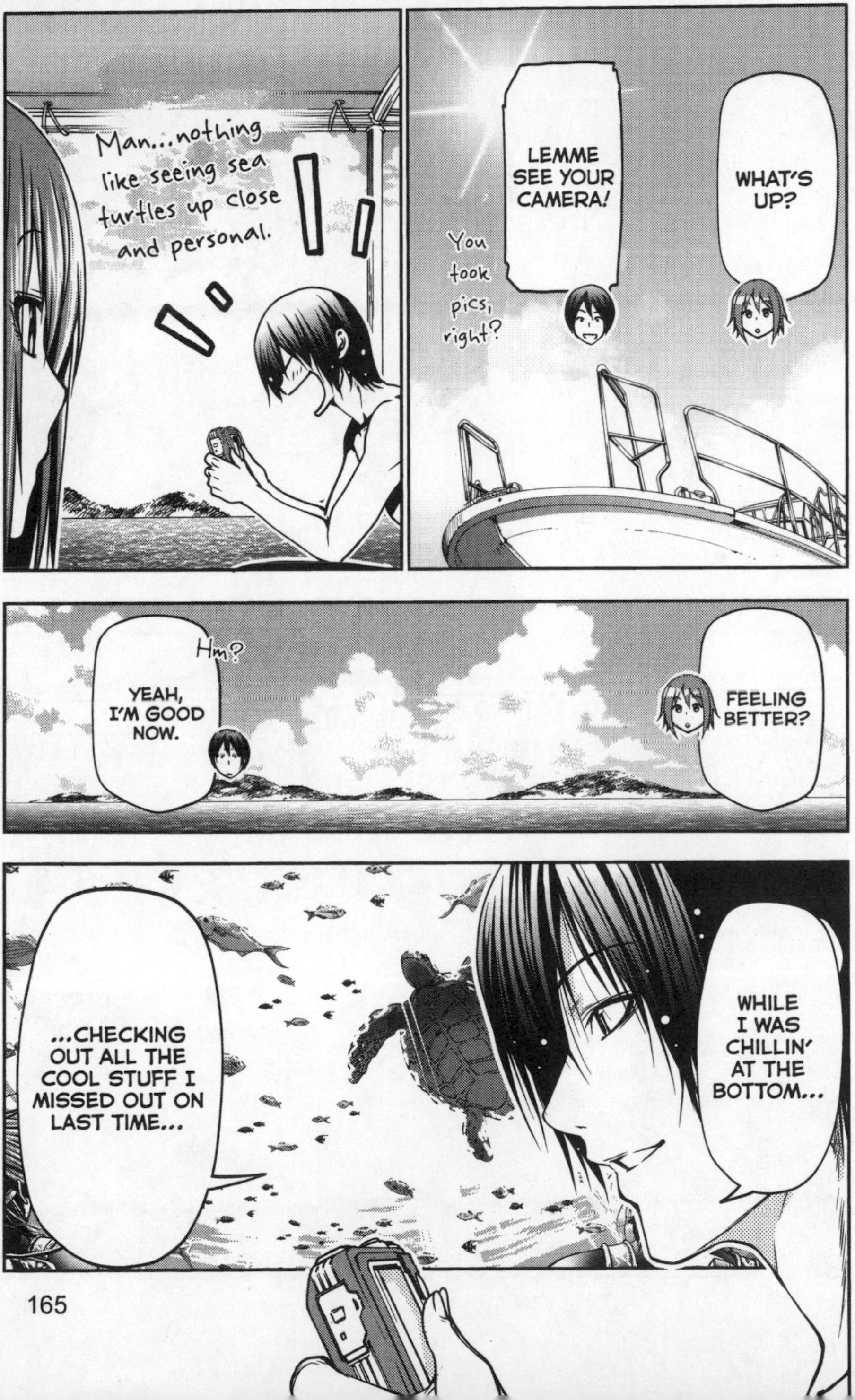
WHAT'S UP?
LEMME SEE YOUR CAMERA!
You took pics, right?
Man...nothing like seeing sea turtles up close and personal.
FEELING BETTER?
Hm?
YEAH, I'M GOOD NOW.
WHILE I WAS CHILLIN' AT THE BOTTOM...
...CHECKING OUT ALL THE COOL STUFF I MISSED OUT ON LAST TIME...

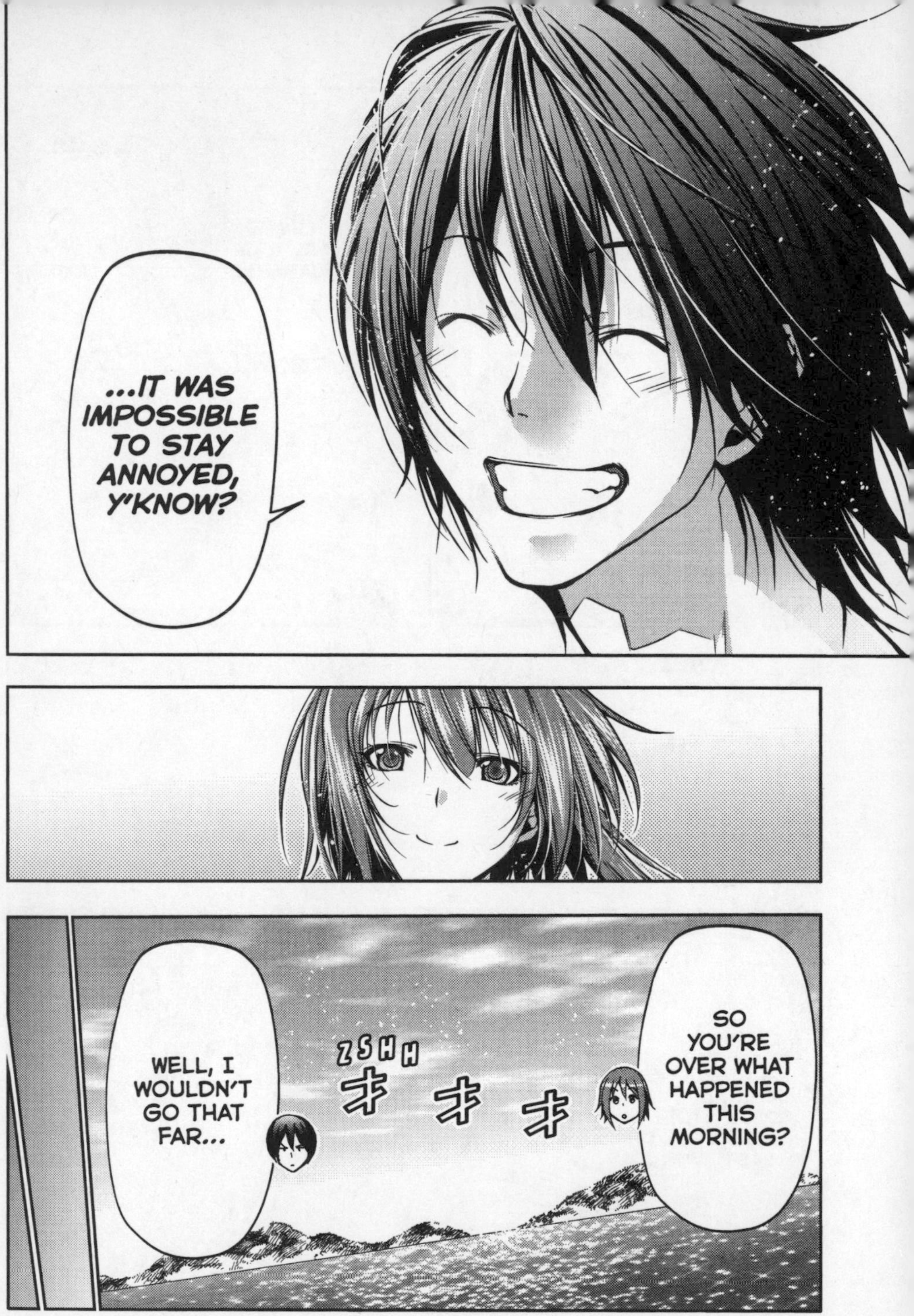
...IT WAS IMPOSSIBLE TO STAY ANNOYED, Y'KNOW?
SO YOU'RE OVER WHAT HAPPENED THIS MORNING?
ZSHH オ オ オ
WELL, I WOULDN'T GO THAT FAR...

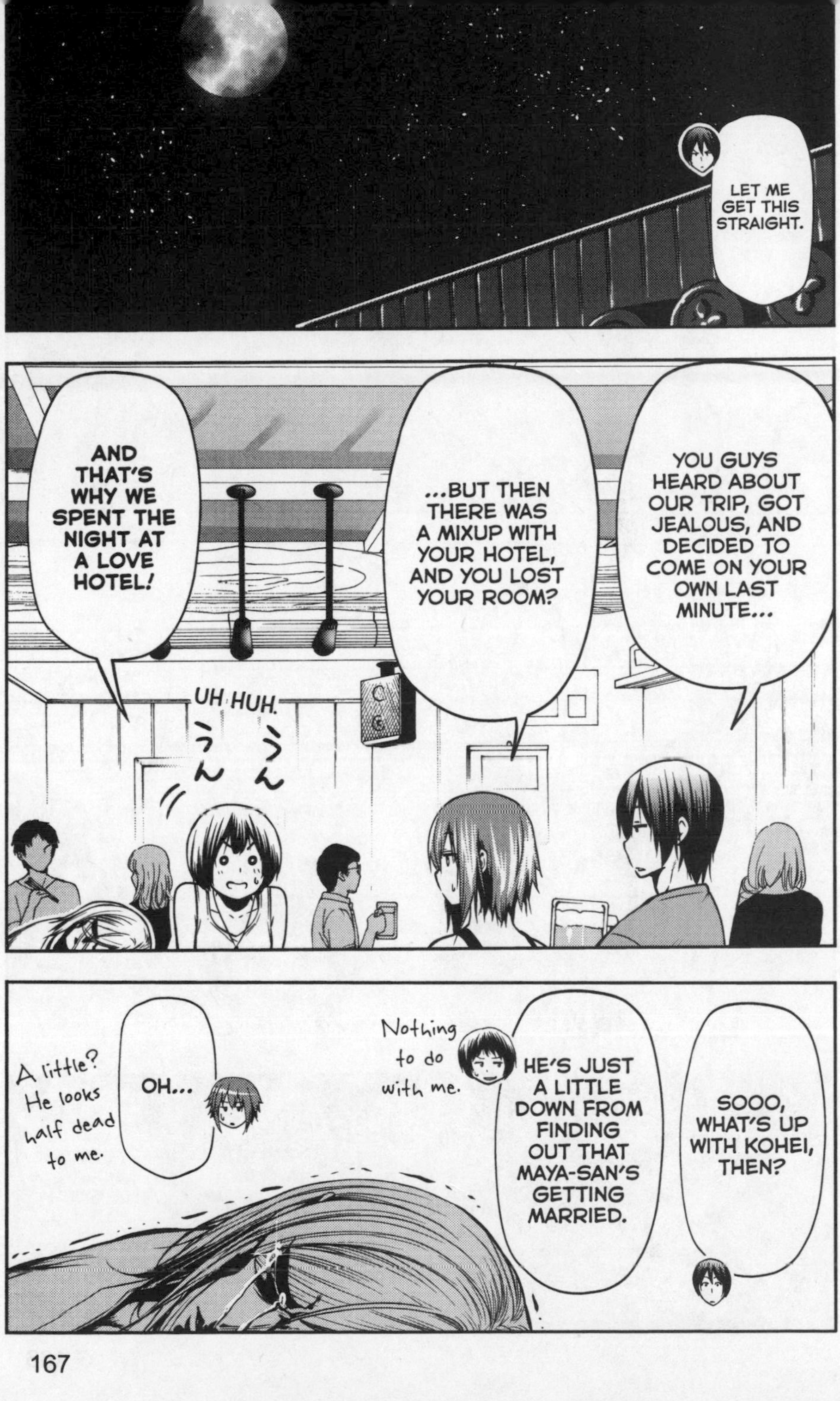
LET ME GET THIS STRAIGHT.
YOU GUYS HEARD ABOUT OUR TRIP, GOT JEALOUS, AND DECIDED TO COME ON YOUR OWN LAST MINUTE...
...BUT THEN THERE WAS A MIXUP WITH YOUR HOTEL, AND YOU LOST YOUR ROOM?
AND THAT'S WHY WE SPENT THE NIGHT AT A LOVE HOTEL!
UH HUH.
うん うん
SOOO, WHAT'S UP WITH KOHEI, THEN?
HE'S JUST A LITTLE DOWN FROM FINDING OUT THAT MAYA-SAN'S GETTING MARRIED.
Nothing to do with me.
OH...
A little? He looks half dead to me.

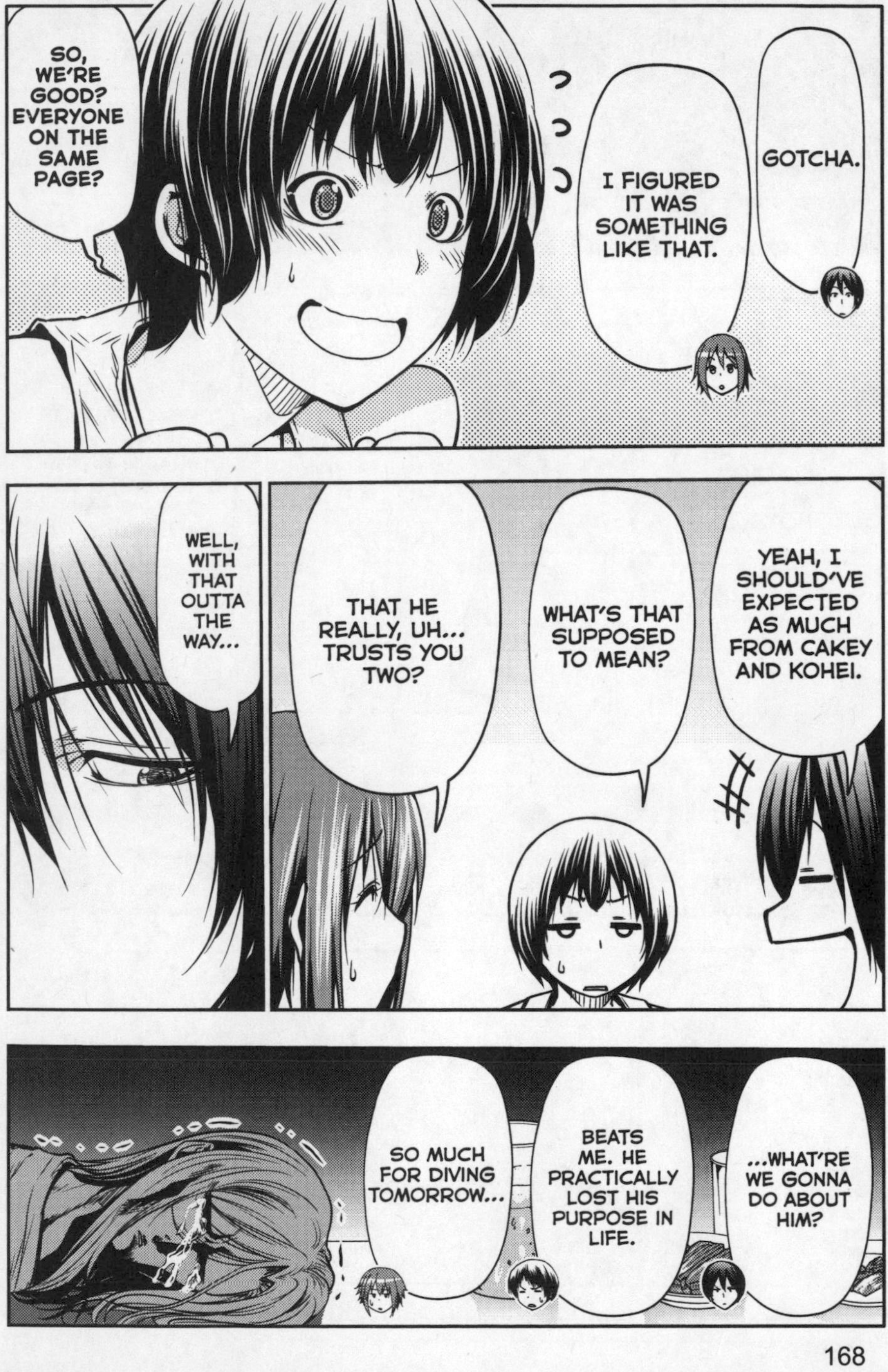
GOTCHA.
I FIGURED IT WAS SOMETHING LIKE THAT.
SO, WE'RE GOOD? EVERYONE ON THE SAME PAGE?
YEAH, I SHOULD'VE EXPECTED AS MUCH FROM CAKEY AND KOHEI.
WHAT'S THAT SUPPOSED TO MEAN?
THAT HE REALLY, UH... TRUSTS YOU TWO?
WELL, WITH THAT OUTTA THE WAY...
...WHAT'RE WE GONNA DO ABOUT HIM?
BEATS ME. HE PRACTICALLY LOST HIS PURPOSE IN LIFE.
SO MUCH FOR DIVING TOMORROW...

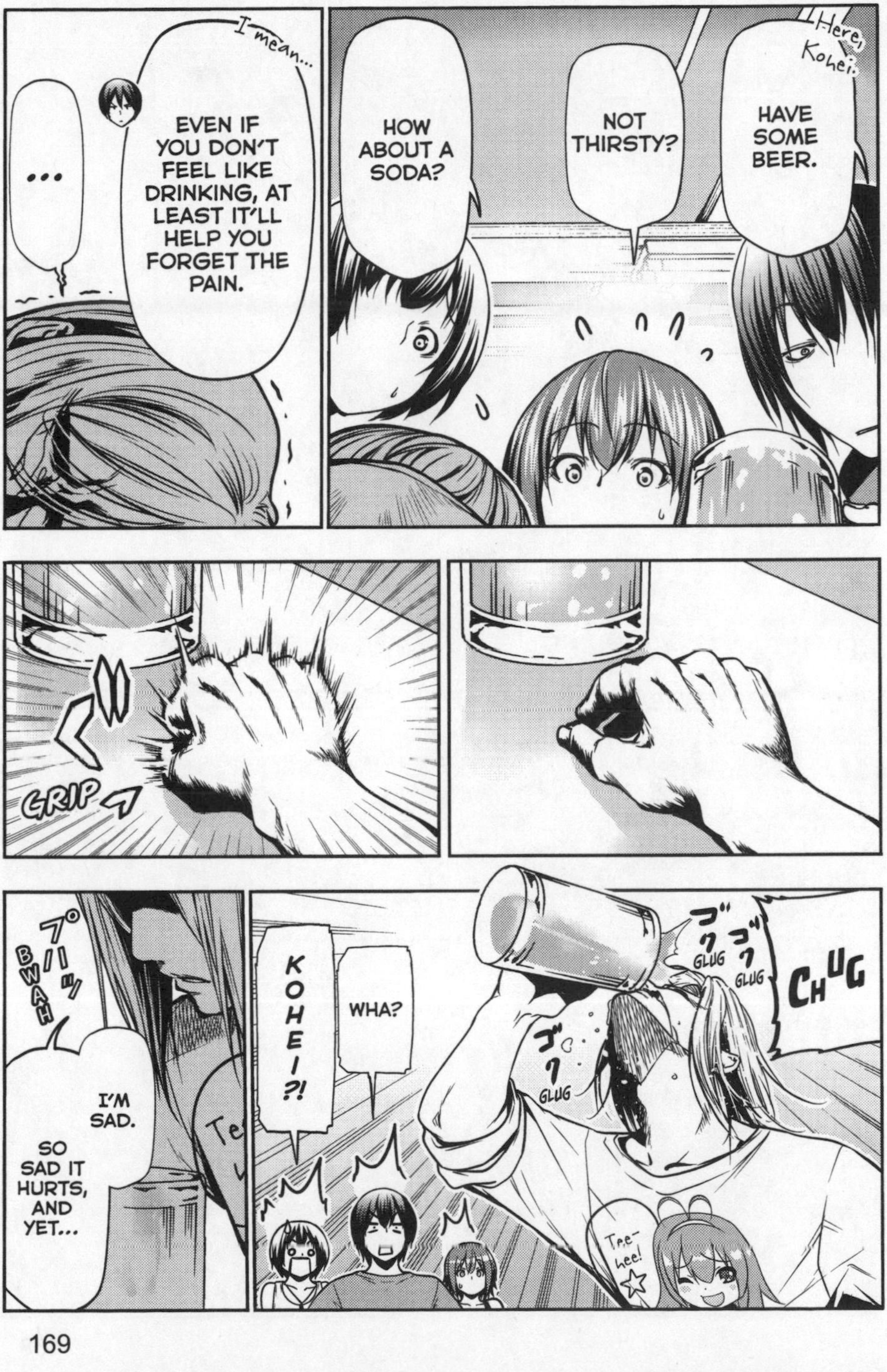
Here, Kohei.
HAVE SOME BEER.
NOT THIRSTY?
HOW ABOUT A SODA?
I mean...
EVEN IF YOU DON'T FEEL LIKE DRINKING, AT LEAST IT'LL HELP YOU FORGET THE PAIN.
...
GRIP
CHUG
GLUG
GLUG
GLUG
WHA?
KOHEI?!
Tee-hee!
BWAH
I'M SAD.
SO SAD IT HURTS, AND YET...

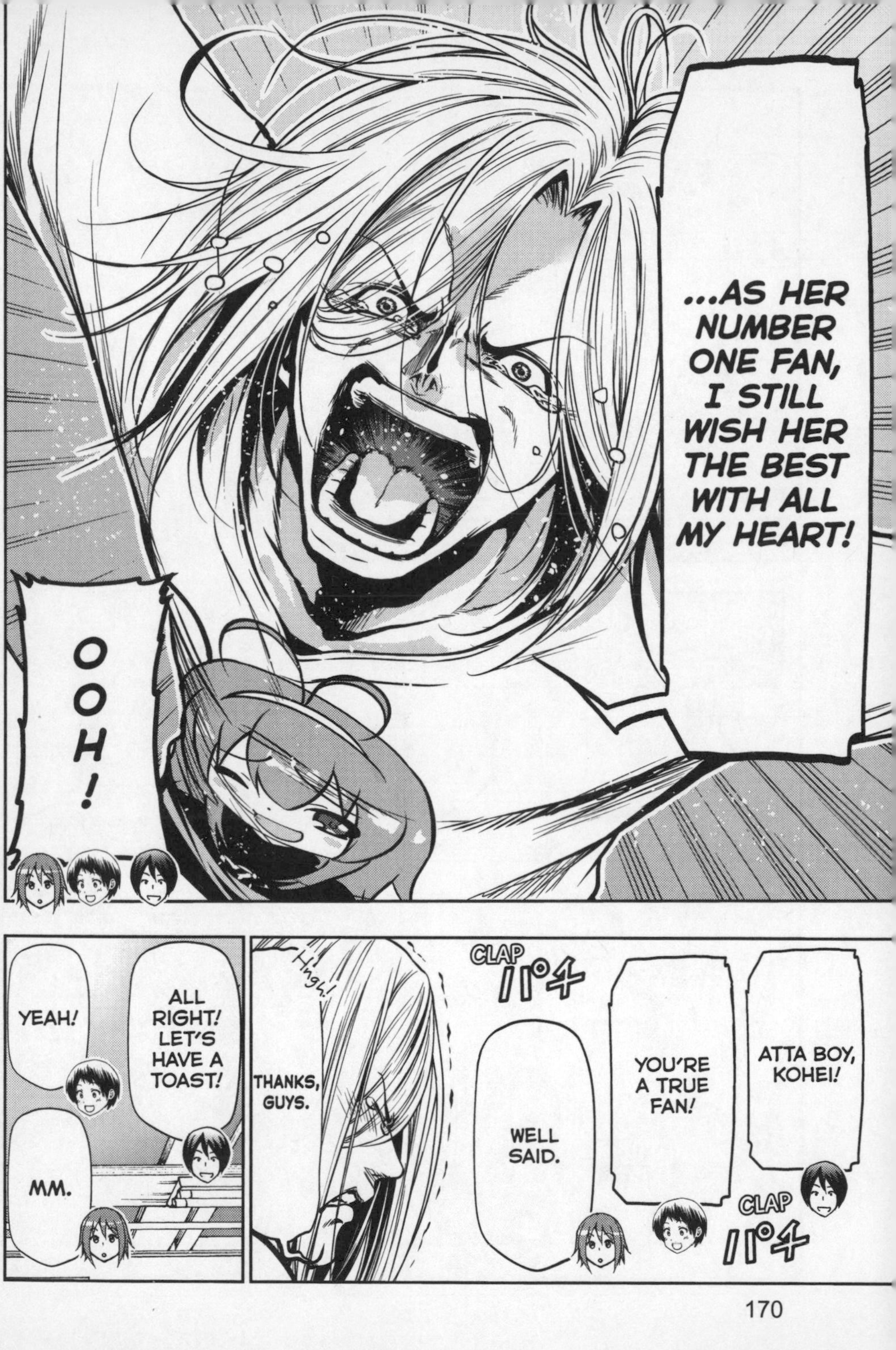
...AS HER NUMBER ONE FAN, I STILL WISH HER THE BEST WITH ALL MY HEART!
OOH!
ATTA BOY, KOHEI!
CLAP
YOU'RE A TRUE FAN!
WELL SAID.
CLAP
Hngh!
THANKS, GUYS.
ALL RIGHT! LET'S HAVE A TOAST!
YEAH!
MM.

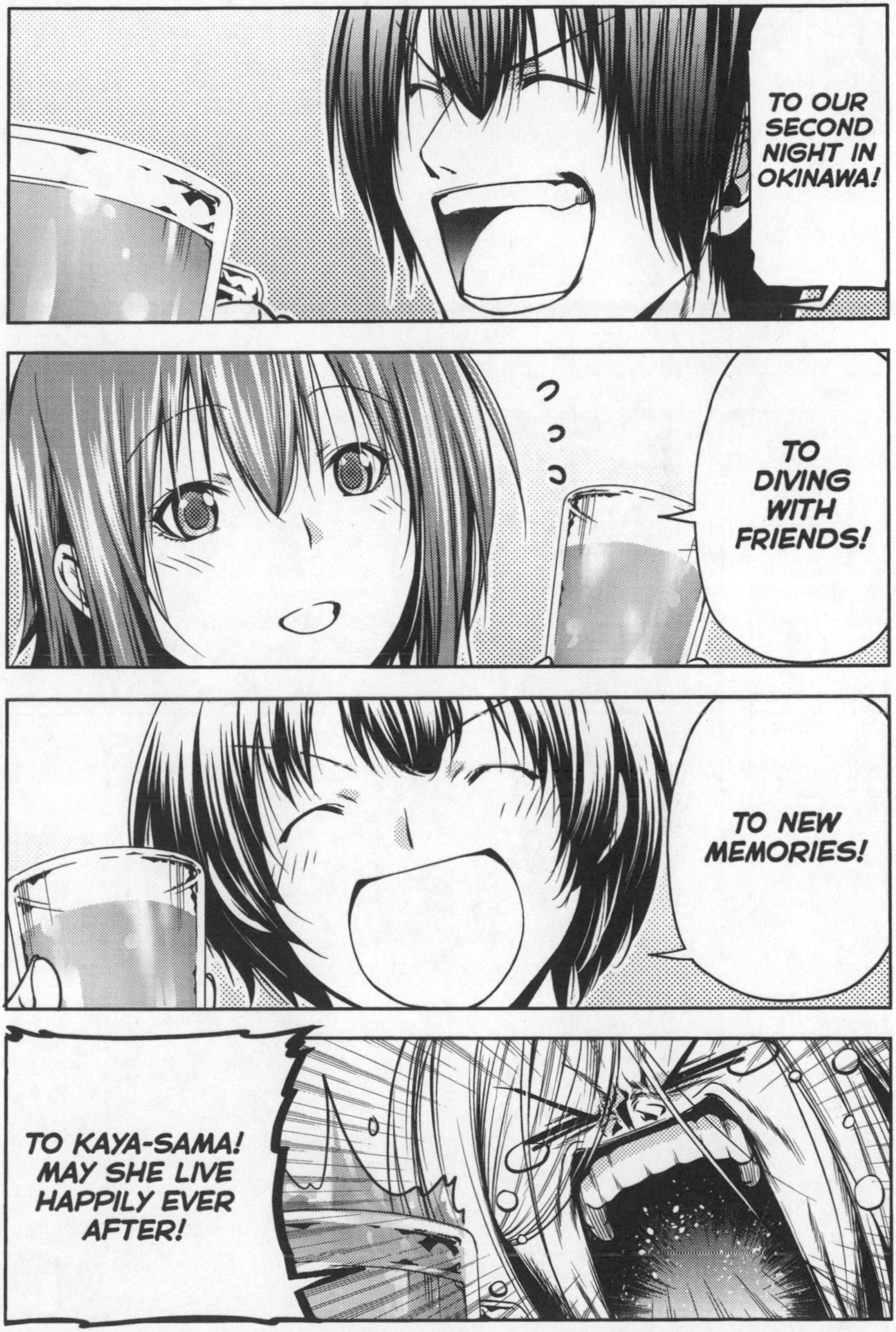
TO OUR SECOND NIGHT IN OKINAWA!
TO DIVING WITH FRIENDS!
TO NEW MEMORIES!
TO KAYA-SAMA! MAY SHE LIVE HAPPILY EVER AFTER!

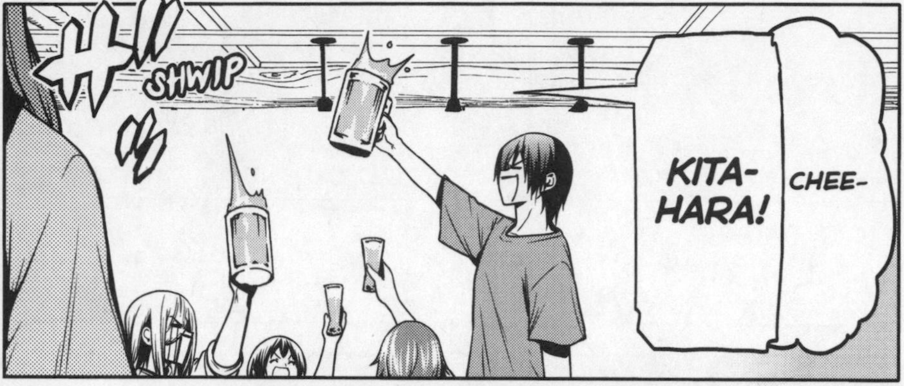
SHWIP
CHEE-
KITA-
HARA!
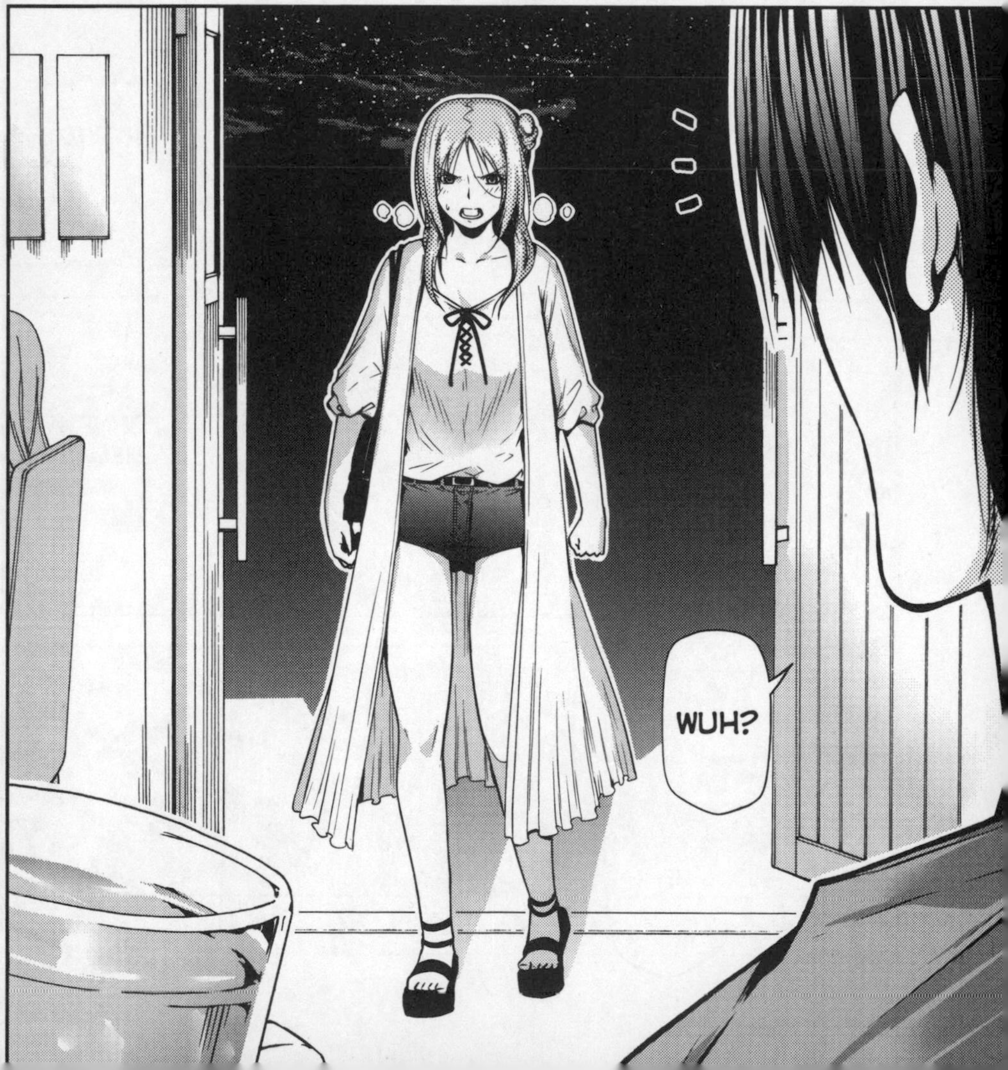
WUH?

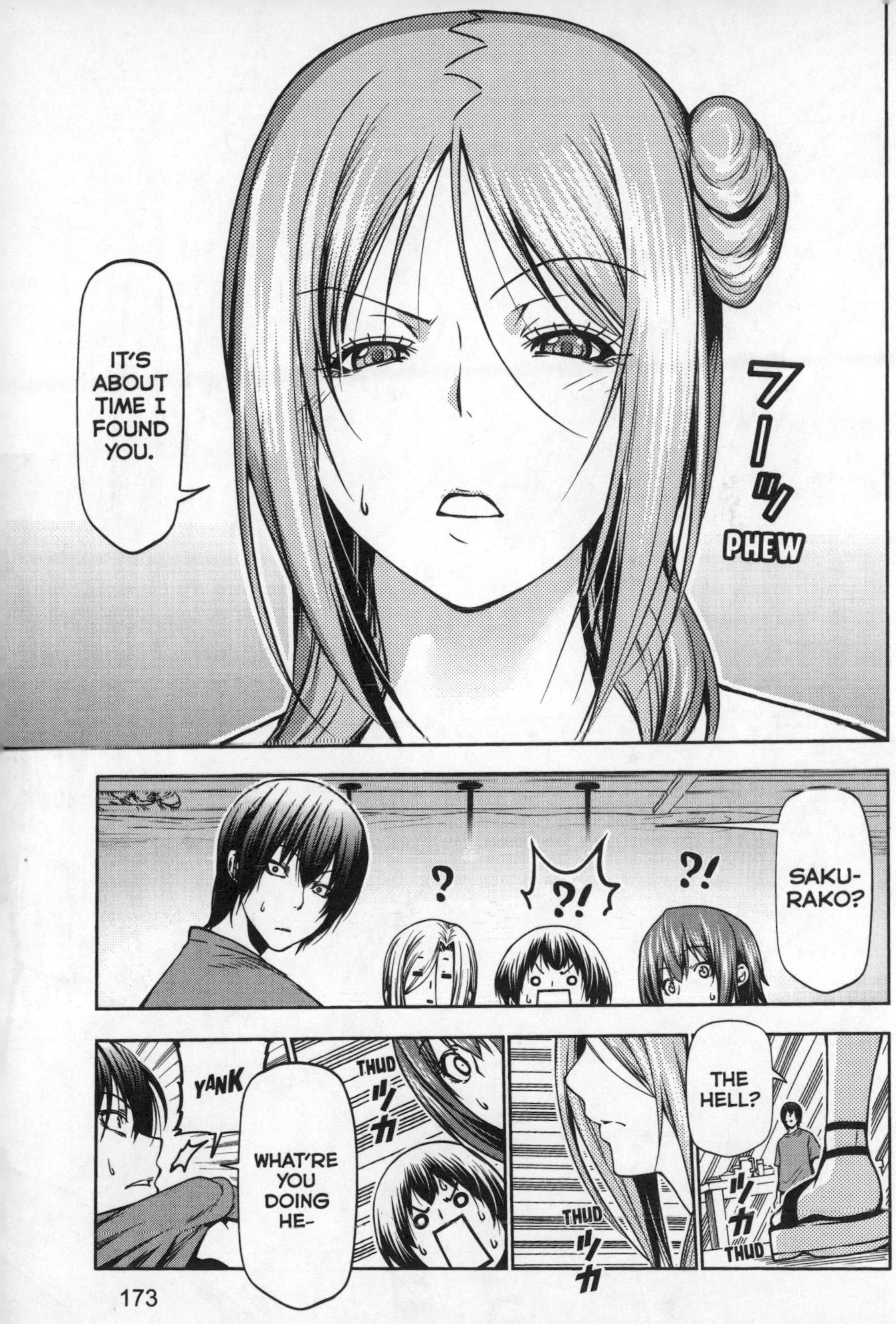
IT'S ABOUT TIME I FOUND YOU.
フーッ
PHEW
SAKU-RAKO?
?!
?!
?
THE HELL?
ツカ
THUD
THUD
ツカ
THUD
ツカ
WHAT'RE YOU DOING HE-
YANK

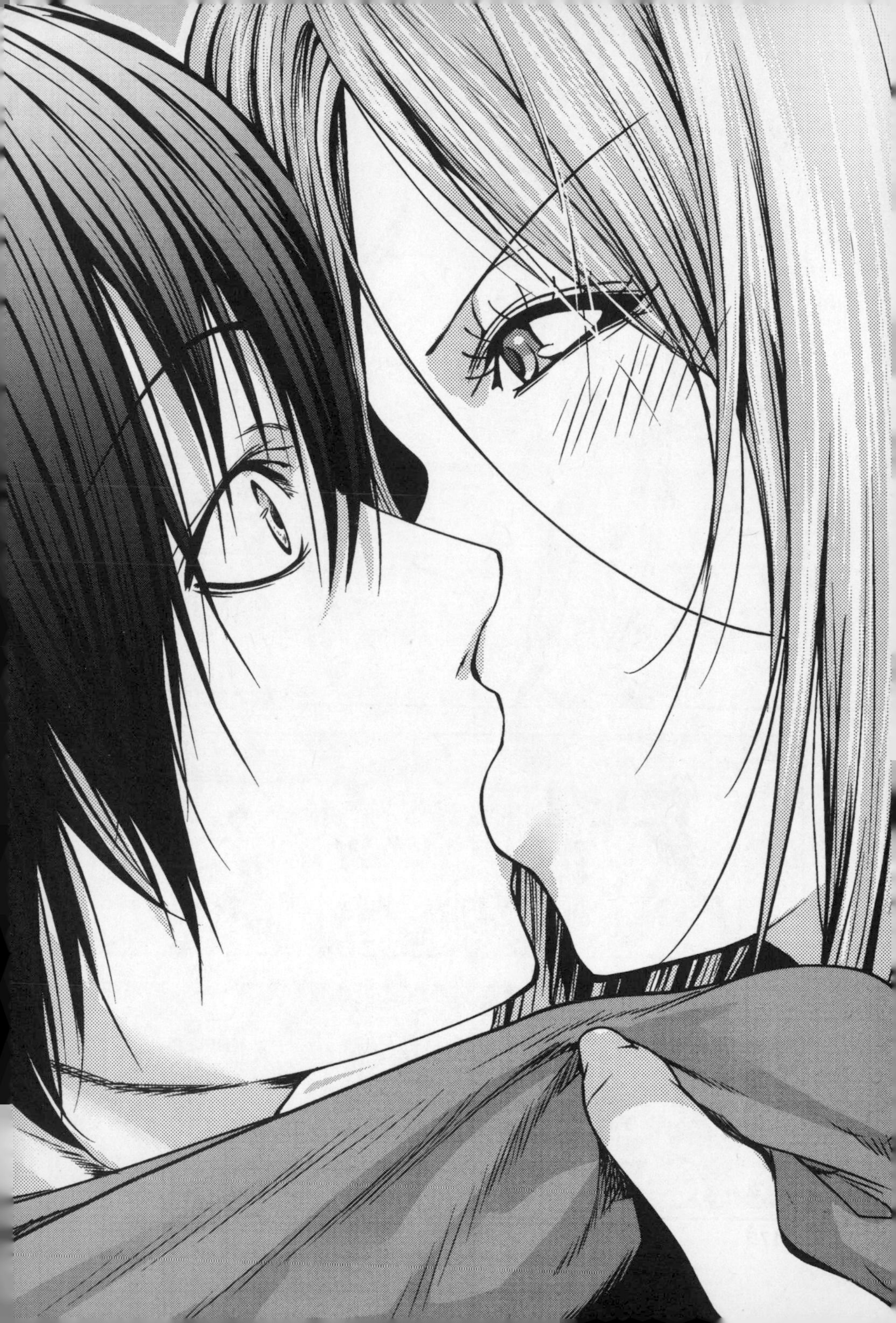

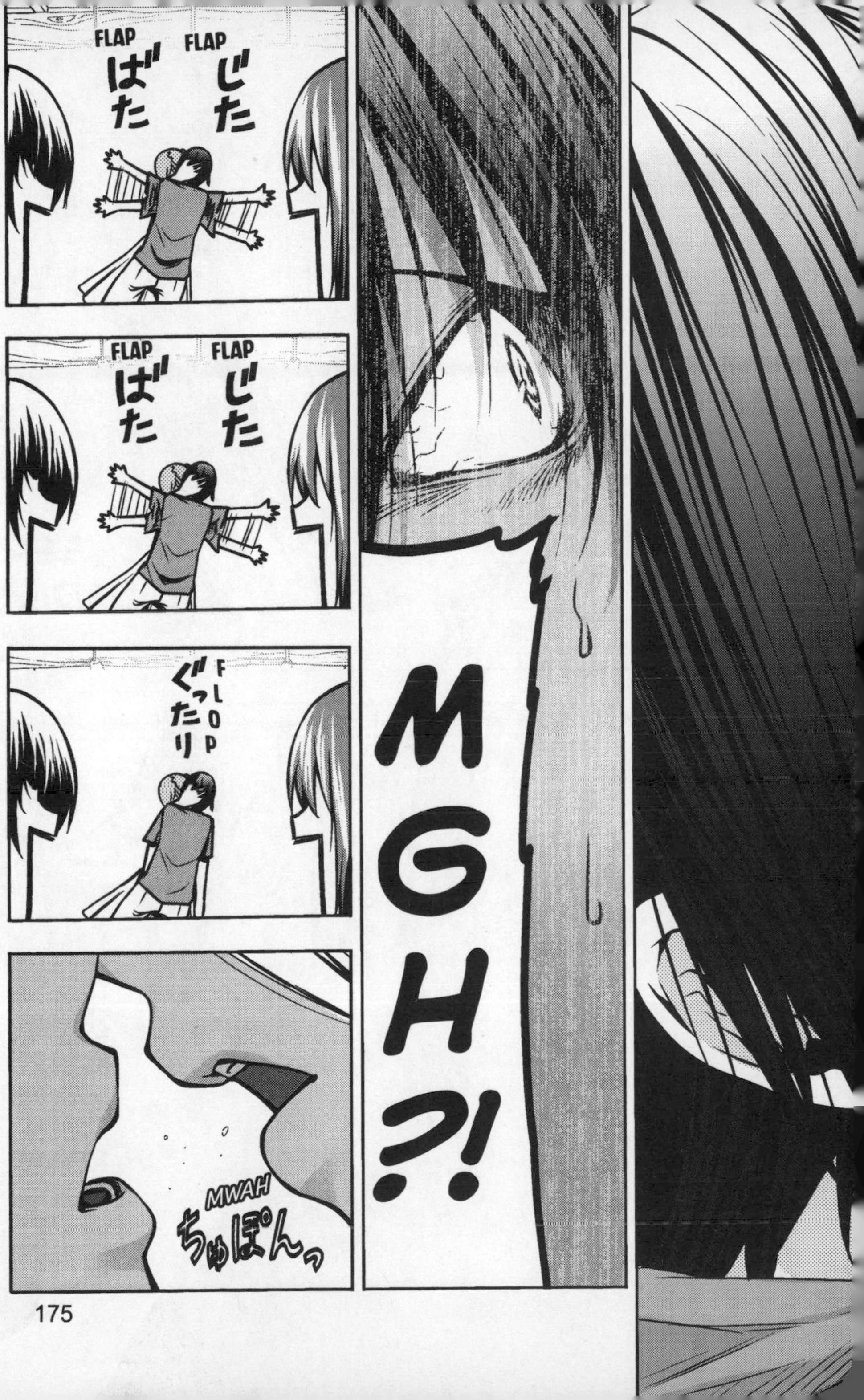
MGH?!
FLAP FLAP
じたばた
FLAP FLAP
じたばた
FLOP
ぐったり
MWAH
ちゅぽんっ

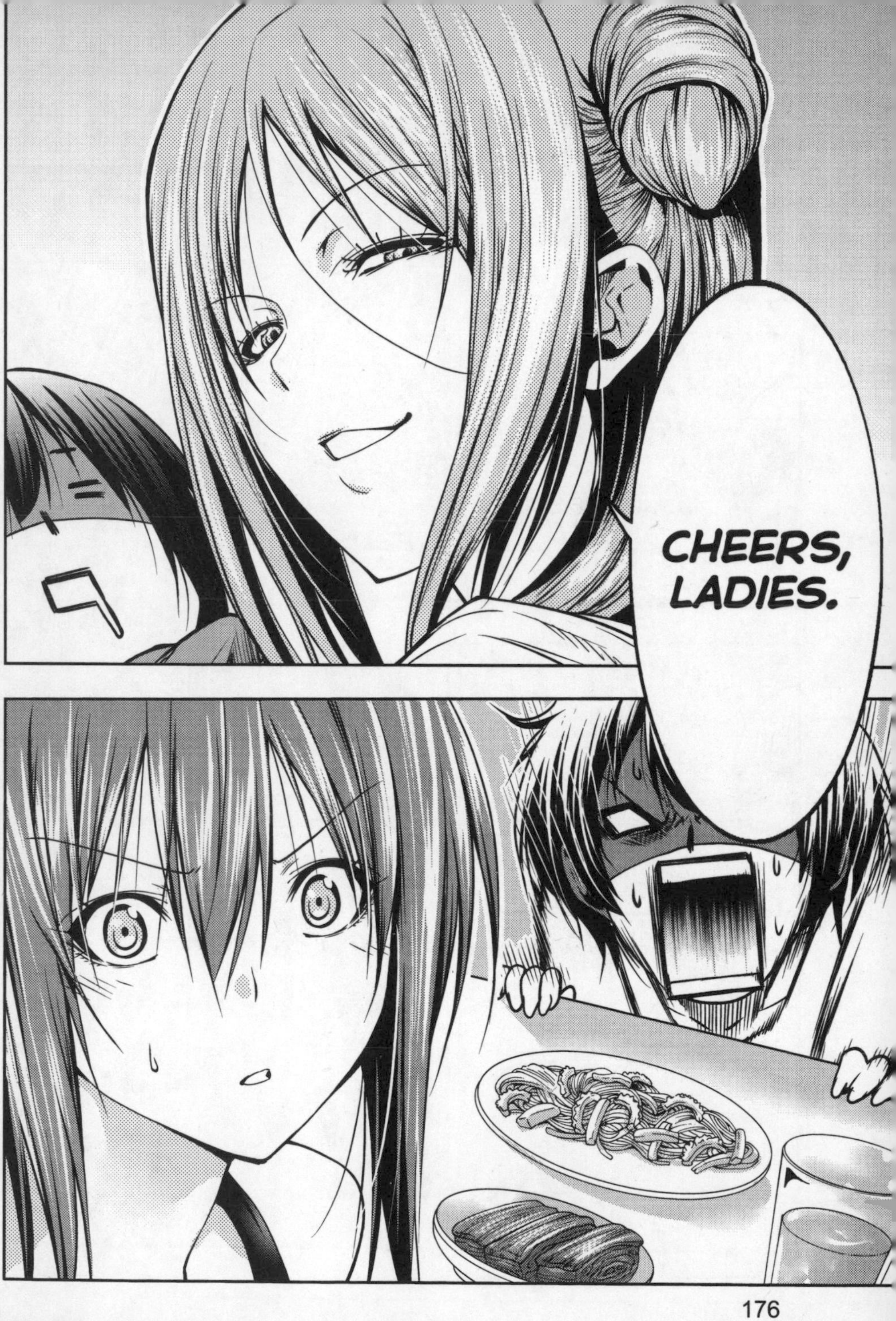
CHEERS, LADIES.

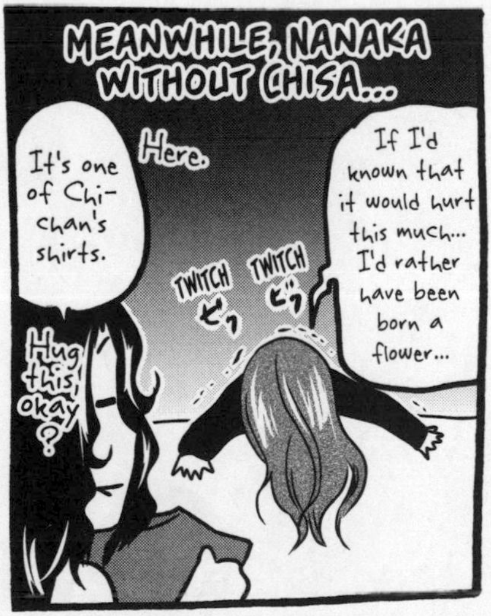
MEANWHILE, NANAKA WITHOUT CHISA...
If I'd known that it would hurt this much... I'd rather have been born a flower...
TWITCH ビッ
TWITCH ビッ
Here.
It's one of Chi-chan's shirts.
Hug this, okay?

Grand Blue Dreaming

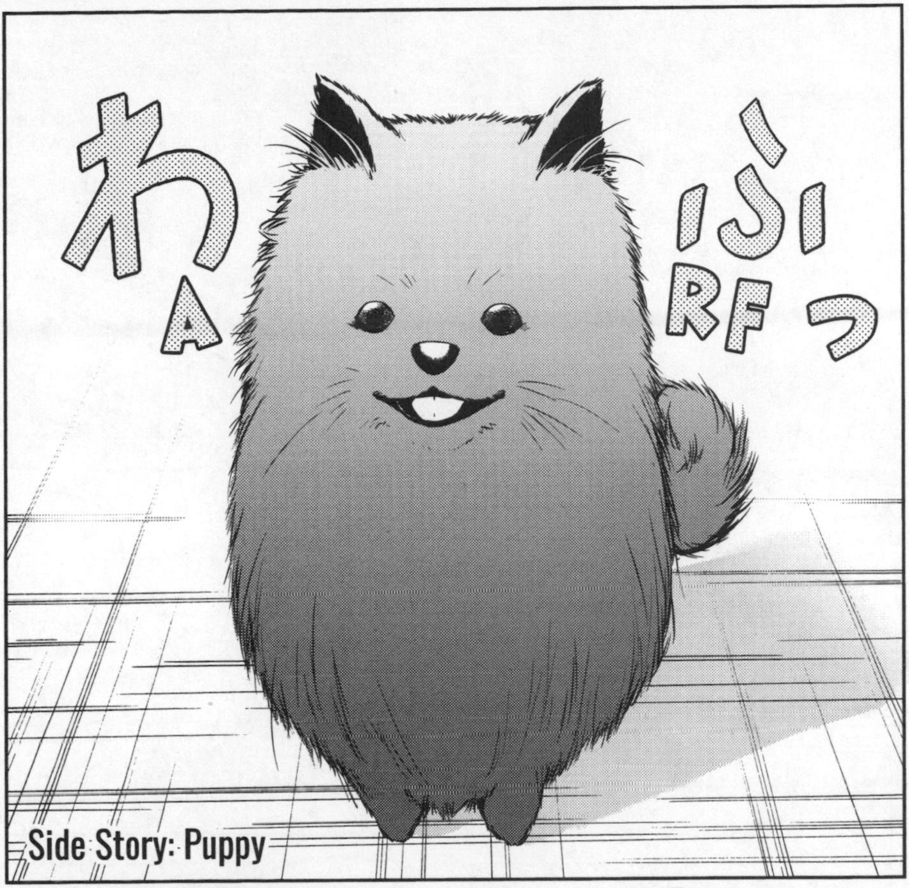
わふっ
ARF

Side Story: Puppy

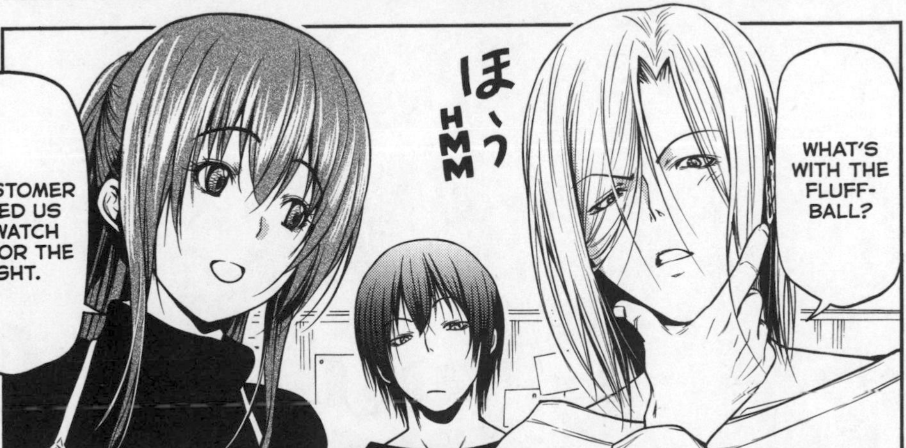
WHAT'S WITH THE FLUFF-BALL?
ほぅ
HMM
A CUSTOMER ASKED US TO WATCH HIM FOR THE NIGHT.

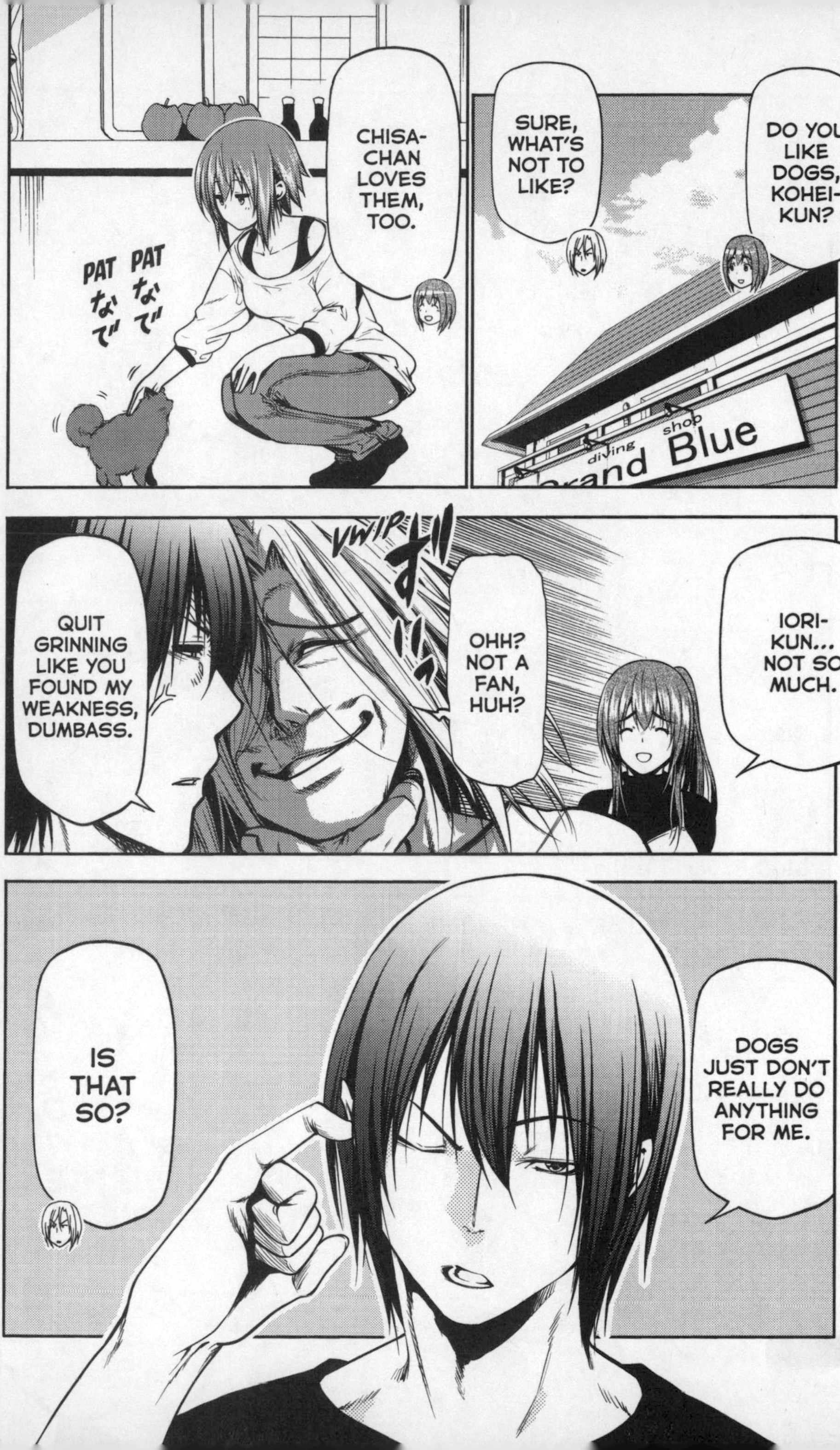
DO YOU LIKE DOGS, KOHEI-KUN?
SURE, WHAT'S NOT TO LIKE?
diving shop
rand Blue
CHISA-CHAN LOVES THEM, TOO.
PAT PAT
なでなで
IORI-KUN... NOT SO MUCH.
OHH? NOT A FAN, HUH?
VWIP
ず
QUIT GRINNING LIKE YOU FOUND MY WEAKNESS, DUMBASS.
DOGS JUST DON'T REALLY DO ANYTHING FOR ME.
IS THAT SO?

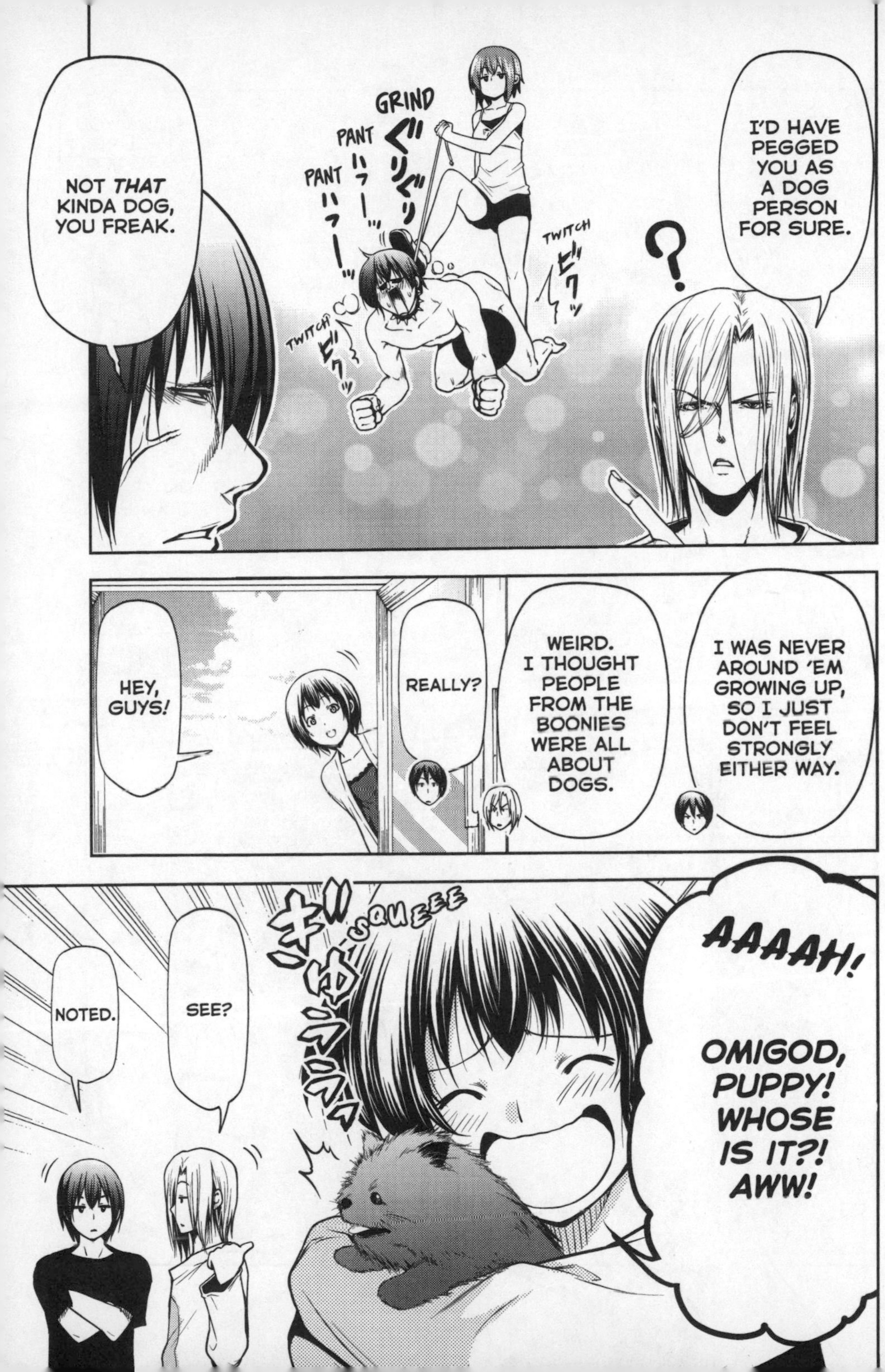
I'D HAVE PEGGED YOU AS A DOG PERSON FOR SURE.
?
TWITCH
GRIND
PANT
PANT
TWITCH
NOT *THAT* KINDA DOG, YOU FREAK.
I WAS NEVER AROUND 'EM GROWING UP, SO I JUST DON'T FEEL STRONGLY EITHER WAY.
WEIRD. I THOUGHT PEOPLE FROM THE BOONIES WERE ALL ABOUT DOGS.
REALLY?
HEY, GUYS!
AAAAH!
OMIGOD, PUPPY! WHOSE IS IT?! AWW!
SQUEEE
SEE?
NOTED.

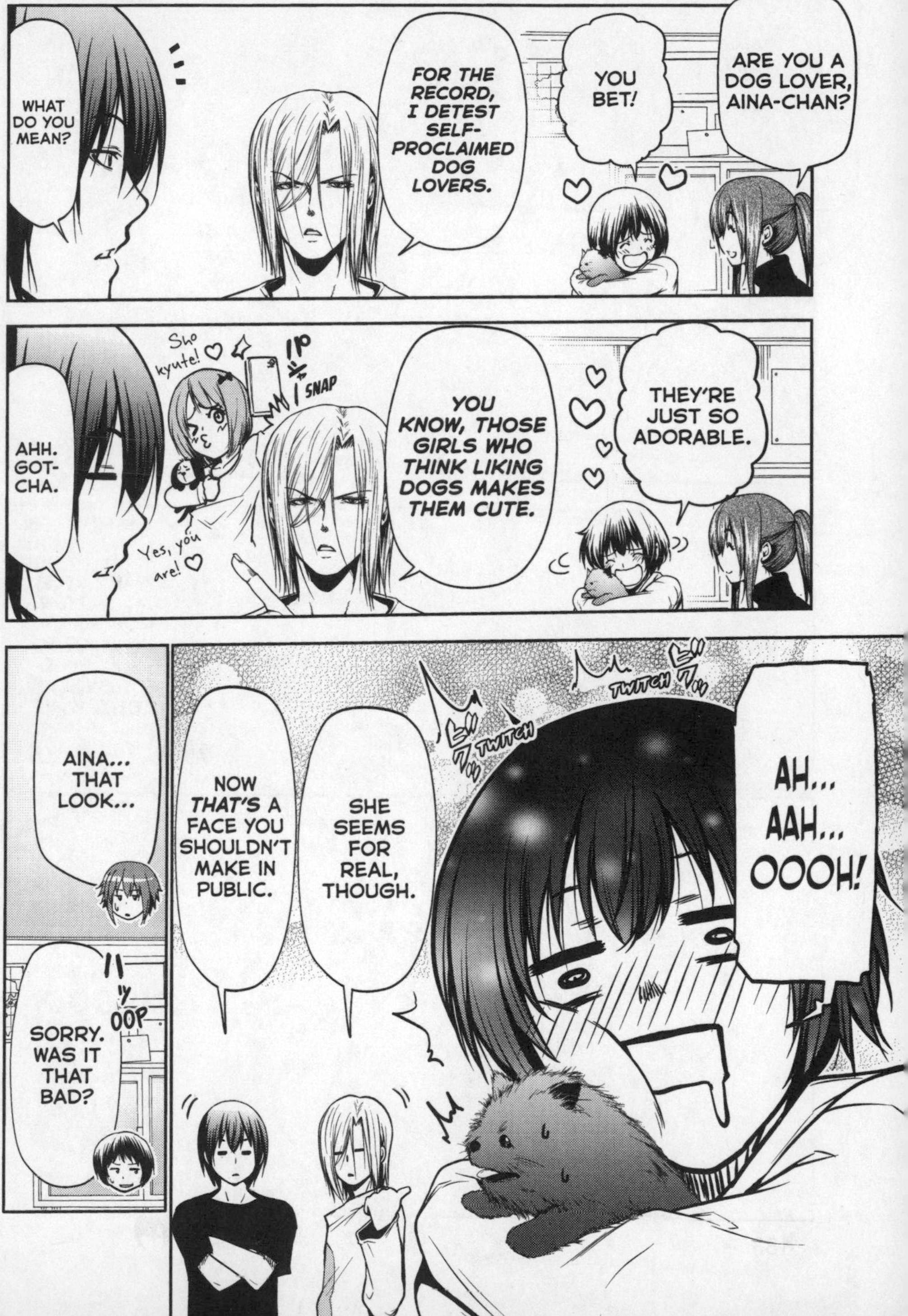
ARE YOU A DOG LOVER, AINA-CHAN?
YOU BET!
FOR THE RECORD, I DETEST SELF-PROCLAIMED DOG LOVERS.
WHAT DO YOU MEAN?
THEY'RE JUST SO ADORABLE.
YOU KNOW, THOSE GIRLS WHO THINK LIKING DOGS MAKES THEM CUTE.
SNAP
Sho kyute!
Yes, you are!
AHH. GOT-CHA.
TWITCH
TWITCH
AH... AAH... OOOH!
SHE SEEMS FOR REAL, THOUGH.
NOW THAT'S A FACE YOU SHOULDN'T MAKE IN PUBLIC.
AINA... THAT LOOK...
OOP
SORRY. WAS IT THAT BAD?

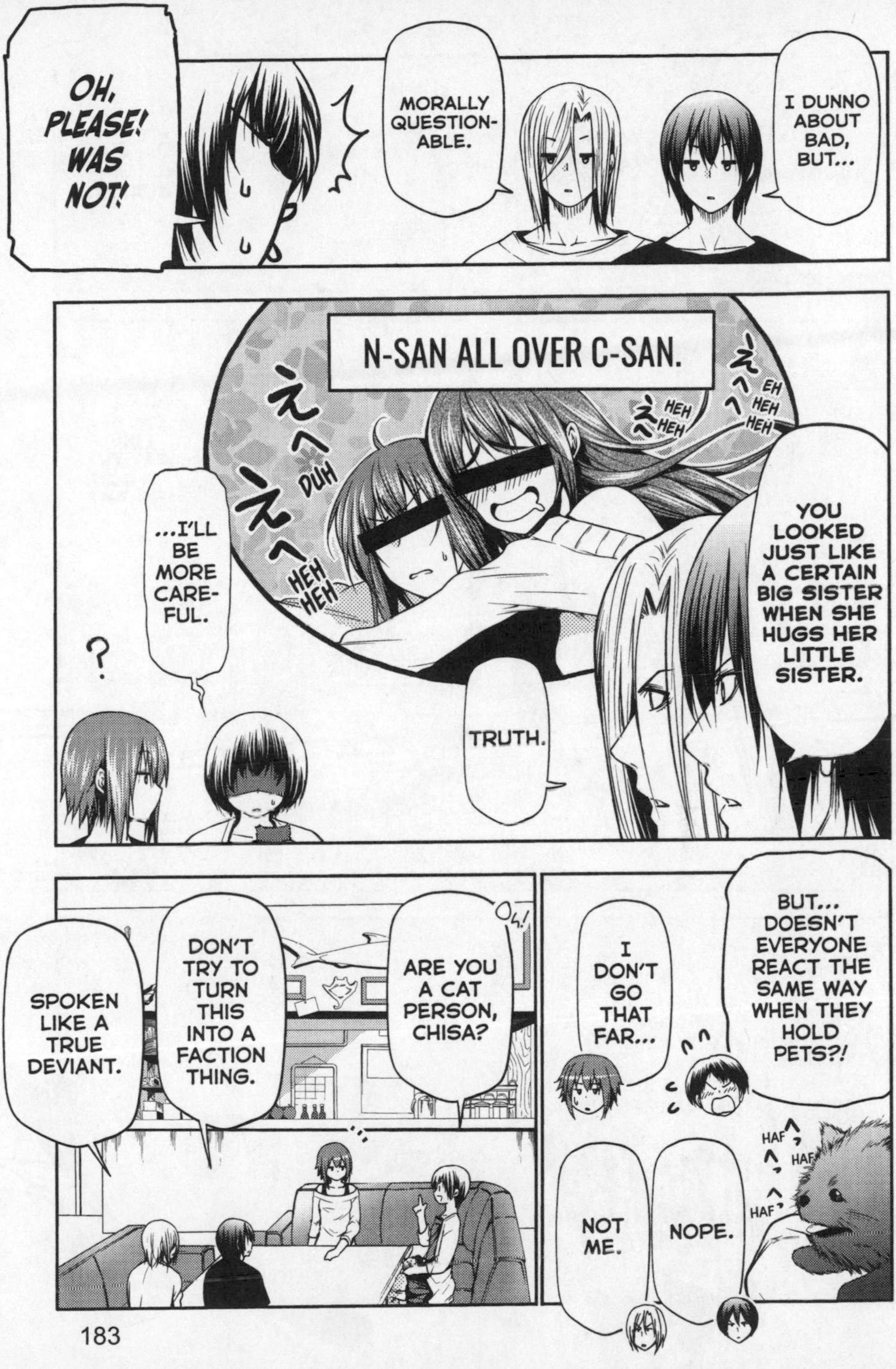
I DUNNO ABOUT BAD, BUT...
MORALLY QUESTION-ABLE.
OH, PLEASE! WAS NOT!
N-SAN ALL OVER C-SAN.
えへ EH HEH HEH
えへ HEH HEH
YOU LOOKED JUST LIKE A CERTAIN BIG SISTER WHEN SHE HUGS HER LITTLE SISTER.
TRUTH.
えへ DUH
えへ HEH HEH
...I'LL BE MORE CARE-FUL.
?
BUT... DOESN'T EVERYONE REACT THE SAME WAY WHEN THEY HOLD PETS?!
I DON'T GO THAT FAR...
HAF HAF HAF
NOPE.
NOT ME.
OH!
ARE YOU A CAT PERSON, CHISA?
DON'T TRY TO TURN THIS INTO A FACTION THING.
SPOKEN LIKE A TRUE DEVIANT.

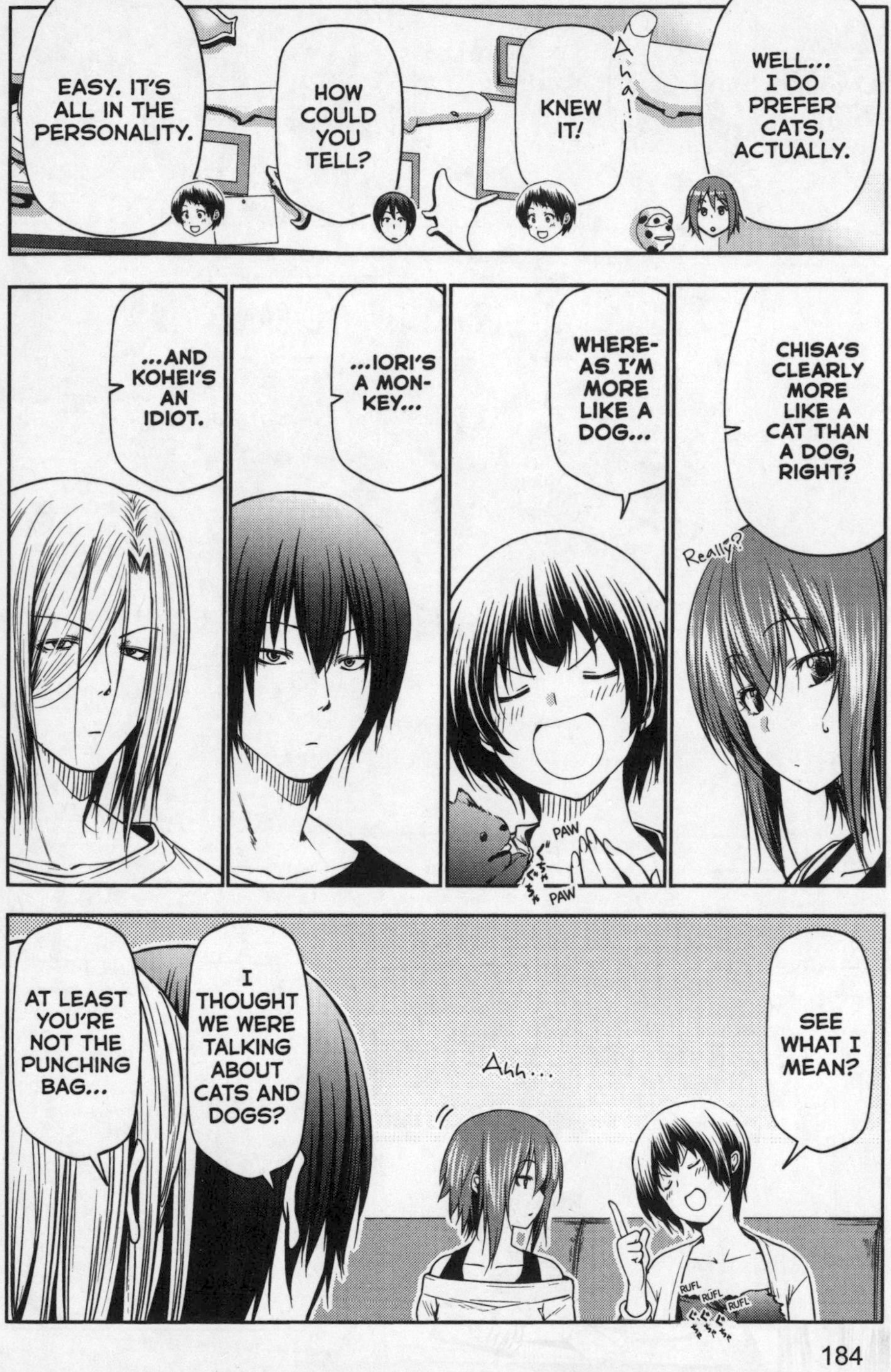
WELL... I DO PREFER CATS, ACTUALLY.
Aha!
KNEW IT!
HOW COULD YOU TELL?
EASY. IT'S ALL IN THE PERSONALITY.
CHISA'S CLEARLY MORE LIKE A CAT THAN A DOG, RIGHT?
Really?
WHERE-AS I'M MORE LIKE A DOG...
PAW
PAW
...IORI'S A MON-KEY...
...AND KOHEI'S AN IDIOT.
SEE WHAT I MEAN?
RUFL
RUFL
RUFL
Ahh...
I THOUGHT WE WERE TALKING ABOUT CATS AND DOGS?
AT LEAST YOU'RE NOT THE PUNCHING BAG...

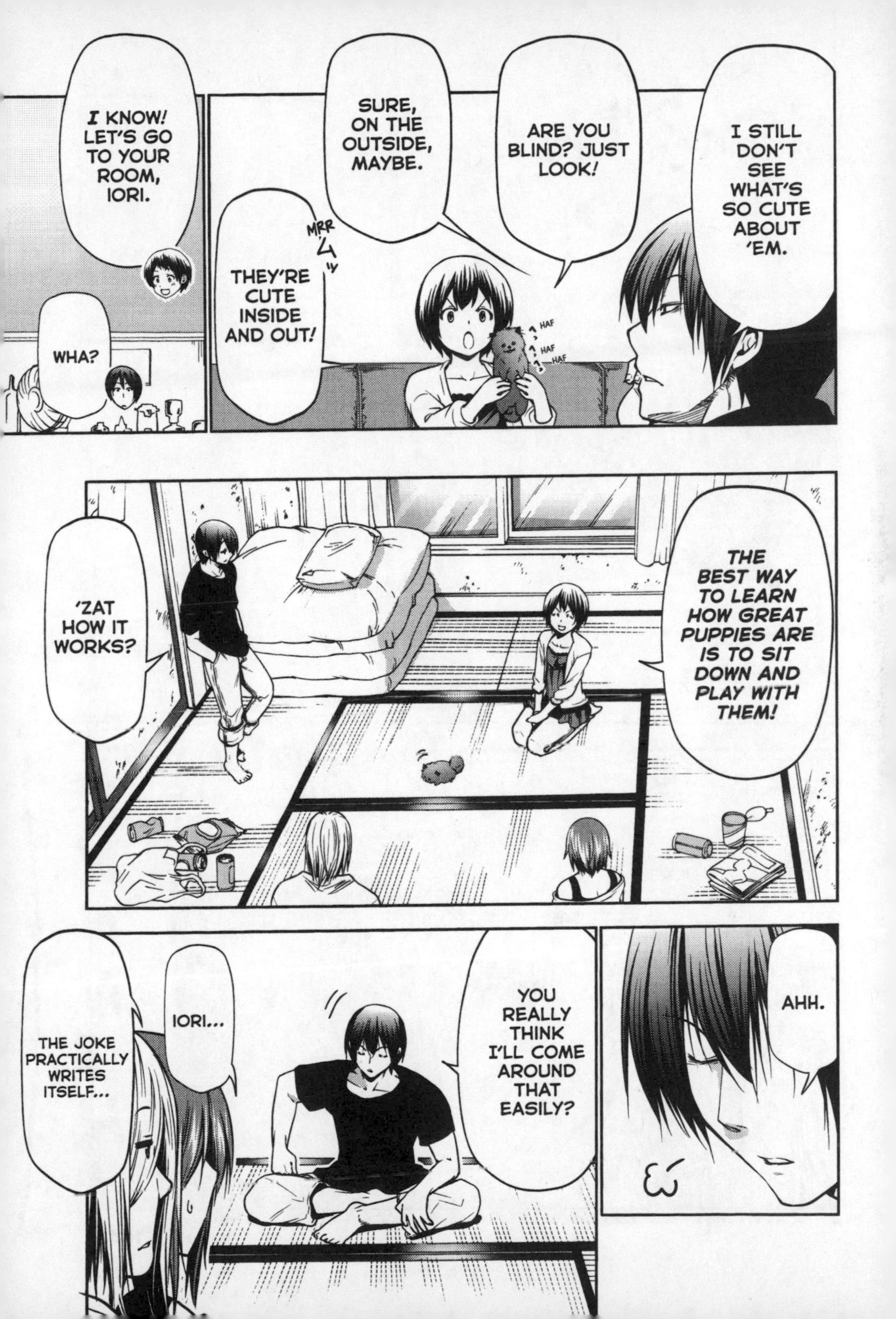
I STILL DON'T SEE WHAT'S SO CUTE ABOUT 'EM.
ARE YOU BLIND? JUST LOOK!
HAF HAF HAF
SURE, ON THE OUTSIDE, MAYBE.
MRR
THEY'RE CUTE INSIDE AND OUT!
I KNOW! LET'S GO TO YOUR ROOM, IORI.
WHA?
THE BEST WAY TO LEARN HOW GREAT PUPPIES ARE IS TO SIT DOWN AND PLAY WITH THEM!
'ZAT HOW IT WORKS?
AHH.
YOU REALLY THINK I'LL COME AROUND THAT EASILY?
IORI...
THE JOKE PRACTICALLY WRITES ITSELF...

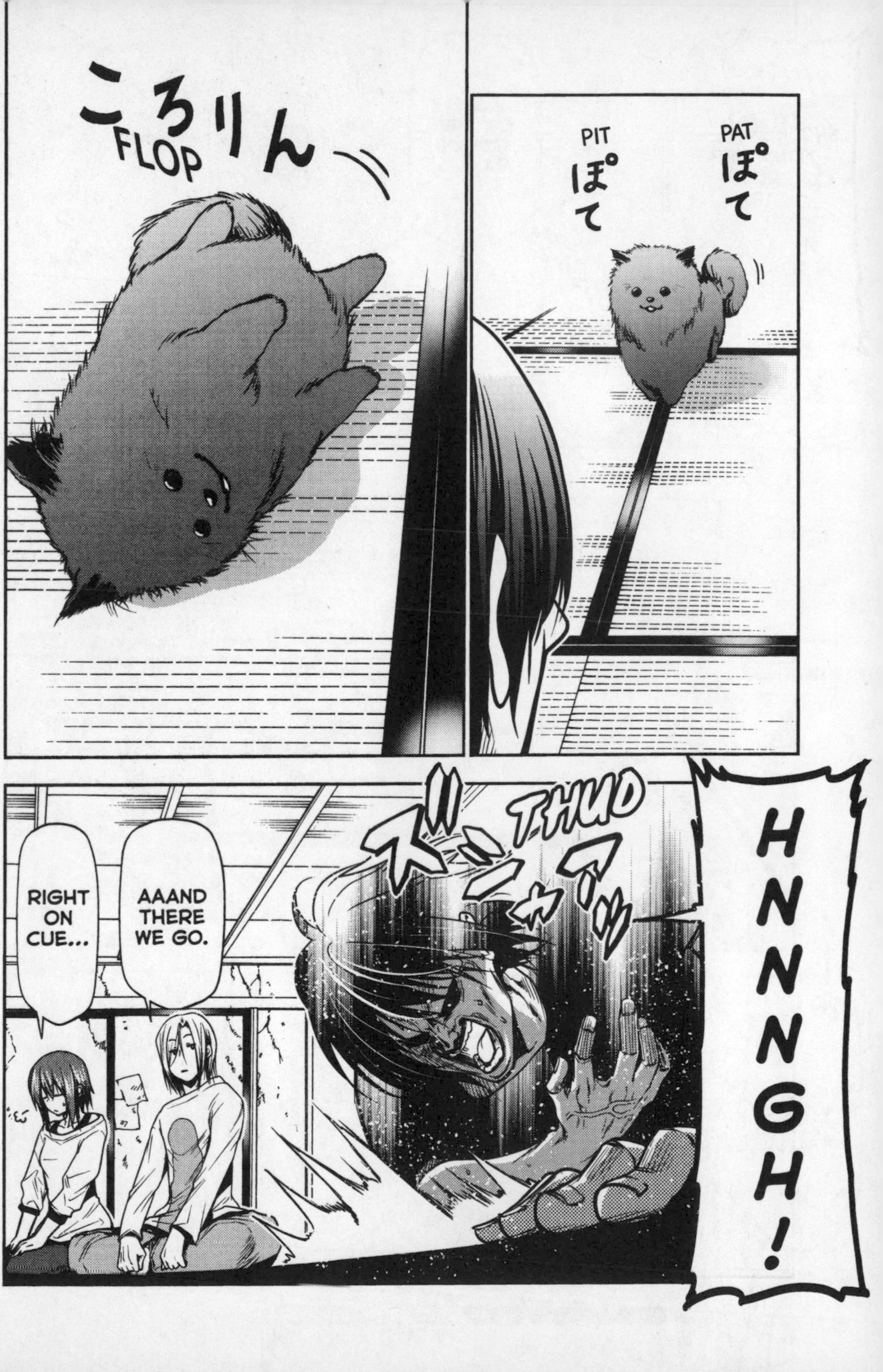
PAT
ぽて
PIT
ぽて
ころりん
FLOP
HNNNGH!
THUD
AAAND THERE WE GO.
RIGHT ON CUE...

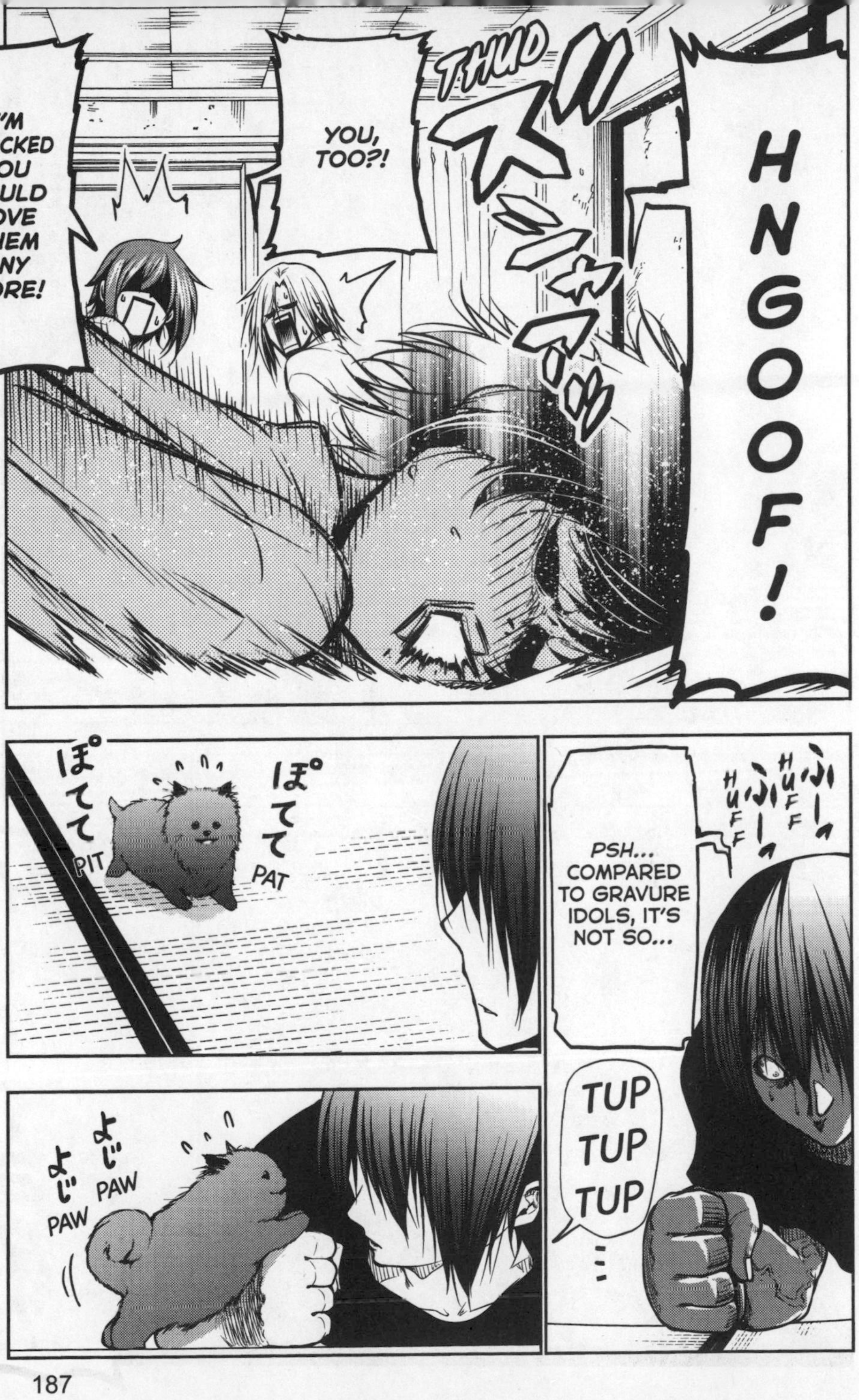
HNGOOF!
THUD
YOU, TOO?!
I'M SHOCKED YOU COULD LOVE THEM ANY MORE!
ふーふー
HUFF HUFF
PSH... COMPARED TO GRAVURE IDOLS, IT'S NOT SO...
TUP TUP TUP
ぽてぽて
PAT
ぽてぽて
PIT
よじよじ
PAW
よじよじ
PAW

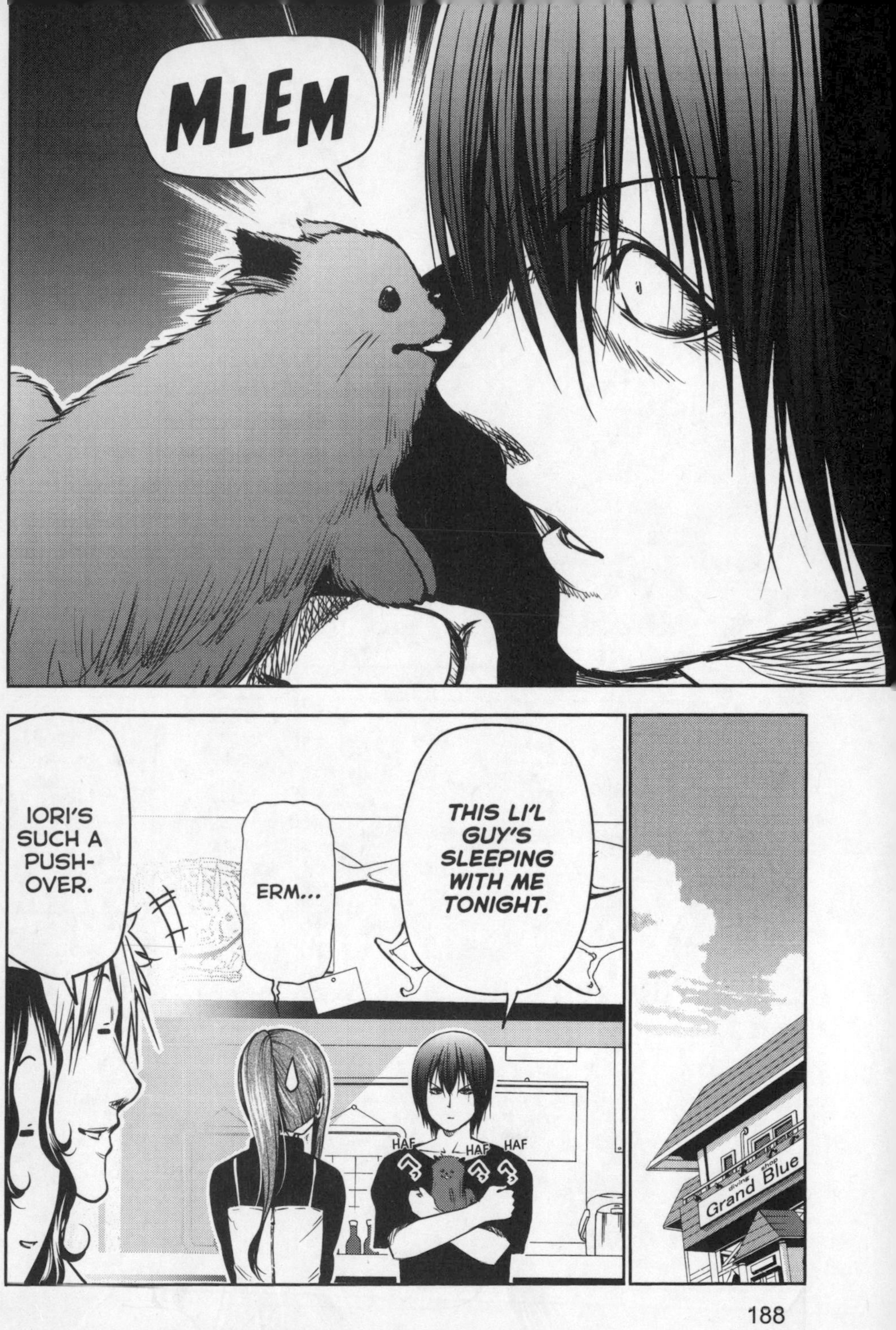
MLEM
diving shop
Grand Blue
THIS LI'L GUY'S SLEEPING WITH ME TONIGHT.
HAF HAF HAF
ERM...
IORI'S SUCH A PUSH-OVER.

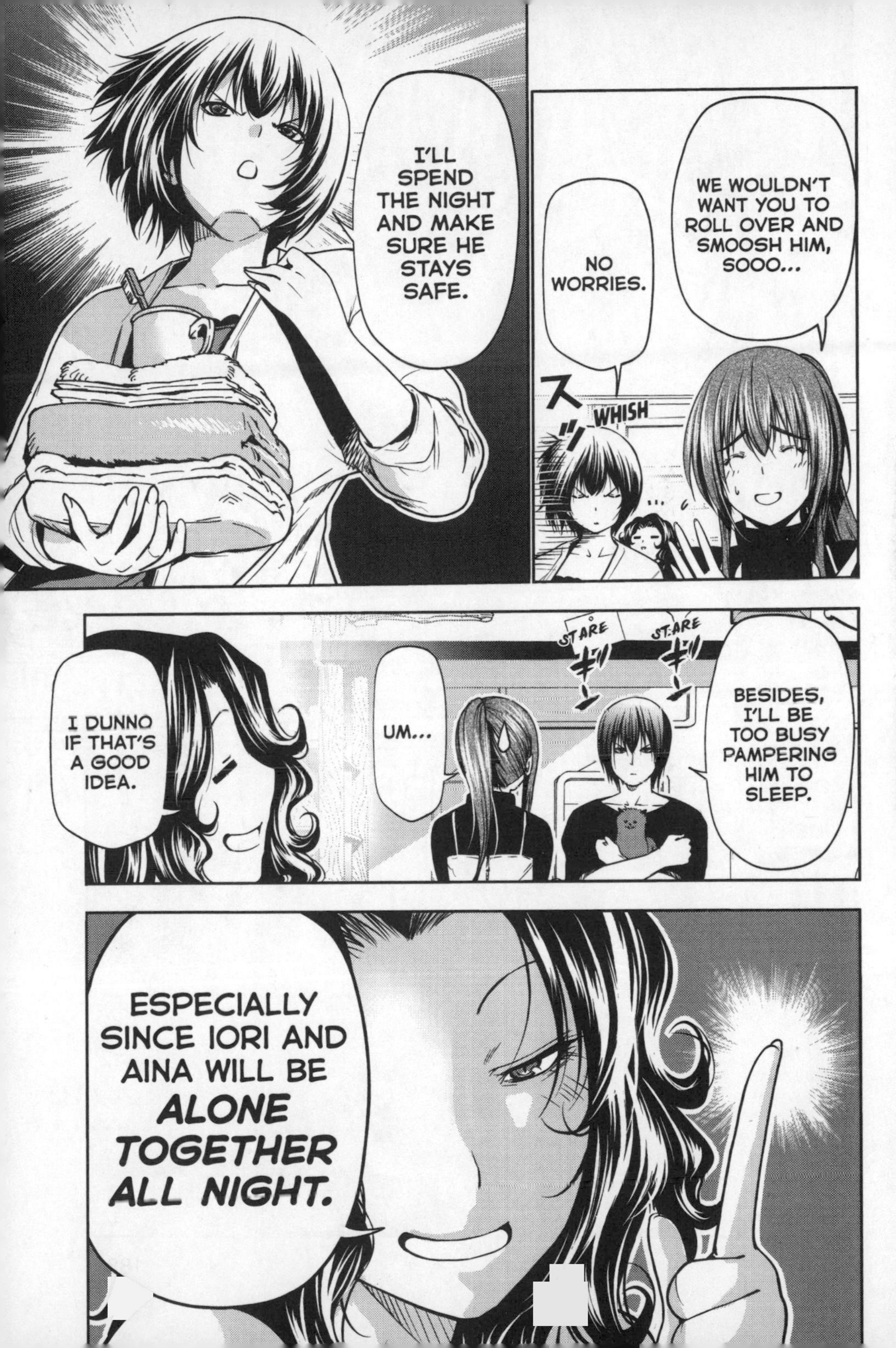
WE WOULDN'T WANT YOU TO ROLL OVER AND SMOOSH HIM, SOOO...
NO WORRIES.
WHISH
I'LL SPEND THE NIGHT AND MAKE SURE HE STAYS SAFE.
BESIDES, I'LL BE TOO BUSY PAMPERING HIM TO SLEEP.
STARE
STARE
UM...
I DUNNO IF THAT'S A GOOD IDEA.
ESPECIALLY SINCE IORI AND AINA WILL BE ALONE TOGETHER ALL NIGHT.

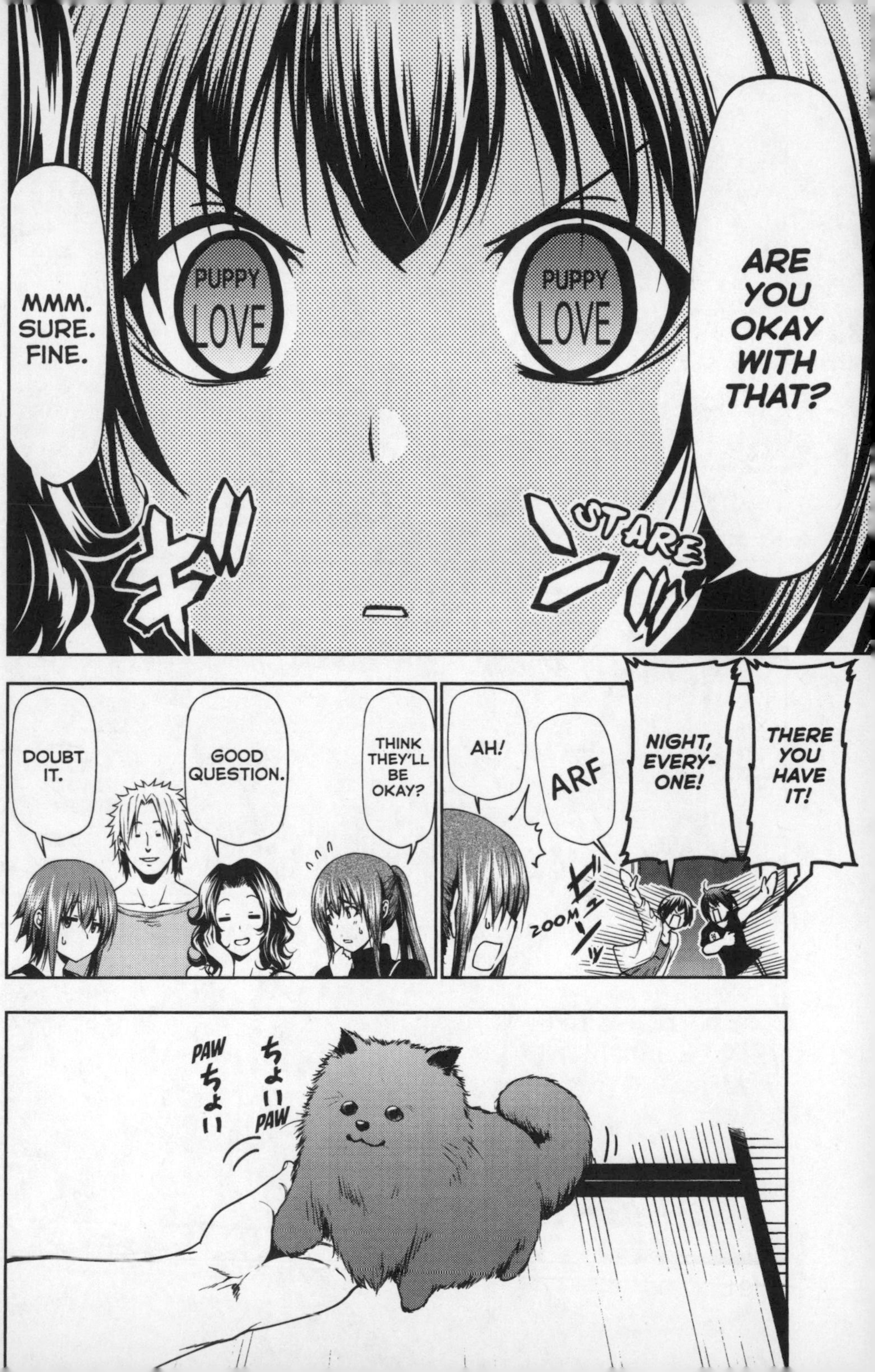
ARE YOU OKAY WITH THAT?
PUPPY LOVE
PUPPY LOVE
STARE
MMM. SURE. FINE.
THERE YOU HAVE IT!
NIGHT, EVERY-ONE!
ARF
AH!
ZOOM
THINK THEY'LL BE OKAY?
GOOD QUESTION.
DOUBT IT.
ちょい PAW
PAW ちょい

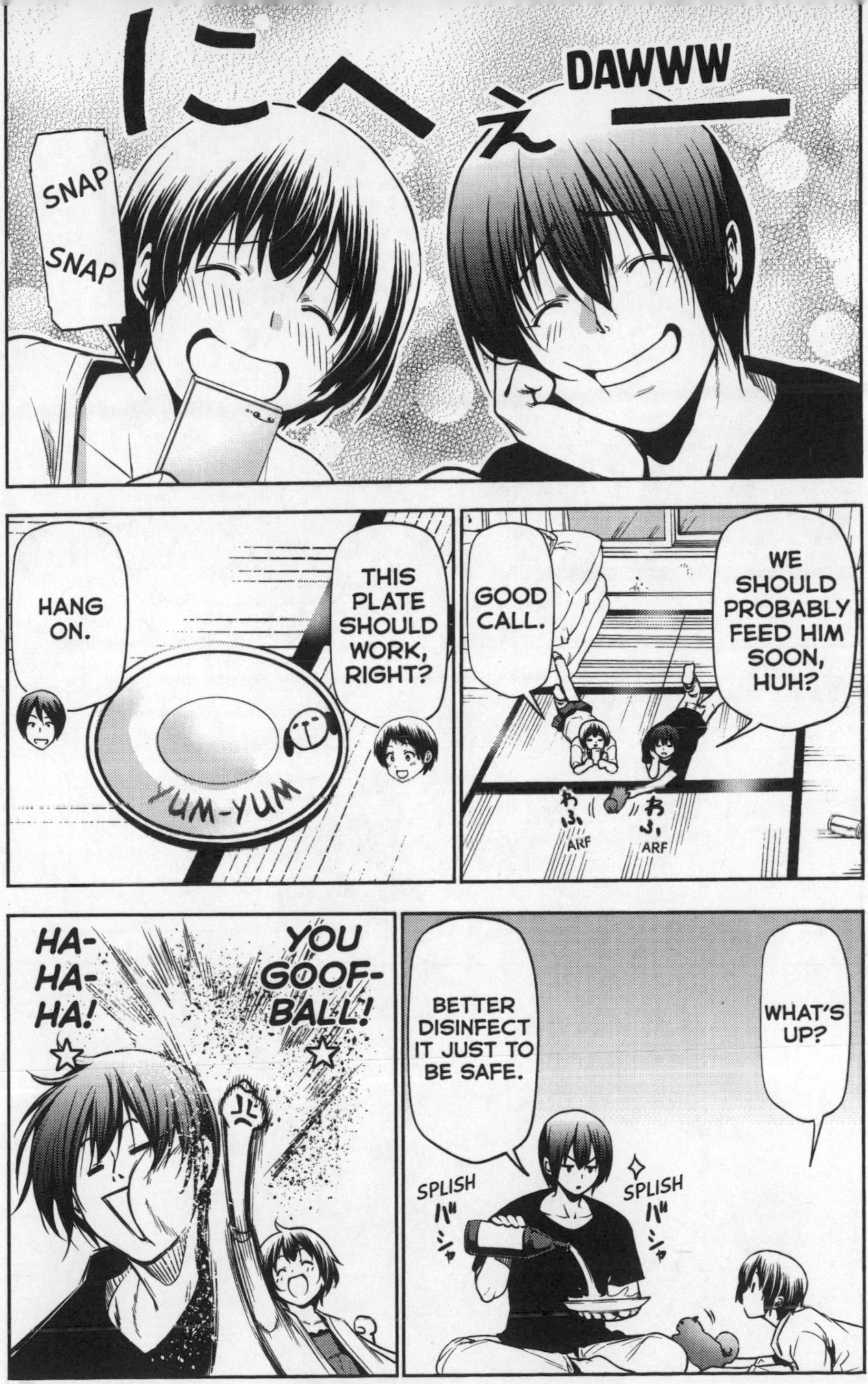
にへえー
DAWWW
SNAP
SNAP
WE SHOULD PROBABLY FEED HIM SOON, HUH?
GOOD CALL.
わふ
ARF
わふ
ARF
THIS PLATE SHOULD WORK, RIGHT?
HANG ON.
YUM-YUM
WHAT'S UP?
BETTER DISINFECT IT JUST TO BE SAFE.
バシャ
SPLISH
バシャ
SPLISH
YOU GOOF-BALL!
HA-HA-HA!

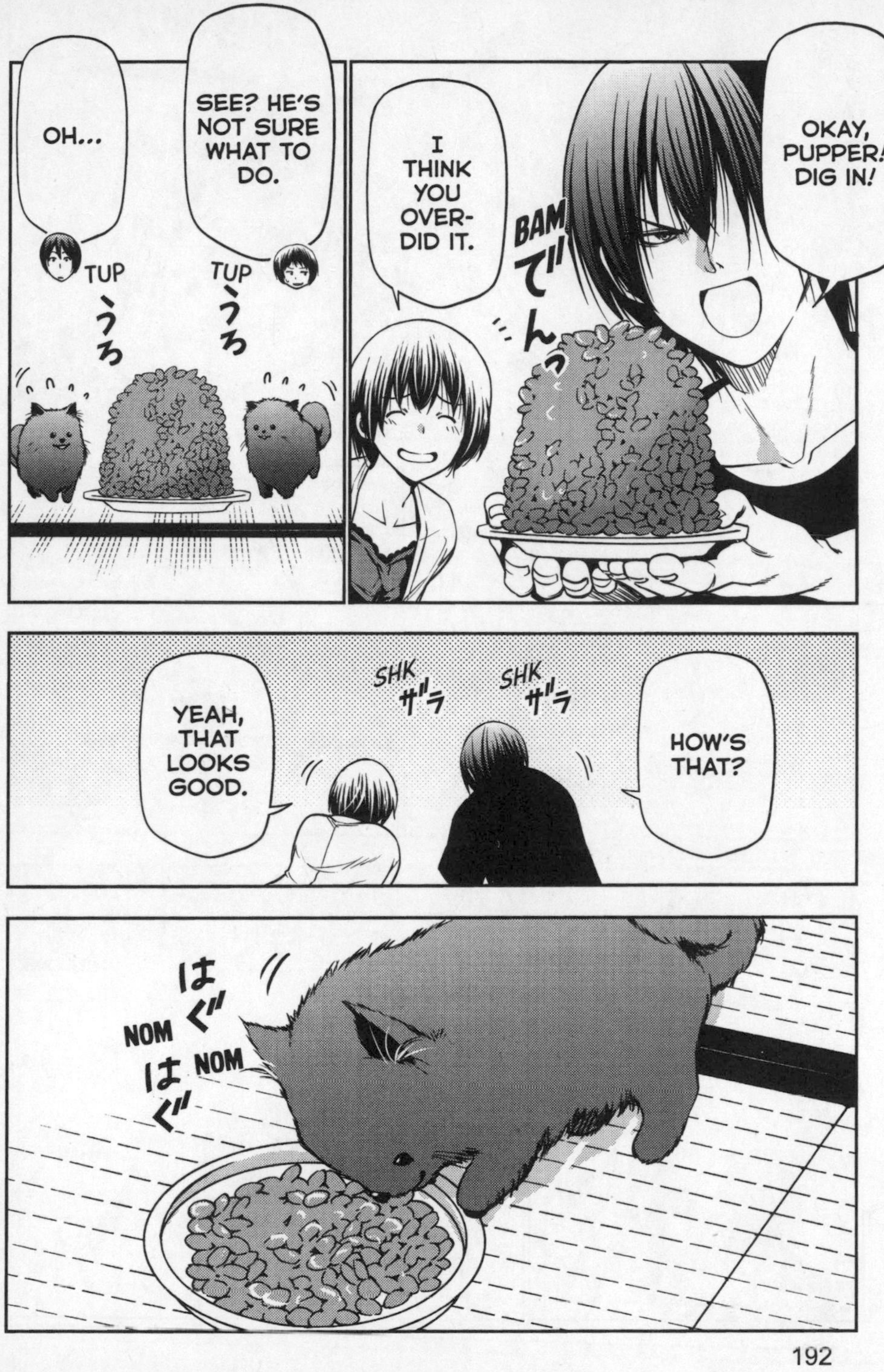

OKAY, PUPPER! DIG IN!
BAM
でんっ
I THINK YOU OVER-DID IT.
SEE? HE'S NOT SURE WHAT TO DO.
TUP
うろ
OH...
TUP
うろ
HOW'S THAT?
SHK
ザラ
SHK
ザラ
YEAH, THAT LOOKS GOOD.
はぐ
NOM
はぐ
NOM

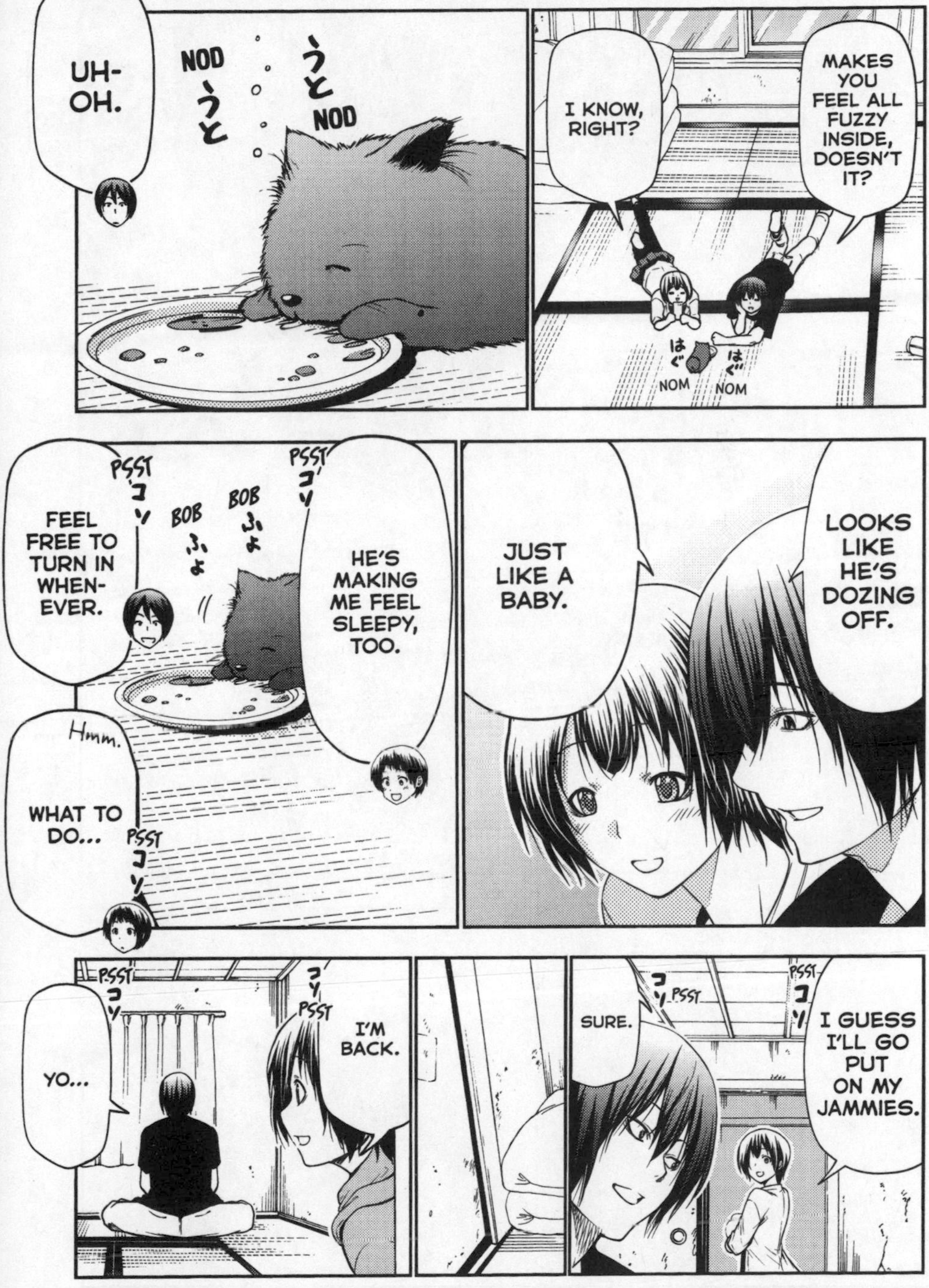

MAKES YOU FEEL ALL FUZZY INSIDE, DOESN'T IT?
I KNOW, RIGHT?
はぐ NOM
はぐ NOM
うと NOD
うと NOD
UH-OH.
LOOKS LIKE HE'S DOZING OFF.
JUST LIKE A BABY.
PSST コソ
HE'S MAKING ME FEEL SLEEPY, TOO.
BOB ふよ
BOB ふよ
PSST コソ
FEEL FREE TO TURN IN WHEN-EVER.
Hmm.
WHAT TO DO...
PSST コソ
PSST コソ
I GUESS I'LL GO PUT ON MY JAMMIES.
コソ PSST
SURE.
コソ PSST
I'M BACK.
PSST コソ
YO...

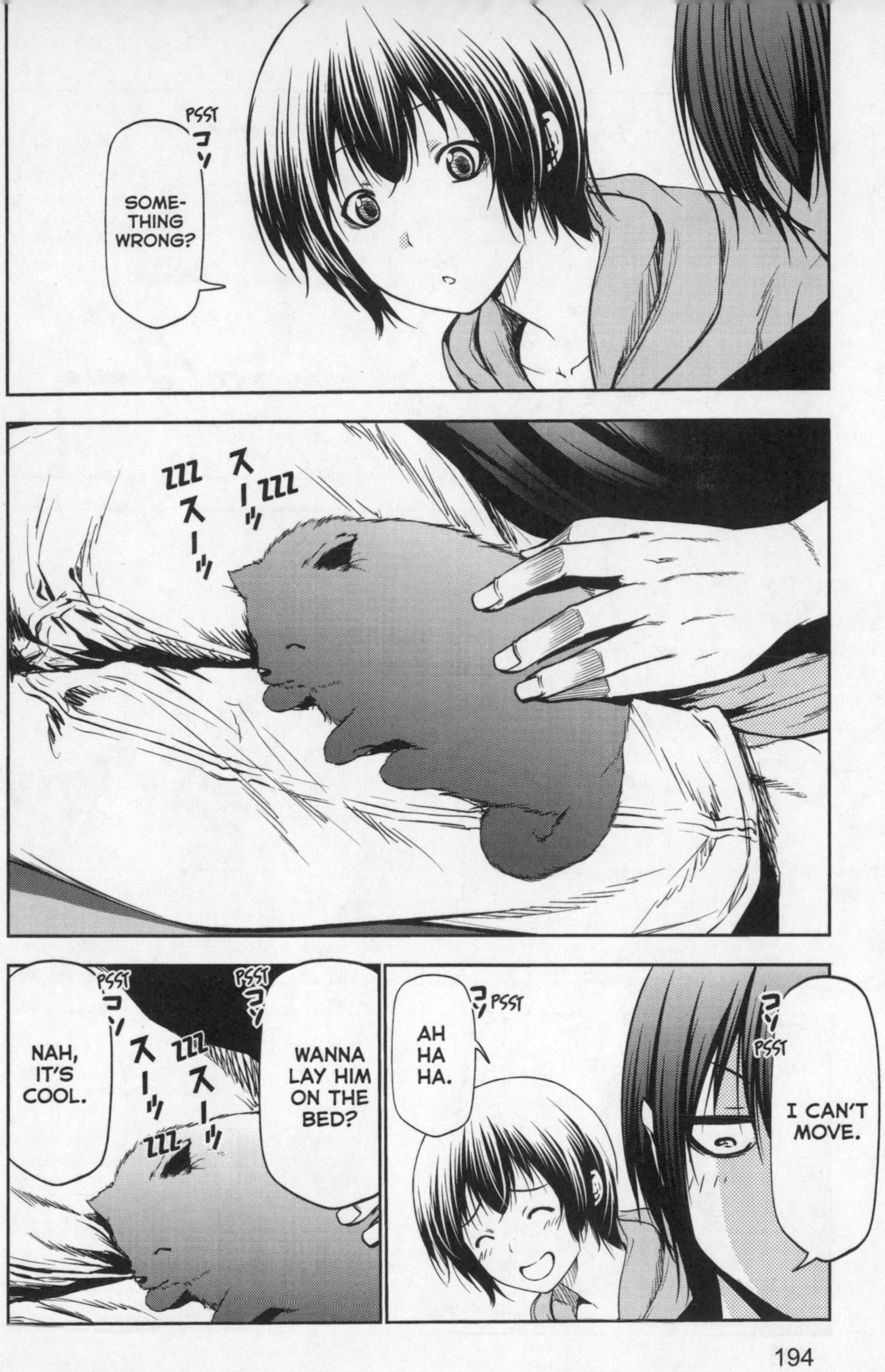
PSST
コソ
SOME-THING WRONG?
ZZZ
スーッ
ZZZ
スーッ
コソ
PSST
I CAN'T MOVE.
コソ
PSST
AH HA HA.
PSST
コソ
WANNA LAY HIM ON THE BED?
ZZZ
スーッ
PSST
コソ
NAH, IT'S COOL.
ZZZ
スーッ
ZZZ

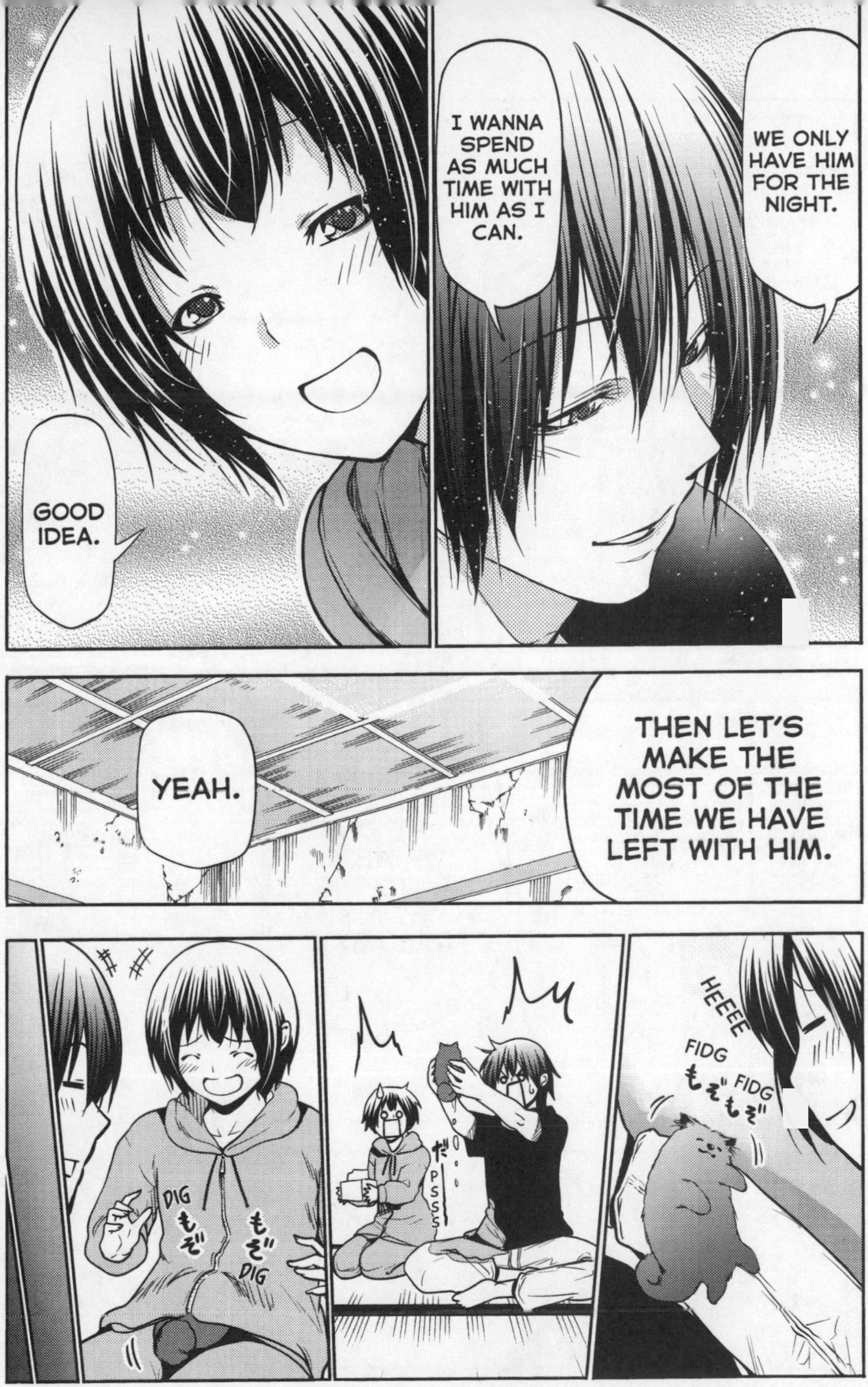
WE ONLY HAVE HIM FOR THE NIGHT.
I WANNA SPEND AS MUCH TIME WITH HIM AS I CAN.
GOOD IDEA.
THEN LET'S MAKE THE MOST OF THE TIME WE HAVE LEFT WITH HIM.
YEAH.
HEEEE
FIDG もぞ FIDG もぞ
だ PSSS
DIG もぞ
もぞ DIG

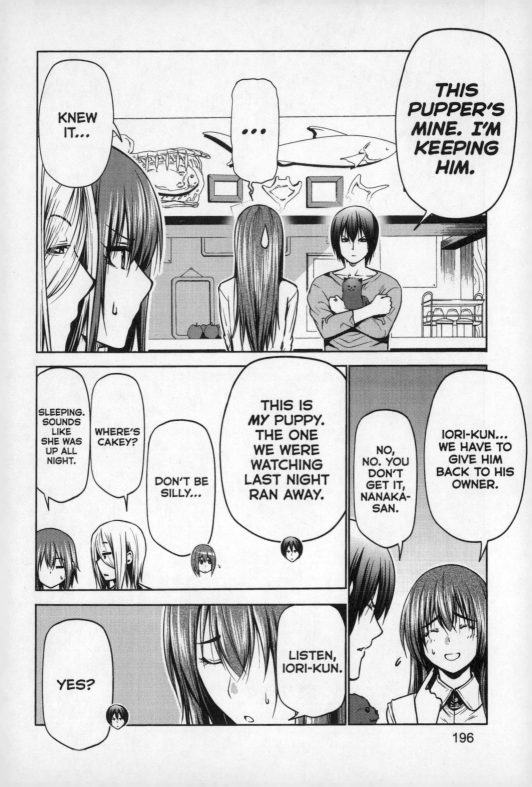

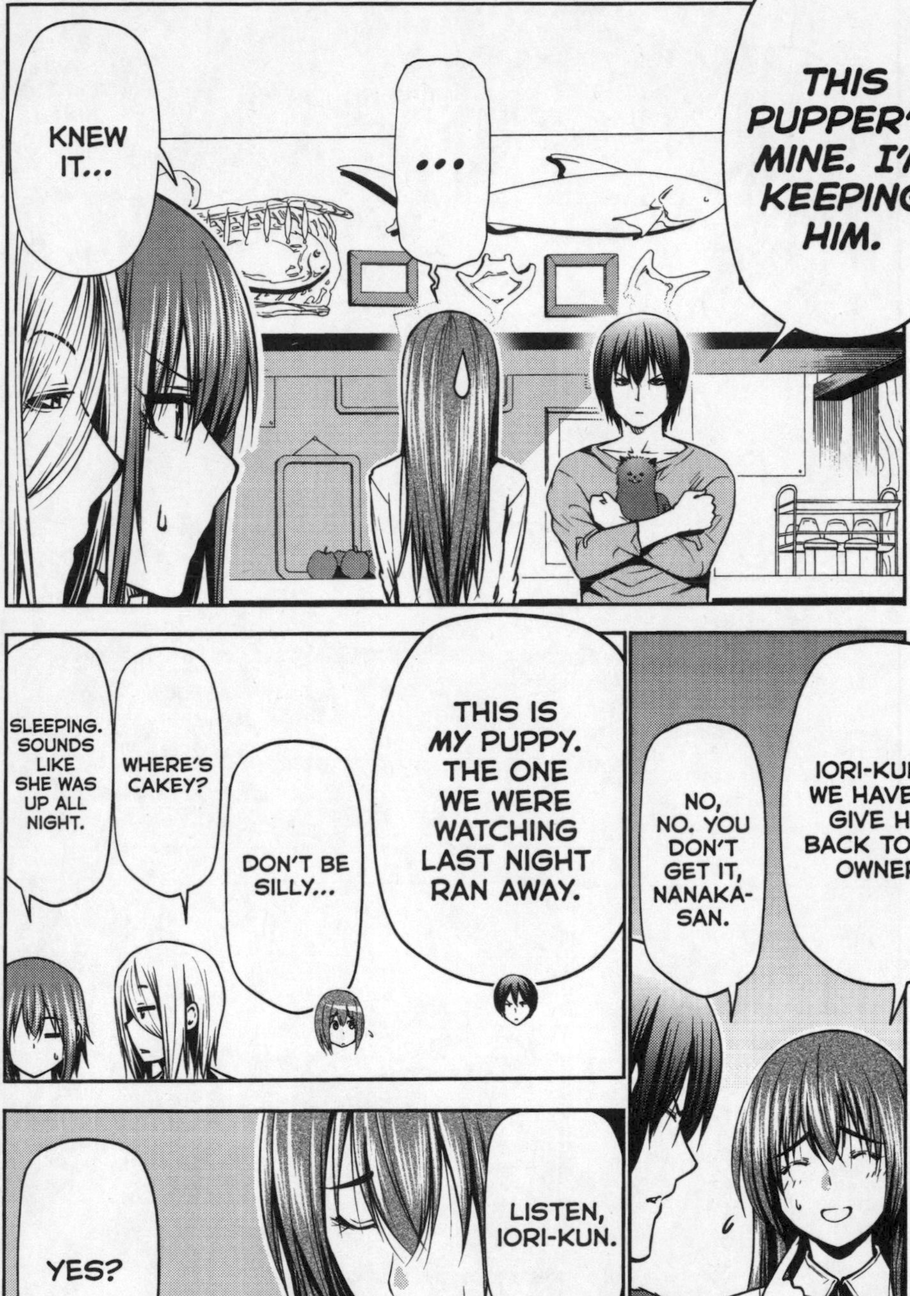
THIS PUPPER'S MINE. I'M KEEPING HIM.
...
KNEW IT...
IORI-KUN... WE HAVE TO GIVE HIM BACK TO HIS OWNER.
NO, NO. YOU DON'T GET IT, NANAKA-SAN.
THIS IS *MY* PUPPY. THE ONE WE WERE WATCHING LAST NIGHT RAN AWAY.
DON'T BE SILLY...
WHERE'S CAKEY?
SLEEPING. SOUNDS LIKE SHE WAS UP ALL NIGHT.
LISTEN, IORI-KUN.
YES?

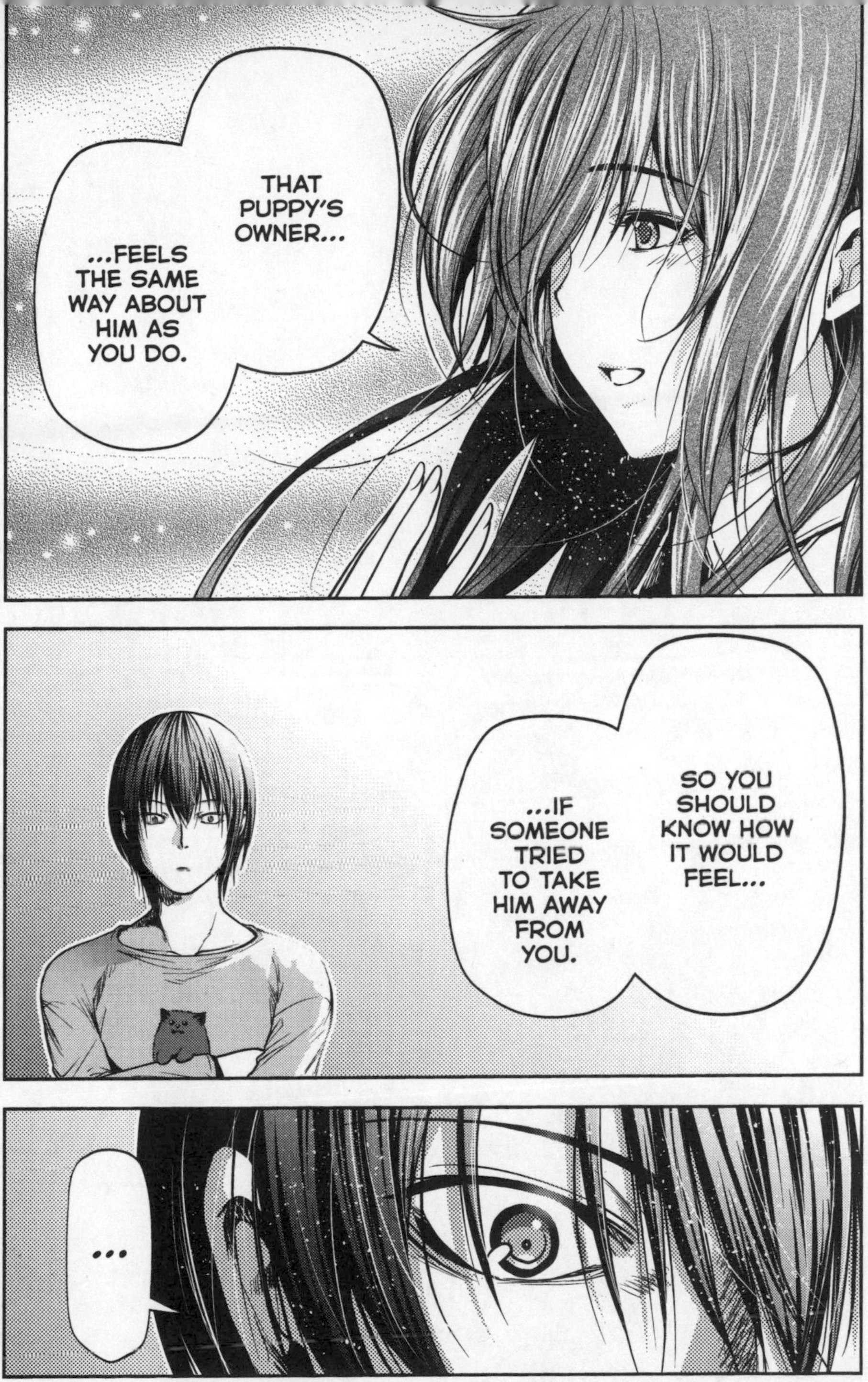
THAT PUPPY'S OWNER...
...FEELS THE SAME WAY ABOUT HIM AS YOU DO.
SO YOU SHOULD KNOW HOW IT WOULD FEEL...
...IF SOMEONE TRIED TO TAKE HIM AWAY FROM YOU.
...

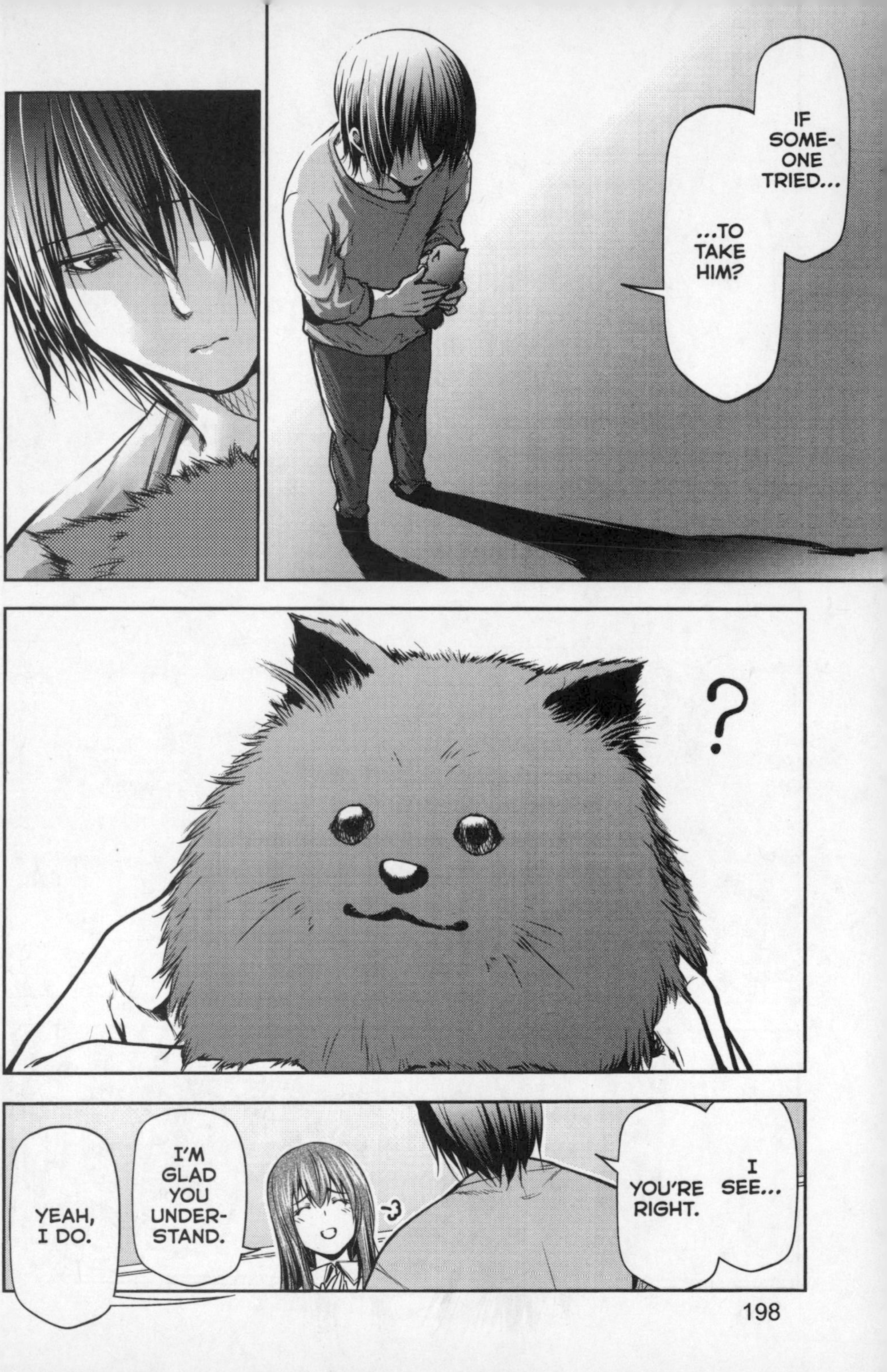
IF SOME-ONE TRIED...
...TO TAKE HIM?
?
I SEE... YOU'RE RIGHT.
I'M GLAD YOU UNDER-STAND.
YEAH, I DO.

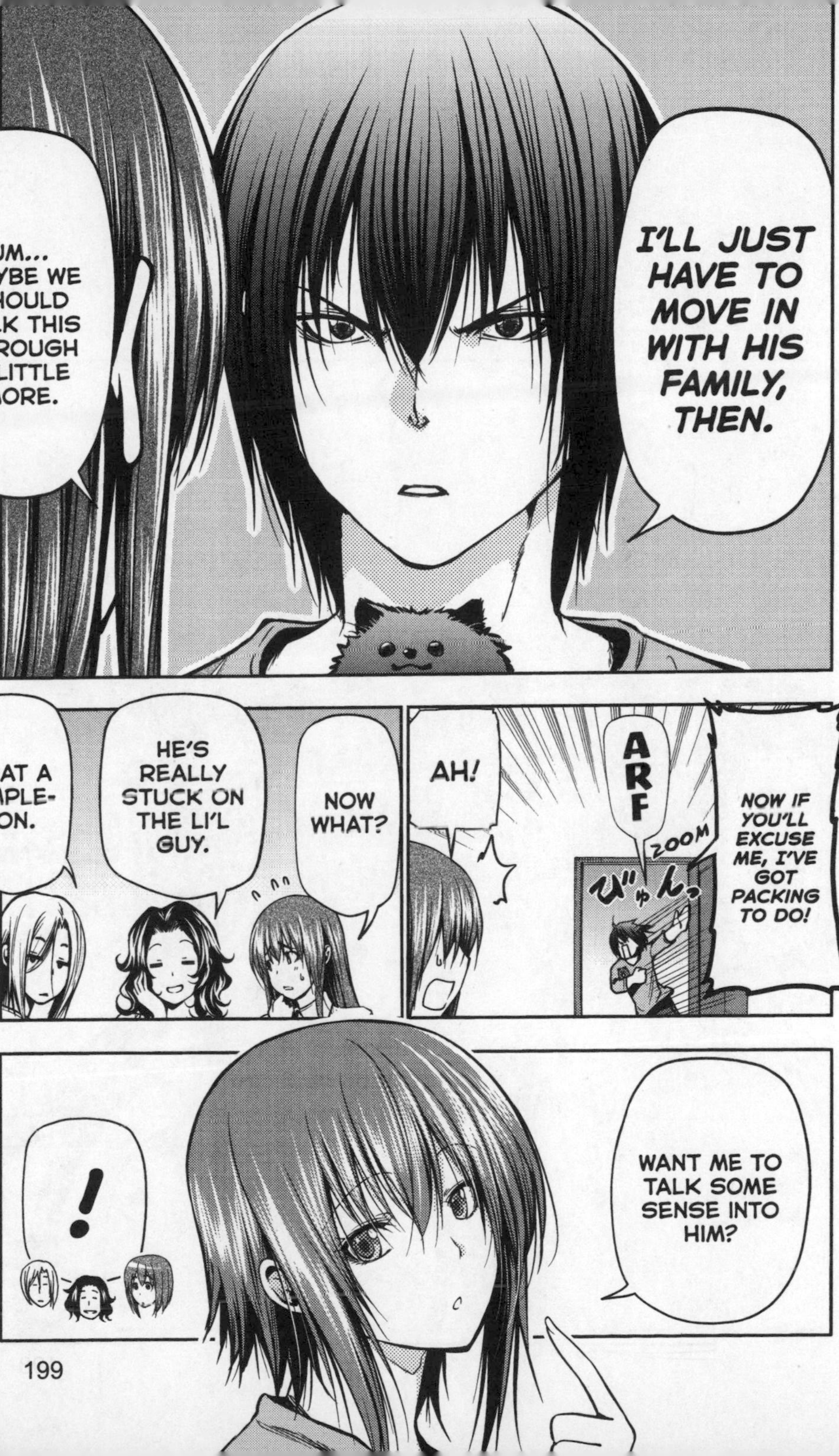
I'LL JUST HAVE TO MOVE IN WITH HIS FAMILY, THEN.
UM... MAYBE WE SHOULD TALK THIS THROUGH A LITTLE MORE.
NOW IF YOU'LL EXCUSE ME, I'VE GOT PACKING TO DO!
ARF
ZOOM
びゅんっ
AH!
NOW WHAT?
HE'S REALLY STUCK ON THE LI'L GUY.
WHAT A SIMPLE-TON.
WANT ME TO TALK SOME SENSE INTO HIM?
!

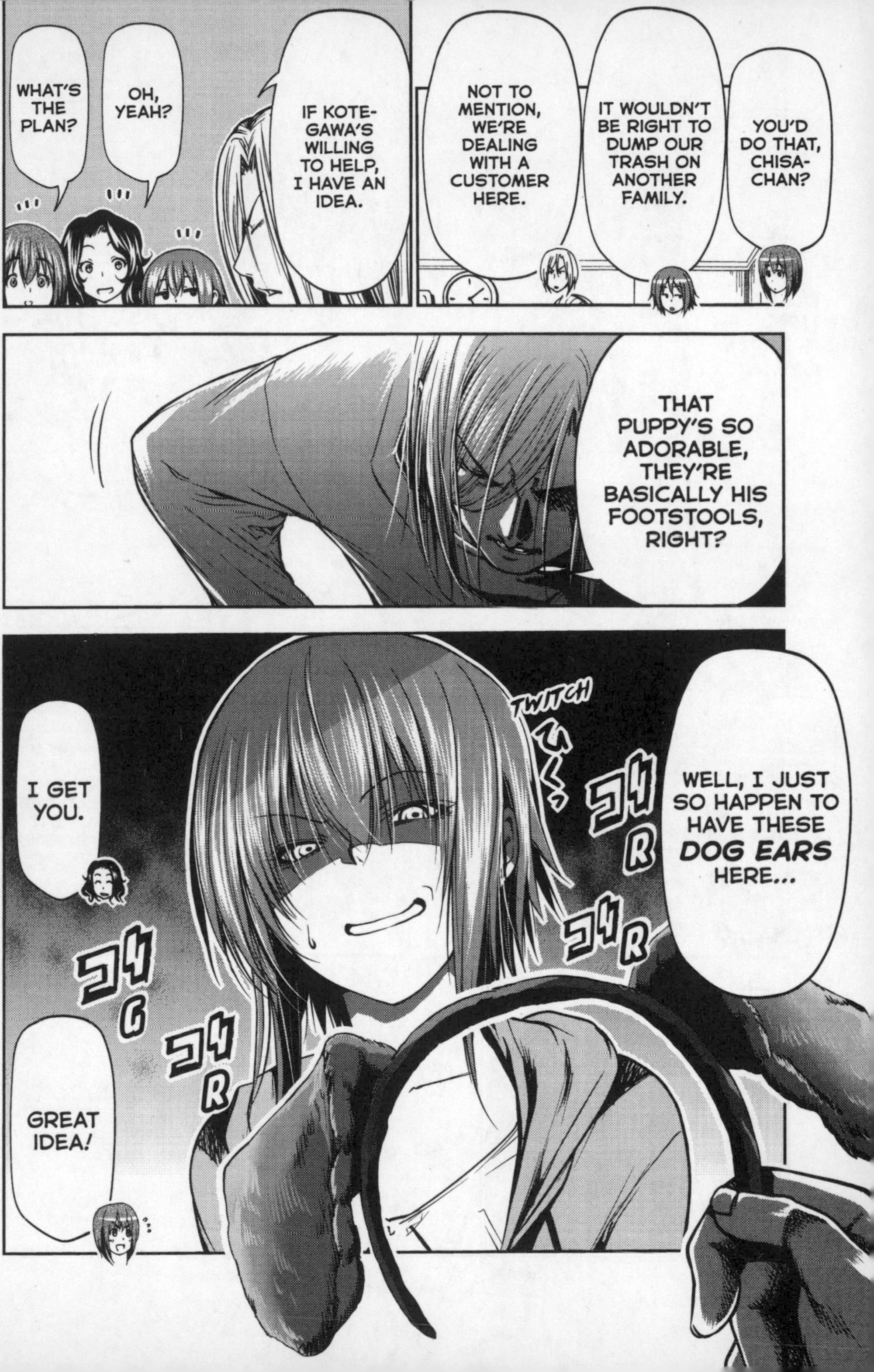
YOU'D DO THAT, CHISA-CHAN?
IT WOULDN'T BE RIGHT TO DUMP OUR TRASH ON ANOTHER FAMILY.
NOT TO MENTION, WE'RE DEALING WITH A CUSTOMER HERE.
IF KOTE-GAWA'S WILLING TO HELP, I HAVE AN IDEA.
OH, YEAH?
WHAT'S THE PLAN?
THAT PUPPY'S SO ADORABLE, THEY'RE BASICALLY HIS FOOTSTOOLS, RIGHT?
WELL, I JUST SO HAPPEN TO HAVE THESE ***DOG EARS*** HERE...
TWITCH
I GET YOU.
GREAT IDEA!

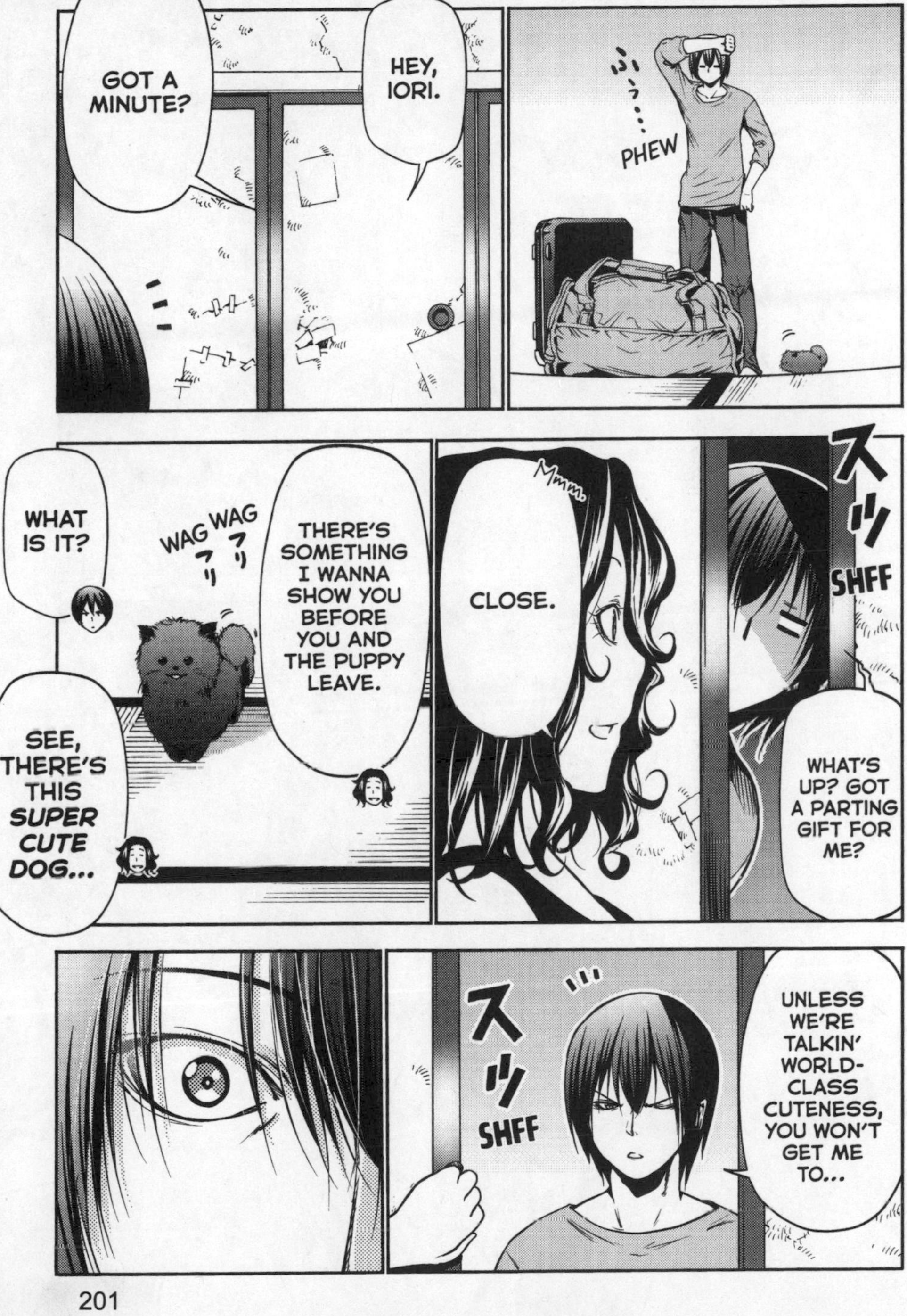
ふぅ…
PHEW
HEY, IORI.
GOT A MINUTE?
スッ
SHFF
WHAT'S UP? GOT A PARTING GIFT FOR ME?
Mmm.
CLOSE.
THERE'S SOMETHING I WANNA SHOW YOU BEFORE YOU AND THE PUPPY LEAVE.
WAG WAG
フリフリ
WHAT IS IT?
SEE, THERE'S THIS *SUPER CUTE* DOG...
UNLESS WE'RE TALKIN' WORLD-CLASS CUTENESS, YOU WON'T GET ME TO...
スッ
SHFF

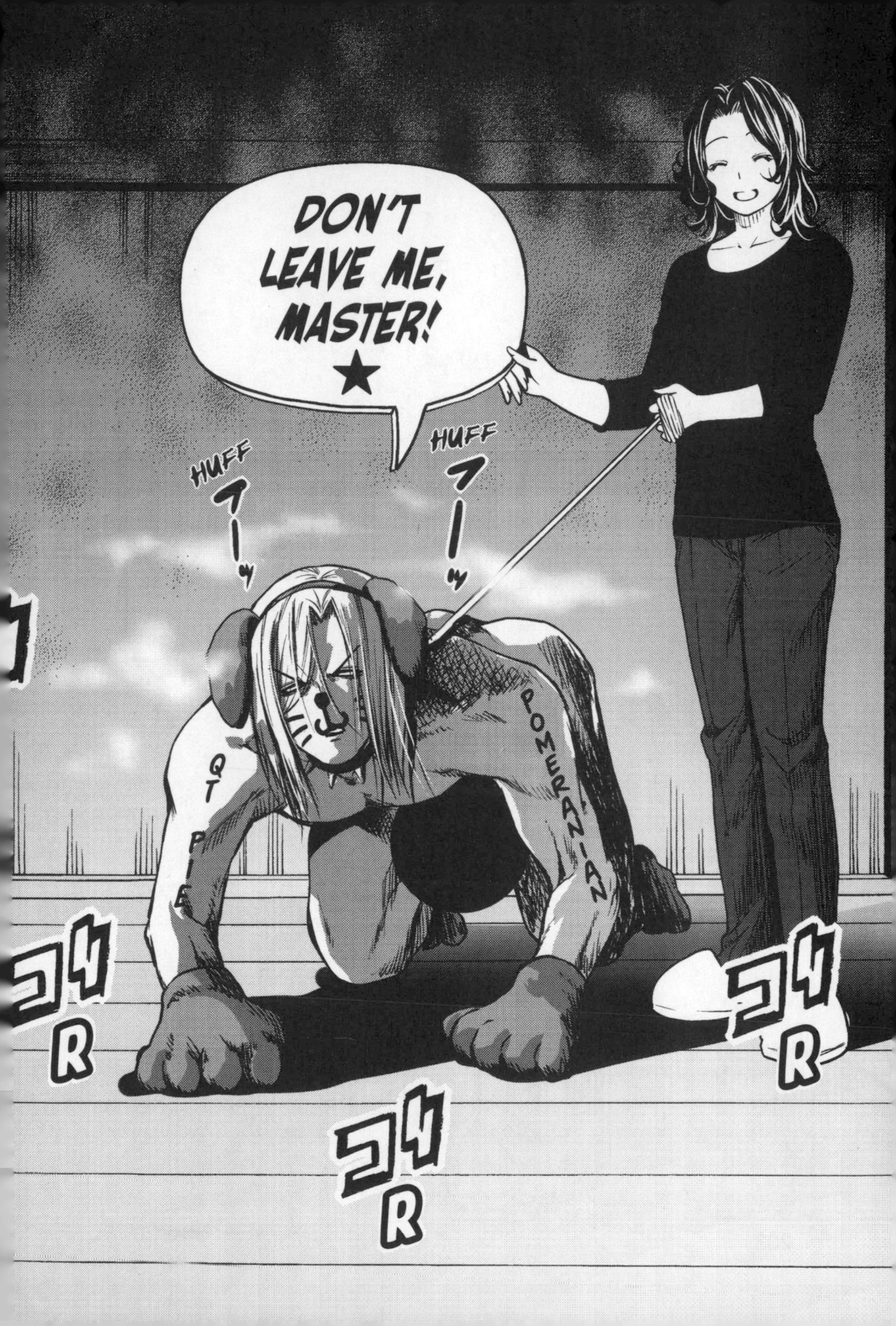
DON'T LEAVE ME, MASTER! ★
HUFF
HUFF
QT PIE
POMERANIAN
R
R
R

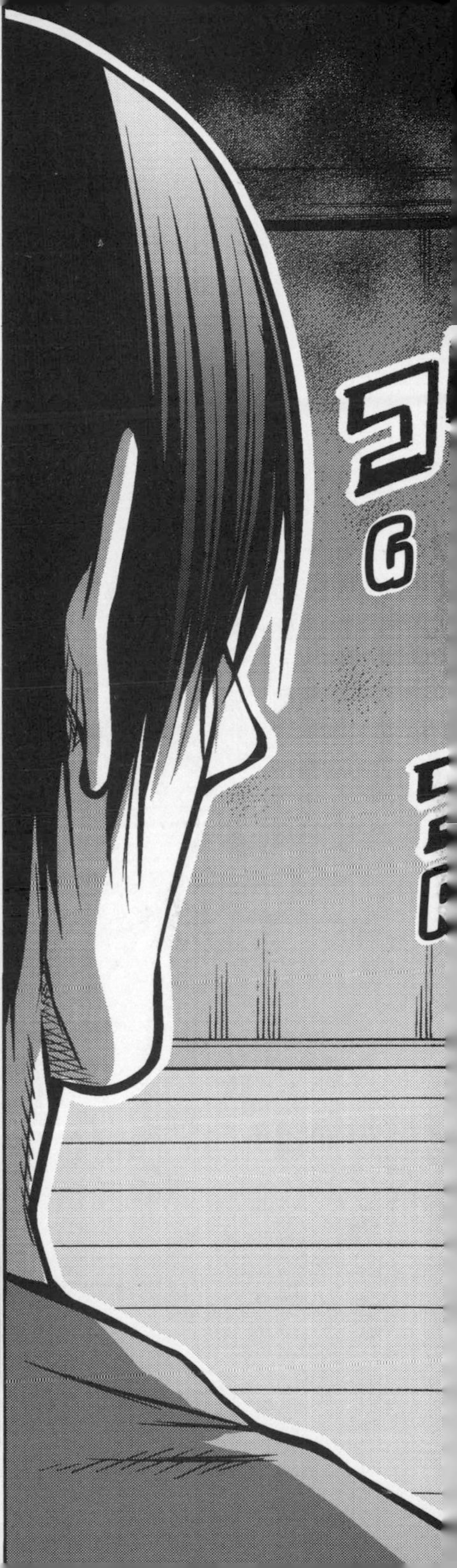
G

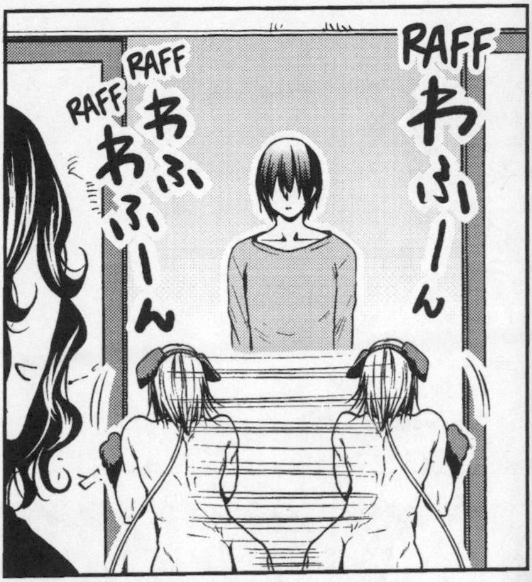
RAFF
わふーん
RAFF
わふ
RAFF
わふーーん

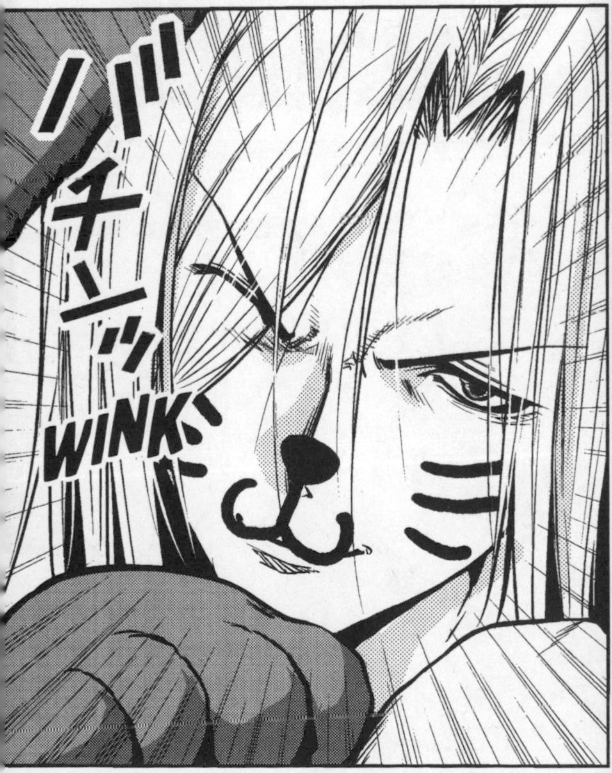
バチーーッ
WINK!

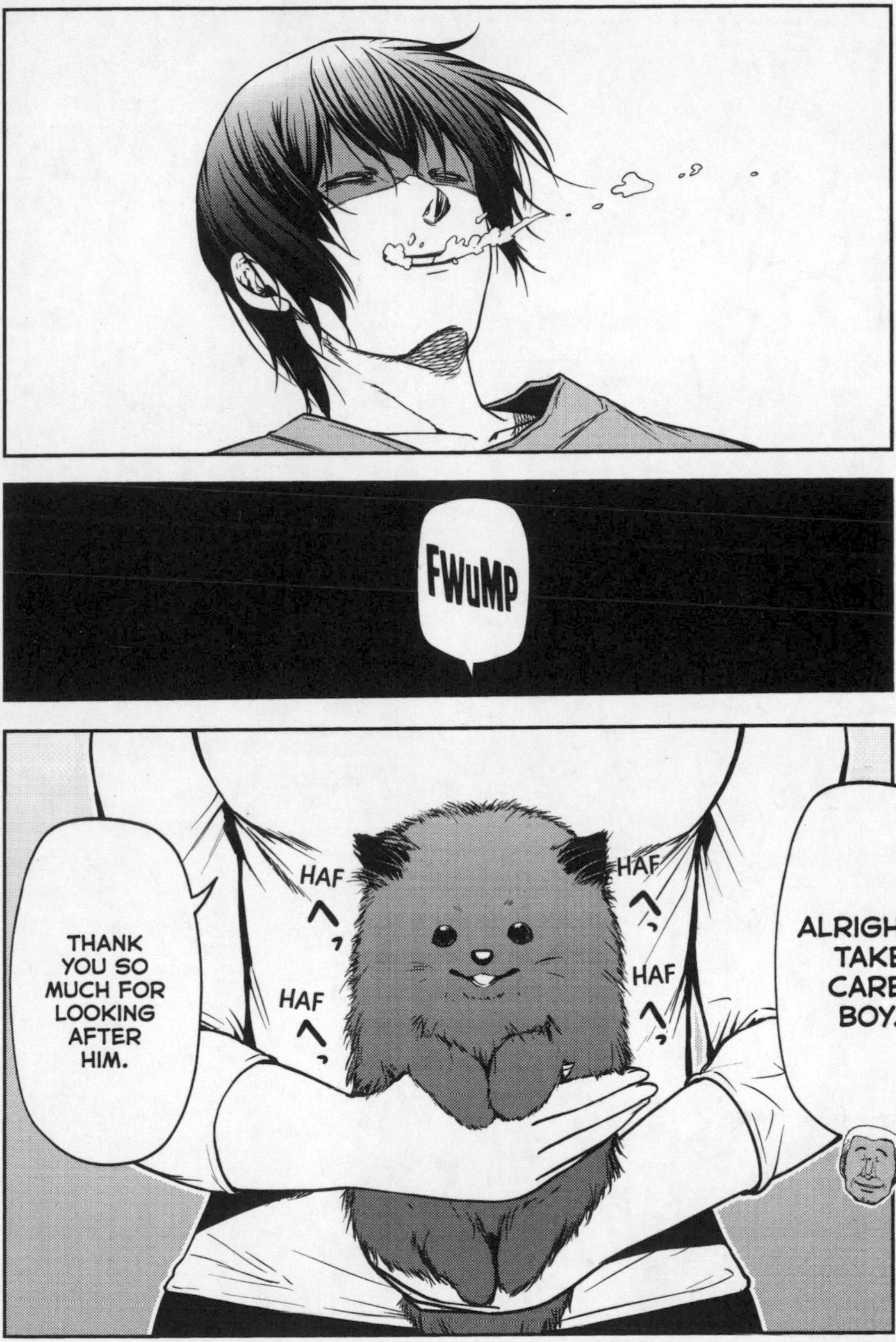
FWUMP
ALRIGHTY. TAKE CARE, BOY.
HAF
HAF
HAF
HAF
THANK YOU SO MUCH FOR LOOKING AFTER HIM.

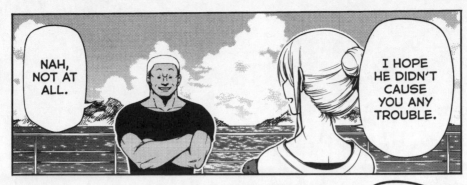

I HOPE HE DIDN'T CAUSE YOU ANY TROUBLE.
NAH, NOT AT ALL.
HE WAS AS WELL-BEHAVED AS CAN BE.
I CAN'T BELIEVE YOU ASSHOLES GAVE HIM BACK WHILE I WAS OUT!
DON'T LOOK AT ME! I DIDN'T WANNA WEAR THAT STUPID OUTFIT!
YEAH, WELL, CHI-CHAN WASN'T HAVING ANY OF IT, SO WE HAD TO IMPROVISE.
REEE
REEE
I'D RATHER DIE!
I REALLY WANTED TO SEE HER WITH THE EARS ON, TOO...
BOO HOO HOO

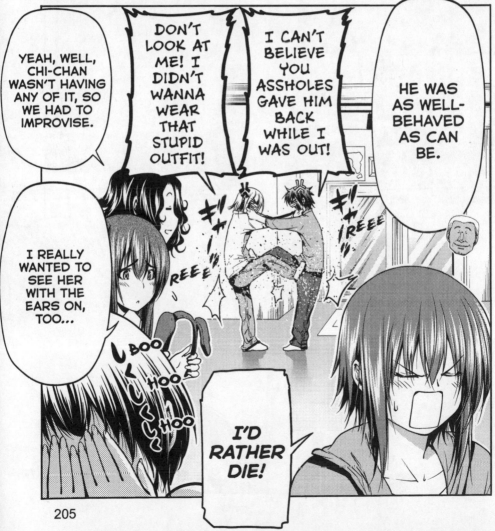

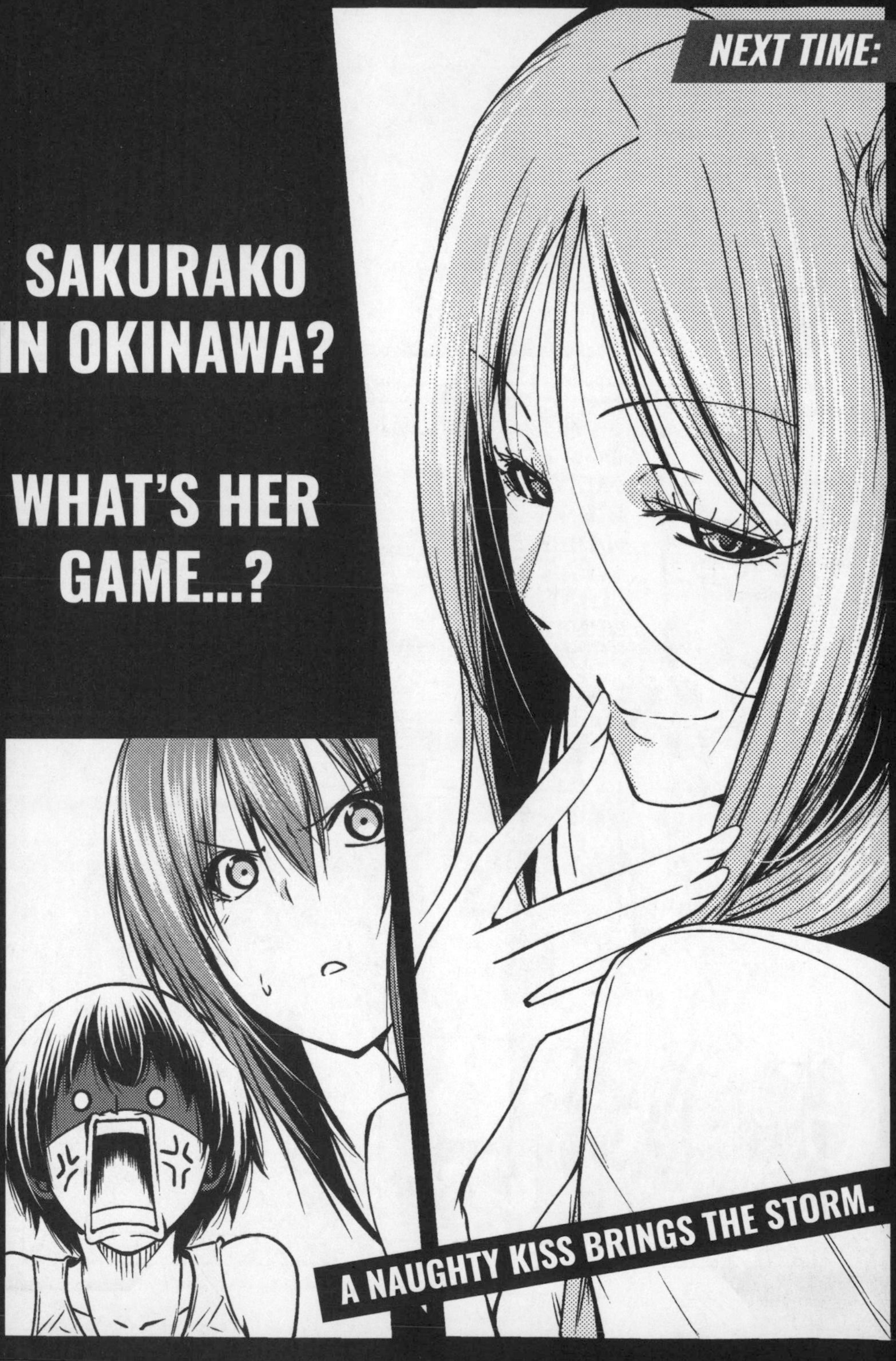
NEXT TIME:
SAKURAKO IN OKINAWA?
WHAT'S HER GAME...?
A NAUGHTY KISS BRINGS THE STORM.

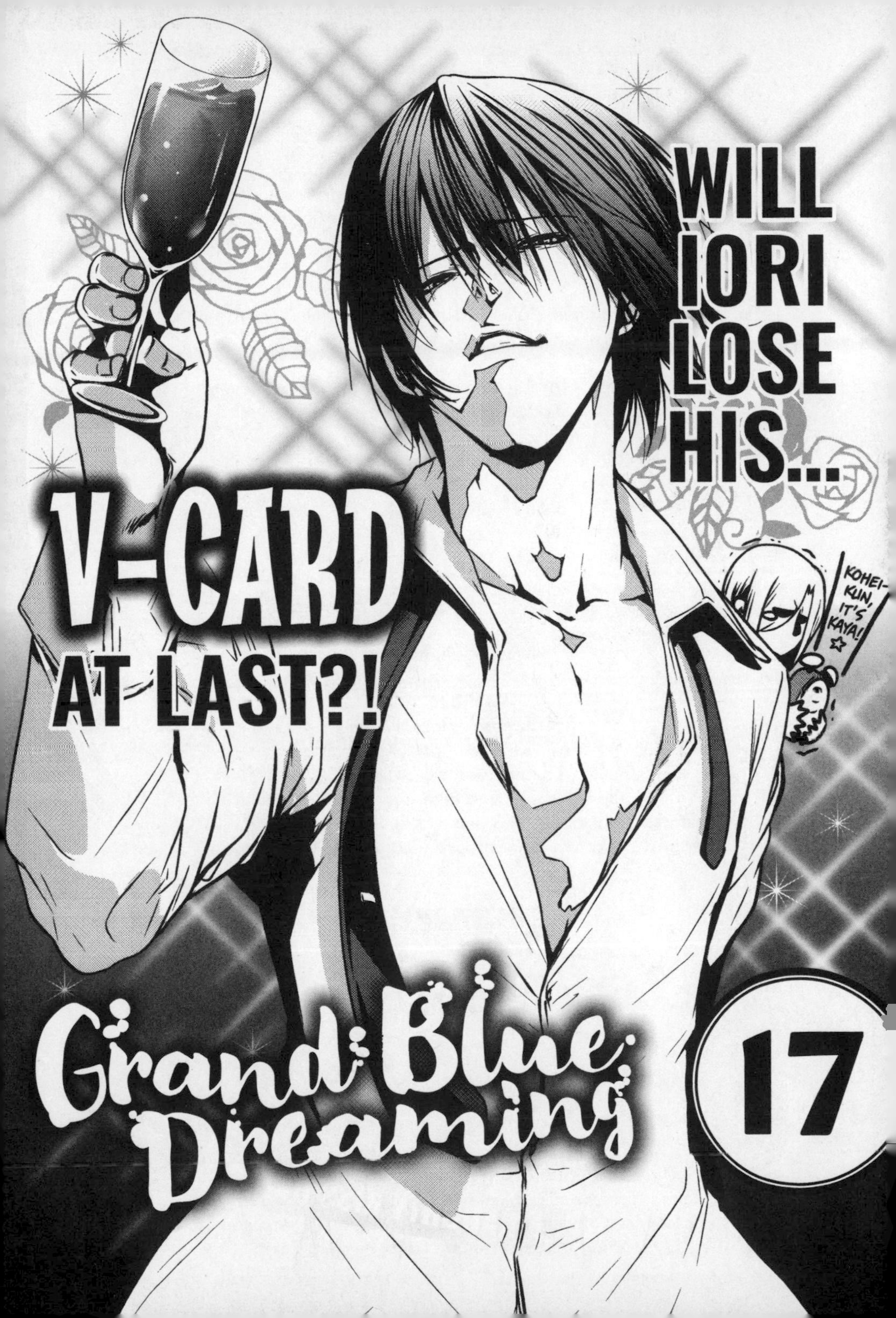
WILL IORI LOSE HIS...
V-CARD AT LAST?!
KOHEI-KUN, IT'S KAYA! ☆
Grand Blue Dreaming
17

A Kodansha Comics Trade Paperback Original
Grand Blue Dreaming 16 copyright © 2020 Kenji Inoue/Kimitake Yoshioka
English translation copyright © 2022 Kenji Inoue/Kimitake Yoshioka

All rights reserved.

Published in the United States by Kodansha Comics, an imprint of Kodansha USA Publishing, LLC, New York.

Publication rights for this English edition arranged through Kodansha Ltd., Tokyo.

First published in Japan in 2020 by Kodansha Ltd., Tokyo.

ISBN 978-1-64651-402-1

Original cover design by YUKI YOSHIDA (growerDESIGN)

Printed in the United States of America.

www.kodansha.us

1st Printing
Translation: Adam Hirsch
Lettering: Jan Lan Ivan Concepcion
Editing: Andres Oliver
Additional layout and lettering: Sara Linsley
Editorial Assistance: YKS Services LLC/SKY Japan, INC.
Kodansha Comics edition cover design by Phil Balsman

Publisher: Kiichiro Sugawara

Director of publishing services: Ben Applegate
Director of publishing operations: Dave Barrett
Associate director of publishing operations: Stephen Pakula
Publishing services managing editors: Alanna Ruse, Madison Salters
Production managers: Emi Lotto, Angela Zurlo